Computer Auditing, Security, and Internal Control Manual

Computer Auditing, Security, and Internal Control Manual

Javier F. Kuong

Prentice-Hall, Inc. Englewood Cliffs, New Jersey

Prentice-Hall International, Inc., *London*
Prentice-Hall of Australia, Pty. Ltd., *Sydney*
Prentice-Hall Canada, Inc., *Toronto*
Prentice-Hall of India Private Ltd., *New Delhi*
Prentice-Hall of Japan, Inc., *Tokyo*
Prentice-Hall of Southeast Asia Pte. Ltd., *Singapore*
Editora Prentice-Hall do Brasil Ltda., *Rio de Janeiro*
Prentice-Hall Hispanoamericana, S.A., *Mexico*

Material in Part I, "How to Test Internal Control and Integrity in Computerized Systems," is reproduced, and further updated, from the book of the same title, published by Management Advisory Publications, Wellesley Hills, MA, with permission of co-author, William E. Perry.

10 9 8 7 6 5 4 3 2 1

Library of Congress Cataloging-in-Publication Data

Kuong, Javier F.
Computer auditing, security, and internal control manual.

Bibliography: p.
Includes index.
1. Computers—Access control. 2. Electronic data processing departments—Security measures.
I. Title.
QA76.9.A25K86 1987 005.8 87-2555

ISBN 0-13-162967-0

Printed in the United States of America

About the Author

JAVIER F. KUONG is a management consultant and president of Management Advisory Services and Publications, an organization devoted solely to the EDP audit, security, and controls fields. Mr. Kuong is the editor of two well-established journals: *COM-SAC, Computer Security, Audit and Controls* (published since 1973), and *COM-AND, Computer Audit News and Developments*. Both journals are devoted to analyzing, digesting, and reporting on the latest developments in these fields worldwide.

The author has lectured throughout the world and is well known in the audit and security communities. He has co-authored and authored numerous books, among them a series of books and audit practice manuals, including *Computer Security, Audit and Controls; Audit and Control of Computerized Systems; Checklists and Guidelines for Reviewing Computer Security and Installations; Operational Audits of EDP; EDP Risk Analysis and Controls Justification; How to Train and Develop the EDP Audit and Control Function; EDP Systems Auditability;* and *How to Prepare an EDP Contingency Plan for Business Continuity*.

Over the years, Mr. Kuong has conducted numerous consulting engagements ranging from EDP operational audits to organization for EDP security, audit and quality assurance, and development of standards and guidelines for EDP internal controls.

Mr. Kuong holds a Master's degree in Chemical Engineering from the University of Pennsylvania and a Master of Business Administration from Babson College. He has held positions in industrial chemical operations and in corporate planning and computing at Atlas Chemical (now ICA America); also as Director of Management Information Systems for Cabot Corporation, and Managing Associate for Arthur Young and Company.

Acknowledgments

I would like to express my appreciation to the thousands of audit, security, and control professionals with whom I have had the privilege of coming in contact throughout the world for the many valuable exchanges of information and for the many ideas that contributed to mold my view of EDP audit, internal controls, and security. In particular, I would like to mention William E. Perry for concepts on testing internal controls.

Likewise, I would like to thank the Prentice-Hall management and editorial staff. In particular, I thank my editor, Nina Diamond, for her untiring efforts in the planning and structuring of the contents of the manual and for her encouragement and excellent efforts during the preparation of a difficult but challenging manuscript. Last, but not least, I would like to express my appreciation to Kathy Dix, production editor, for her singular thoroughness and endless efforts in polishing the manuscript and for seeing it through to successful completion.

Preface

Over the past two and a half decades, data processing and information system technologies have brought about dramatic developments and benefits. However, along with this explosive growth there has surfaced a corresponding set of potentially adverse situations, risks, and associated exposure problems for both those who use computer-based information and those who provide computer-related services.

The *Computer Auditing, Security, and Internal Control Manual* provides solutions to these problems. Within this manual you will find important facets of the security, audit, and internal control aspects of managing, securing, and auditing computer systems and the information systems facility. A commonly used term that encompasses all the computer and information science fields into one is Information Resources Management (IRM). This manual is about the security, audit, and control (S.A.C.) aspects of IRM.

As a manager, data processing professional, auditor, financial executive, controller, and information systems user you must consider the security, audit, and control implications of computer systems to ensure that your organization's assets and information are not only effectively processed but also secure and well controlled to preserve their integrity.

This timely book covers two major topics of great importance to you, the busy practitioner, in your quest to harness and control EDP activities. It then provides a third area of backup. You will learn: (1) how to test EDP internal controls, and (2) how to train professional personnel in EDP audit and controls. The third section provides you with a comprehensive set of checklists to enable you to review the most important areas of computer installations and computer-based information systems.

Section I on internal controls testing helps you gain a sound understanding of internal controls assessment and testing and provides you with a structured methodology for preparing detailed test plans, including knowledge of the most important test techniques to aid you in testing computerized systems.

Section II on training shows you the fundamental aspects of developing and training effective EDP audit- and controls-oriented staff and presents the most important skills required to equip personnel to test internal controls, conduct EDP system applications audits, and review data processing installations in an effective and knowledgeable manner.

Section III provides a comprehensive set of guidelines and checklists to assist you in the review of internal controls and security provisions for computer installations and computer-based systems run in these installations. This section can easily constitute a whole audit plan for the comprehensive operational review of data processing installations, and is based on information used in the conduct of actual audits of data processing installations during the course of consulting and audit engagements.

These three areas have been selected because they provide the structure and practicality that you, the busy manager and practitioner, require in your everyday activities. This blend of coverage of two specific and important topic areas with an in-depth set of guidelines for reviewing all areas of computers and computer-based systems has been written using a practical, pragmatic, and how-to-do-it approach.

You will find the manual easy to use, and it will save you many hours of painstaking development effort. The material in the manual has been applied by the author in countless consulting situations and has been used by hundreds of professionals who have attended seminars conducted by the author all over the world. The manual was drawn from text materials from Management Advisory Services and Publications and from the author's personal files.

Computer Auditing, Security, and Internal Control Manual closes a gap in the literature and, most importantly, provides you with a working-level guide on computer security and internal controls testing and training that you can apply in your daily practice.

Javier F. Kuong

Contents

PART III

Checklists Provided in Part III

PART I

How to Test Internal Control and Integrity in Computerized Systems

Preface to Part I

The great drive toward computerization of business sytems and operations over the past few decades has created a situation where computer systems in industry, government, and service organizations have become the basis upon which these organizations are able to function. As systems become more integrated and intertwined into a cobweb of information systems for daily decision making, the extent to which functions previously performed by humans have been incorporated into computer systems has assumed monumental proportions. The advent of microcomputers and networked systems now makes it possible for computer power and data bases to be dispersed to the most remote locations, further increasing the possibility of risks and exposures to organizations all over the world.

Thus, the need to control the integrity of data, assets, and proprietory information flowing through computerized information systems has indeed become quite critical. In order to determine whether a sound system of internal controls exists in operational systems or is being provided in new systems in development, managers, users, data processing professionals, auditors, and security and quality assurance specialists all need to know how to test the system of internal controls in computer-based systems. This raises the need for practical approaches and a methodology on how to test the system of internal control in computerized systems.

This section provides you with the fundamentals of, and a practical methodology for, assessing and testing internal controls and integrity in computerized systems. The material presented fills a major gap in the literature and provides you with the necessary knowledge and structured approach to test the system of internal controls in a manner that is understandable and usable by managers and professionals with a minimum of data processing technical skills.

The subject of internal controls testing is presented here in a broader context than is the case in traditional accounting and data processing textbooks. For example, this section presents five major approaches to testing internal controls showing the advantages and disadvantages of each approach. Next, it presents a sound methodology for testing internal controls that would be applicable to any type of computer-based system.

Since the characteristics and environment of traditional manual systems have changed dramatically in the computerized environment, this section also presents a variety of tools and techniques that you will need to consider to be effective in the testing of internal controls in today's computerized environment. Through a thorough bibliography and by quoting other sources of information throughout, this section directs you to other important sources of information for details of these new techniques.

I would like to emphasize that the testing approaches and techniques presented in this manual are not limited in application only to existing or so-called "operational" computer-based systems. Quite the contrary. The method presented is most applicable to the testing of internal controls in systems at the development stage and indeed it can be applied to the testing of the business provisions and capabilities of any system. In other words, although testing of internal controls is emphasized, the system analyst, EDP professional, user of systems, quality assurance specialists, and system project managers can apply the methodology presented in the manual to the preparation of "detailed" testing and validation plans for the whole of the computerized business application system that is being developed and tested. In fact, knowing that it is always more profitable to build the appropriate system of internal controls at design and development time, rather than after the fact, you will find the methodology presented in this section immensely useful as you prepare overall "system test plans" as well as "internal control test plans."

I have made every attempt to present practical information that you can apply immediately after studying this manual. It is based on my actual experience as well as on that of other colleagues with whom I have been very fortunate to have been associated over the years. In particular, I wish to mention the work of William E. Perry in the course of our joint seminars and publishing projects related to internal controls testing. Chapter 1 provides you with an understanding of the needs and objectives of internal control testing. The second chapter presents the main approaches to testing internal control. The third chapter details the approaches for internal control testing. The fourth chapter presents a detailed illustration of how to test internal controls and how to prepare actual test plans. The fifth chapter provides you with important considerations in testing controls. The sixth chapter presents an array of tools and techniques for testing internal control in the computerized environment and suggests other sources of information. The seventh chapter shows you how to determine the approach and depth of testing to be used. The eighth and final chapter provides you with an advanced view of the testing methods that will probably become prevalent in future years so that you may prepare for them and do further investigation.

The subject of this manual is indeed very timely in view of increasing pressure from various legislative pronouncements, such as the Foreign Corrupt Practices Act of 1977, Office of Management and Budget (OMB) 123, the various privacy acts, and the host of governmental and bank statutory and regulatory pronouncements enacted in the past few years throughout the world. All of these place direct responsibility on the shoulders of boards of directors, managers, internal and external auditors, and, increasingly, on the designers and users of information systems for the quality and integrity of computerized systems.

Assessing and testing internal control in computerized systems will become increasingly important with the advent of advanced, on-line, data base systems and with the increase in distributed network systems for both large and small organizations. You will need to increasingly rely on the system of internal controls and place less emphasis on data verification. Therefore, testing of internal controls becomes more important than data verification to justify reliance on the system of internal controls present in the systems in question.

Testing of internal controls should be an integral part of building and maintaining systems with a sound level of integrity. Since systems designers and users are primarily responsible for building internal controls into systems, knowledge of how to test internal controls must also be a vital part of the skills of data processing professionals, system users, and EDP quality assurance professionals.

I earnestly hope that this section of the manual will provide material help to all concerned with the important subject of testing internal control.

1

Understanding the Need for and Objectives of Testing Internal Control

THE NEED TO TEST THE SYSTEM OF INTERNAL CONTROL

The system of internal controls or management controls is an essential aspect of running a successful business or governmental operation to protect assets, control activities, and promote operational effectiveness at all levels of the organization.

As computers penetrated business and governmental operations in increasing levels of complexity and sophistication, the need to respond with adequate EDP controls has surfaced over the past few decades. In today's increasingly sophisticated computerized systems, controls are becoming less and less visible as they are being embedded or built into the systems. Despite this—or more accurately, because of it—the need is ever more urgent for those responsible to test and assess the systems of EDP controls.

Beyond management common sense in building and testing controls, boards of directors, audit committees, external and internal auditors have had, as a matter of special interest and duty, the responsibility for ascertaining that an adequate level of internal controls exists to fend off potential risks to the organization. The enactment of the 1977 Foreign Corrupt Practices Act and the flurry of pronouncements by regulatory agencies, has added great impetus to the need for building a sound system of internal controls as well as the need to assess it. In order to do an effective job of assessing internal control, one must test it.

Most professional auditors and system reviewers may be familiar with how to test conventional and visible controls. However, with the sizable proliferation of computerized systems and with the increase in the handling of business operations by computerized applications, the obvious need is for all concerned to become more intimately familiar with approaches, methodologies, and techniques for testing internal control in computerized applications.

This manual presents alternative approaches and methods for testing internal control and integrity in *computerized applications*. As instruments of the broader role of testing, it discusses the various types of techniques that one can use to aid in the testing process, including some of their advantages and limitations.

OBJECTIVES OF TESTING IN A COMPUTERIZED ENVIRONMENT

Prior to the computer, auditors concentrated their efforts on examining processed transactions. When people process transactions, there is no guarantee of consistency. The fact that one transaction is processed correctly is no indication that the following transaction will also be processed correctly.

In a computerized environment, the processing rules are predetermined and coded into computer programs. The advantage of the computer is that processing is consistent from transaction to transaction. If the processing rules are correctly implemented, all of the transactions will be processed correctly. On the other hand, if there are errors in the implementation of the processing rules, those errors will be applied to all affected transactions. Thus, if the system is properly implemented, there is a much higher reliance on internal controls in computerized applications.

The increased reliance on internal controls in computerized applications is causing auditors to shift audit emphasis. In manual systems, the emphasis was upon evaluating transactions, while in a computerized environment, the emphasis should be upon the evaluation of internal control.

As a system reviewer, you have three basic questions on testing that should be answered prior to conducting the audit. These questions are:

1. *What* tests should be performed?
2. *How much* testing should occur?
3. *Which* transactions should be tested?

What Tests Should Be Performed?

In a manual system, you check the steps performed by bookkeepers. In other words, you follow the bookkeepers' footsteps to verify that each step of the process is performed correctly. In the initial audits of basic or simple computerized applications, these same procedures were feasible and were followed. However, this approach does not take advantage of the capabilities of the computer. Also, in many cases, such as in advanced systems, it is not feasible to follow the process steps.

Most computer systems are integrated networks of applications. Thus the information from one application flows to another. In this environment, a company normally enters one-half of the accounting transaction which automatically generates the other half. For example, when cash is received to be applied against accounts receivable, the cash is entered into a cash application. This records the cash for posting to the cash account, but at the same time cash is automatically applied against accounts receivable. Thus, it may not be necessary to test both cash receipts and accounts receivable. The test of cash receipts in effect proves the postings to accounts receivable.

We can also narrow our scope of testing by concentrating upon the primary area of concern (the major risks) for each account. Let's look at what is normally the primary concern for each type of account:

- Asset accounts—The primary concern is that assets will be overstated.
- Liability accounts—The primary concern is that liabilities will be understated.
- Income accounts—The primary concern is that income will be understated.
- Expense accounts—The primary concern is that expenses will be overstated.

Identifying these areas of primary concern[1] helps us develop more effective testing. It also helps us understand the relationship between accounts. For example, if we audit cash and find that it is overstated, it would tell us that accounts receivable are understated. In other words, too much cash has been applied to accounts receivable. These rules of relationship are understood by accountants, but many times they are not applied to the design of system testing.

How Much Testing Should Occur?

The amount of testing to be undertaken should be directly related to the risk present in the area being audited. The higher the risk, the greater the amount of testing, and the lower the risk, the lower the amount of testing. Therefore, you must first identify and assess the extent and severity of the risk before testing. It is ineffective to conduct extensive tests in an area of low risk and few tests in an area of high risk.

Risks can be identified and assessed by four general approaches, which are:

- **Intuition/judgment**—The auditor uses a combination of experience, guesswork, tips, and other heuristic criteria to pick areas where the auditor believes the risks exist.
- **Application experience**—The auditor knows where the errors and losses have been occurring, and concentrates future tests in those same areas.
- **Common sense analysis**—For example, if all the employees of an organization were paid the minimum wage and the latter multiplied by the number of employees equalled the actual gross payroll, then the auditor could assume minimal payroll risk.
- **Risk scenario**—The auditor, in conjunction with other knowledgeable people, spends time identifying risks and then, working with individuals accountable for the application, assesses the severity of those risks.

---

[1] This presumes that the reviewer becomes familiar with the system by conventional audit procedures and uses audit techniques such as control flowcharting. For flowcharting methods, the reader may refer to C. E. Bellamy, et al., "Flowcharting in the Audit Environment," *The Australian Accountant,* May 1979, pp. 224–235.

Once the risks have been identified and the severity established, the auditor has the basis for determining what tests should occur. The auditor should concentrate tests of internal control in the areas of high risk.

Which Transactions Should be Tested?

Four factors must be considered in determining which transactions should be tested. These four considerations are:

- **Strength of internal control**—The stronger the system of internal control the less the need for extensive testing, while the weaker the system of internal control the greater the need for extensive transaction testing.
- **Sampling audit risk**—The auditor should test based on the sampling audit risk as opposed to the maximum audit risk. For example, if there are five people on the payroll and the payroll is $1,000 per week, then a maximum audit risk is $1,000. However, let's say that the minimum wage is $3 per hour, so that the minimum each of the employees would get based on a 40-hour week, is $120 per week. Then, a $600 payroll is the minimum pay by law, assuming all worked forty hours a week. The audit risk is then $400 (i.e., the maximum audit risk of $1000 less the minimum legal payroll of $600 equals $400). The auditor would then concentrate the tests on those people earning over the maximum in order to concentrate the tests on a sampling audit risk, as opposed to the maximum audit risk.
- **Precision**—The auditor must determine how much of an error can be tolerated in the audit area. This is the auditor's definition of audit materiality.
- **Reliability**—This determines how certain the auditor wants to be that the results of testing are representative of the population. In statistics this is expressed as confidence. For example, if the auditor wants to be 95 percent confident that the test is representative of the population being tested, an adequate sample to achieve that level of confidence can be developed.

TESTING INTERNAL CONTROLS

The computerized environment is composed of both manual and computerized segments. The auditor should test the two segments of the computerized environment together. For example, when cash is received the manual mail room procedures of opening the envelopes and restrictively endorsing the checks should be reviewed as closely as the procedures for entering that information into the computer applications and applying the cash to the appropriate accounts.

This manual provides the auditor with step-by-step guidance in determining areas for control evaluation, and conducting the control assessment. The manual is designed to permit a reviewer with minimal EDP skills to be *effective* in the assessment of control in a computerized environment.

The testing of internal controls in a computerized environment comprises four major components. These components embody the considerations and procedures involved in testing internal control. The components are:

- **Risks**—Identifying situations which can result in error, financial loss, or loss of data integrity.
- **Approaches**—The alternative postures for testing
- **Methods**—The tools and techniques used for conducting the test
- **Level**—The various component parts of the computerized application and its environment that will be tested

Risks

You must identify the risks in order to effectively test internal controls in a computerized environment. If there were no risks of losses and errors, there would be no need for control. In a perfect operating environment, controls are unnecessary. It is only when imperfections (which are risks) are introduced into the environment that controls need to be implemented. Controls should not be considered a cost of doing business but, rather, *a cost-effective means of reducing risks to an acceptable level.*

Few systems designers identify risks prior to building systems of internal control. Most systems of internal control are built using the intuition and judgment of users and systems personnel. Risks are neither identified nor measured. In this environment it is easy to miss or misapply controls.

If you begin by evaluating only a control, you may fall into the same trap the systems designer often does. In other words, you may examine the controls to determine if they are well implemented and effective, but never determine the two more important aspects, namely: (1) What are the risks? and (2) Have the risks inherent in the system been reduced to an acceptable level? This more important aspect of internal control assessment can be accomplished only by first identifying the risks and their attendant consequences.

Approaches

You must determine the type of test needed to *evaluate controls relating to a specific risk.* The specific risk will lead you to pinpoint the area that should be subject to the testing of controls. For example, if the risk or concern to you is in the security area, then you would probably concentrate the testing of internal controls in the system environmental areas.

Methods

The methods or means for testing internal control are provided by the tools and techniques available to you to conduct the test. You have several methods available from which to select to arrive at the most effective tool or techniques to solve a specific audit concern. You should be familiar with the tools and techniques available for testing internal control, which are covered in detail in several books. (See the literature references in the Bibliography and the lists of current journals and publications in the field, Figures 10-13 through 10-15.)

Level

You must determine what major components and elements of the computerized environment need be tested to measure the adequacy of controls. It may be possible to restrict testing to a single processing module, or the testing may need to encompass several application systems. The level of testing can be determined only after the risk has been isolated to specific points in the computerized environment. This isolation of risk is performed using testing methods.

HOW TO USE THIS MANUAL

This manual is designed to help you with a complex test situation. You basically face three problems in assessing internal control in computerized applications. These are:

- **Lack of control documentation**—Few systems designers identify and document internal controls separate from the documentation for their normal processing. In many instances, the systems designer is uncertain as to what is and what is not a control. Therefore, in many applications you must search through all the documentation in an effort to identify controls. This is a very time-consuming task. In the future, the auditor should recommend that internal controls documentation be provided by the design and user team as part of the total documentation package.
- **Lack of EDP skills**—Surveys indicate that only a small percentage of auditors have good EDP skills. This has prevented many auditors from attempting detailed control evaluations. This manual is designed to help those auditors become effective with minimal skills.
- **Lack of tools and techniques**—Few professionals are aware of the tools and techniques available to them to assess internal control. This manual explains the available tools and techniques and points where to find additional information on them.

2

How to Use the Different Approaches for Evaluating Internal Control

CONSIDERATIONS IN TESTING INTERNAL CONTROL

The objective of testing internal control is twofold:

1. To assess the adequacy of the system of internal control
2. To delimit the scope of system audit testing

The stronger the system of control the fewer the tests that need to be made to ascertain the integrity of the system in question.

It has been estimated that there are 50,000 different payroll systems in the United States. This means that there are 50,000 different systems of internal control, as controls are normally structured around system requirements and processes. A different process may require different controls.

The auditor can expect each review of internal controls to be different. For example, the review of internal control in payroll in one organization will be different from that in another organization. This means that uniformity in review must come from the approach as opposed to coming from similarities in the systems.

As explained in Chapter 1, the following four major considerations shape your approach to testing internal control:

- **Risk** in control
- **Method** of testing
- **Approaches to** or **types** of testing
- **Level** of testing

You need to evaluate each of these considerations prior to reviewing the controls. This chapter discusses each of the four considerations.

RISK IN CONTROL AND RISK ASSESSMENT

In a "perfect" operating environment, everything works smoothly. There are no errors in input, programs function properly, operations are completed on time, reports are delivered to the appropriate people and meet their needs. The users understand and use the information properly, and no one attempts to defraud the system. Unfortunately, such an environment does not exist. There are risks which must be dealt with.

Thus, the first consideration in any review of internal control is risk assessment. The objective of risk assessment is to determine the types and severity of risks which the system of internal controls is designed to reduce. Without risk, there is no need for control.

The systems analyst who designs the system of internal control should also begin with risk assessment. However, few systems analysts go through a formal risk analysis process, usually because of lack of training in this subject. Thus, when the auditor attempts to determine the types and severity of risk, he probably will not find it documented.

In most instances the assessment of risk by the systems analyst is not the primary thrust of control design. At present, the rationale for most systems of internal control is one or several of the following:

- Controls are installed in all systems (whether they need them or not).
- Systems analyst intuition.
- User intuition.
- Controls are included to prevent or detect problems familiar to the systems analyst from other experiences (the extraorganizational syndrome).
- Controls are dictated by auditors and/or senior management.
- Controls required by regulatory agencies.

Most of the above reasons for establishing control are based on "symptoms," personal bias, or rules, rather than responsiveness to risks. Sometimes control symptoms have little effect on reducing the losses associated with risk. For example, in all payroll systems there is a risk that people will be included on the payroll master who are not authorized employees. An individual might be terminated and yet still remain on the payroll master. A control that reconciles the number of checks to the number of people on the payroll master is ineffective against this risk. It treats one of the symptoms: that unauthorized checks may be prepared. However, it does not deal with the issue of preventing or detecting, the inclusion of unauthorized people on the payroll master. This can best be accomplished by risk analysis.

The following four types of risks need to be considered when reviewing systems of internal control:

- **Product risk**—The system does not do what the user wants it to do. This can also result from forcing a system to perform functions it was not designed to do.
- **Technology risk**—Problems in mastering the technology result in systems problems

- **Use risk**—The user does not understand the information and limitations in reports and/or makes faulty decisions based on that information. Violations of the boundaries of applicability of the system can lead to this.
- **Security risk**—Valuable information of the organization is stolen or compromised (the privacy and confidentiality implications).

Product Risk

The product from the development of a system is the application system. The risk is that the needs of the user will not be met. The specific product risks include:

- Inaccurate data.
- Incomplete data.
- Unauthorized data.
- Inadequate audit trail.
- Inconsistent data.
- Untimely data.
- Data not prepared in accordance with generally accepted accounting procedures.
- Unreliable data.
- The system does not cover the operational boundary needs of the user.

These general product risks can be used as a guide, or the auditor can develop a more specific list. It is recommended that a specific list be developed for each application under audit. Experience has shown that there are only approximately fifteen to twenty major risks per application.

Let us examine a payroll application to determine the type of risks in that application. These risks can be specified in terms of application processing such as:

- Unauthorized people will be on the payroll master.
- Gross pay will be too large.
- Deductions will be inaccurately calculated.
- Payroll amounts will not be accumulated properly.
- Employees will not receive their pay on a timely basis.

You must also determine the severity of the risk. For example, is there a low, medium, or high risk that unauthorized employees will be on the payroll master, and thus paid when they should not be paid? This determination forms the basis of the types and quantity of controls installed.

If the risk of having extra people on the payroll is low, then only minimal controls need be installed. However, if the risk of having extra people on the payroll is very high, then extensive controls should be established. Once the controls are established, the condition should be monitored to, first, determine that the severity assumption was correct and, second, to make any adjustments to controls necessary based on actual practice.

Technology Risk

Automating systems involves the risk of the misuse of the automation technology. This risk affects not only the efficiency, economy, and effectiveness of automated applications, but also the integrity of data. For example, problems in data base technology can result in a broken pointer, which may result in lost data, or the loss of a key password or encryption key may result in irreparable loss of data or a file.

The specific types of risks that are associated with technology include:

- Hardware failure
- Software failure
- Failure to incorporate desirable vendor-provided controls
- Ordering too much hardware
- Ordering more sophisticated software than needed
- Improperly assembled software
- Failure to control high-risk situations, such as concurrent updates in a data base

The proper use of hardware and software has traditionally fallen to the systems programming function. This function is normally given the responsibility to select both hardware and software, and then to effectively utilize it. However, frequently the personnel in the systems programming group are not fully aware of the application needs. Thus, in many organizations the hardware and software is out of synchronization with the true application needs.

The definition of risk with computer technology may require extensive technology skills. This may require the assistance of a computer audit specialist. However, there are some alternatives to assessing technological risks.

The auditor with minimal computer skills who wants to gain insight into technology risks should:

- Review the vendor's control considerations, if any, to ascertain the conditions the vendor believes need controlling
- Ask the systems programmers what they believe are the more serious problems associated with achieving a successful installation and operation (i.e., the EDP risks)
- Interview users to determine their assessment of the possible technology problems involved in meeting their needs

- Review various technical services and publications covering hardware and software capabilities to keep abreast of technological problems

Use Risk

Computer applications provide information to users. Users act upon this information in the performance of their job function. If the information is erroneous, improperly described, or misunderstood, those user decisions may be improper.

In advanced computer systems, the use risk may be higher. For example, in batched systems, time is available between processing steps to do checking and to think about a situation. In on-line data base sytems, the action may occur concurrently with the information in seconds. For example, when a bank depositor requests the account balance, and then withdraws funds based upon that balance, the transaction is complete and the funds may be gone.

The risk of improper use of computer information is a difficult one to assess. The auditor must make this determination using information such as:

- The sophistication of the report format
- The sophistication of the procedures to be followed when using the information
- The skill of the people using the information
- Past history of errors and omissions associated with the use of information
- Past history of errors and omissions associated with the application system

The larger the gap between the skill required to use the system successfully, and the actual skill of the people using it the higher the risk. In other words, highly skilled people can normally make a poorly structured and complex computer system workable, while people with lower skills would have only a minimal chance of success using that system.

Security Risk

The increasing concentration and accessibility of data in corporate data bases increases the risk of loss, destruction, and compromise of data. The loss of data is the physical removal of data media, destruction results in data obliteration, and compromise is the transfer of that same data to an unauthorized media. The first and third, both, result in the data going into the hands of an unauthorized source, but compromise can be more serious because it is more difficult to detect.

Privacy is a subset of the security risk. Privacy deals specifically with the loss of confidential information about people while the security risk includes all types of information affected. However, privacy may also involve violations of laws, as employees' and customers' rights are protected under numerous federal and state privacy laws.[1]

The security risk is broad. It encompasses a wide range of compromise, from the very casual through the most sophisticated, made possible by advanced electronic equipment. Most control-oriented personnel can be effective in designing controls to restrict the casual perpetrator, but compromise by a professional using advanced electronic equipment and penetration methods is difficult to prevent or detect. When the use of electronic equipment is suspected, experts should be involved in the design and evaluation of security controls.

The specific types of security risks that an organization might encounter include:

- Disgruntled employee manipulating or destroying data for revenge purposes
- Dishonest employee manipulating or stealing information for personal gain
- Outside individual manipulating or stealing information for personal gain
- Casual observer who stumbles upon valuable information
- Water damage
- Fire
- Acts of nature
- Accidental sources (byproducts of imperfect technology, e.g., unsafe operating system)

METHODS FOR TESTING INTERNAL CONTROL

You must select among the available methods for testing internal control. The method which you select will be based upon the attributes of the system of internal control being tested, the available time/budget constraints, and your skills. You should be familiar with the testing options available.

In manual systems, internal control does not have the same significance as in automated systems. When people process transactions, the processing can be inconsistent. The random nature of errors makes testing of data a more important segment of auditing. In computerized applications, processing is performed using automated routines. Processing is more consistent than for manual systems in that transactions of a single type are normally all processed correctly, or all processed incorrectly.

This means that the amount of data testing performed in an audit can be

[1] CBEMA, "Privacy and Security, State Legislation Status Report," Computer and Business Equipment Manufacturers Association, 1828 L Street, N. W., Washington, DC 20036.

reduced by the adequacy of internal control. The stronger the system of internal control, the less data testing required, while the weaker the system of internal control, the more data testing that should be performed. Therefore, you need to conduct tests of internal control that will enable the auditor not only to determine the adequacy of the controls but also to be able to rely upon them during the data testing phase of the audit.

The five general methods that you can use to test systems of internal control are:

1. **Checklist method**—Using a series of questions to interrogate the adequacy of the system of internal control.
2. **Static method**—Examining the system of internal control from a policy and procedure perspective or on paper.
3. **Test data**—Developing test transactions to be processed through the application to test the system of internal control.
4. **Live data method**—Using live transactions as a means of testing the adequacy of internal control.
5. **Parallel method**—Running live data through the same application twice, or using two applications designed to achieve the same purpose to compare the results for consistency of control.

Each of these methods of testing internal control will be discussed individually. You should be familiar with these methods so that you can apply them where necessary.

Checklist Method

The checklist method is the most common method for assessing internal control. It attempts to provide a comprehensive series of encompassing questions to probe the adequacy of control provisions and procedures. The checklist is used both to assess controls and to identify areas of weakness for testing.

Most checklists are general purpose checklists. That is to say, the questions contained in the checklists are applicable to any system of internal control. Thus, they are transferable between application systems and across organizations.

The checklist method offers the advantages of being:

- An organized approach to the assessment of control
- A consistent approach to the review of internal controls
- A comprehensive approach to the review of internal controls
- A useful reminder of sound control practices

The disadvantages of the checklist method include:

- Some of the questions in the checklist may not be applicable to the system being reviewed.

- The questions may mislead you because they force responses into specific categories.
- You may not understand the implications of the questions.
- You may rely too heavily on the checklist and not use other review methods.
- The checklists do not uncover the cause-and-effect relationships of control problems.
- There may be areas that should be probed that are not included on the checklist.

The checklist should be *a part* of any review of internal control. It provides a quick assessment of the strengths and weaknesses of a system of internal control. However, it should be only the starting point of the review, and not the basis for the total review, especially in the context of computerized applications. A sample internal control checklist is included in Chapter 3, Figure 3–5.

Static Method

A review of a system of internal control by the static method entails an assessment of the controls in a nonfunctioning mode. You review the control methods and procedures in existence in an effort to determine their effectiveness. For example, you would look at the controls over the preparation and issuance of payroll checks in order to determine whether the checks are adequately controlled. However, the static method does not involve the examination of the processed checks themselves.

The static method of reviewing controls can be used both for a system under development and for a system in operation. The techniques that have proved most effective for static analysis are:

- Transaction flow analysis
- Transaction conflict matrix

These two techniques are explained in Chapter 3, Step 6.

Test Data Method

The test data method utilizes dummy transactions created for the purpose of evaluating internal control. The dummy transactions are processed through the application and the results compared to predetermined results. The assumption here is that if controls are properly executed, the actual processing results will equal the predetermined "perfectly controlled" results.

The test data method demonstrates whether or not the controls function in practice. The validity of the test results is dependent upon the ability of the tester to construct a realistic sample of test data. If the sample is *comprehen-*

sive, then the test data method provides a positive indication of the functioning of controls, and thus of the adequacy of controls. However, the process of creating and validating test data is time-consuming.

Test data provides the advantage of testing unusual conditions. For example, test data can simulate error conditions, high volume transactions, and other exceptional conditions which might be difficult to find in a live environment. Thus, test data offers the advantage that it can evaluate the controls over processing conditions that have *yet* to occur. In other words, control deficiencies detected through the use of test data can be corrected *prior* to the actual occurrence of the processing condition or loss. Thus, the use of test data becomes a preventive tool, as one could simulate special test conditions *before* implementation.

The types of conditions for which test data is best suited include:

- Normal processing conditions
- Anticipated error or abnormal conditions
- System limits or boundaries of operation
- Adequacy of system changes

The situations where the use of test data is not as effective include:

- Tests of manual procedures
- Interface between manual and automated procedures
- Unanticipated conditions not included in the test data

Live Data Method

Traditionally, auditing has used the results of live processing to validate internal controls. Auditors examine the *results of processing* in an effort to determine if the results are processed in accordance with management's intents. In other words, they validate whether controls were sufficient to ensure that the desired results were achieved.

The advantage of testing with live data is that the results of actual processing conditions can be verified. Occasionally, test conditions might not properly simulate live conditions. This frequently occurs because, in other methods, only segments of the total system are tested, as opposed to testing all aspects of systems, from transaction origination through to use.

The benefits accruing to use of the live data method include:

- Assets can be verified for the audit test periods involved.
- All aspects of the system are involved.
- Actual processing conditions are evaluated.
- The severity of risks can be determined through the evaluation of actual errors and losses incurred.

The disadvantages to testing using the live data method include:

- Only those conditions which have occurred can be evaluated since the test is based on the results of processing.
- It is frequently difficult to find the desired type of transaction to evaluate.
- Potential control weaknesses cannot be tested unless a live transaction of the type containing the weaknesses can be found.

The use of *live data to evaluate controls* should *not* be confused with the use of *live data to test the validity of processing*. Only one or two transactions of a type are needed to test controls. For example, the evaluation of a single product in inventory may test the adequacy of inventory controls. However, the validation of the inventory totals, based on many transactions, may require extensive data testing. This is often referred to as "substantive" testing. On the other hand, the amount of testing can be limited by first determining the strength of the controls.

Parallel Test Method

Parallel testing involves processing the data twice using two different processing means. The results of the parallel processing are then compared to identify differences. The differences are investigated to determine if there are control and/or processing errors in one of the two processing means.

The types of parallel testing that can be performed to test internal controls include:

- **Before and after conversion of systems**—If a system has been rewritten, the data can be run through both the old and the new versions of the application system to test controls. However, if the conversion causes data to be reformatted or otherwise modified, such changes must be taken into account when comparing the results of the parallel runs.
- **Task or function testing**—A single task or function in an application system can be tested by simulating the processing rules in a special *separate* program. For example, if you wanted to test the FICA deduction in payroll, a special routine could be written for that purpose. The production version of the program would then: (1) calculate the FICA deduction using the current application system, (2) pass the data through a *simulated* FICA deduction routine, and (3) compare the results.
- **Control copy**—A control copy of a program can be maintained by the auditor, and then its results compared to the results obtained from the production version. This variation proves valuable in identifying change between two periods of time, and in identifying unauthorized changes.

Parallel system operation uses more data to test controls than do the other methods of testing internal control. However, parallel testing offers these advantages:

- Comprehensive testing using live data
- Automatic checking of results because two versions of the same process or function have taken place
- Ability to identify differences in control between two versions of the same application system

The disadvantages of parallel testing include:

- Slight variations in processing may result in thousands of differences requiring reconciliation, depending on the volume and type of data processed.
- The execution of parallel testing is time-consuming, both on and off the computer. For functional tests, a *separate* program version must be written which can become costly.
- Normally an extensive knowledge of the application system is required because the testing occurs on computer records in their coded format.
- For very large and complex systems, it is difficult to justify the effort in dual redundant system preparation.

TYPES OF TESTING

There are five types of testing that the auditor can utilize. Each type of testing is designed to test different aspects of a computerized application. It is important for you to understand both the similarities and differences between the types of testing.

The five types of testing are:

- **Stress**—Pushing the application system to its limits
- **Functional**—Verifying that the system performs the functions it was designed to perform
- **Regression**—Determining that changes to an application system have not adversely affected existing functions
- **Environmental**—Testing the interrelationship between hardware and software and chains of applications
- **Performance**—Testing the efficiency, economy, and effectiveness of the application system

Another type of test that will become important with the advent of distributed data processing is **Portability testing** to ensure that a system works in several intended locations.

You may desire to perform one type of testing at a time, or perform several types concurrently. The audit objective and the type of system involved should tell you which type of test (or tests) is needed to achieve that objective. Each type of testing will be explained individually.

Stress Testing

Computer applications are designed with built-in restrictions. You should identify these limitations and test them through stress or saturation testing. The more common limitations in computerized applications include:

- Size of fields
- Size of accumulators
- Size of internal tables
- Size of queues
- Dating restrictions
- Volume of transactions, especially as it affects response time

These types of problems can be uncovered only when the system is fully loaded. Stress testing is designed to put a sufficient saturation load on the system to test these problem areas. Stress testing attempts to approximate real-life processing situations and peak loads.

Good stress testing attempts to simulate real-life processing as much as possible. In order to do this, you need to understand the type, mix, and volume of work that the user might be entering. In other words, you would have to develop a user profile of work and then enter that type of work to develop a stress test situation approximating that in the real world.

In advanced operating environments, a user profile can be obtained by analyzing one or more of the operating logs and data base logs. An analysis of these logs gives an appreciation as to the mix, volume, and type of transaction entered by various users. In development systems the workload must be anticipated and simulated.

Functional Testing

Functional testing is the type of test most commonly used in application systems testing. The objective of functional testing is to assure that the functions of the application system operate as intended and correctly. This normally involves preparing one transaction of each functional type. The results of processing then determine whether or not the function is properly executed.

Functional testing not only tests proper transactions, but must test improper transactions. Improper transactions should test all of the possible error conditions which might occur to assure that they are properly detected and that the appropriate error messages are produced. A traditional weak point in test ing, from a systems analyst/programmer perspective, has been the completeness of testing of error conditions.

Regression Testing

One of the problems that has plagued data processing is that of a current change made to an application affecting other aspects of processing. It is possible to change one part of a program, and due to some "quirk" in the system or through a clerical error in making the change, some unrelated aspect of the program is changed or the interactions between the change and the rest of the program can result. In some instances, a change in one program has caused errors to be initiated in or *propagated* to other programs. This is referred to by some as the "ripple effect."

The objective of regression testing is to assure that changes made do not adversely affect the intended results, and that everything else executes precisely as it did before the changes were made. Many times, "quick and dirty" fixes are incorporated under the pressure of deadlines without conducting regression testing. Thus, a cursory look by the involved party tends to give assurance that the new change operates correctly without any attempt being made to verify whether existing segments also function correctly.

Regression testing is effective only when an existing set of test data exists to provide a frame of reference. This accumulation of test data can be modified to test the new function, but at the same time it is used to verify that the existing functions perform correctly.

Environmental Testing

In the real world, the application program and/or system operates in an environment which includes actual hardware, specific vendor-supplied software, and other application systems contending for computer resources. It is therefore necessary to test that the application functions properly in the *actual* operating environment. Processing peculiarities of an application may cause it to malfunction in the operating environment even though other applications function correctly.

Environmental testing attempts to evaluate the following three environmental conditions:

- **Hardware**—The application system functions properly on the operating hardware.
- **Operating software**—The application system operates properly when interconnected with the operating software, such as operating systems, communication systems, data base management systems, etc.
- **Other applications**—The application is tested together with other interconnected applications to determine that the proper information is passed between applications.

Performance Testing

Performance testing evaluates the economy, effectiveness, and efficiency of an application system. It is designed to identify bottlenecks which cause application systems to be poor performers. However, prior to undertaking performance testing, measures of performance should be predetermined.

Performance testing is normally executed using large volumes of data. The testing attempts to determine that the system meets its performance criteria, and that bottlenecks are identified so that appropriate action can be taken. This type of testing helps fine tune the application so that the maximum performance levels are achieved.

Performance testing is frequently conducted with hardware and software monitors. These monitors pinpoint potential bottlenecks so that they can be analyzed and/or corrected. In some instances, the bottlenecks will be associ-

Figure 2-1
Approaches to Testing Internal Control

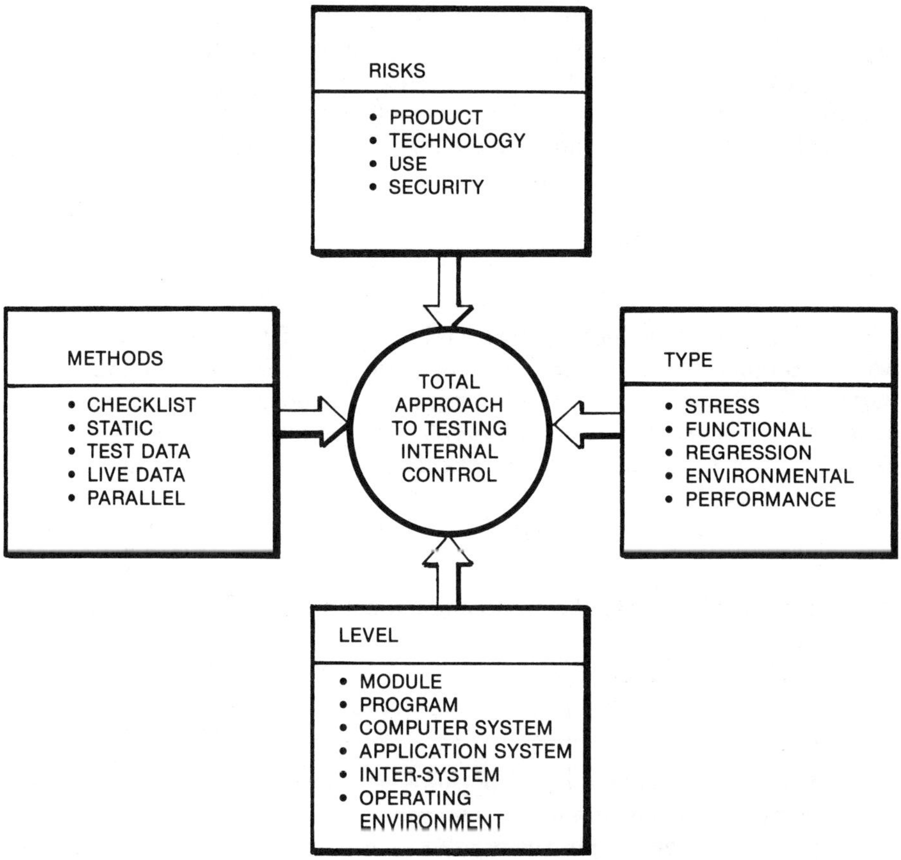

ated with the environment, such as insufficient storage or communication capabilities, and these too must be addressed if performance is to be improved.

LEVEL OF TESTING

The level of testing determines which components of the operating environment will be tested. Again, the audit objectives will, to a large measure, determine which level or what components of the application system need to be tested.

The six levels of testing to consider are:

- **Module**—The testing of a *segment* of a program that performs a specific task, such as the interest calculation on savings accounts, or the FICA deduction on payroll.
- **Program**—The testing of *all of the modules* that are linked and compiled into a single program. This is sometimes labeled ''string'' testing.
- **Computer system**—The testing of a *series of programs* that are interconnected as one processing unit, such as all the programs needed to produce weekly payroll checks, or to bill customers for products ordered.
- **Application system**—The testing of both the *computer system and the manual interfaces*. This test level would test from the point where data is originated through the use of that data in a user area. In other words, from human to human.
- **Intersystem**—This test *validates the links between two or more computer systems* or application systems.
- **Operating environment**—Testing *the functioning of all the operating support systems* needed to enable computer systems to function properly.

Figure 2-1 summarizes the key elements that converge to help you develop a sound and total approach to testing internal control in computerized systems.

3

How to Evaluate the Approaches to Testing Internal Control

THE IMPORTANCE OF PLANNING

Studies have shown that the time of the day and day of the week, as well as people's attitudes at a particular point in time, affect the accuracy and completeness of processing. On the other hand, computers are machines. They follow, precisely, the instructions they have been given. Thus, while auditors cannot rely on the consistency of people, they can rely on the consistency of machines, when the machines are properly programmed.

However, if you are to place greater reliance on the internal controls in an automated application, then the auditor must develop an assessment methodology that justifies that reliance. In a manual system, auditors tended to rely upon internal control questionnaires. These questionnaires established the atmosphere in which controls flourished, but did little to show the interrelationships between and the inner workings of controls. This was often not necessary because the auditor would do extensive testing.

In a computerized application, the total system of control must be assessed if the auditor is going to place reliance upon that control system. This involves a clear understanding of the application, the controls over the application, and the interrelationship of the controls. This requires that the auditor develop a *plan* for assessing the controls which takes these considerations into account.

In this section, we will review the steps for assessing internal control in computerized applications. The section provides a step-by-step methodology that will lead the auditor or test specialist through the test process. However, the final audit judgment must still rest with the auditor. The procedure presented will aid the auditor materially in providing the information and documentation needed to make that judgment.

Main Steps for Assessing Internal Control

The four main parts in the conduct of a test of internal control in any environment are:

1. Determine *what to test*

2. Determine *how to test*
3. *Perform the tests*
4. *Evaluate and report* results

These four parts of testing do not change in an automated environment. However, the methods by which these steps are performed may change significantly depending upon the type and characteristics of the application system under review. The more the application relies on automated information, the more important it becomes to assess the adequacy of the system's internal controls.

The four parts of the assessment process can in turn be subdivided into detailed audit steps. While these detailed audit steps also apply to a manual environment, the discussion will be devoted to automated applications. The steps to test internal control are summarized in Figure 3-1 and further described below.

- **Step 1—Risk analysis.** You identify the threats to an application system which may result in a loss. Threats are ever present, such as the potential for erroneous input. The threats, or the events that may damage the organization, must be identified before the adequacy of control can be evaluated. Next, a risk analysis process should take place to quantify the likelihood that the threat will occur and the severity of the risk so that the auditor can determine the degree of audit effort that should be allocated to each risk.

  A **threat** *represents the potential for an adverse event to take place, given a set of prevailing circumstances or conditions. A* ***risk*** *represents the* ***probability*** *that a threat will materialize.* ***Risk analysis*** *is the* ***process*** *of establishing risk occurrence as well as the severity of the risks for a number of situations to enable the assessor to concentrate on those areas of highest risk severity.*

- **Step 2—Establish testing objectives.** Based on the risk analysis process, the auditor should determine what to test. Ideally, the tests would be based upon the high-risk situations. For example, if you assess that there is a high risk of erroneous input, and the impact or damage that could be caused by the fruition of that risk is high, then the assessment of controls over that risk should become an objective of the test (testing objective).
- **Step 3—Determine expected results.** The auditor must determine or anticipate the results of conducting an assessment of internal control. When using questionnaires, this is determined by knowing that, for example, a yes answer is good and a no answer is bad. If the test data method is used, the actual test results would be determined. It is against these predetermined or expected results that you assess the adequacy of internal controls.
- **Step 4—Select type of testing.** The type of system testing approach to be

Figure 3-1
Main Steps to Testing Internal Control

MAIN STEP	PURPOSE
1. Risk Analysis	☐ Identify the threats, or damaging events that may result in a loss
2. Establish Testing Objectives	☐ Determine what to test
3. Determine Expected Results	☐ Establish the criteria to determine whether or not the test is successful
4. Select Type of Testing	☐ Determine which aspects of control are to be tested
5. Select Level of Testing	☐ Determine which components of operating environment will be tested
6. Select Method of Testing	☐ Determine which testing technique will be used
7. Prepare for Test	☐ Gather and/or create the needed input for the test
8. Verify Integrity of Operating Environment	☐ Assure that the test environment simulates the actual operating environment
9. Conduct Test	☐ Perform the test
10. Evaluate Results	☐ Determine differences and the causes of the differences from predetermined processing results
11. Prepare and Disseminate Test Results	☐ Inform management of test results and any required action

used is dependent upon the established testing objectives. Knowing the testing objectives, you can select the type of testing that will achieve the audit objectives. For example, if the objective is to determine that the system can handle X messages per hour, then the obvious type of testing to be used is stress testing. Stress testing is used to push the system to its limits, and thus would be valuable in determining whether X messages can be processed per unit of time.

- **Step 5—Select level of testing.** The level of testing determines which components of the operating environment will be tested. Again, this is dependent upon the established testing objectives. If the objectives are to determine that parameters passed between systems are accurate and complete, then intersystem testing would be the required level.
- **Step 6—Select method of testing.** The method of testing is determined by the actual testing technique utilized. A single testing method can be used on multiple levels and for different types of testing. For example, the preparation of test data (e.g., a method of testing) can be used for all the levels of testing, and for all the types of testing with the possible exception of environmental testing.
- **Step 7—Prepare for test.** Once the testing objectives have been established, and the type, level, and method of testing determined, then the preparation for testing begins. This includes the gathering and/or creating of the needed input for the test. In addition, it covers the procedures to be followed in conducting the test, and any documentation necessary.
- **Step 8—Verify the integrity of the operating environment.** You must be assured that the environment in which the testing occurs is the same environment as that operating in production. In many instances this will require verifying that the programs used for testing are the same programs used in production.
- **Step 9—Conduct test.** The conduct of the test is the actual performance of the test procedures. In a simple case, conducting the test may mean only completing an internal control questionnaire. However, in more complex controls testing, it may involve flow charting the system, preparing test matrices, developing test data, and processing the test data.
- **Step 10—Evaluate results.** The expected results determined in Step 3 should be compared to the actual results produced in Step 9. You should investigate any differences. Differences can be attributable to control weaknesses, errors in testing, or unexpected conditions.
- **Step 11—Prepare and disseminate test results.** Testing is of little value until the appropriate people are informed of the test results. The type of test, as well as the findings, determines who is the appropriate person to inform. Management is interested in serious and aggregate control weaknesses, or weaknesses in testing procedures, while systems and user personnel are interested in specific findings of a smaller scope which could help them fine tune the system application.

The steps involved in testing internal control, together with a synopsis of the purpose of each step, is illustrated in Figure 3-1. This figure is helpful in orienting auditors on the overall steps of the testing process. The process of testing, and the eleven testing steps involved, are illustrated in flowchart form in Figure 3-2. The flowchart of the process is designed to show which steps fall into the four previously discussed major parts of testing. In addition, the flowchart illustrates where auditors must make decisions. The decisions are indicated by a diamond-shaped symbol, while the actions are illustrated by a square or rectangular flowchart symbol.

Determining *what to test* requires the first three steps. The first is a decision process in which you must determine which risks require testing. When this has been determined, you can establish testing objectives. For each objective, you must determine the expected results, so after the test is conducted you can assess whether or not the controls are adequate.

The part of testing that determines *how to test* involves three decisions by you. The first is to select the type of testing from among the following options:

- Stress testing
- Functional testing
- Regression testing
- Environmental testing
- Performance testing

After the type of testing has been determined, you select the *level of testing* from among the following options:

- Module testing
- Program testing
- Computer system testing
- Application system testing
- Intersystem testing
- Operating environment testing

The last option in how to test is *selecting the method of testing* from among the following alternative methods:

- Checklist
- Static
- Test data
- Live data
- Parallel

The next part of testing is actually *performing* the test. This includes two procedural steps and one decision step. First, you must prepare the necessary data and instructions to conduct the test. The next step is to determine whether

Figure 3-2
The Process of Testing Internal Control

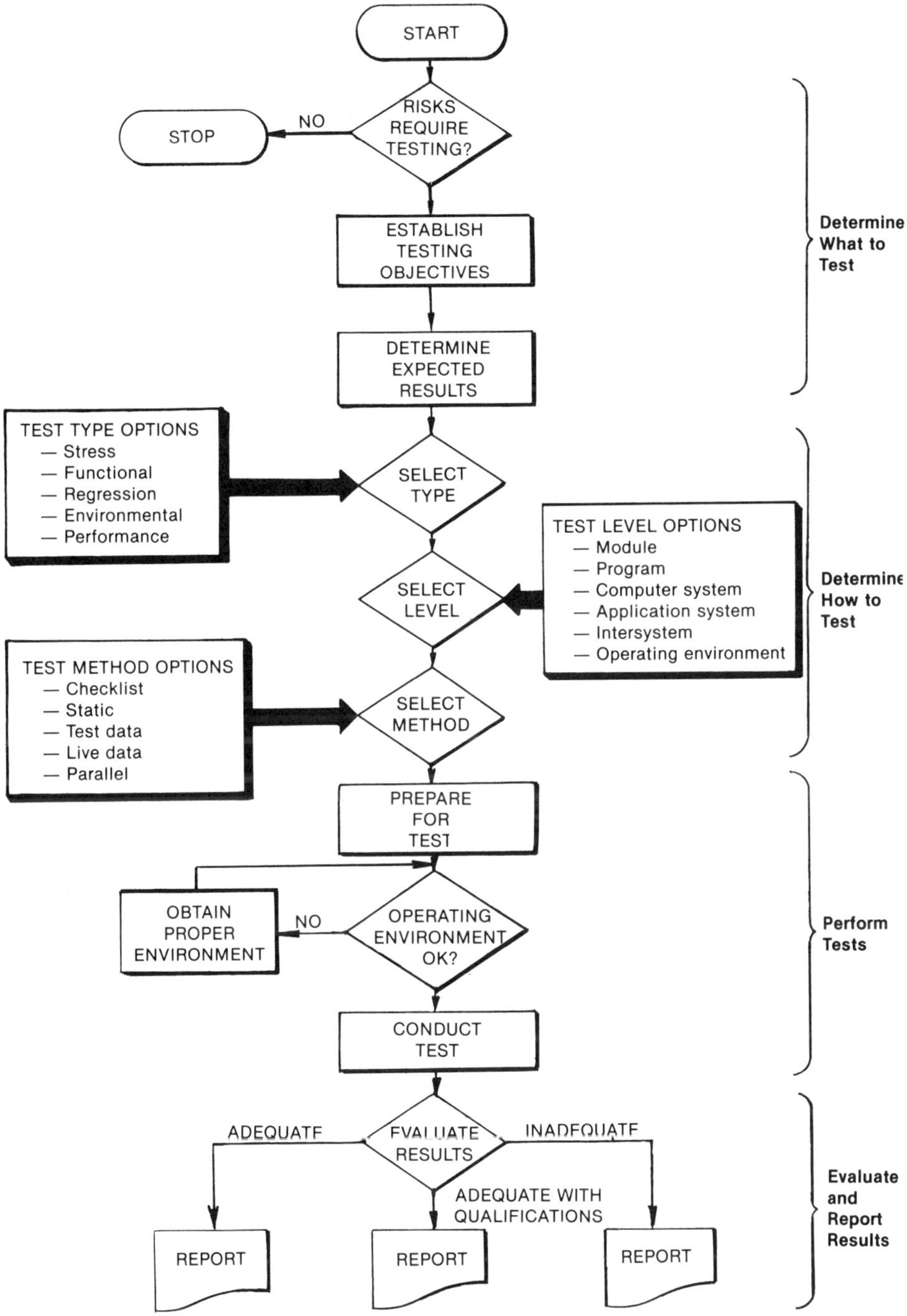

the operating environment is equivalent to the test environment. If there are discrepancies between the environments, these must be reconciled prior to conducting the test. The last part of performing the test is the *actual conduct of the test.*

The last part of the test process is to *evaluate and report results.* The evaluation is a decision step, while the reporting step is procedural. You must assess whether the test results are adequate, adequate with qualifications, or inadequate. Depending upon the evaluation, you will prepare a report with appropriate findings and recommendations.

Each major part of the testing process, as well as each step within that part, will be discussed individually.

DETERMINING *WHAT* TO TEST

The foundation upon which the test is built is the determination of *specific* test objectives. The more specific the test objectives, the easier it is to determine whether or not the test has been successful. Unfortunately, too much of the testing in the computer environment is never successfully completed because the criteria for completion is not established in the first place. This is in great measure caused by a lack of definition of *a set of specific test objectives,* which can be incorporated into a test plan.

The three aspects of determining *what should be tested* are:

- Identifying the **risks requiring testing**
- Establishing **specific testing objectives**
- Determining **expected test results**

Determining what to test involves establishing a *test plan.* The establishment of the testing objectives is, in fact, a test plan. This assumes that the objectives are established in enough detail so that the test can be derived and conducted from those objectives. Obviously, this entails a lot more than stating the testing objectives; it also involves ascertaining that the system produces accurate and complete results.

The amount of time allocated to test internal controls should be divided into approximately thirds (see Figure 3-3). One-third of the total test time should be allocated to determining what to test and how to test. The second one-third allocation of time should be for performing the test, and the remaining one-third to analyzing and reporting results.

Step 1—Risks Requiring Testing

The objective of risk analysis is to identify the threats to an application system. Until the threats are known, it is difficult to design an adequate system of internal control and to assess the adequacy of that system.

As mentioned before, in an ideal environment, controls are not necessary.

Figure 3-3
Allocation of Test Time

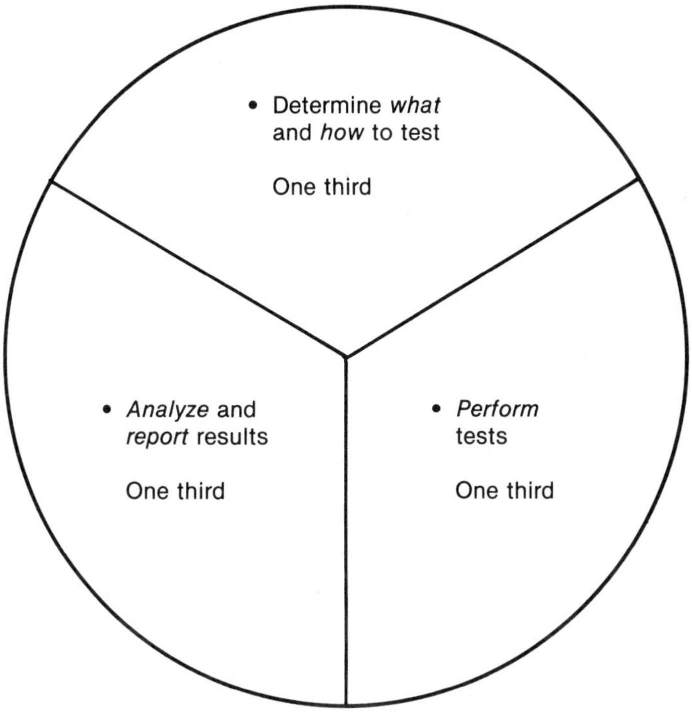

Controls are necessary only when problems or departures from the ideal situation occur. These problems are the results of damaging events which turn risks into financial or data integrity losses.

The risk assessment process tells us what type of test we should develop. Obviously, it makes little sense to test a risk or condition in which there is very little probability of loss. For example, the risk of someone stealing a building is very low, and thus to design tests to assess the adequacy of control over someone stealing the buildings is probably a poor use of auditor time. While this example is obviously remote, there are many risks of a similar nature in a computerized application which the auditor should discern. Some risks which appear remote include:

- Issuing duplicate payroll checks
- Electronic eavesdropping
- Not paying an employee

These are real risks, and they could happen, depending upon the type of activity in which your company or organization is engaged. The point is that the probability is so low that the estimated annual loss that might be determined through risk analysis would be considerably less than the assessment process for evaluating the controls. On the other hand, some risks appear to be quite high, such as:

- Creating an automatically computer-generated record for an unwanted product or service
- Cascading of errors through a series of computerized applications
- Input errors to master data

When these types of risks are subjected to a risk analysis evaluation, the estimated annual loss might be so high that they warrant extensive internal control assessment and testing. It is through this process that the auditor can fully appreciate both the risks, and the annual dollar loss from these risks as they impact the application under audit.

Chapter 2 identified the four types of risks that need to be considered when reviewing systems of internal control. These are the product risk, technology risk, use risk, and security risk.

The overall risk assessment process involves the following nine steps:

- Set the audit objectives.
- Develop an audit strategy (e.g., preliminary review) planning phase.
- Understand the system (i.e., identify the control structure).
- Evaluate the individual controls employed in the system.
- Evaluate the total system of control employed by the system.
- Determine the degree of reliance to be placed on the system of controls.
- Design the audit tests.
- Conduct the audit tests.
- Use audit judgment to reach an opinion and issue recommendations (i.e., evaluate the results of audit tests).

The risks developed from this process should be identified as specifically as possible. It is difficult to assess a general risk, but relatively easy to assess the controls needed over a specific risk. However, understanding the general risks makes it easier to develop some specific risks, by a process of delineating the highly specific risks that might result from each of the general risks.

The general risks were described in Chapter 2. For example, some product risks that were general in nature included:

- The data produced by the system will be inaccurate.
- The data produced by the system will not be prepared on a timely basis.

From these general risks, the auditor should develop a series of specific risks to be quantified during the risk assessment process. For example, in a payroll application, the specific risks for the general risk that data might be inaccurate include:

- The hours reported by employees will be inaccurate.
- The pay rate used for the gross pay calculation will be inaccurate.
- Overtime hours will be inaccurately reported.
- The year-to-date deductions will be inaccurately calculated.
- Net pay will be inaccurately calculated.
- The days of vacation taken will be inaccurately reported.
- Changes to the payroll master will be inaccurately entered.

The auditor should attempt to develop an exhaustive list of risks. This is not as time-consuming as it may appear at first. Experience has shown that in major computer systems there are normally only twenty to forty risks. In some systems, the number may be lower than twenty.

For each general risk, the auditor should then devise a list of specific risks. Again, for each general risk, there may be an average of five specific risks. Therefore, the total number of risks for an application is probably between 100 and 200.

For each of the specific risks, you must attempt to quantify an annual loss. This again is not as complex as it may sound.[1] Using some of the simpler risk analysis techniques, an auditor should be able to quantify five to ten risks per hour. However, during this process it is helpful to have someone from the user area furnish additional input. For example, if payroll is being audited then someone from the payroll department should be asked to participate in this risk assessment process.

At the end of the risk assessment process, you should have developed a prioritized list of risks. The risks are prioritized in accordance with their potential annual dollar loss. See Figure 3-4 for an example of such a listing. This listing then becomes the basis for establishing audit and test objectives.

Step 2—Establish Testing Objectives

This step involves establishing not only testing objectives, but a test plan. The establishment of the testing objectives is based heavily on the results of the risk analysis step. Next, the test plan should be prepared using auditing test procedures.

The eleven steps outlined in this book are, in fact, a test plan. The eleven steps cover all the items required for testing internal control in an automated application. Auditing procedures and techniques for testing systems should provide the auditor with the testing methodology. This could be accomplished by requiring auditors or system test specialists to read this manual prior to testing internal control in an automated application and by consulting other sources for details of audit techniques. Also, Figure 3-5 provides you with a

[1] Refer to W. E. Perry and J. F. Kuong, *EDP Risk Analysis and Controls Justification* (Wellesley Hills, MA: Management Advisory Publications, 1981) Chap. 3.

Figure 3-4
Prioritized Application System Risk

APPLICATION SYSTEM: Payroll			
Risk Priority	**General Risk**	**Specific Risk**	**Annual Dollar Risk**
1	Data is inaccurate	a. Hours incorrectly reported	$86,000
2	Data is inaccurate	b. Payroll master data incorrectly entered	51,000
3	Data is untimely	a. Federal tax deductions are deposited late	26,000
4	Data is inaccurate	a. Employee unexcused (i.e., unpaid) absences are not reported	13,800
5	Etc.		

checklist to be used as a guide when testing controls in automated applications.

The test objectives are established by analysis of the prioritized application system risks. If the risks appear minimal, you may wish not to test that particular risk, or to conduct only minimal tests. On the other hand, the areas of high risk are the areas where the majority of the audit time should be allocated.

In this step, you should determine if there are any actions in the test plan that need to be determined quickly. For example, if there are limited retention periods on computerized data, you may have to take action quickly.

The testing objective is developed from the specific risks. If we analyze the risks outlined in Figure 3-4, we can see how this process is performed. For example, the highest risk in this example is that the work hours will be incorrectly reported. The annual dollar risk has indicated that the organization could lose $86,000 per year from this risk. The thinking that went into setting the annual dollar risk can be used in setting specific test objectives. There may be several test objectives for a specific risk, or, on the other hand, one test objective may encompass two or more specific risks.

In the example, "hours incorrectly reported," you must determine where the greatest points of risks are so that controls at those points can be tested. In this example, we can see three control points. These are:

- The point at which the employee records the hours worked
- The point at which the supervisor approves the hours worked
- The point at which the hours are transcribed to computer media

At any of these points, there can be an error in the hours reported. For example, the employee might make a mistake in recording the hours, the super-

Figure 3-5
Internal Control Assessment Checklist

Question No.	Control Task to be Performed	Task Performed By	Date Task Performed	Comments
1	Identify application system risks.			
2	Determine the annual dollar loss for the risks.			
3	Prioritize the risks.			
4	Establish detailed testing objectives.			
5	Document the steps needed to achieve the testing objective (a detailed test plan).			
6	Determine the expected result for each test objective.			
7	Select the level of testing required to achieve each testing objective.			
8	Select the test technique for each testing objective.			
9	Prepare necessary test data for each test objective.			
10	Have the test data prepared into machine-readable format if required.			
11	Arrange for computer time to run the test if required.			
12	Prepare the necessary job control language statements or equivalent needed to conduct the test if required.			
13	Make specific assignments to individuals to conduct the test.			
14	Arrange to acquire all the necessary computerized data required to conduct the test, if necessary.			
15	Determine that the operating environment for the test is the same as the actual operating environment.			
16	If the environment is different, take whatever steps are necessary to ensure the integrity of the operating environment.			
17	Conduct the test in the controlled environment.			
18	Make arrangements to save all the documentation produced by the test.			

(Continued)

Figure 3-5
Internal Control Assessment Checklist
(Continued)

Question No.	Control Task to be Performed	Task Performed By	Date Task Performed	Comments
19	Compare the test results to the expected test results.			
20	Investigate differences between the actual and expected test results.			
21	If there were problems in conducting the test that caused problems, rerun the test.			
22	Evaluate actual problems to determine their potential impact on the application being reviewed.			
23	Develop recommendations to correct control weaknesses if possible.			
24	Prepare a report outlining the results of the test.			
25	Disseminate the report to the appropriate people.			
26	Follow up on a continuing basis to determine that the findings and recommendations are acted upon on a timely basis.			

visor might not perform sufficient checks to verify that the hours are correct, and a data entry error can be made as the data is transcribed to computer media.

Thus, there are three test objectives that could be established for this one risk. Determine that:

- Employees record hours worked correctly
- Supervisors verify hours worked prior to approval
- Hours worked is properly recorded on computer media

The testing objectives should be recorded on a test plan form. Figure 3-6 illustrates such a form. The example previously discussed has been recorded on this to illustrate how the form should be used.

Step 3—Determine Expected Results

The establishment of the expected results from a testing objective is a two-part process. The first part establishes a generic test result, and the second

Figure 3-6
Testing Objectives Test Plan

Testing Objective	Expected Generic Test Results	How to Test			Test Preparation Steps
		Type	Level	Method	
Determine that: Employees record hours worked correctly					
Determine that: Supervisors verify hours worked prior to approval					
Determine that: Hours worked is properly recorded on computer media					

part establishes a specific test result. It is helpful in designing and evaluating tests to go through the two-part process.

Determining the generic test result is equivalent to designing a computerized application, while determining the specific test result is more closely allied to programming. One is high level and conceptual in nature, while the other is low level and detailed in scope. Just as it is difficult to develop good programs without system design specifications, so is it difficult to determine the expected results from a test without first establishing a generic result.

The generic test result can be specified in terms of a *control action;* the specific test results are equated to the actual results of processing data. For example, when analyzing an error condition, the generic test result may be to "reject" the transaction. The specific test result would be to issue error message "number 1, 2, 3, 4, 5, which says transaction X has been deleted."

The most common generic control actions in a computerized application are:

- **Reject**—*The event which is being evaluated is prohibited from completing the processing cycle*. The rejection can occur at any point during the application system. This can be in a manual or automated segment of processing. In most cases where data is rejected, an error message is produced.

- **Accept with warning**—*the condition being evaluated is accepted but the attributes of what is being accepted are questionable.* For example, an employee may indicate that he worked sixty hours overtime in a week. This might be acceptable by the system, but is questionable because it is impractical that an employee would work that many overtime hours. The acceptance with warning enables people to make a judgment as to whether or not it is an actual situation. In our example the employee either did or did not work sixty hours overtime. But unless someone takes a specific action, the condition or event will be processed.
- **Modify with notice**—*The event or condition being monitored is changed based on the processing rules.* For example, a customer orders product X, but product X is temporarily out of stock. The organization may substitute product Y, which is an improved version of product X, and accept and process the order. The customer is notified of the substitution, but the order is processed. In computer terminology, this is frequently referred to as a "default option."
- **Update**—*The event or condition is changed based upon the processing rules.* Update is one of the most common results of a control action. For example, in accounts receivable or banking the customer's balance is changed or updated by each transaction. Normally, certain conditions have to be met prior to updating or changing a quantity or balance.
- **Lookup**—*The desired information is retrieved from storage for the purpose of decision making.* For example, a sales clerk may desire to know the status of a customer's credit prior to selling merchandise on credit.
- **Delete**—*The elimination of a condition or data.* For example, when employees are terminated their information may be removed from the personnel file and other files within the organization. This deletion may occur immediately, or it may occur at a specified point in time after the deleting condition has occurred.
- **Create**—*Information is added to the organization's records.* For example, a new customer is added to the customer master, a new employee to the payroll file, etc.
- **Calculate**—*A mathematical operation is performed.* The mathematics can involve addition, subtraction, multiplication, or division or other functions. However, an action involving the changing of an account balance should be considered an update process. Calculations normally involve intermediate actions resulting in an amount that may update an account balance. For example, the federal withholding tax in payroll is the result of a mathematical calculation, and the tax withheld for a specific pay period "updates" the federal withholding tax year-to-date totals.

- **Replace**—Here, one value is substituted for another value. This is very common on master files when, for example, the price of a product is replaced with a new price or an employee's wage rate is replaced with a new wage rate.

In determining the expected result from a testing objective, you should analyze that objective to determine generically what to expect.

Figure 3-7 illustrates this process. For example, the testing objective "employees record hours worked correctly" would have only one expected result, which is the creation or recording of hours. Thus, any tests would revolve around the employee creating the hours-worked figure. The testing objectives of "supervisors verify hours worked prior to approval" and "hours worked is properly recorded on computer media" both have the same expected generic test results. These are that improperly recorded hours would be rejected, whereas questionable recorded hours might be accepted with a warning, or modified with notice. For example, a supervisor may not have authorized an employee to work overtime, but accepts the hours for overtime payment with a warning that the employee should not do it again, or the supervisor may compromise with the employee and pay only partial overtime hours. The computerized application would go through many of the same analyses. For example, if

Figure 3-7
Testing Objectives Test Plan

Testing Objective	Expected Generic Test Results	How to Test			Test Preparation Steps
		Type	Level	Method	
Determine that: Employees record hours worked correctly	•Create				
Determine that: Supervisors verify hours worked prior to approval	•Reject •Accept with warning •Modify with notice				
Determine that: Hours worked is properly recorded on computer media	•Reject •Accept with warning •Modify with notice				

hours worked was alphabetic, it would be rejected; or, if over a certain number of hours, it would be rejected. Within a limited range such as 20 to 50 hours, the overtime may be accepted with a warning for people to determine if it is actual hours worked or a data entry error. In other instances, the hours worked may be modified, such as ninety hours overtime may be changed to nine hours and a notice put out to verify if that is truly the correct amount.

You should enter the expected test results onto the testing objective test plan, Figure 3-7. The completion of this worksheet will provide the audit plan for testing the adequacy of internal controls in computerized applications.

DETERMINING *HOW* TO TEST

The tests you design should achieve the testing objectives established in Step 2. This part of the test process is the completion of test planning. The objective of this aspect of planning is to select the type, level, and method of testing to be used to achieve the test objectives.

Step 4—Select Type of Testing

There are different types of testing available to you. Each type of test subjects the computerized application to different types of analyses. These analyses should complement the characteristics of the test objectives.

It should be readily apparent from the test objectives which type of testing is most appropriate. As described in Chapter 2, and Figure 3-2, the five options and the testing objectives they best accomplish are:

- **Stress testing**—This type of testing satisfies testing objectives designed to push the application system to its limits; for example, testing objectives designed to determine the volumes of transactions that an application can process, or test objectives designed to determine what happens when tables or disk packs or diskettes have been exceeded. Stress testing is normally high-volume testing. It enables the auditor to determine, in a test environment, the breaking point in a system.
- **Functional testing**—A large majority of the auditor's test objectives will fall into the functional category. This is analogous to compliance testing. Computerized applications are designed to achieve certain objectives for a function. For example, a payroll system function is the calculation of net pay, an accounts receivable function would be to check credit limits, and an inventory function would be to automatically replenish stock when it falls below a predetermined point. Any test objective involved in verifying that the system performs as specified would be achieved through functional testing.
- **Regression testing**—One of the problems that has plagued data processing from its inception is the introduction of one change causing appar-

ently unrelated problems. For example, if a specification is changed, such as changing the FICA percentage deduction in a payroll system, that change would be verified using functional testing. However, if your test objective is to verify that all other functions in the application system perform as they did prior to the FICA change, then you should use regression testing. Regression testing applies to those test objectives related to assuring the integrity of unchanged segments of computerized applications and is used to determine that no "cascade" or "domino" effect has taken place.

- **Environmental testing**—The testing objectives that can best be achieved by environmental testing are those related to the control atmosphere in which the applications function. In most systems, these are manual policies and procedures. However, in many advanced data processing systems, many environmental controls are automated. For example, in a data base environment, security procedures may be automated through the implementation of security profiles (a profile of what a function or entity is allowed to do). Test objectives relating to more than one application are verified through environmental testing. This is similar to functional testing, but at the environmental level.
- **Performance testing**—The testing objectives that relate to operational economy, effectiveness, and efficiency are verified through performance testing. Performance testing covers the operational and efficiency aspects of computerized applications. For example, test objectives that relate to response times, turnaround times, efficient use of code, and interface between the application and the operating system, are best verified through performance testing. This type of testing may require special hardware or software monitors to measure the operational performance. It is normally a very technical aspect of testing because the auditor must not only verify that the results are correct, but that the methods of achieving those results are properly designed and implemented. This may require measuring the execution time of routines within programs.

You should enter the type of testing selected onto the testing objective test plan form. See Figure 3-8 for an example of a completed test plan form. Note on this form that for the testing objective "employees record hours worked correctly" the environmental-type testing has been selected. This is because recording hours applies to all employees and is considered to be general in nature. The test objective "supervisors verify hours worked prior to approval" is also environmental in nature because it, too, applies to all areas within the organization. However, the test objective "hours worked is properly recorded on computer media" is reviewed using functional testing because the program rules for editing and validating the hours field are included in a single payroll program. This would involve compliance testing of the application rules.

Figure 3-8
Testing Objectives Test Plan

Testing Objective	Expected Generic Test Results	How to Test			Test Preparation Steps
		Type	Level	Method	
Determine that: Employees record hours worked correctly	•Create	12/10 Environmental	12/10 Application system	12/10 Checklist	
Determine that: Supervisors verify hours worked prior to approval	•Reject •Accept with warning •Modify with notice	Environmental	Environmental	Checklist	
Determine that: Hours worked is properly recorded on computer media	•Reject •Accept with warning •Modify with notice	Functional	Environmental and Module	Test data	

Step 5—Select Level of Testing

The level of testing performed is dependent upon where the routines covered by the test objective are located. You should attempt to test at the lowest level possible. This makes the test function easier by concentrating the test on a smaller segment of the computerized application.

You analyze the test objective and then determine what processing logic is responsible for the area covered by the test objective. For example, if you are going to evaluate the FICA deduction, then you would be looking for the processing logic that calculates the FICA deduction. You would then inquire of the computer systems personnel where that processing logic is located. The answer to that question would determine the lowest level of processing that can be evaluated to satisfy the desired testing objective.

There are six levels of testing, which are listed below in order of increasing size:

- **Module**—*A routine within a program.* This would be used when processing logic can be isolated to a segment within a program. For example, the FICA deduction logic is probably performed in a program module.
- **Program**—*A grouping of one or more modules tied together to achieve a common objective.* A program normally groups together one type of

function such as input edit. Testing objectives that deal with one specific function could be achieved at the program level.

- **Computer system**—*The automated aspects of an application.* If the test objectives were limited to the automated segments of an application system, they could be achieved by testing at the computer system level.
- **Application system**—*The processing that occurs from the inception of a transaction through the use of processing results.* Test objectives that involve the manual aspects of computerized applications, or the manual automated interface, require application system testing.
- **Intersystem**—*The interface between two or more application systems.* For example, product usage may be fed into an inventory system for the purpose of automatic inventory replenishment. If the testing objectives involve the interface between application systems, this level of testing must be utilized.
- **Operating environment**—*This level of testing is unique to automated applications.* It covers the large software systems provided by vendors to aid and govern the processing of application systems. The operating environment includes operating systems, communication systems, data base management systems, the operating system library, and various system software utilities.

The selected level of testing should be recorded on the testing objectives test plan form. See Figure 3-8 for a completed example. In this example, all three test objectives must be evaluated at the application system level. This is because there are manual procedures involved in verifying all of the test objectives. However, the test objective "hours worked is properly recorded on computer media" can also be verified at the module level. You would want to look at or test that module of a program that edits the hours field.

Step 6—Select Method of Testing

The method of testing involves the specific testing technique to be used by the auditor. You must evaluate the test objectives and then determine which technique is the most appropriate to achieve the test objectives. The five options for *method* of testing along with the test objectives for which they would be most appropriate are listed and summarized below:

- **Checklist**—*The use of checklists is most effective for reviewing manual operations and identifying general control weaknesses.* The advantages of checklists are that they provide a degree of consistency in reviews between reviewers, and they provide a guide for you to follow so that control areas are not overlooked. However, relying too heavily on a checklist may result in overlooking potential control weaknesses which might otherwise be uncovered with additional probing. You can use generalized checklists, or develop specific checklists for a specific test purpose. If time permits, the preferred way is to develop a specialized checklist for an individual test using a generalized checklist as a guide. This is a part of the test plan.

- **Static testing**—*Static analysis analyzes a situation without the use of test data*. For example, it would involve the analysis of procedures, policies, documentation, and computer programs. Using the available processing methodology, you simulate the effective processing and make an audit judgment based on that simulation. Using computer programs, this is often referred to as "what if" or "ask" debugging.

  When referring to static testing in Chapter 2, reference was made to two popular techniques to assist you in doing static testing, namely, "transaction flow analysis" and "transaction conflict matrix." *Transaction flow analysis* consists of using a system flowchart of the domain one wishes to test and then superimposing on it a set of key control points at which activity takes place. The auditor then selects a test transaction and follows it through the system logic, in fact, doing what amounts to the conventional walk-through, except this time doing the walking on paper. When one uses the "structured walk-through" technique used by data processing professionals to explain a system to users, the test professional is essentially applying a form of the transaction flow technique. The difference in the two techniques is that the transaction flow analysis emphasizes the flow of the transaction past the controls and the control points, whereas the structured walk-through tends to emphasize data processing flow.

  The transaction conflict matrix is a test technique that helps the auditor identify transactions which are contradictory or incompatible with one another. In other words, sets of transactions that should not occur in the presence of one another or that are mutually exclusive. For example, in a payroll system, the transaction "pay exempt employee" is incompatible with the transaction "pay overtime to exempt employee." The matrix is constructed by simply listing all key transactions of a system in a matrix vertically and across the matrix. All the diagonal cells in the matrix are possible and legal. However, upon further analysis, the auditor tries to determine those pairs or sets of transactions that are "incompatible or not allowed to happen." Based on this matrix, the auditor may then set up test conditions to validate whether the conflicting transactions can occur in the system.

- **Test data**—*The objectives best accomplished through the use of test data* are those that are compliance oriented. Test data is used in the automated aspects of computerized applications. While the static testing uses flowcharts and matrices, the test data testing requires that you create actual test transactions. The two most common methods for creating test transactions are:

  –**Input forms:** You prepare the input using the normal input forms of the application system. The data is then entered into the application through the normal data entry means. Note that the integrated test facility test technique makes heavy use of this type of test data creation.

-**Computer records:** You create the actual computer record images complete with codes and other computer system data characteristics. This is often technically complex because you must understand both the data characteristics of the computer, as well as the codes and data structure of the application being tested.

- **Live data**—*Using actual transactions enables you to assess the results of actual processing*. You can select actual transactions as they are being entered and follow them through processing, or use audit software to extract the results of processing of certain types of transactions. This method of testing not only verifies the actual results of processing data, but also permits you to evaluate compliance to processing rules and procedures.
- **Parallel testing**—*This method utilizes the same data through two versions of the processing rules*. The two versions may be a before and after image of a program or application reflecting a change. The two versions may be a controlled version of an application system and the current version, or it may be an *old version* and an independently *rewritten version* of a program or application system. Parallel testing is frequently performed to determine whether programs and/or systems have been converted to a new computer language or version properly. Also, you may wish to simulate computer processing as a means of testing. For example, you may wish to write the FICA deduction computation using audit software and then run all of the application data through the test routine that you wrote. The results from your program are then compared to the actual processing results and the differences investigated.

Upon completing the selection of the testing method, you should enter the selected method onto the testing objectives test plan form. An example is illustrated in Figure 3-8. In this example, the checklist method is suggested for the first two testing objectives. This is because those objectives require analysis of manual procedures, and can best be checked through specially designed checklists. The last objective "hours worked is properly recorded on computer media" can be tested through the use of test data. You prepare test data showing the different types of input that might be entered and then determine that the processing result is in compliance with the payroll policies and procedures.

PERFORMING THE TEST

The test may be performed by an individual other than the one determining the what and how aspects of the test. A higher level of skill is required to properly determine what and how to test. A lesser-skilled auditor can prepare for and conduct the test. Further, determining that the operating environment is the proper environment is a highly technical area. However, it may not be necessary to perform this step each time testing occurs if the auditors have assured themselves of the integrity of the operating environment at another time.

Step 7—Prepare for Test

Preparations for a test will vary significantly depending upon the test objectives, type, level, and method of testing. However, adequate preparation involves a number of tasks and many of those tasks are common to all testing processes.

Preparing for the test involves detailed test planning. The test objectives, methodology, and expected results were documented in the test planning part of testing. Now the auditor must work out the detailed procedures to execute that plan. The same type of function is performed in the computer field when EDP takes program specifications and converts them to program code.

The tasks that you should perform in preparing for the test include:

- **Ascertain computer media retention**—Frequently, needed computer media will not be saved until the time that you desire to conduct the test. Therefore, you must determine all the needed computer media for the test and then ascertain that that media will be available at the time the test is to be conducted. If normal EDP retention periods are insufficient for audit purposes, you must take the necessary steps to assure that the data will be retained.
- **Reserve computer time**—If computer time availability is tight, or the test will require extensive computer time, it should be reserved sufficiently in advance to assure there will be no delays in conducting the test. However, if only minor amounts of computer time are needed this task may not be necessary.
- **Prepare detailed test data**—If test data is to be prepared, it should be prepared sufficiently in advance so as not to delay the test. The test planning part will have given general specifications for test data. However, the actual test records are prepared during this step. This is normally a mechanical process which involves understanding computer codes and which is not required to specify the type of conditions that should be tested.
- **Prepare test programs**—If audit software or other computer language is used, the program must be written and tested. This is a lengthy and time-comsuming process, which may require many weeks to accomplish.
- **Document test procedures**—Work papers should be prepared that docu-

ment the detailed test procedures. This can be accomplished using the testing objective test plan form. (See Figure 3-6.)

- **Prepare job control language (JCL) instructions/cards**—Many operating environments require that you prepare special job control language instructions so that your program can be run in the operating environment. Some audit software languages include this step as part of the coding of the audit software programs.
- **Determine verification procedures**—The test plan has determined the expected results. However, it may be a very time-consuming task to perform that step. Therefore, you may wish to automate that aspect of testing. Some organizations use testing utility programs that compare the actual results to expected results. If these types of automated tools are available, they should be used.
- **Develop a detailed "testing type" plan**—You should work out the detailed implementation of the proposed testing type. This would involve such things as determining how to create enough transactions to conduct the stress test, and what type of monitors are needed to execute the performance test, if the latter is included in the test.
- **Develop detailed level testing plan**—You must isolate and identify the specific module, program, systems, etc. needed for the specified level of testing. This may involve discussions with both the application system personnel and the computer operations personnel. You must also determine that the appropriate version of the testing level will be available when needed.
- **Develop detailed "testing method" plan**—You must determine the procedures for utilizing the proposed testing method. For example, if a checklist is to be used, you must either obtain or create the appropriate checklist.

Prepare and enter the test preparation steps on the testing objectives test plan form. The type of documentation and tasks resulting from this step are illustrated on Figure 3-9. Our example shows three testing objectives and previous figures have illustrated the creation of the test plan. Now you must define and document the detailed test preparation steps.

For the testing objective "employees record hours worked correctly" two test tasks are needed. The first is to develop a checklist to assess the procedures for employees recording their time. For example, you would be interested in knowing if this is to be done daily, or whether it is only done monthly. The more controlled the procedures, the higher your confidence that the task will be performed correctly by employees. The second step is for you to execute the test and assess the results. This involves performing the steps outlined in the checklist and then evaluating the answers to the questions.

The second testing objective is to determine that "supervisors verify hours worked prior to approval." This involves the same two steps that were

Figure 3-9
Testing Objectives Test Plan

Testing Objective	Expected Generic Test Results	How to Test			Test Preparation Steps
		Type	Level	Method	
Determine that: Employees record hours worked correctly	•Create	12/10 Environmental	12/10 Application system	12/10 Checklist	1. Develop a checklist to assess the procedures for employees recording their time 2. Execute and assess tests
Determine that: Supervisors verify hours worked prior to approval	•Reject •Accept with warning •Modify with notice	Environmental	Environmental	Checklist	1. Develop a checklist to assess a supervisor's procedures for verifying and approving employee hours 2. Execute and assess tests
Determine that: Hours worked is properly recorded on computer media	•Reject •Accept with warning •Modify with notice	Functional	Environmental and Module	Test data	1. Develop a checklist to assess data entry procedures 2. Prepare test data to test hours reported 3. Execute and assess tests

used in preparing to test the previous objective. You would want to develop and use a checklist which interrogates the procedures used by supervisors to verify that the hours recorded by employees were authorized and actually worked.

The third testing objective is to determine that "hours worked" is properly recorded on computer media. This involves both a manual and an automated process and thus is more complex to test. In this example, you have again chosen to use a checklist to verify the adequacy of the manual controls over data entry. However, to test the automated edits and verification procedures, you have elected to develop test data. This test data would include not only normal working hours, but a series of error conditions to verify that the system will recognize and reject or identify these questionable or erroneous conditions.

These test procedures accomplish the test objectives outlined during the test plan. However, you could have established other testing objectives or methods which would have altered the planning process. For example, you may have determined that regression testing would be necessary; this would require extensive preparation of test data.

Step 8—Verify Integrity of Operating Environment

One aspect of testing in a computerized environment that has plagued auditors is the verification of the integrity of the operating environment. Specifically, this involves knowing with certainty that:

- The program being tested is the same program used in the operating environment
- The operating environment prohibits unauthorized modification of data and/or programs during the test process
- The data files used for the test are accurate and complete
- Your extract mechanism cannot be modified during execution

With few exceptions, the current state of the art in operating environment control makes it difficult to achieve this certainty. This is especially true for the nontechnical person who has little understanding of the loopholes embedded in operating systems. For example, most vendor-produced software has "user exits" which enable knowledgeable personnel to insert routines for execution during operating times. This would enable these routines to modify data in buffer areas where there would be no audit trail to detect the occurrence of unauthorized processing.

Your real concern should be the integrity of the operating environment on a day-to-day basis, and not just the integrity during the specific test process. If you cannot rely upon the day-to-day integrity of processing, then you cannot rely on the integrity of the operating environment during the test process. In those instances where the integrity is uncertain, you should conduct an extensive audit on the strengths and weaknesses of controls in the operating environment. This is accomplished by means of a separate operational audit.

If the operating environment appears reasonable, the following steps can be taken to ensure the integrity of the operating environment:

- **File integrity**—The files used in the test environment should be verified to prove file integrity. This may involve:
  –Footing key fields and verifying to external control totals
  –A printout of internal file header and trailer records
  –A count of records on the file
  –Extracting data on a random basis and verifying those records, and then making a statistical inference as to the integrity of the file.

–In data base systems, a check for broken links or other data base anomalies

- **Application program verification**—You must verify that the program used in the test environment is the same program used in the operating environment. Some of the techniques helpful in this verification include:
  –*Verifying from the operating system log that the version used during the test is the same version number that is in production,* if your organization uses program version numbers.
  –*Maintaining control copies of programs that have been verified in the audit department* to compare them to the programs used in the test environment. Hash totals or time/date stamps can be used to determine uniqueness.
  –*Extracting the programs being used in the production environment and then comparing them to a control copy of the same program* taken as a result of operating the test. Do this on an after-the-fact surprise basis. Utility programs can be used for this task.
- **Data or program modifications during execution**—The most technically difficult aspect of verifying the integrity of the operating environment is the determination that data and/or programs are not modified during execution. This may not be a practical step for other than a highly skilled EDP auditor, but the type of steps that can be taken include:
  –*Reviewing the use and execution of very powerful utilities.* These types of utility programs have the capability to modify the operating environment during execution, often without a trail.
  –*Identifying the purpose and execution of "user exit" routines* from operating software.
  –*Reviewing operating system logs* for unusual operator intervention and/or messages.

At a minimum, you should take some preliminary precautions to assure that the integrity of the operating environment can be relied upon. If the operator feels insecure about the technical operating aspects, then your efforts should be oriented toward data control. You should take those steps necessary to ensure the integrity of data before, during, and after processing.

Step 9—Conduct Test

The actual conduct of the test of internal control should be a mechanical process. This does not mean that your inquisitiveness and experience will not be brought into the test but, rather, that the procedures and process should be well enough established so that you need not devise the testing methodology during the conduct of the test.

If the test indicates that additional testing should be required, such additional testing should be performed by rethinking the eleven-step process. Additions to the test process during execution time can be very time-consuming and produce questionable results. In the audit of a manual application, these added steps were often valuable and necessary because of the lack of preciseness of the controls in manual systems. However, in an automated system the controls are predetermined and thus the analysis logic must be as well thought through as the logic that developed the system of controls.

The following is a list of conditions to which you should be alert during the conduct of tests of internal controls in computerized applications:

- Conditions in the automated segments of computerized applications:
  - –Lack of documentation to explain codes, error messages, or other system outputs
  - –Uncertainty as to the data input preparation steps
  - –Lack of understanding of the computerized applications by user personnel
  - –Too much control over manual processes by computer personnel
  - –Too much control residing in one person or department
- Conditions in the automated segments of computerized applications:
  - –Special operator procedures during the conduct of the test
  - –Special instructions given to the operator via operator terminal and/or logs
  - –Special operating personnel needed to run the test
  - –Missing the data files

These conditions are symptomatic of conditions that may indicate control problems. They do not necessarily represent control problems but, rather, represent conditions that should call for further investigation. To familiarize yourself with the operating environment, observe the computerized system in operation in its normal environment so that you will have a basis of comparison when the application system is run in a test environment.

EVALUATING AND REPORTING RESULTS

Many individuals conduct tests of internal control, but they really do not place heavy reliance on the outcome of those tests. This is because reviewers have found it difficult to evaluate the strengths of individual controls, and of the total system of control. In a manual environment, this approach works reasonably well because extensive testing was still required due to the inconsistency of manual processing.

In a computerized environment, the amount of testing can be truly limited when reliance can be placed on the system of internal control. Thorough analysis of controls over a single transaction type can be relied upon because the controls will be applied consistently for all other transactions of that type. When the results of the test are documented, this documentation can be used as the basis for analyzing the adequacy of internal control. The attendant results should then be disseminated to the appropriate levels of management.

Step 10—Evaluate Results

The test step for which you should be uniquely equipped is the assessment of the adequacy of internal control. However, this is a difficult step for data processing personnel to perform, mainly because they are neither trained nor experienced in control assessment. To do a proper job of control assessment, the individual assessing controls should have experience in control, the application in question, and data processing.

The control assessment process involves the following three tasks:

- Comparison of the actual results versus expected results
- Assessment of compensating controls
- Exercising auditor judgment

We will examine each of these evaluation tasks individually.

Comparison of Actual Versus Expected Results

A testing objective test plan outlines the generic results that are expected. During the "prepare for test" step the auditor should have extended the generic test results into data test results. Thus, upon completing this step, you know specifically what is the desired result from the test.

At the completion of the test, you must either manually or by automated means compare the results of actual processing to anticipated processing results.

In the simpler testing methods such as checklists, the desired answer becomes apparent through the construction of the checklist. In the more complex methods using large volumes of data, the verification of expected versus actual results may be done only on a sample basis. It may be impractical timewise for the auditor to verify the correctness of several hundred transactions. Also, in a computerized environment, this may not be necessary because all transactions of a single type should be processed by the same controls.

Assessment of Compensating Controls

In a computerized environment, it is possible to have very weak controls in one area and very strong controls in another. The concept of compensating controls suggests that the strong controls will compensate for the weaker controls. For example, a credit card company may be very *lax in issuing cards,* but have very *strong* controls regarding *the use of those cards*. The controls provide them the ability to stop issuance of credit at the time a credit card is presented. Thus, the strong use controls compensate for the weaker card issuance controls.

You should document the controls throughout a computerized application as they apply to each testing objective. You will then have in one spot all the controls that relate to the test objective. From this document, you can *relate* various internal controls and then make an assessment as to whether the totality of the controls is adequate.

A matrix for documenting the controls relating to specific test objectives is illustrated in Figure 3-10. This matrix lists the test objectives in the left-hand margin and the segments or key activities of a computerized application across the top of the matrix. The three test objectives are those used in our testing objectives test plan example (see Figure 3-6). The computer application is broken into the following segment or activities subject to control:

- **Transaction initiation**—The recording and/or initiation of the transaction
- **Authorization**—The approval to process the transaction
- **Communication**—The movement of data from initiation (source) to the processing unit
- **Input validation**—The verification of the accuracy, completeness, and authorization of data
- **Processing**—The application of the processing rules to the data
- **Storage**—The retention of manual and computerized data
- **Output**—The preparation of information for manual use
- **Use**—The use of the application-produced data or results

In the matrix on Figure 3-10, the controls are listed by number. As shown, the controls would have to be either standard controls for the organization, or there should be a supplementary list explaining what the meaning of the controls is. However, the matrices can be made big enough or you can write in the cryptic description of the control in small enough print so that the latter can be placed in the cells of the matrix.

You evaluate the adequacy of control across the horizontal span and then make a judgment on whether or not it is adequate to achieve the control objectives. The previous data analysis step provides an indication as to whether or not the control is functioning as specified. Obviously, the matrix shows only those controls that are functioning as specified and/or shows them as they are actually being executed.

Step 11—Prepare and Disseminate Test Results

The final step of the test process is to prepare and disseminate the results of the test. This step is normally dependent upon the organization's practices. For example, audit reports often have predetermined distribution lists. However, listed below are some tips and techniques that can be of value in the reporting process.

Figure 3-10
Example of a Matrix for Relating Test Objectives to Controls Solutions

CONTROL / TESTING OBJECTIVES	TRANSACTION INITIATION	AUTHORIZATION	COMMUNICATION	INPUT VALIDATION	PROCESSING	STORAGE	OUTPUT	USE
• Employees record hours worked correctly	Controls #1 #2	Control #17			Control #33		Control #106	
• Supervisors verify hours worked prior to approval		Control #17					Control #106	
• Hours worked is properly recorded on computer media				Controls #62 #63 #64 #65			Controls #62 #63 #64 #65	Control #115

Numbers given in the columns do not refer to any other material in this book; rather, they refer to predetermined controls solutions you would have set up under your own compendium of numbered controls.

- **Words of Caution**—The following items should be taken into consideration when preparing reports on the assessment of internal controls in computerized applications:
  - –*Avoid the use of technical jargon on the adequacy of control* in computerized applications. The terminology on this subject is not well understood by many and thus is best avoided.
  - –*Avoid the use of data processing jargon.*
  - –Controls never provide 100 percent assurance for anything. *The report should reflect what is meant by adequate.*
  - –The assessment process should state very specifically what *is* as well as what is *not* being assessed.
- **Report Tips and Techniques**—The following suggestions will make your reports more valuable to their recipients. These suggestions reflect the needs of users as expressed over the years:
  - –*Prioritize the control weaknesses.* It is very confusing to read about and be confronted with numerous control weaknesses and not be able to evaluate their relative importance.

–*Quantify the potential impact of the control weakness.* Nothing is more valuable to management than an annual dollar estimate of the loss that might materialize or that is now occurring because of the control weakness.
–*Write the report in terms that management can understand* and not for data processing or auditing professionals alone.
–*If statistical inference is used, explain it in simple everyday terminology.*
–*Spell out clearly and in detail the action steps that need to be taken* and recommend who should perform them.
–*Review the report with and obtain agreement from the auditee on the facts and findings prior* to issuing the report. The auditee does not need to agree with the conclusions derived from the facts and findings, but should agree with the facts as stated in the report.
–*Review the report, its findings and conclusions, with the auditee prior* to presenting the report to management.
–*Include in the report the auditee's reaction to the report along with any plan of action the auditee has or action steps he plans to take* as a result of the audit report. Do this if it is practical or if the organization's procedure calls for it.

4

Specific Steps to Conducting Tests on Internal Control

TESTING OF INTERNAL CONTROL

The American Institute of Certified Public Accountants' Statement on Auditing, Standard No. 3, requires CPA's to evaluate the adequacy of systems of internal control in computerized applications; *Standards for the Professional Practice of Internal Auditing* also encourages the involvement of auditors in assessing the adequacy of control in computerized applications. The supplemental standards issued by the United States General Accounting Office require government auditors to be involved in assessing the adequacy of controls in computerized applications under development. The trend is clear: Auditors need to evaluate control in computerized applications.

Two problems have faced auditors in this assessment process. First, the EDP skills needed to assess controls in automated applications exceed the skills needed for verifying data in automated applications. Second, the methodology for evaluating controls has not been outlined in an easy to follow step-by-step format. Most control assessment performed is now done by highly skilled EDP auditors, who are in short supply. Thus the need to disseminate practical information on internal control evaluation is indeed great.

Assessing the adequacy of internal control achieves two objectives for auditors. First, by conducting the assessment the auditors fulfill their professional obligation to evaluate controls in computerized applications, leading to increased system integrity. Second, by performing the assessment the auditors may be able to significantly reduce the extent of their testing, and thus possibly reduce audit costs.

EXPLANATION OF CASE HISTORY

The test of internal controls in a computerized application is normally a complex and lengthy process. There is no easy way to assess controls. What the auditor must do is to:

- Understand the system
- Identify the risks

- Identify the system of controls
- Test the functioning of the system of controls
- Assess the adequacy of the functioning system of controls

Done properly, the assessment follows the same systematic approaches used by computer systems analysts in designing computerized applications. It is a detailed process of understanding and documenting and analyzing. However, at the completion of the process, the auditor will have a high degree of confidence about the integrity or lack of integrity of data processed by the application.

The following case history is an example of the testing of internal controls in a computerized payroll application. The case is detailed and extensive. While it is recognized that some of the testing objectives are unique to the organization which undertook this audit, they are presented to provide an overview of the scope of an internal control assessment as well as to illustrate the type and extensiveness of test objectives and testing methods used.

You will observe from reading the case that the risk analysis process led the auditors to a large number of test objectives. Each one of these test objectives addresses a given risk in the payroll application. This is the type of procedure that auditors and system reviewers and designers should follow in assessing control in a computerized application.

Explanation of the Test Plan

The test plan for this case history is presented in a slightly different format than the structured procedure that was given in Chapter 3. The reason for this is that it is unnecessary in many cases to repeat the testing type, level, and method if they are common for each test objective. You will also note in the following test plan that the expected results are more specific than some of the generic expected results outlined in Chapter 3.

This change in format is normal in the conduct of tests of systems of internal control. Auditors should adjust these test plan forms to meet their specific test needs.

The test plan (Figure 4-1 on page 63) has three main sections. These are:

- **Test objective**—The objective established as a result of the risk analysis process.
- **Expected results**—The detailed expected results that are applicable to this specific computerized payroll application.
- **Nature of test transaction**—In this case, the test method is to use test data, and thus the nature of the test transaction is more appropriate than a generalized description of the test methodology. Note that, based upon the test objective and the nature of the test transaction, an auditor familiar with the records in a computerized application could generate specific test data during the step to prepare for testing.

TESTING INTERNAL CONTROLS IN PAYROLL

Background

Organization X computerized its payroll application on a medium-sized computer. Their auditors were given the assignment of reviewing the adequacy of the system of internal controls. They proceeded as follows:

The auditors conducted a risk analysis to identify the potential risks. From this exercise, they established a series of detailed test objectives, and established expected generic results for each test objective.

1. They *conducted a risk analysis* to identify the potential risks.
2. From this exercise, they *established a series of detailed test objectives.*
3. They *established expected generic results* for each test objective.

Testing Methodology

The selected test methodology was as follows:

Testing	Option
• Testing Type • Testing Level • Testing Method	• Functional • Computer System • Test Data

The test data method used included a set of simultaneous transactions designed to test for the existence and effectiveness of programmed controls and procedural operations in the computer systems. The transactions represented both expected and conceivable transactions that could happen in the course of actual data processing operations. Before the transactions were run, expected test results were "predetermined" (calculated on the assumption that the computer program being tested contained effective internal controls and would perform as specified). On this basis, actual results could be compared with the predetermined results.

Preparing for the Test

Prior to conducting the test, the auditors reviewed all available documentation for the manual and automated parts of the payroll system. They obtained an understanding of the manual operations, interviewed the payroll supervisors and clerks, reviewed laws and regulations relating to pay and leave, and familiarized themselves with standard payroll operating procedures. For the automated part of each system, they interviewed system designers and programmers and reviewed system and program documentation and operating procedures.

After acquiring a working knowledge of the system, they decided to test computer programs used to update payroll master records and those used to calculate biweekly pay and vacation pay. Although they were concerned primarily with these particular programs, they decided that other programs used in the normal biweekly payroll processing cycle (such as programs for producing pay and vacation history reports, vacation records, and savings bond reports) should also be tested to determine the adequacy of their controls.

They then designed a test data of simulated pay and vacation transactions to test the effectiveness of internal controls, compliance with applicable laws and regulations, and the adequacy of standard payroll operating procedures. The test data included transactions made up of both "valid" and "invalid" data. These transactions were based on specified procedures and regulations and were designed to check the effectiveness of internal controls during payroll processing. They used one transaction for each master record chosen.

They decided that the best method of obtaining suitable payroll master records for the test would be to use copies of actual master records, supplemented with simulated records tailored for test conditions not found in the copied records.

Accordingly, they obtained a duplicate of the payroll master file and had a section of it printed in readable copy. From this printout, they selected a specific master record to go with each test transaction. When none of the copied records on the printout fitted the specifics of a particular transaction, they made up a simulated master record by preparing source documents and processing them with the program used by each installation to add records for new employees to its master file. They then added the simulated records to the copied records to create the test master file.

They next prepared working papers on which were entered, for each test transaction, the control number assigned to the transaction, the type of input document to be used, and the nature and purpose of the test. They predetermined the correct end results for all test transactions and recorded these results in their working papers for comparison with actual results.

With some help from payroll office personnel, they next coded the test transaction onto source documents. The data was then transcribed onto computer media and key verified. They then processed the test data against actual payroll programs and compared the test results with the predetermined results to see whether there were any differences.

They found the payroll systems accepted and processed several invalid test transactions that should have been rejected or flagged by programmed computer controls. Alternative manual controls were either nonexistent or less than fully effective because they could be bypassed or compromised through fraud, neglect, or inadvertent error. The auditors recommended that the systems' automated controls be strengthened to ensure accurate payrolls and protect the organization from improper payments.

Testing Tasks

In designing and using test data, the auditors performed the following tasks:

1. Determined the types of transactions to be included in the test.
2. Determined the types of master records to be used.
3. Obtained copies of master records and/or prepared simulated master records for processing with the test transactions.
4. Printed out the contents of all such master records before the test.
5. Predetermined the correct end result for each test transaction for comparison with actual processing results.
6. Verified that the programs used for processing the test transactions were the same as those used for normal payroll processing.
7. Ascertained that any changes to these programs during the review were documented and that the changes were tested and approved by the organization.
8. Arranged with data processing personnel for processing of test transactions and producing output in a useful form.
9. Printed the contents of all master records used in the test and compared them with the predetermined results to see whether the programs performed as expected.
10. Determined what impact weaknesses in automated controls have on the accuracy of master file data and computer output.

Figure 4-1
Test Objectives Test Plan

TEST OBJECTIVE	EXPECTED RESULTS Reject	Print error message	Reject certain circum- stances	Cut back to allowable maximum	Process without cutback	Automat- ically compute correct amount	Automat- ically adjust leave records	NATURE OF TEST TRANSACTION
•To determine whether the system will accept a master record with essential data missing. - If missing data will cause an incorrect payment, the master record should be rejected with appropriate warning. - If missing data is for administrative purposes only, the condition should be flagged by an error message.		X (administrative purposes only)	X (incorrect payment)					•Leave a mandatory field blank on a new employee's master record.
•To determine whether the system will accept invalid data into employees' master records. The program should - Print error messages to identify invalid data - Reject further processing of such transactions.		X	X					•Enter erroneous codes, such as charity donations, life insurance, union dues, marital status, etc. (Note—one erroneous code per master record.)
•To determine whether the system will accept an invalid annual vacation category.	X	X						•Enter an invalid annual vacation category.
•To determine whether it is possible to change fields in inactive master records and whether adequate controls exist over such changes. Processing of inactive records should be separated from the normal processing of active records to eliminate the possibility of unearned salary payments or the manipulation of records for persons who are not in a pay status.	X	X						•Change a field in an inactive master record.

(Continued)

Figure 4-1
Test Objectives Test Plan (Continued)

TEST OBJECTIVE	EXPECTED RESULTS: Reject	Print error message	Reject certain circum-stances	Cut back to allowable maximum	Process without cutback	Automat-ically compute correct amount	Automat-ically adjust leave records	NATURE OF TEST TRANSACTION
•To determine whether the system will reject invalid up-dates. The annual vacation category is based on the amount of creditable service an employee has, computed from the employee's service computation date. Employees with less than 3 years of serv-ice get 2 weeks; employees with 3 to 15 years of service get 3 weeks; employees with more than 15 years of service get 4 weeks. - The program should reject any attempt to change a vacation category before it is due to be changed.	X	X						•Change an employee's an-nual vacation category before it is due to be changed.
•To determine whether the system rejects an invalid transaction. Organization's policy states that an hourly employee above grade 5 must be in grade at least 1 year before being promoted.	X	X						•Promote an hourly employee above grade 5 before 1 year in grade has passed.
•To determine how the system handles this transaction. Or-ganization policy states that an exempt employee must be in a grade at least 1 year be-fore being eligible for a within-grade salary increase. The system should "flag" the transaction as being a quality step increase (which has the same effect as a within-grade increase but can occur with-out the employee's having been in grade for 1 year).		X						•Give an exempt employee a within-grade salary increase before 1 year in grade condi-tion has passed.

Figure 4-1
Test Objectives Test Plan (Continued)

EXPECTED RESULTS								
TEST OBJECTIVE	Reject	Print error message	Reject certain circum-stances	Cut back to allowable maximum	Process without cutback	Automat-ically compute correct amount	Automat-ically adjust leave records	NATURE OF TEST TRANSACTION
•To determine whether the system accepts incompatible data. The program should have salary and grade controls which will reject transactions of this type from further processing.		X	X					•Change an employee's grade or annual salary so that the the grade/step and annual salary rate are incompatible.
•To determine whether the annual vacation category is correctly changed, with a message printed to indicate the change. - If the vacation category is not automatically changed, a message should be printed.		X						•Change an employee's service computation date to indicate that vacation category is due to change
•To determine whether the system will compute pay for an inactive employee (an employee who has been separated but whose record is maintained in the same master file used for active employees).	X	X						•Pay an inactive employee.
•To determine whether the system will compute pay for an employee with no record in the master file.	X	X						•Pay a nonexistent employee
•To determine whether the system will compute pay twice for the same employee.	X	X						•Input two times and attendance cards for the same employee.

(Continued)

Figure 4-1
Test Objectives Test Plan (Continued)

	EXPECTED RESULTS							
TEST OBJECTIVE	Reject	Print error message	Reject certain circum-stances	Cut back to allowable maximum	Process without cutback	Automat-ically compute correct amount	Automat-ically adjust leave records	NATURE OF TEST TRANSACTION
•To determine whether the system rejects overtime, shift differential payments for exempt employees.	X	X						•Pay an exempt employee for 80 hours work on a second-shift entitlement for an hourly employee.
•Same as above.	X	X						•Pay a GS employee for 80 hours work on a third-shift entitlement for an hourly employee.
•To determine whether the system rejects exempt em-ployee entitlements for hourly employees.	X	X						•Pay an hourly employee for 80 hours work on a night-differential entitlement for an exempt employee.
•To verify the accuracy of premium (overtime) pay computation. Overtime pay is 1½ times regular pay.						X		•Pay an hourly employee for 20 hours of overtime.
•Same as above. Premium = 10 percent.						X		•Pay an exempt employee for 20 hours of night-differential pay.
•Same as above. Premium = 7½ percent.						X		•Pay an hourly employee for 80 hours on second shift.
•Same as above. Premium = 10 percent.						X		•Pay an hourly employee for 80 hours on third shift.
•Same as above. Holiday pay is double regular pay.						X		•Pay an exempt employee for 8 hours of holiday pay.
•Same as above.						X		•Pay an hourly employee for 8 hours of holiday pay.

Figure 4-1
Test Objectives Test Plan (Continued)

	EXPECTED RESULTS							
TEST OBJECTIVE	Reject	Print error message	Reject certain circumstances	Cut back to allowable maximum	Process without cutback	Automatically compute correct amount	Automatically adjust leave records	NATURE OF TEST TRANSACTION
•Same as above. Sunday premium is 25 percent of regular pay if Sunday is a regularly scheduled workday.						X		•Pay an exempt employee for 8 hours of Sunday pay (for Sunday work that is not overtime work).
•Same as above.						X		•Pay an hourly employee for 8 hours of Sunday pay.
•Same as above.						X		•Pay exempt employees for 10 hours of environmental pay at the following premiums: a. 4% b. 8% c. 25% d. 50%
•Same as above.						X		•Pay hourly employees for 10 hours of environmental pay at the following premiums: a. 4% b. 8% c. 25% d. 50%
•To verify accuracy of premium pay computation. For exempt employees whose basic pay rate does not exceed the salary of a pay grade 7, the overtime rate is 1½ times the basic pay rate.						X		•Pay exempt employees in grades 1-7 for 10 hours of overtime.
•Same as above. For an exempt employee whose basic rate is equal to or exceeds the rate of pay for grade 8, the overtime rate is 1½ times the hourly rate for the middle of pay grade 8.						X		•Pay an exempt employee in pay grade 8 or higher for 10 hours of overtime.

(Continued)

Figure 4-1
Test Objectives Test Plan (Continued)

	EXPECTED RESULTS							
TEST OBJECTIVE	Reject	Print error message	Reject certain circum-stances	Cut back to allowable maximum	Process without cutback	Automat-ically compute correct amount	Automat-ically adjust leave records	NATURE OF TEST TRANSACTION
•To test maximum salary limitation. - Additional pay, such as overtime, night-differential, holiday, and Sunday pay, may be paid to the extent that it does not cause the aggregate pay for a biweek-ly period to exceed the rate of pay of grade 15. - The program should cut back pay to this maximum.		X		X				•Pay a pay grade 14 em-ployee enough overtime pay to exceed the maximum salary limitation.
•Same as above. Program should not cut back environ-mental pay because it is not subject to the maximum salary limitation.					X			•Pay a pay grade 14 em-ployee enough environ-mental pay to exceed the maximum salary limitation.
•Same as above. Program should not cut back pay be-cause hourly employees have no maximum salary limita-tion.					X			•Pay an hourly employee enough premium pay to ex-ceed the maximum salary limitation.
•To determine whether the system will pay less than the 2-hour minimum of holiday pay.		X				X		•Pay an exempt employee for 1 hour of holiday pay.
•Same as above.		X				X		•Pay an hourly employee for 1 hour of holiday pay.
•To determine whether the system limits Sunday pay to 32 hours maximum allowed.		X		X				•Pay an exempt employee for 40 hours of Sunday pay.

Figure 4-1
Test Objectives Test Plan (Continued)

	EXPECTED RESULTS							
TEST OBJECTIVE	Reject	Print error message	Reject certain circumstances	Cut back to allowable maximum	Process without cutback	Automatically compute correct amount	Automatically adjust leave records	NATURE OF TEST TRANSACTION
•To verify the accuracy of premium pay. - Organization policy states pay for an employee regularly working the second or third shift will be computed at 1½ times the second or third shift rate, respectively.						X		•Pay an hourly employee for 80 hours on second shift and 10 hours for overtime into the third shift.
•Same as above.						X		•Pay an hourly employee for 80 hours on third shift and 10 hours for overtime into the first shift.
•To determine whether sick and annual vacation will accrue when a full-time employee charges 80 hours vacation without pay. - The sick leave credit should be reduced by 4 hours and the annual vacation credit should be reduced by 4, 6, or 8 hours, depending on the annual vacation category.							X	•Charge a full-time employee for 80 hours of vacation without pay.
•To determine whether excess annual vacation is charged to vacation without pay. (The system should automatically reduce employee's pay for vacation without pay.)		X				X	X	•Charge a full-time employee for more annual vacation than the employee has.

(Continued)

Figure 4-1
Test Objectives Test Plan (Continued)

	EXPECTED RESULTS							
TEST OBJECTIVE	Reject	Print error message	Reject certain circum-stances	Cut back to allowable maximum	Process without cutback	Automat-ically compute correct amount	Automat-ically adjust leave records	NATURE OF TEST TRANSACTION
•To determine whether excess sick leave is charged to annual vacation or vacation without pay. (The system should automatically adjust vacation records and reduce pay for vacation without pay, if required.)		X				X	X	•Charge a full-time employee for more sick leave than the employee has.
•To determine whether the system will cut back to the maximum of 80 hours for regular pay in a pay period.		X		X				•Charge a full-time employee for 99 hours of annual vaca-tion (19 hours more than a regular biweekly period).
•Same as above.		X		X				•Charge a full-time employee for 99 hours of sick leave.
•Same as above. Total hours of work and vacation cannot exceed 80 in a two-week pay period.	X	X						•Charge a full-time employee for 80 hours of regular pay and 80 hours of annual vacation in the same two-week pay period.
•To determine whether the system flags military leave in excess of 120 hours. Organi-zation policy states that an employee cannot charge more than 120 hours to mili-tary leave in a pay year.		X						•Charge a full-time employee for enough hours of military leave to exceed 120 hours total.
•To determine whether the system appropriately ex-cludes excess annual vaca-tion in a lump sum leave payment.		X		X				•Make a lump sum annual vacation payment to a sepa-rated employee in excess of annual vacation balance.

Figure 4-1
Test Objectives Test Plan (Continued)

	EXPECTED RESULTS							
TEST OBJECTIVE	Reject	Print error message	Reject certain circum-stances	Cut back to allowable maximum	Process without cutback	Automat-ically compute correct amount	Automat-ically adjust leave records	NATURE OF TEST TRANSACTION
•To determine whether the system correctly accrues annual and sick leave for part-time employees. For each 20 hours worked, a part-time employee receives 1 hour of sick leave; an employee needs 20 hours of work to earn 1 hour of annual leave.							X	•Pay a part-time employee for 32 hours of regular pay.
•To determine whether the system will make a lump sum annual vacation payment to an active employee. These payments should be made only to separated employees.	X	X						•Make a lump sum annual vacation payment to an active employee.

5

Key Points to Consider in Testing Internal Control

BASIC QUESTIONS AND CONSIDERATIONS

The major aspects that you should consider in internal control testing are:

- *The degree of risk* inherent in the computerized application
- *The completeness of hard copy documentation* to substantiate transaction processing
- *The relative economics of auditing without internal control assessment compared to incurring substantial amounts of substantive testing* (the latter requires the testing of large volumes of transactions to prove the validity of financial records).

The most difficult criterion to assess is that of risk. Auditing is a risk-oriented business. You should attempt to do the minimal amount of work possible consistent with reducing the risk of erroneous audit judgment to an acceptable level. We can learn much about the audit risk in computerized applications by analyzing the results of audits of computerized applications. The U.S. General Accounting Office[1] has summarized the problems encountered in such audits. These results were supplemented with a questionnaire sent to key officials regarding the causes of problems in computerized applications. The results of that study provide some guidance to auditors in identifying high-risk situations in computerized applications.

This discussion of risk in computerized applications is divided into the following three areas:

- Automated decision-making applications can make bad decisions
- Common software problems
- Common data problems

These are summarized in the following sections.

[1] General Accounting Office, "Improvements Needed In Managing Automated Decision-Making By Computers Throughout the Federal Government," Comptroller General of the United States, Report FGMSD 76-5, 1976.

AUTOMATED DECISION-MAKING APPLICATIONS CAN MAKE BAD DECISIONS

Whether actions initiated automatically by the computer are correct or not depends largely on:

1. The internal logic of the program
2. The data that is fed into the system

Computers will produce bad decisions (1) if programmers and analysts make misjudgments or errors in establishing the decision-making criteria, or (2) if the application is not designed and/or coded in a manner that properly implements the decision-making criteria. Changing circumstances can make adequate decision-making criteria in the software obsolete, and bad decisions will occur if the software is not changed. Failure to design appropriate checks on input data, such as edit checks, can contribute to bad decisions. These applications can also make bad decisions if the data supplied to them is incomplete or incorrect or if the data is not obtained or processed quickly.

Some internal audit groups have reported on bad decisions made by automated decision-making applications. These computer-initiated actions caused their organizations to incur unnecessary costs, premature costs, and overpayments. Such bad decisions may also harm individuals and impair an organization's ability to carry out its objectives effectively.

Adverse conditions common to several organizations have been reported. These conditions, resulting in the applications' automatically initiating uneconomical or otherwise incorrect actions, can be broadly categorized as (1) software problems, and (2) data problems.

Software Problems

Several software problems that can cause bad decisions by automated decision-making applications include:

- *Designing software with incomplete or erroneous decision-making criteria.* Actions have been incorrect because the decision-making logic omitted factors that should have been included. In other cases decision-making criteria included in the software were inappropriate, either at the time of design or, later, because of changed circumstances.
- *Failing to program the software as intended by the customer (user) or designer.* This resulted in logic errors often referred to as programming errors.
- *Omitting needed edit checks for determining completeness of input data.* Critical data elements have been left blank on many input documents, and because no checks were included, the applications processed the transaction with incomplete data.

Data Problems

Input data quality is frequently a problem. Since much of this data is an integral part of the decision-making process, its poor quality can adversely affect the computer-directed actions. Problems include:

- *Incomplete data used by automated decision-making applications.* Some input documents prepared by people omitted entries in data elements which were critical to the application but which were processed anyway. The documents were not rejected when incomplete data was being used. In other instances data which the application needed and which should have become part of EDP files was not put into the system.
- *Incorrect data used in automated decision-making application processing.* People have often unintentionally introduced incorrect data into the EDP system. This incorrect data affected application decisions.
- *Obsolete data used in automated decision-making application processing.* Data in the EDP files became obsolete due to new circumstances. The new data may have been available but was not put into the computer.

COMMON SOFTWARE PROBLEMS

Examples of software problems are presented to demonstrate the problems frequently experienced with automated decision-making. The two basic automated decision-making application problems, software and data, are often interdependent. For example, automated decision-making applications' making bad decisions because of incomplete data elements on input documents illustrates both a data problem and a software problem because:

1. Input documents have not been properly prepared (data).
2. Edit checks for completeness have not been properly designed (software).

Other problems, such as when incomplete or erroneous decision-making criteria are used (software) and incorrect data is put into the application (data), can occur independently. The problems in each of these two areas are caused by a variety of factors.

Computer programs are usually developed and modified by a combination of people: the user (or customer); the designer (or analyst), who translates the requirements of the user into a logical structure; and the programmer, who translates the logic into program instructions which can be recognized and used by the computer.

The user initiating the work sets forth many of the specifics regarding the internal decision-making criteria to be used. Often the designer makes some decisions. Both act on the basis of their knowledge of the function, the available guidelines in terms of management instruction or legislation, their perceptions of the transactions to be processed, and their communications with each other. Sometimes they will call on operations research experts to help them design new criteria, while sometimes they will use existing criteria to process similar transactions.

The designer takes the established criteria and prepares more specific documentation which is used for programming. The design and programming documents thus developed become very detailed and complex, because the computer is instructed to operate in a logical step-by-step manner on a large number of different conditions. Even less complex applications can consist of thousands of individual instructions that must be designed and programmed to do what the user and designer perceive to be correct.

The user and designer are usually responsible for designing edit checks into the program. This includes checks for the completeness of data elements on input documents. According to government agency officials, edit checks are placed in the software for data that is critical to decision-making, such as when incomplete or erroneous data can affect the determinations made by the computer. Some officials said that edit checks are placed for almost every data element. One agency is making an overt effort to limit edit checks to reduce the number of documents rejected by the computer.

In developing software, it is generally accepted that the lines of communication between user and designer and between designer and programmer must be effective.

A schedule that lists and ranks the major causes of software problems is shown in Figure 5-1. A discussion of each cause follows.

The problems identified can occur at various phases of the software development cycle including:

- User determinations
- Designer actions
- Program coding

Many problems are not detected through the review and test phases of the process and are therefore continued through implementation and operation of the automated decision-making application. Most people believe that it is impossible to ensure the design of completely error-free software under the current state of the art, but a knowledge of the more common problems can help reduce the incidence of errors.

Inadequate Communications Between the Parties to Software Design

At least three groups of people (general management, users, and EDP) must adequately communicate to develop or modify the applications success-

Figure 5-1
A List of Causes of Software Problems

RANK	CAUSE
1	*Inadequate communications* between the parties to software design
2	*Incorrect perceptions* of the nature of actual transactions to be processed
3	*Inadequate documentation* preventing adequate reviews of software
4	*Time constraints* hampering the effectiveness of the design process
5	*Absence of written criteria* or guidelines for designers to follow
6	*Detail and complexity* involved in designing, coding, and reviewing software
7	*Reliance on the expertise and experience of people* doing the work (state of the art)
8	*Undetected changes in circumstances* making the application obsolete
9	*State of the art* in software testing which prevents testing all possible conditions

fully. Assuming that the users know what they want the computer to do and that their criteria are correct, inadequate communication of this information to EDP can result in the development of software that is not exactly what the user wants.

Much has been written about the communications problem in software development, and it is generally recognized as primarily a problem of human source.

Incorrect Perceptions of the Nature of Actual Transactions to be Processed

Decision-making criteria used in these applications have sometimes been erroneous, because people developing them made wrong assumptions about the nature of the transactions that were to be processed. They may have relied on limited data about the transactions and established the criteria on their judgment.

It is believed that a large percentage of automated decision-making application software problems are caused at the very beginning of the design process by people involved in defining requirements and establishing decision-making criteria. In other cases, the designer may have used criteria contained in existing software to process transactions in a similar, but not identical, environment. Sometimes this is done to shorten design and programming time, but it can and has caused problems.

Inadequate Documentation Preventing Adequate Reviews of Software

Many organizations have not developed adequate guidelines for preparing good documentation. This is a problem because the documentation for many computer applications (including automated decision making) is inadequate.

The same audit report stated the following about documentation:

> In one case documentation explaining the objectives of the computer system was not prepared by the systems analyst. Without this information, management could not adequately monitor the system's development. . . . the system did not accomplish the results originally intended by management. . . . Inadequate documentation was cited as causing management to spend over a year to determine how the various programs in the complex system operated.[2]

Thus, adequate design documentation is needed to allow:

- Review of the work during application design and modification
- Making the necessary modification
- Correcting errors when they are detected
- Ensuring that the application is operating as intended

Time Constraints Hampering the Effectiveness of the Design Process

Many systems containing these applications are designed or modified because of legislation or other high-priority requirements imposed by top management. Often this calls for implementation by a specific date. Developing and/or modifying software within the required time frames can hamper efforts to ensure its adequacy.

Absence of Written Criteria or Guidelines for Designers to Follow

There is a need for written guidelines for the designers of software. Many organizations have varying degrees of formal guidelines, but few provide instructions on how to do design work.

Some believe that written criteria and guidelines on how to design soft-

[2] General Accounting Office, "Improvements Needed In Managing Automated Decision-Making By Computers Throughout the Federal Government," Comptroller General of the United States, Report FGMSD 76-5, 1976.

ware are not desirable because they consider the process an art that cannot be guided or improved by written instructions. However, the consensus of many knowledgeable people is that the absence of criteria or guidelines can be a major cause of some automated decision-making application problems.

Detail and Complexity Involved in Designing, Coding, and Reviewing Software

Even smaller applications can be extremely complex and detailed when designing and coding the processing logic and edit checks. The complexities and detail involved may also hamper the review process that may exist. The sheer detail and complexity of the process can cause design and programming errors and omissions which are not caught at review and testing time. Therefore, bad decisions can occur.

Reliance on the Expertise and Experience of People Doing the Work

The nature of the design process causes organizations to rely on designers who must be experienced both in the software design and in the business function to be supported by these applications.

Most system designers fall into one of these categories. They are either:

- Schooled in the art of software design and learn the function to be supported,
- Experienced in a business function and learn the art of software design, or
- Former programmers who are promoted to the design function. Programmers are generally schooled in writing code in specific computer languages but not schooled in business functions.

Much reliance is placed on the individual designer's ability to convert user requirements to the type of detailed logic needed for programmer coding. Reliance is also placed on the programmer's ability to write code according to the logic given him. Because of the detail and complexity involved, it is difficult for management to review and assess every aspect of the designer's and programmer's work, thereby creating an additional source of problems.

Undetected Changes In Circumstances Making the Application Obsolete

Another cause for erroneous decision making derives from the failure to identify and/or to relate changes in processing circumstances to the operation of the application. Once the application is operational, it will make decisions—good or bad—on the same basis until it is modified.

Not recognizing changed circumstances so that applications can be modified could result in bad decisions based on criteria that were correct when designed, but which no longer apply.

State of the Art in Software Testing Which Prevents Testing of All Possible Conditions

The current state of the art makes it difficult for organizations to test for all conditions that may occur during the transaction processing. Most organizations cannot even be sure that the tests have exercised every line of code. As a result, accepted software can contain design and/or coding errors not identified during the test phase. Some of these errors may not be detected until long after the application becomes operational.

The inability to test for all conditions also precludes a full evaluation of user and designer criteria built into the program (if and when such evaluation is attempted).

COMMON DATA PROBLEMS

Control over the completeness, accuracy, and currency of data depends largely on the source. Obviously, the correctness of an application where all the data comes from outside sources depends largely on the quality of data submitted. Some controls can be applied to incoming input, but they cannot guarantee completely error-free data.

There are two basic types of controls for ensuring the completeness, accuracy, and currency of data input into a computer in making decisions.

1. **External controls** which are procedures developed outside the computer system. The objective is to check the quality of data to be put into and contained in the computer system. The controls include such things as manual procedures designed to determine if data is recorded completely and accurately on input documents and whether documents are being received and/or processed on time.
2. **Internal controls** which generally do not involve human intervention. Many of these controls are built into the software. They include edit checks for completeness, logical relationship tests (does the data make sense?), and reasonableness checks (to isolate predetermined out-of-bounds conditions).

As part of the external controls that should exist, the people doing the work should be qualified and adequately trained. Adequate guidelines should be given to these people on a timely basis instructing them how to fill out the documents involved, including what entries should be made under varying circumstances. The forms (hard copy and input) should be designed to be as simple as possible to allow for easy reading. Procedures should exist for reviewing (e.g., statistical sampling) input documents to test their completeness and accuracy. Controls should also provide for timely processing of the data.

If incomplete or inaccurate data enters the computer system undetected, automatic actions can be incorrect. The actions will continue to be incorrect if the data is stored in EDP files and reused. These applications can also make incorrect decisions if current data is not put into the system. A list that summarizes some of the major causes of data problems is provided in Figure 5-2. A discussion of these causes follows.

Forms Designed and Used for Input Preparation Are Too Complex

Using simple forms to record, collect, transmit, and process information for input to computers improves the completeness and accuracy of the data eventually used by all computer application programs. The more complex the forms, the more prone they are to data errors, which can affect the correctness of actions initiated by automated decision-making applications.

EDP Files Are Not Always Adequately Reviewed to Assure That Good Data Is Being Used

A recognized external control technique is to output and review data contained in EDP files. Failure to do this can result in obsolete or otherwise incorrect data used in automated decision-making applications. Incorrect decisions are therefore initiated. Without reviews, it is possible for some data errors to remain undetected for years and to allow for an accumulation of errors compounding the problem.

Instructions to People Preparing Data Input Are Not Always Provided, Are Provided Late, or Are Not Adequate

It is important to provide clear instructions to people preparing input documents. Timely updating of these instructions when changes occur is also

Figure 5-2
A List of Causes of Data Problems

RANK	CAUSE
1	Forms designed and used for input preparation are too complex.
2	EDP files are not always adequately reviewed to assure that good data is being used.
3	Instructions to people preparing data input are not always provided, are provided late, or are not adequate.
4	Preparers of data input are not always adequately trained.
5	Manual reviews of input documents are not always adequate.
6	High volumes of transactions cause input preparers to make errors (workload pressures).

important. The failure to issue clear and timely instructions can cause data errors that may not be detected by internal controls.

Preparers of Data Input Are Not Always Adequately Trained

Most training in the input data preparation area is done by individual departments, because the training must be geared toward the individual application, each with its own special forms, data content, and related input media.

Inadequate training of persons involved in processing data to the computer (such as filling out forms and punching cards) can lead to high error rates which result in bad decisions being made by these applications.

Manual Reviews of Input Documents Are Not Always Adequate

External controls include selective manual reviews of input documents to determine completeness and accuracy. These reviews, made by supervisors or quality control groups, should be geared toward measuring the quality of data entering the system, including determining trends, significance, and sources of errors.

When there are different types and sources of input, review procedures should cover them all. Developing and monitoring statistical error rates is important. The review procedure, however, should also include determining the potential materiality of errors so that management can make judgments on where corrective actions should be taken.

Manual reviews supplement internal controls by (1) disclosing needed software data validation (such as edit checks) that is missed because of software problems, or (2) identifying trends of material data errors which are not detected by software data validation.

High Volumes of Transactions Cause Input Preparers to Make Errors (Workload Pressures)

Automated decision-making applications are designed, in part, to help organizations cope with the high volumes of transactions that have to be processed. Although the computer processes the data once it is entered, the volumes of documents (hard copy and machine readable) that must be prepared are often tremendous.

These tremendous volumes of data can lead to workload pressures on the people who record material on original documents and prepare machine-readable documents, thus resulting in data errors.

Summary

It is clear that you should seriously consider the factors discussed above in the evaluation of internal control.

6

How to Obtain Tools and Techniques for Testing Internal Control

THE NEED TO TEST INTERNAL CONTROL

No single package or technique by itself assesses the adequacy of control in computerized applications. The process is complex and time-consuming. You can, however, make use of several computer-aided techniques to simplify the controls assessment and test process.

In a manual environment, internal control is usually assessed using checklists and walk-throughs. The auditor can physically observe who does what and make a judgment regarding the adequacy of control. The test involves examining hard-copy evidence produced at the various manual control points by people who are visible and can be interviewed.

In a computerized application, walk-throughs involve much more detail. It is not uncommon for a computer system to have several hundred thousand instructions. Thus, it is difficult for anyone to comprehend the totality of and the interrelationship between these instructions.

Computerized applications, in addition to having many thousands of instructions, have literally millions of paths through the system. Thus, it would be impractical to attempt to assess controls over all the paths. The only possibility of doing a reasonably good job is to use computerized tools and techniques to aid in the process.

TOOLS FOR TESTING INTERNAL CONTROL

Auditing in a computerized environment should incorporate the use of computer-aided tools. To be effective in a computerized environment, you need to use the computer to audit the computer. In the test of internal control, this involves using tools to help you perform the process.

Too many auditors still attempt to assess the adequacy of internal control using pencil and paper. This not only increases the time required to conduct the audit, but increases the opportunity for an invalid assessment. The invalid assessment can occur because you would not have sufficient time to assess the many control risks in a computerized application. Some of the techniques and tools which you can use in testing the adequacy of internal control include:

- Audit software
- Test data generators
- Data dictionary
- Automatic flowcharting packages
- Static analyzer
- Tracing
- Utilities (dumps)
- Privileged commands
- User exits
- Logs
- Query languages
- Consultants
- Job accounting systems
- Hardware and software monitors

These are but a few of the many tools that can help you assess internal control. An examination of your own organization's operating environment will probably identify many more. As you become proficient in the use of these aids, you can perform reviews of internal control more effectively.

A brief description of the above tools follows.

Audit Software

Audit software is by far the most versatile audit tool for analyzing and extracting computerized data. Refer to the book, *Generalized Computer Audit Software—Selection and Application,* for an overview of the capabilities and the application of audit software.[1]

Test Data Generators

Software packages are available which automatically generate test data. The user enters parameters of the desired test data and quickly generates as many test records as required. This is particularly useful in conducting stress testing or performing testing on a computerized application. Depending on the

[1] W. E. Perry, and J. F. Kuong, *Generalized Computer Audit Software—Selection and Application* MAP–14 (Wellesley Hills, MA: Management Advisory Publications, 1980).

characteristics of the test data generator used, you can specify the contents of the fields, lengths of the fields, and many other data characteristics. This enables you to generate both valid and invalid test data and save a considerable amount of time in test data preparation.

Automatic Flowcharting Packages

Automatic flowcharting packages are software packages used for documenting programs. They are generally limited to high-level languages such as COBOL, PL/1, and FORTRAN. These automatic flowcharting routines use language source statements as input and from program source statements create flowcharts. These flowcharts can be used by you to pinpoint points where control should be established, and also to identify areas of risk. The flowcharts can also be used to follow the logic, and thus determine if controls are adequate.

Static Analyzer

Static analyzers help analyze the *execution* of computer programs to determine those specific instructions, modules, as well as segments, of programs which are not used. This is helpful in determining the number of times routines are entered to process a single transaction or series of transactions. They could also be used to uncover "Trojan Horse" or fraudulent routines which do not activate under normal circumstances, but only when some special event occurs, under the control of a defrauder.

Tracing

Many languages include a trace option. This trace option shows which instructions have been executed during the processing of a specific transaction or piece of data. Using the trace option, you can positively identify the path taken and the controls executed over the processing of that transaction. The latest versions of ANSI COBOL and PL/1 provide tracing capabilities which can be of value in the internal control assessment process.

Utility Programs

Most operating systems, data base management systems, communication systems, security systems, and in general, most large vendor operating software include one or more utility programs. Examples include report writers, sorts, memory dumps, etc. The vendors provide these utilities so that organizations can perform miscellaneous EDP tasks, analyses, or actions to assess the operating environment. You can use these same utilities for such purposes as file dumps, extracting programs from libraries, and analyzing operating statistics.

Privileged Commands

Many operating software systems contain a series of commands that are privileged. These are specialized commands to perform specialized actions which are very powerful from a control perspective. For example, passwords can be changed only through the use of these privileged commands. These are a series of actions which tend to bypass the normal controls in the system to enable administrative actions to occur. Many of these have potential audit implication for testing controls and thus should be considered.

User Exits

Most operating systems and other large vendor software packages provide the capability for their customer base to enter special routines. The purpose of these user exits is to make it possible for users to add and/or to perform specialized functions which would not be economical for the vendor to include because of the highly specific nature of the user tasks. However, these same exits provide the capabilities to avoid most of the control and security mechanisms of the system. The reason they enable a bypass is because they are connected to the operating system, and they can read and manipulate data in the buffer areas. Programs not being executed are just another form of data. However, you can use these user exits to do your own unobserved analysis to evaluate controls.

Logs

In on-line/data base environments, logs are established for the purpose of restart and recovery. They contain the necessary information on transaction processing so that if an error occurs these logs can replay processing like a motion picture playing scenes backwards or forwards. These logs constitute one of the most extensive sources of audit trails, providing the data necessary to substantiate processing. They provide a wealth of information to help you assess the adequacy of controls and evidence of transactions. The logs can be used to validate transactions entered against contents of the data base.

Query Languages

These are high-level powerful languages, associated with data base management systems, that can extract, manipulate, and present data stored within the data base. With the exception of statistical sampling, these query languages can perform most of the functions in major audit software languages. In addition, the query languages are often simpler to use and more powerful in capabilities than other routines. They can assist the auditor in control analysis in the data base environment.

Consultants

One of the skills listed for auditors in a computer environment is the ability to know when their own technical competence has been exceeded. In other words, a highly skilled auditor knows when to call in a technical expert, or consultant to help him in a difficult audit situation. Consultants are available within an organization, from outside consulting groups, from similar organizations, and from vendors. Auditors recognizing the fact that the control assessment requirements exceed their own technical capability should call in the expert help needed to complete the assignment successfully.

Job Accounting Systems

Job accounting systems—usually provided by vendors for resource accounting purposes—record what resources are used, by whom, and for what purposes. Within the job accounting system is a complete record of who has accessed what files, how frequently, and what resources have been utilized in processing that data. A wealth of control-oriented information awaits the person who spends the time necessary to learn how to use this valuable source of data.

Monitors

Hardware and software monitors are available to record the operational performance of the computing environment. These monitors are primarily performance-oriented. The monitors indicate which facilities are used, and the operating performance of the use of those facilities. The hardware and software monitors can be used to fine tune the performance of the operating environment. These tools could be helpful if the level of testing were to include performance tests.

VARIOUS VENDOR-SUPPLIED SOFTWARE TEST PACKAGES

In order to facilitate the testing and debugging of systems, mainframe vendors often furnish EDP shops with a number of useful software test aids that can be adapted by the system reviewer to help in testing internal controls. These aids vary from vendor to vendor and depend upon individual needs in system testing and the type of systems involved, such as basic versus complex. See Chapter 8 for more information on this subject and also for other ideas and potential approaches to test internal control in the future.

7

How to Arrive at the Best Approach and Method of Testing Internal Control

THE NEED FOR IMPROVED INTERNAL CONTROL ASSESSMENT APPROACHES

The business community's need to perform in-depth assessments of internal controls in computerized applications is increasing. The pressure exerted by audit committees, regulatory agencies, and professional auditing associations on the audit profession to conduct these assessments is ever increasing. It is quite likely that you will have to issue formal statements on the adequacy of the system of internal control in your organization. In most organizations, the majority of business operations are computerized and many applications are moving to the advanced/on-line/data base environment, which will require further attention in the building and assessment of internal control. The subject of internal control testing is by no means confined to the auditor alone. It is also of vital concern to the designers and users of systems, since they are the parties responsible for building sound EDP system controls. It is thus natural to expect that EDP professionals and users of systems will also feel an increasing pressure to acquire skills in EDP internal control and how to test it. The methodologies for testing internal control presented in this manual should be equally valuable to auditors as to EDP professionals and system users.

Existing methodologies, including the one outlined in this manual, are highly labor intensive. In other words, while some automated aids can be used, much of the process still requires that you analyze situations with pencil and paper and a great deal of judgment.

The amount of time and skill required to do a proper in-depth assessment of internal controls in computerized applications is prohibitive for some organizations. At present, they do not have either sufficient staff or sufficient skills to conduct the needed assessment. Thus, there is greater need now than ever before for new tools and techniques to aid auditors in becoming more productive in this process of internal control assessment and testing.

ADVANTAGES AND DISADVANTAGES OF CURRENT APPROACHES

This manual has proposed that you consider risks, type, level, and methods of testing in testing control. This testing framework provides you with an approach to testing internal control in computerized applications. However, it is within these areas that new tools and techniques are very much needed to improve the assessment and testing process.

This manual has not attempted to provide detailed procedures for the risk analysis process. These are covered in other books listed in the bibliography at the end of this manual. However, the four main risk concerns of product, technology, use, and security were briefly described. These risks are applicable to any internal control assessment situation.

The advantages and disadvantages of the five types of testing are pre-

Figure 7-1
Advantages and Disadvantages of Types of Testing

TESTING TYPE	ADVANTAGES	DISADVANTAGES
•STRESS	1. Approximates operational conditions in the real world. Tests boundaries of operation of the system. 2. Tests storage limits 3. Tests response times	1. Requires large amounts of test data 2. Requires large amounts of computer time
•FUNCTIONAL	1. Tests compliance to application rules 2. Tests compliance to regulations 3. Tests compliance to organization's policies & procedures	1. Requires a detailed knowledge of programs 2. Requires a detailed knowledge of application rules, regulations and organization's policies and procedures
•REGRESSION	1. Tests unchanged parts of application in consort with changed portions 2. Tests stability between unchanged parts of multiple connected systems	1. Requires testing beyond immediate confines of change 2. Requires large amounts of test data 3. Requires large amounts of computer time
•ENVIRONMENTAL	1. Tests manual parts of computerized applications 2. Tests control atmosphere 3. Tests integrated flow of application strings	1. Manual controls may not be implemented consistently 2. Control atmosphere may have been evaluated in a test of another application
•PERFORMANCE	1. Tests efficiency, economy, effectiveness of application system processing 2. Tests effectiveness, economy, effectiveness of application system/operating environment interface	1. May require costly hardware and software monitors 2. May be difficult to demonstrate that a more efficient, economical, or effective way of processing could be developed

Figure 7-2
Advantages and Disadvantages of Levels of Testing

LEVEL OF TESTING	ADVANTAGES	DISADVANTAGES
MODULE	1. Isolates control evaluation to smallest possible processing unit 2. Concentrates test on control	1. May not be representative of true operating environment 2. Would not detect regression errors
PROGRAM	1. Easy to test level 2. Often organizations have good program testing aids for programs	1. May not be representative of true operating environment 2. Would not detect inter-program regression errors
COMPUTER SYSTEM	1. Tests full function of the automated part of the application 2. Can use standard input forms to generate much of the test data	1. Does not evaluate manual parts of application 2. Does not evaluate the interface between manual and automated portions
APPLICATION SYSTEM	1. Allows full testing of all the interrelated parts of the application 2. Tests manual parts of the application	1. Requires the assistance of application user and support personnel 2. May be a costly and time consuming but necessary test
INTER-SYSTEM	1. Tests inter-relationships between systems 2. Tests regression error problems between systems	1. Requires the cooperation of two independent systems/ audits 2. May be a costly and time-consuming test
OPERATING ENVIRONMENT	1. Tests the operating softwore surrounding the application 2. Test the application system/ operating environment interface	1. Is technically difficult to perform 2. Requires advanced EDP skills to evaluate 3. May be a costly and time-consuming task

sented in Figure 7-1. The advantages and disadvantages of the six levels of testing are presented in Figure 7-2. The advantages and disadvantages of the five methods of testing are presented in Figure 7-3. These figures are designed to summarize and provide a perspective on the material described in earlier chapters of this manual.

SUMMARY AND PROGNOSIS

Auditors (especially external) currently spend their time in two basic audit areas, the assessment of controls and the verification of data. In most audits, auditors spend significantly more time in data verification than they do in control assessment.

As automation advances, the division of audit time between control as-

Figure 7-3
Advantages and Disadvantages of the Testing Methods

TESTING METHOD	ADVANTAGES	DISADVANTAGES
1. CHECKLIST	1. Aids in covering all important areas with a low level of effort 2. Helps organize the test approach 3. Provides consistency in reviews 4. Helps uncover areas of weakness and points the direction for detailed audits.	1. The danger exists of being relied upon too extensively, as key complex system aspects can be missed. 2. Portions of the checklist may not be applicable to the audit being conducted. 3. Usually, symptoms are primarily uncovered which do not give a cause-and-effect relationship to permit prescription of solution.
2. STATIC	1. It can be performed manually 2. Identifies inefficient coding 3. May identify "Trojan Horse" routines	1. May not be representative of a "live" situation 2. May require the use of a costly software audit tool 3. Requires significant programming knowledge
3. TEST DATA	1. Tests any desired or anticipated conditions 2. It can easily test error conditions 3. Can be used to simulate test conditions *before* adverse situations occur.	1. May not be representative of a "live" situation 2. Requires advanced skills in EDP 3. Requires a detailed knowledge of the application
4. LIVE DATA	1. Is representative of the real world 2. It can be used to substantiate "data" findings 3. With use of proper technique, it can help test the software environment	1. May be difficult to find specific desired transactions to test 2. It may be difficult to test error conditions
5. PARALLEL	1. Provides an "independent" assessment of functions being tested by separate auditor-prepared logic 2. Verifies processing of all data 3. Verifies system-produced totals	1. May be difficult to verify results because minor differences can result in numerous differences 2. It is often a costly and time-consuming method

sessment and data verification will change significantly. Within a few years the majority of audit effort will be spent in control assessment. This is because the automation of both application and general controls will take place. By testing controls, you will be able to know that controls in place function consistently.

As organizations become more dependent upon the controls in automated applications, fewer hard-copy documents will be in existence and more of the processing will be machine-oriented. For example, in the banking business, the automatic cash dispensing terminal, as well as electronic funds transfer, are significantly changing the methods of banking. The traditional sources of evidence (e.g., checks, signatures, etc.) and people are being replaced by machine processing. People can move funds by entering instructions to a computer over touch-tone telephones, and can withdraw money through cash-dispensing terminals or automatic teller machines (ATM's).[1] In this type of environment, control is considerably more important to the organization than is data validation alone.

The methodology presented in this manual is designed to lead anyone with minimal skills through the process of testing internal control. You are encouraged to practice and perfect this methodology as soon as possible. It is only through a mastery of this methodology that you will be prepared to utilize the newer tools and techniques outlined in the preceding and following chapters. But the primary reason for you to adopt improved internal control testing methodologies lies in the professional obligation you have to management to carry out your duty of "providing assurance to management, stockholders, etc., of the *integrity* of computerized systems," at a higher level of thoroughness and excellence than has been the case heretofore. Furthermore, there is a need to move forward and adjust previous methodologies to cope with demands imposed by the associated changes in the nature of internal control, especially with regard to advanced EDP systems.

---

[1] C. M. Winters, *ATM Control, Auditing and Security* (Wellesley Hills, MA: Management Advisory Publications, 1986).

8

Preparing for New Approaches, Techniques, and Developments in Testing

PRESENT STATUS OF TESTING

It has been stated that testing of EDP systems has been a neglected area of EDP, especially when it comes to the testing of advanced/on-line/data base systems.[1] The approach most commonly used has been to try to force outdated methods onto new, more complex, system test situations. The result of this approach is that systems and audit professionals may perform a less-than-adequate job of testing.

This chapter reviews and summarizes some of the new approaches and means for enhancing testing which you should consider applying to the process of testing internal control in the foreseeable future. The previous chapters have presented practical material for immediate application. It is, however, just as practical and important for you to be aware of new ideas, approaches, and trends, so you can begin to prepare for the future. This is particularly important because it takes time to think, evaluate, adapt, sell, and implement new approaches. The lead-lag time resulting from the adoption of new methodologies and the changeover from existing to new methodologies is indeed sizable, caused primarily by sheer human inertia to change at all levels of any organization.

NEW DEVELOPMENTS IN TESTING COMPUTERIZED SYSTEMS

The methodologies for testing computerized systems, usually used by data processing professionals, provide useful approaches, means, and techniques for the testing of internal control. Many of the well-known techniques for testing and debugging EDP systems, such as test decks, integrated test facility, parallel simulation, actually originated from the field of data processing. It is therefore natural that those interested in control testing should be

[1] J. F. Kuong, *How To Prepare Audit Plans for EDP Systems,* MAP-21 (Wellesley Hills, MA: Management Advisory Publications, 1987) Chap. 5.

constantly aware of new developments in EDP testing and keep abreast of published works in the literature.

Developments of interest in testing can be classified, rather arbitrarily, as follows:

- Vendor-provided software test packages or capabilities
- Software reliability and engineering approaches and techniques
- Microcomputer approaches

Following is a discussion of the developments in each of these classifications as well as the potential applicability to EDP internal control assessment.

VENDOR-PROVIDED SOFTWARE TEST PACKAGES

As EDP technology and system development methodologies advance, vendors have had to ease the process of testing for client's systems. Both specific packages and generalized provisions are often provided by mainframe vendors. Upon attending briefings by vendors on new hardware and software architectures one gets the feeling that this trend will continue as vendors feel the pressure to develop safer and more secure products, following implications of legislation such as the Foreign Corrupt Practices Act. Auditors and EDP professionals should be on the watch for these developments.

Examples of these software test packages or capabilities are:

- Batch Terminal Simulator (BTS)
- Back-out capability from recovery provisions in data base management systems (DBMS) used with logs.

- **Batch Terminal Simulator (BTS).** This is essentially a software capability that enables system personnel to test on-line programs, and program strings using card input and printer output which simulates the operation of a production system. With modifications in approach, the method can be adopted by auditors to test on-line systems. This capability is available for IBM and DEC computers.
- **DBMS Back-out Capability.** This is an adaptation of the DBMS transactions back-out capability used for recovery purposes. The auditor could apply the approach to a copy of the production data base and write the test data added on the transaction logs to test the DB update process and test the data base on-line. (See Reference 43 in the Bibliography, Part I.)
- **User Query Languages.** The DBMS system provides query language capabilities for users to interrogate the data base. These packages could be adapted to aid in data base auditing in a manner similar to audit

software packages, except the process can take place interactively and permit "probing" or "adaptive" auditing of a data base to take place. The testing expert should look into these new capabilities for future use in data base-oriented systems.

SOFTWARE RELIABILITY AND ENGINEERING

As the EDP industry matures, professionals have seen the need to move EDP out of the *art* stage and closer to the *science* stage. A great deal of activity is noticeable in the literature on the field, with attempts by many to develop "software engineering" methodologies leading to software products with a greater level of reliability and integrity than previously.

In the process, many new ideas and techniques for testing software are being developed. The following is a partial list of these developments. Note that many of these are being built by EDP for software quality assurance purposes. When this is the case, the auditor can facilitate the subsequent process of testing by participating in the development cycle of these techniques and then using them as "auditability" provisions to test internal control when the systems become operational.

- **Software probes.** These consist of especially designed analytical software modules that can be placed in or invoked to analyze the behavior of regular functional logic for diagnostic, debugging, and testing purposes. In the future, it is possible that auditors may specify such software probes to test internal controls in complex systems. This concept parallels that used in applying software monitors for performance improvement purposes.
- **Ongoing or embedded testing.** In the past the trend has been to develop elaborate testings methodologies, routines, and data for use during the period of system debugging and prior to the acceptance phase. Thereafter, all these provisions were disposed of and never used again. In fact, a completed system is never tested again until a major modification is made to it. This amounts, from a testing viewpoint, to "throwing the baby out with the wash." Under an *ongoing testing philosophy* EDP, quality assurance, or auditing could build *permanent* testing facilities in systems which could be used on a continuing or invokable basis to test and ascertain internal control and system integrity. For example, such provisions may enable auditors to evaluate the impact on control of changes made to previous versions of software, or to perform periodic tests of system logic functioning.
- **Built-in testing/Self-testing computers.** Considerable attention is being given to the subject of *automatic computer testing,* whereby testing approaches become an integral part of the system design by built-in

tests (BIT), using hardware and software redundancy concepts. A number of alternative test approaches have been described by J. B. Clary and R. A. Sacane. (See Reference 12 in the Bibliography, Part I.) Speculating on this topic, it is conceivable that if EDP built in these capabilities, the auditor may be able to review the testing methodology and rely on it and thus reduce the scope of his own testing in the future.

- **The computer security and quality assurance monitor.** This concept, recently discussed in the literature,[2] involves the use of a "dedicated" separate computer to control and monitor the processing computer. Depending on the capabilities built into the computer monitor, the latter can be used for doing testing, performing security checks, or conducting quality assurance reviews of the processes in the main computer on an ongoing basis. This is similar to the patient monitoring systems used in hospitals for 24-hour surveillance of patients. When this concept is practiced for certain types of business systems that may warrant it, it will essentially amount to testing the system of internal controls on a continuous basis and reporting any deviations from normal for subsequent action or correction.
- **Dual-and-distinct software.** In this approach the designer or auditor develops and builds, *independently,* a dual code version of key portions or all of the system's logic for ongoing or sporadic verification of the system of internal control. The dual code can be a *replica* of the functional logic or *that plus additional analytic logic* at key steps to do what amounts to "in-situ" analysis of internal control "using the computer to test the computer system." With some imagination, the independent dual logic could be built into a separate minicomputer under auditor control, as shown in Figure 8-1.

  For an approximation of the concept, read the article by Hulme and Aiken in Australia. (See Reference 21 in the Bibliography, Part I.) Their approach did not make use of a separate computer, however. Although this approach appears expensive at the present time, it will not be in the context of the risks that will be present in future complex systems. It further offers the advantage of independence in the testing process. See also Chapters 6 and 10 of Reference 31 for a detailed explanation of these approaches. NASA has used this concept for years to monitor the correctness of critical programs in the space program. The duplicate programs test each other continuously to detect possible errors.
- **Twin data base test approach.** In this approach one uses essentially a similar technique for testing internal control as is used by EDP profes-

[2] C. Riddle, and J. Austin, "Updating Security, Auditing, and Quality Assurance—The Dedicated On-Line Computer Security Monitor," *COM-SAC, Computer Security, Auditing and Controls,* Vol. 13, No. 1, 1986.

Figure 8-1
Dual-and-Distinct Software Testing
Using a Minicomputer for Dual Resources

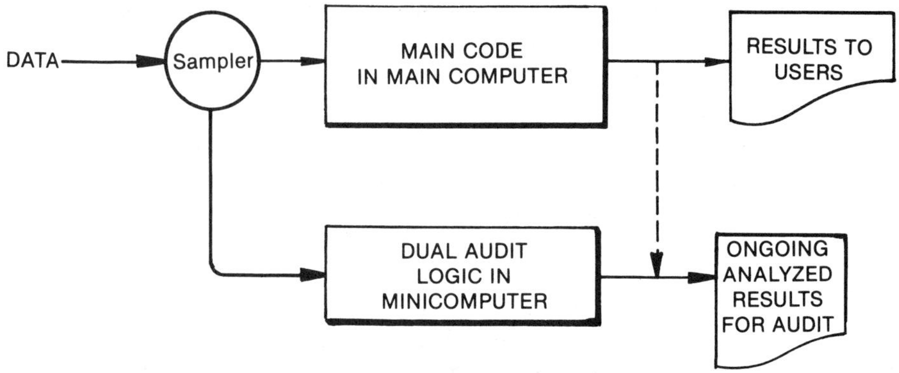

sionals when they are in the process of improving (testing) a new version of an operational system's programs. Twin data bases are created by copying the production data base onto a test data base residing in a separate drive and the version of the programs under internal control evaluation onto another partition or "test region." This separates the test data from the real data. The test system is then run in parallel with and independently of the production system, to test its functioning.

This techniquc is described in detail in Reference 47 of the Bibliography, Part I. An illustration of the technique is presented in Figure 8-2, which shows the essence of the test method.

MICROCOMPUTER APPROACHES

The advent of microcomputers in all aspects of business activity and their widespread use in performing a number of versatile functions opens up many new possibilities for using them in testing. As auditors are becoming quite adept at the use of microcomputers in auditing functions, it is just a matter of time before microcomputers are used in a testing mode.

The microcomputer can be used essentially in two main modes:

1. "Stand-alone" mode
2. "Micro-to-mainframe" connected mode

Stand-alone mode. In this mode of use, many of the traditional audit test functions that were conducted via generalized software packages, can now be programmed for a microcomputer. This process is greatly aided by the availability of so-called "user-friendly fourth generation (4GL) languages" which permit a user without much training in programming to write application programs. It is therefore quite possible for the auditor or test specialist to practice

Figure 8-2
Illustration of Twin Data Base and Test Region Approach

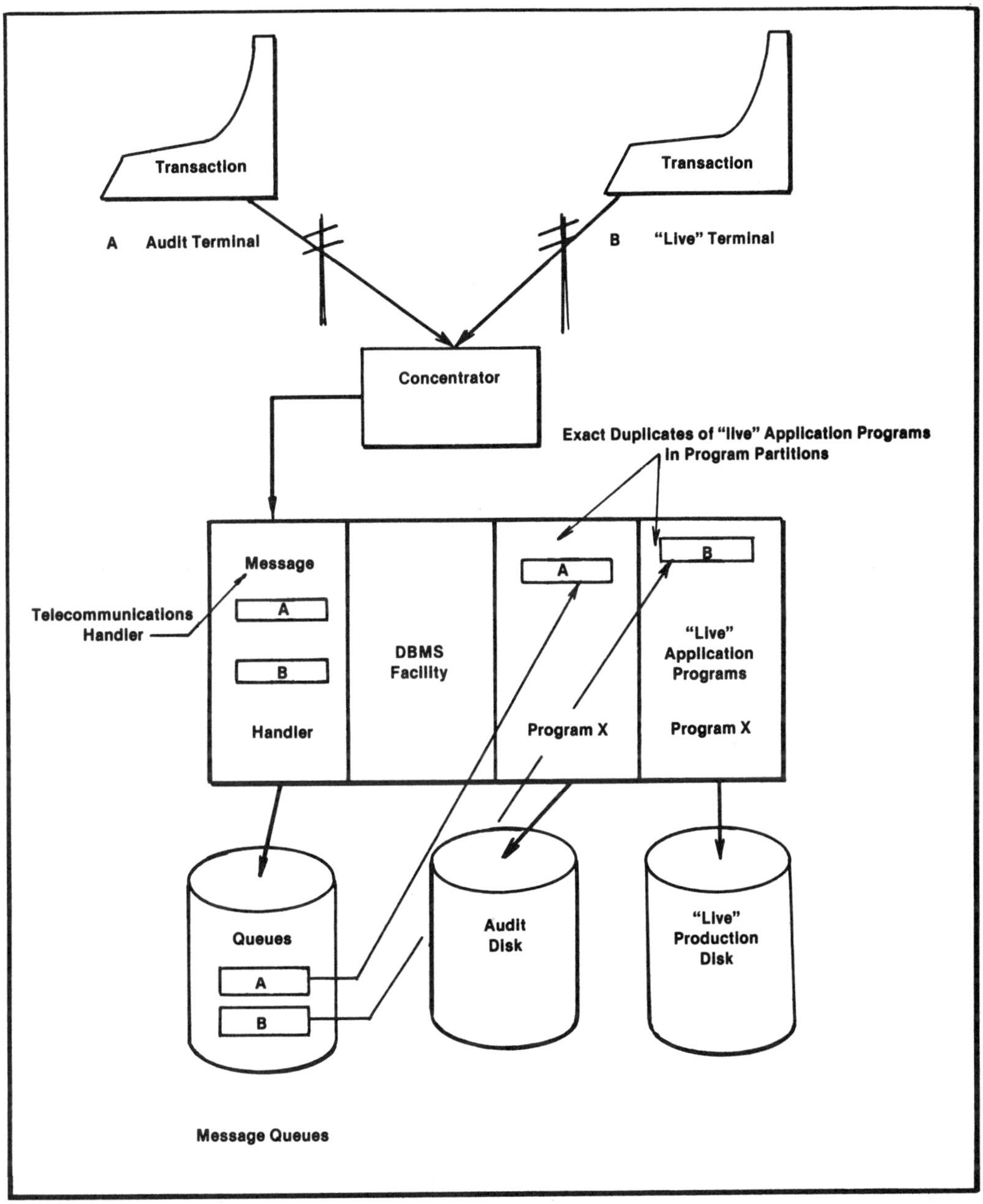

Reprinted by permission from B. P. Wess and L. D. Hunt, "Virtual Transaction Testing—An Audit Technique for On-Line Data Bases and Computer Networks," COM-SAC, *Computer Security, Auditing and Controls,* Vol. 5, No. 2, July 1978, p. A-4.

the technique of parallel simulation by reprogramming vital portions of the application logic in a fourth generation language, process a set of transactions subject to test through the parallel programs, and then compare the results to those obtained during the production period under test.

Micro-to-mainframe connected mode. The capability now exists, and many new avenues are underway, to permit the auditor or test professional to link a microcomputer to a large system mainframe (or to other microcomputers via local area networks—LAN's). This makes possible a whole array of new possibilities to either (1) download data from the mainframe or corporate data base and then test its contents in the microcomputers, or (2) through the use of intelligent software capabilities, permit the auditor to interact with the mainframe system's data base to extract target data from the mainframe system for auditing and subsequent analysis, either in the microcomputer or through the more powerful capabilities of the mainframe itself. When data is downloaded from the mainframe to the microcomputer, the microcomputer behaves essentially as just another terminal in an on-line system network. The use of interactive intelligent software capabilities permits a wider choice of selection and analysis capabilities for testing the main system via the microcomputer, than when using the microcomputer in a terminal emulation mode.

Alert and forward-looking auditors and test professionals should look into these continually evolving new avenues and capabilities to enhance their cadre of audit tools and techniques, thus facilitating their internal controls testing efforts.

PART II

How to Train EDP Audit and Control Staff

Preface to Part II

The first part of this manual dealt with the fundamentals of and a methodology for testing internal control in computer-based systems. This presumes that your organization has the professional personnel with the proper level of skills ready to undertake the complexities of auditing computer systems and testing internal controls. Experience indicates that, because of the major transition in skills brought about by the advent of computerization, organizations either do not have professionals skilled in *EDP* internal controls and auditing or their existing professionals need a considerable amount of reindoctrination and upgrading to be able to effectively cope with their responsibilities in the conduct of EDP audits, EDP internal controls evaluation and testing, and operational reviews of data processing installations.

We should realize that it is people, equipped with the proper skills and methodologies and tools, that test internal controls and conduct EDP reviews. Methodologies and techniques by themselves do not get the job done. The purpose of this section is therefore to provide you with information and practical guidelines on how to train and develop the new breed of computer audit and control specialists required to conduct effective audits of computer systems and how to upgrade the personnel already in your organization.

The topics selected present information that will be useful to you both in assessing the current strengths and weaknesses of your staff and upgrading them and in developing new personnel to work in this increasingly important area of internal control. Chapter 9 presents a practical and proven method to help you assess the skills of your present staff if you are a manager or assess the state of your own skills if you are a concerned professional, and spot weaknesses in skills that need to be addressed. The method presented has been successfully used in many consulting engagements and is based on a skills inventory program. Chapter 10 shows you a training program in computer audit and controls which can form the basis from which you develop your own program to meet your particular objectives and needs. Relating back to Part I, which concentrates on internal controls testing, this chapter provides a specific profile of desirable skills for personnel involved in EDP internal controls testing. Chapter 11 provides ideas and insight to the kinds of skills and training that may be required as new developments in computer and communications technology bring a need for further innovation and upgrading of computer audit and control personnel.

If you are serious about embarking on the assessment and testing of internal controls in computer systems and installations, it is essential that you become proficient in the cadre of new skills needed to function effectively in your work and to maintain a high level of professional excellence.

I am confident that the information contained in this section will be as useful to you as it already has been, in earlier versions, to hundreds of professionals I have worked with in consulting assignments and seminars throughout the world.

9

How to Assess the Skills Profile and Spot Weaknesses

IMPORTANCE OF ASSESSING YOUR SKILLS PROFILE

Organizations and individuals cannot do much to improve their skills until they know the *present* status of their capabilities. This is akin to the old proverb that says "you cannot fight and overcome an enemy that you do not know."

The way to raise the level of competency is to make an assessment of one's present skills in relation to the overall panorama of skills that would ideally be needed to cope with the problems of controlling EDP. One mechanism for doing this is to prepare a *skills inventory profile* for the EDP audit and control unit.

The skills inventory profile will be useful in at least these ways:

- It will enable each individual in the group to identify personal strengths and become aware of personal weaknesses.
- It will provide a panoramic view of the group's strengths.
- It will provide a sound basis upon which to develop an ad-hoc training and development program to overcome the discovered weaknesses.
- It can be used as a tool for staffing. If the unit is in the process of acquiring new staff (organizations usually always are) the profile will suggest the type of staff backgrounds to look for.
- It can be used as an aid in recruiting and attracting high-quality personnel. Through seeing the training and development program your organization has developed, prospective employees may be induced to join your organization because of your demonstrated concern for and established steps in keeping your personnel abreast of the technology and required skills.
- It can be a useful tool in the manning of audit and control projects with the proper skills mix.

The effort required to prepare the skills profile is relatively small but the benefits derived from it are most worthwhile.

HOW TO PREPARE A SKILLS INVENTORY AND PROFILE

There are two aspects to this program:

1. Developing an inventory of useful skills
2. Preparing the specific profile for your organization

SKILLS INVENTORY

The skills inventory involves listing all the skills that would be desirable to have as regards: *basic* knowledge in EDP, *applied practice* subjects in EDP audit and control subjects and *supporting* disciplines. The *basic EDP skills* consist of the topical subjects which anyone dealing with data processing should possess, such as knowledge of programming, a programming language, etc. The *applied practice subjects* refer to courses or subject matter related to the particular field of EDP auditing and controls, such as testing, tools and techniques for auditing systems, methodologies for involvement in the development cycle, data center audits, etc. *Supporting subjects* refer to knowledge from the fields of accounting, auditing, statistics, operations research, and the behavioral sciences.

It is clear then that the competent EDP audit and control professional needs to bridge three related fields of knowledge to discharge his or her duties in a competent fashion, namely, data processing fundamentals, applied EDP audit and controls, and supporting disciplines in accounting, management sciences, and personal skills.

A Sample Skills Inventory

An example of the skills inventory is shown in the vertical part of Figure 9-1. This listing is by no means general or complete for every organization but it provides a good initial basis for the preparation of your own. For instance, there may be items in the list that your organization may need to include in view of the highly specific nature of types of equipment, programming languages, or other unique features present in a given organization.

The list of skills for the EDP audit and control field can be pinpointed more definitively, although it will naturally change as the field evolves and new skills or techniques become available.

THE SKILLS PROFILE

The skills profile for any one individual and for the group as a whole has to do with the determination of the "pattern" of knowledge or, if you will, the "clusters" of available knowledge in the group under review.

Figure 9-1
Skills Inventory and Profile

NAME:________________________
Position:________________________
Department:________________________

SKILLS PROFILE SHEET
(Auditor and EDP)

HOW TRAINED → / SKILL	Academic College	Seminar	Reading	On-the-Job	Proficiency BAS	INT	ADV	COMMENTS
FUNDAMENTALS **Introduction to EDP**								
Programming Concepts								
Programming Languages								
Machine (BAL, NEAT, etc.)								
FORTRAN								
COBOL								
BASIC								
RPG								
PL-1								
APL								
Other								
File Design Concepts								
Sequential								
Random								
Index-sequential								
Other								
Data Base Concepts								
Data Communications								
On-Line Systems								
Basic								
Advanced								
Operating Systems								
DOS								
OS								
V-OS								
Other								
Job Control Language								
Systems Analysis								
EDP Systems Design								
Systems Testing								
Computer Operations								
Terminals								
Distributed Data Processing								
Knowledge of Equipment								
EDP/AUDITING & CONTROLS								
EDP Management								
Computer Operations								
Applications audit								
–manual								
–computerized								
Documentation								
EDP Standards								
Operational Audits								

Figure 9-1
Skills Inventory and Profile (Continued)

SKILL	Academic College	Seminar	Reading	On-the-Job	Proficiency			COMMENTS
					BAS	INT	ADV	
Audits using Programs								
Project Control Methods								
Audit during Design Cycle								
Post-Installation Audit								
Financial Audits								
Operational Audits in general								
SYSTEM DEVELOPMENT AUDIT								
1. Feasibility Phase								
2. General Design								
3. Detailed Design								
4. Programming/Implementation Planning								
5. System Test								
6. System Acceptance								
7. Conversion Phase								
8. Post-Installation Review								
9. Auditability Building								
10. Controls Design								
DATA CENTER AUDITS								
1. Data Center Audit Plan Prepn.								
2. Admin. General Controls								
3. Organization Review								
4. Physical Security –Access Control –Location –Building/Construction –Environmental Support –Fire Protection –Protected Storage –Housekeeping Practices								
5. Data Security Practices								
6. Backup & Recovery								
7. Data Control Section								
8. Maintenance Practices								
9. Insurance Provisions								
10. Legal Reviews								
11. Data Preparation								
12. Planning and Scheduling								
13. Data Center Measures of Perfm.								
14. Cost Charge-out								
15. Personnel Security								
16. New System Installation Stnds.								
17. Operating Software Op. Practs.								
18. DC Operating Statistics								
DATA BASE AUDITING								
1. Data Base Substantive Testing								
2. Data Base Controls								
3. Data Base Integrity Review								
4. Data Base Recovery								
5. Data Base Admin. Function								

(Continued)

Figure 9-1
Skills Inventory and Profile (Continued)

SKILL	Academic College	Seminar	Reading	On-the-Job	Proficiency BAS	INT	ADV	COMMENTS
6. Data Base Interface Lang. Use.								
7. DBMS Software Packages: –IMS –IDBMS –ADABAS –TOTAL –Other CICS								
8. DATA DICTIONARY SYSTEMS Data Manager Lexicon, others Review Procedures								
9. DB. Accuracy Controls								
10. DB. Security Controls								
11. DB. Generalized Audit Packages ASI-ST EDP Auditor Audex, Mark IV, etc.								
AUDIT TECHNIQUES								
1. TEST DECKS								
2. ITF								
3. PARALLEL SIMULATION								
4. TAGGING & TRACING								
5. PROGRAM BEHAVIOR ANALYSIS TOOLS –COMBI –COTUNE –COBOL TRACE –PLI-TRACE								
6. BATCH TERMINAL SIMULATOR								
7. DUAL AUDIT CODE								
8. MAPPING								
9. SCARF								
10. EDIT ROUTINES SIMULATION								
11. ROLL-IN/ROLL-BACK TESTING TECHNIQUE								
12. EMBEDDED TEST ROUTINES								
Techniques for System Selection								
1. SCORING								
2. CRITICALITY INDEX								
Techniques for Testing Files								
1. GASPS								
2. SPECIAL AUDIT ROUTINES								
3. PARALLEL SIMULATION								
4. RANDOM SAMPLING								
Techniques for Interactive Auditing								
1. Interactive ITF								
2. Audit Terminal								
3. Audit Minicomputers								

Figure 9-1
Skills Inventory and Profile (Continued)

SKILL	Academic College	Seminar	Reading	On-the-Job	Proficiency			COMMENTS
					BAS	INT	ADV	
4. Virtual Transaction Test								
5. In-line System Simulation								
6. Batch Terminal Simulation								
7. Audit System Monitor (internal system to check main system)								
Techniques for Data Collection and Audit Trailing								
1. Embedded Data Collection								
2. Extended Records Reference File								
3. SCARF								
4. Auditor Data Base Segment								
Techniques for Monitoring and Surveillance								
1. Threat Monitoring								
2. On-line Acknowledgment								
3. Control Terminal								
4. SMF Use								
5. Other________								
Techniques for System Acceptance								
1. Base Case Acceptance								
2. Acceptance Matrix								
Techniques for Program/ Library Integrity								
1. Hash Total Modules								
2. Load Library Reviews								
3. Compare								
4. Authorization Matrix								
5. Re-entrant Code								
Other Techniques								
NEW TECHNOLOGY AREAS								
1. Operating System Review —Operating Standards								
—Testing								
—Security Flaws								
—Controls								
2. Distributed DP —Architecture								
—Testing Techniques								
—Controls								
3. Data Communication Networks Review —Front end processors								
—Concentrators								
—Message Switching								
(Continued)								

(Continued)

Figure 9-1
Skills Inventory and Profile (Continued)

SKILL	Academic College	Seminar	Reading	On-the Job	Proficiency BAS	INT	ADV	COMMENTS
–Types of Lines Services								
–Data Communication Controls for								
–Data Accuracy								
–Data Security								
–Data Privacy (encryption)								
4. Controls for Software Environment –TSO								
–Program Change Control & Load Library Audits								
–System Utilities Use & Controls								
5. MINI-MICRO COMPUTERS –MINICOMPUTERS AUDIT –MICROCOMPUTER CONTROLS								

To develop the skills inventory and profile, the following steps should be followed:

1. *Prepare a skills inventory list* as shown in Figure 9-1. Update it to reflect your organization's needs.
2. *Distribute a blank copy of the skills inventory sheet to each member of the group.* Ask the group to check those skills they feel they have, how they were acquired, what is their level of proficiency in the skills, and have they actually applied these skills in the field.
3. *Have a supervisor review and discuss the completed forms with the staff.*
4. *Overlay or superimpose the skills profile sheets for the whole group* by either plotting the skills onto one single sheet, or even better, by preparing transparencies of the individual sheets and then, by overlaying the sheets, obtaining an aggregate view of the skills possessed by the whole group.
5. *Analyze the "clusters" of knowledge which indicate the strengths of the group and identify the "sparse" or "light" areas which indicate lack of or weaknesses* in these particular areas of knowledge. (See Figure 9-2.)

EXAMPLE OF AN ACTUAL APPLICATION

The procedure described above has been used by the author in a number of consulting assignments and when he was a data processing director with good results. The procedure is applicable to both EDP and EDP audit and

Figure 9-2
Strengths and Weaknesses of Audit Staff

NAME:____________________ SKILLS PROFILE SHEET
Position:____________________ (Auditor and EDP)
Department:____________________

HOW TRAINED → / SKILL	Academic College	Seminar	Reading	On-the-Job	Proficiency BAS	Proficiency INT	Proficiency ADV	COMMENTS
FUNDAMENTALS Introduction to EDP					√√√√√	√	√	
Programming Concepts					√√			
Programming Languages								
Machine (BAL, NEAT, etc.)					√			
FORTRAN					√	√√√		
COBOL						√√	√	STRENGTHS
BASIC					√√√			
RPG					√			
PL-1					√			
APL								
Other					√	√		
File Design Concepts								
Sequential					√	√		
Random					√	√		
Index-sequential					√			
Other								
Data Base Concepts					√√			
Data Communications					√√			
On-Line Systems								
Basic					√			
Advanced								
Operating Systems					√			
DOS								
OS								WEAKNESSES
V-OS								
Other								
Job Control Language					√			
Systems Analysis					√	√√		
EDP Systems Design								
Systems Testing					√			
Computer Operations								
Terminals					√√			
Distributed Data Processing								WEAKNESSES
Knowledge of Equipment								
EDP/AUDITING & CONTROLS								
EDP Management					√			
Computer Operations								
Applications audit					√√√	√√	√	
–manual					√√	√√		
–computerized					√√			STRENGTHS
Documentation					√	√		
EDP Standards					√√			
Operational Audits					√√	√		

control personnel. The only difference lies in the contents of the skills inventory matrix.

In a major organization, the procedure was applied as one of the steps in determining the state of readiness and the effectiveness of an EDP audit department. Through field interviews with various auditee department managers, we obtained a number of critical observations about the EDP audit group's ability to conduct competent audits as well as many comments about their lack of skills in auditing advanced systems. Through the skills inventory and profile, the organization was able to confirm the correctness of the auditees' contentions.

A remark often made was that the "EDP auditors are well qualified to assess controls in 'conventional' and batch systems, but thoroughly inadequate to deal with the more 'advanced/on-line/data base systems' which are currently being developed." The skills profile sheets revealed that this was in fact the case.

The findings and the skills inventory sheet enabled the particular organization to revamp the whole training program for EDP auditors and for regular auditors as well. This set other steps in motion, such as determining what types of training courses would be needed from inside or outside the organization to *develop* competent auditors and what skills would be considered minimal before promoting staff members from one category to another. The results helped define what skills would have to be acquired from the outside through recruiting efforts in view of the fact that it could take too long to develop the skills internally.

Essentially the same approach was used by the author in determining the real cause of horrendous bottlenecks in the delivery of on-time and in-quality systems in a financial organization that was developing *twenty-five major* system projects simultaneously. In this case the skills profile inventory was used in conjunction with a tally or accounting of the demand for the skills by all projects under development over the development period. Such an analysis revealed that all projects were bottlenecked and inadequate in quality because there was a terribly lopsided mix of skills in the EDP department. There were only four analyst caliber personnel and *forty* trainees with fancy titles who were not equipped to handle the complex projects, especially in the communications and human relations area, which required seasoned, user-oriented personnel. The problem was resolved when personnel of project-leader caliber were obtained and put in charge of the projects and when the mix of senior, semisenior, and junior skills was balanced.

ASSESSING THE STRENGTHS AND WEAKNESSES OF THE AUDIT/CONTROL GROUP

The strengths and weaknesses of the EDP controls unit can be readily assessed using the results of the Skills Inventory and Profile shown in Figure

9-1. You may recall that the procedure to determine the skills inventory of each staff member is to ask each one to fill out the inventory form and then have a supervisor review its contents to ensure its accuracy and to eliminate biases.

Having obtained all the skills inventory profiles for the group in question, one can obtain the relative strengths and weaknesses of the group as a whole by one of two methods:

1. *Plot all the check marks in each of the skill categories listed in the figure onto one sheet,* showing overlaps where more than one individual has the given skill.
2. *Make transparencies of the various skills profiles sheets filled out by the staff and then overlay them to show the overlap of check marks.*

The areas where the staff is strong will show "clusters" of marks, indicating that the staff has these skills. Conversely, those areas of the skills matrix showing empty cells or a wide scatter of check marks indicate areas of skills which are not possessed by the staff. Upon study of these patterns, the manager or person in charge of training and development can determine the relative criticality of those missing skills to the group's ability to function effectively, and, therefore, prepare the necessary training and development programs required to correct the deficiencies.

Figure 9-2 illustrates how the skills matrix would show a cluster of check marks indicating skills strengths, and a light scatter of check marks indicating skills weaknesses. The figure is based on the actual procedure used in several assignments to determine the skills profile of a group of auditors.

10

The Training Program for EDP Audit and Control

BASIC CONSIDERATIONS

Contrary to what many people think, the training and development of personnel in any discipline must be "designed" and "programmed" for optimum results. This stems from the fact that training and developing staff is not a single, one-time task, but a "process." Even better, it is an "ongoing" process with recognizable stages. Universities and educators talk about a "designed curriculum" for X discipline. Why should training and development of a new professional group of people whose mission is to help meet the goals of the organization be handled with less care and thoughtfulness?

Here are some elements to consider in developing a training program:

- The objectives of the training program
- The learning cycle
- The charter of organization and responsibilities
- The relative complexity of the EDP environment
- The relative sensitivity of the computerized applications
- The degree of statutory or regulatory mandates
- The present level and profile of skills of the staff
- The relative availability of training courses outside the organization
- Resource constraints

The Importance of Setting Training Objectives

Before undertaking the training and development program, the organization (or individual if he/she is pursuing a self-development program) should spell out the objectives and boundaries of the training and development program. In so doing, several of the other factors listed above most likely enter the picture.

Following is a set of questions that the responsible individual should ask in determining the program's objectives:

- What are the present weaknesses in the staff? (The skills profile helps here.)
- Are we trying to develop a separate specialized EDP audit/controls capability or do we wish to train all personnel to be self-sufficient in EDP audit and control?
- What are the short-term needs and long-term requirements?
- Do we plan to develop skills from within the organization only, or supplement with ready-made skills from the outside?
- Do we plan to opt for in-depth audits or simple compliance audits only?
- Will the department plan to do more anticipatory and preimplementation audits than postoperational audits? (System review skills are important.)
- Does the organization have other controls functions besides audit, such as quality assurance, data security, data base administration?
- Is auditing primarily a corporate function or are there divisional audit groups?

An example of training and development objectives follows.

Sample Training and Development Objectives

- To provide a standard program which all members of the group should follow in their natural progression within the group.
- To provide a minimum level of sufficiency for the bulk of the audit/control staff with specialized training supplied on a case-by-case basis.
- To develop a staff capable of conducting total audits of EDP system applications including the field and manual portion of systems.
- To equip EDP audit and control personnel to be fully competent to handle the EDP portions of the system and provide support to regular audit/control staff with responsibility for the opinion resting with the financial auditor. (The audit unit becomes a consulting or supporting agency primarily.)
- To equip personnel to conduct "in-depth" audits of EDP.
- To produce specialist auditors in data centers, system development audits, and operational audits.
- To train auditors on the use of computer-aided audit tools, such as audit software packages. (This is a limited training objective.)
- To provide auditors with good communications skills to convey technical subjects in business terms.

Having a clear set of training objectives serves to delimit the scope and magnitude of the training program. It also helps in tying in the training programs for various types of personnel, such as regular auditors, EDP auditors, and other support technical personnel (for example, technical support specialists). It helps link in-house training to purchased training from outside sources.

The Learning Cycle

The process of developing personnel is multiphased. This all goes back to the concept of the learning curve in industrial engineering. Briefly, in developing good people the following kinds of training must be provided:

- Incubation and indoctrination
- Workshop training
- Field or hands-on training

The *indoctrination phase* is usually taken care of via classroom sessions, seminars, and university courses supplemented by reading. *Workshop training* is basically simulated training with or without the aid of computerized assistance. The latter is usually accomplished via work sessions with cases or via a terminal connected to a computer application. *Field training,* as the name implies, involves the development of personnel in actual assignments under senior supervision, but in a real-world environment.

The existence of the learning cycle has a great deal to do with the time span it takes to develop a proficient audit and control professional. This is illustrated in Figure 10-1, which shows the various stages in human development.

As can be appreciated, the "time span" to become *proficient*[1] varies

Figure 10-1
The Learning Curve in the Development of Professionals

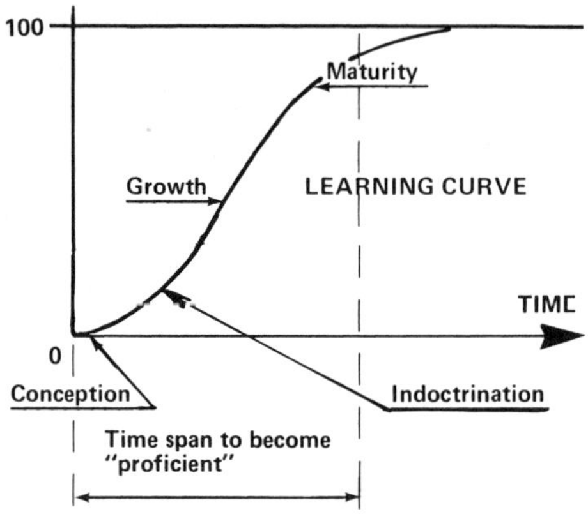

[1] "Proficiency" is taken to mean a level of knowledge which equips the individual to handle assignments with self-sufficiency and which commands the respect and acceptance of peers and superiors.

depending upon the individual's background and his/her level of seasoning and previous experience. As can be expected, an individual with a background quite removed from either EDP or audit will take longer to become proficient. Likewise an individual with no real-world or practical experience or just out of a university will take an even longer period of time to gain meaningful proficiency.

We can provide some rules-of-thumb to estimate the "proficiency time span," as shown in Figure 10-2.

One of the reasons for discussing the learning curve is to emphasize that there is no such thing as "instant geniuses" and that the time span is inexorable and unavoidable. The most managers can hope to do to "accelerate" the development of personnel is to change the slope of the learning curve by one or several of these avenues:

- Choosing people judiciously
- Selecting senior people with many of the fundamental skills and experience
- Implementing a well-planned training program and curriculum
- Providing supervision by or exposure to experienced personnel during assignments
- Offering access to top quality courses and seminars
- Selecting EDP audit assignments carefully to develop experience

The acceleration process is illustrated in Figure 10-3.

The Nature of the Charter of Responsibilities

The functional charter of organization, to a great extent, delimits the scope of responsibilities.

Figure 10-2
Time Span to Gain Proficiency*

TYPE OF INDIVIDUAL	TIME SPAN, YRS.
1. *Senior* Level with experience in EDP or Audit*	2½ to 3½ years
2. *Senior Level with no experience in EDP or Audit*	3 to 4½ years
3. *Inexperienced person being indoctrinated in EDP Audit as a first field of endeavor.*	4 to 6 years

* Implies a level of proven expertise and real-world experience in the field of origin, usually five years in a professional field. Individual has handled major system projects or audit assignments in a competent manner.

Figure 10-3
Accelerating the Learning Process

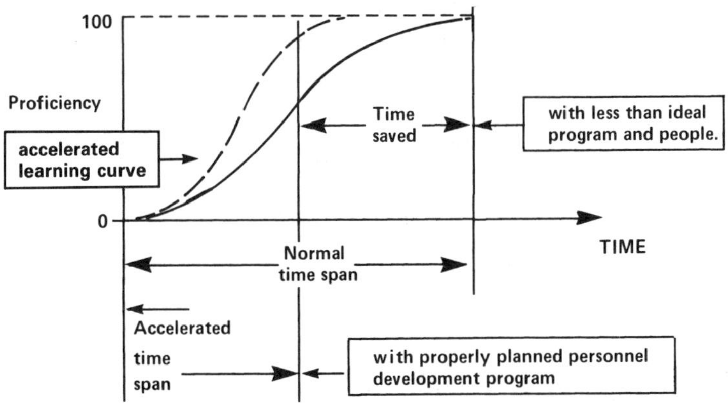

Naturally, those areas that are not covered in the charter will not require corresponding training.

The charter often spells out also the types of roles to be played by the EDP and controls function. In turn, the roles that the auditor will play will call for different skills and the knowledge of a distinct cadre of audit techniques.

For example, following are some roles that audit/control functions can play. (See References 18, 20, and 23 in the Bibliography, Part II.)

ROLE	REQUIRED KNOWLEDGE
• Compliance audit • Substantive • Surveillance/Intrinsic (through the computer auditing)	• Test data decks • Audit software packages • SMF, audit reference logs COMBI (COBOL Missed Branch Indicator), embedded audit modules, embedded audit routines, etc.

EDP Complexity

As can be expected the relative complexity of the EDP environment will significantly influence the extent and the contents of the training program.

If the organization is involved in advanced systems, on-line/data base and telecommunication technologies, training in the fundamentals of these subjects as well as knowledge of controls for these areas must be provided.

The skills profile matrix identifies a number of advanced EDP skills. (See Figure 9-1.)

The advent of distributed data processing (DDP) networks opens up a whole new area of knowledge and the need for novel audit and control approaches.

Sensitivity of Computerized Applications

Needless to say, if the organization's EDP applications are very important to the organization's operations, present a high level of exposure, or could lead to a breach of regulatory provisions, the types of skills that the audit/control staff would require must vary accordingly. For instance, you may need to become more familiar with skills on:

- Compliance testing
- Fraud prevention, detection, and deterrence
- Legislative pronouncements and mandates (see next item)
- Legal implications (see next item)
- Ongoing and monitoring audit/surveillance techniques.

Statutory Regulations

Organizations subject to a number of regulatory or statutory mandates such as financial institutions, utilities, food and drug products, or suppliers of services to governments will most likely face careful scrutiny for compliance of rules and for proper interpretation of established rules in the computer systems they build.

If this applies to you, you should be well versed on legislative pronouncements and their implications on organizations.

The enactment of the Foreign Corrupt Practices Act (FCPA) actually applies to most organizations. The FCPA, in fact, mandates that a sound system of internal control should exist in organizations and that such should be properly documented. If you work for or are connected with the U.S. government, you need to be familiar with the dictates of Office of Management and Budget (OMB) 123, the Financial Managers Integrity Act, and the Data Privacy Act of 1974. These regulations stipulate that internal controls must be present in various aspects of computer systems.

The implication of these laws on the training of audit/control personnel is that the latter should be competently trained on the *assessment and testing of internal controls*. This means that audit/control personnel should acquire the methodologies on how to design and assess internal controls. In view of its importance, this subject has been covered in great detail in Part I of this manual.

Present Levels of Skills or Staff

It is obvious that the level of skills of the existing staff is an important consideration in developing the training program.

If the audit/control staff is specialized, such as on data center audits, system development audits or operational system audits, it is clear that various individuals may receive training along specialized areas of EDP audit and control over and above the regular core courses applicable to all members of the staff.

The other point to consider is training for senior and junior staff members. The emphasis on training for senior staff members might be on the ''acquisition of knowledge'' for new areas. For junior staff, training on the ''foundation'' of audit and control may be more important.

Availability of Training Courses

The availability of training courses and materials will naturally influence both the scheduling of training and the extent of in-house training development.

Considering the real ''opportunity'' value of the senior staff's time, generally speaking, it *is not always cost-effective to deploy internal personnel* to research, develop, and deliver training courses on audit/control for the organization's staff if such are already available outside the organization.

Developing training courses for in-house staff is a time-consuming task which requires professional experience and should be undertaken only when dealing with:

- Company-specific subjects
- Extremely large organizations with a very large audit/control staff
- One-of-a-kind subject matter not available elsewhere and yet needed immediately.

There are a number of reasons for this, such as:

- The economics of scale
- The lack of in-house staff proficiency in *developing and maintaining* suitable text materials
- Large investment in course development yet infrequent use of the in-house training resource
- A tendency to induce ''inbreeding'' and a failure to expose the staff to the views and experiences of other organizations

Because audit and control staffs are usually limited in number, most organizations send their staffs to attend public seminars and conferences or have experts conduct training courses on company premises.

Resource Constraints

Organizations with limited staff *do have a problem* in providing the breadth of skills necessary for effective coverage of the current state of EDP technology.

Because of size, in relation to the broad field of EDP audit and control, generally, the training program may tend to concentrate on the basics with little time left for advanced audit/control approaches. If the organization is engaged in advanced EDP systems and has a very small staff, it is quite difficult to be able to conduct meaningful audits. This is tantamount to management's being willing to accept a significant level of risk or potential exposure.

Somehow, on a selective basis, managers should still train at least someone in the staff on some of the more advanced aspects of audit and control—if for no other reason than to be aware of what the organization may be missing because of the lack of an adequate organization and staff able to encompass the full range of technical EDP audits and to assess exposures.

MAIN BODY OF KNOWLEDGE FOR THE EDP AUDIT AND CONTROL PROFESSIONAL

This subsection lists the main topical subjects that the ideally qualified audit/control professional might possess to handle a wide array of EDP audit and control assignments and to be able to function effectively in both simple and complex EDP environments. It is most unlikely that any one single individual could *amass* and *maintain* fluency in all the subjects listed because of the wide diversity of topics described here.

The implication, therefore, is that *most organizations should seek to build all these skills across a number of people in the staff* and by *specializing some of the staff members* in the more technical topics, such as operating systems.

The knowledge and skills list is presented in two figures. Figure 10-4 lists the basic set of topical subjects or courses that would provide the ideal background for the EDP audit/control professional. Figure 10-5 presents a matrix which indicates the types of training that might be required for various functional categories or levels, such as manager, general auditor, EDP auditor, or quality assurance (QA) or EDP controls expert, based on the list of skills in Figure 10-4.

Figure 10-5 also clearly illustrates a number of interesting points, as follows:

- *Two levels of training are required for personnel, regardless of whether their source background is EDP or audit.* If the individual comes from auditing, he/she must learn topics on basic data processing *and* in EDP auditing, the latter being a new discipline. If the individual comes from EDP, we save ourselves the effort of training him/her on EDP, but must

Figure 10-4
Body of Knowledge in EDP and EDP Auditing

ITEM	SUBJECT
1.	DATA PROCESSING FUNDAMENTALS • BASIC EDP EQUIPMENT AND CHARACTERISTICS • COMPUTER PROGRAMMING
2.	SYSTEMS DESIGN PRINCIPLES
3.	COMPUTER CENTER OPERATIONS
4.	ORGANIZATION AND FUNCTIONAL RESPONSIBILITIES OF EDP
5.	EDP MANAGEMENT PRINCIPLES • ADMINISTRATION • MANAGEMENT STANDARDS
6.	EDP SYSTEM CONTROLS
7.	EDP DOCUMENTATION
8.	DATA, PROGRAM AND FILE PROTECTION TECHNIQUES
9.	COMPUTER COMPLEX PHYSICAL SECURITY
10.	CONTINGENCY PLANNING AND RECOVERY
11.	SYSTEMS AUDITING WITH THE COMPUTER • TEST DECK APPROACH • AUDIT SOFTWARE
12.	OPERATIONAL AUDIT OF EDP ACTIVITIES
13.	REVIEW OF EDP ALTERNATIVES–(SERVICE CENTERS)
14.	ELEMENTS OF OPERATING SYSTEMS
15.	DATA COMMUNICATIONS AND ON-LINE SYSTEMS TECHNOLOGY
16.	CHECKLISTS AND GUIDELINES FOR EDP AUDITING
17.	ORGANIZATION FOR COMPUTER AUDITING
18.	OTHER SUPPORTING DISCIPLINES
19.	SYSTEM DEVELOPMENT (PRE-IMPLEMENTATION) AUDITS
20.	ADVANCED TOOLS AND TECHNIQUES FOR SYSTEMS AUDITABILITY (Chap. 3)
21.	DATA BASE CONCEPTS AND DATA BASE AUDITING APPROACHES
22.	DATA BASE AND FILE RECOVERY APPROACHES
23.	KNOWLEDGE OF ENVIRONMENTAL SOFTWARE CONTROLS (Operating Systems, DBMS)
24.	HOW TO ASSESS AND TEST EDP INTERNAL CONTROLS (Part I of this manual)
25.	EDP RISK ANALYSIS METHODS & CONTROLS JUSTIFICATION
26.	HOW TO DESIGN EDP INTERNAL CONTROLS
27.	DISTRIBUTED DATA PROCESSING (NETWORK SYSTEMS)
28.	MINICOMPUTERS
29.	ON-LINE SYSTEM CONTROLS AND AUDITING
30.	STRUCTURED PROGRAMMING CONCEPTS
31.	SYSTEM CONVERSION EXPERIENCE
32.	EDP QUALITY ASSURANCE STANDARDS
33.	PROTOTYPING

* Denotes that this subject is addressed in Part III of this manual

make the individual competent in auditing *and* EDP auditing. In both cases, EDP audit training is a common element of the training process.

- *Training in the basics of data processing comes primarily from vendor training courses,* university, and programmed learning instruction.
- *Training in EDP auditing, at present, comes primarily from profes-*

Figure 10-5
Suggested Personal Development Plan and Sources of Training

COURSE OR SUBJECT	FOR ITEMS IN FIGURE 10-4	OBTAINED VIA	AUDIT MANAGER	AUDITOR	EDP AUDITOR	EDP CONTROL, QA
1. EDP FUNDAMENTALS						
Introduction to EDP	1,2	V, U, PC	x	x	x	x
Programming (Assembler, COBOL, etc.)	1	V, U, PC	se	se	x	x
EDP File Design Concepts (random, sequential)	2	V, U, S	se	x	x	x
Operating System Concepts	14	V, U, S	—	s	x	x
Data Communications Concepts	15	V, U, S	se	se	x	x
Data Base Concepts	2, 15	V, S, L	—	—	x	x
Systems Analysis and Design	2	V, S, L, U	—	—	x	x
Advanced Programming		V, S, L	—	—	x	x
On-Line Technology	15, 24	V, S, L	—	—	x	x
Service Bureaus, Minicomputers	13, 28	V, L	se	se	x	x
Distributed Data Processing	27	S, V, L	se	se	x	x
Structured Programming, Prototyping	30	S, V, L	se	se	x	x
Systems Conversion Experience	31	E, L	—	—	x	x
2. EDP AUDIT PRACTICE						
A. EDP Audit, Security & Controls Overview	12, 6, 8, 9	S, L, U	x	x	x	x
B. EDP Risk Analysis	25	S, L	x	x	x	x
C. How to Organize & Manage EDP Auditing	17	S, L	x	—	x	x
D. Data Center Audits	12	S, C	x	—	x	x

(Continued)

Figure 10-5
Suggested Personal Development Plan and Sources of Training (Continued)

COURSE OR SUBJECT	FOR ITEMS IN FIGURE 10-4	OBTAINED VIA	AUDIT MANAGER	AUDITOR	EDP AUDITOR	EDP CONTROL, QA
E. System Applications Auditing and Controls	6, 7, 11, 22, 24	S, C, U	x	x	x	x
F. How to Design EDP Internal Controls	26, 24	S, L	se	—	x	x
G. How to Assess EDP Controls	24	S, L	x	x	x	x
H. Audit and Control of On-Line/Data Base Systems	15, 20, 21, 22	S, L	x	se	x	x
I. System Environmental Controls	23	S, L	—	—	x	x
J. Advanced Tools & Techniques for System Auditability and Testing	20, 23	S, L	—	se	x	x
K. Auditing Distributed Systems	27	S, L	se	se	x	x
L. Data Security and Privacy	8	S, L	se	se	x	x
M. EDP Audit Report Writing	29	S, L	x	se	x	x
N. System Development Audits	19	S, L	se	—	x	x
O. EDP Quality Assurance Stds.	32	S, L	—	—	x	x
3. AUDIT & SUPPORTING SKILLS						
A. Audit Evidence		U, L	x	x	x	x
B. Sampling Methods		S, U, L	x	x	x	se
C. Audit Opinions		U, L	x	x	x	se
D. Accounting		U, L	x	x	s	se
E. Auditing Principles		U, L	x	x	x	se
F. Statistics and O.R.		U, L	s	s	x	x
G. Audit Operations		E, U, L	x	x	x	se

Figure 10-5
Suggested Personal Development Plan and Sources of Training (Continued)

COURSE OR SUBJECT	FOR ITEMS IN FIGURE 10-4	OBTAINED VIA	AUDIT MANAGER	AUDITOR	EDP AUDITOR	EDP CONTROL, QA
H. Operational Auditing		U, S, L	x	x	x	x
I. Risk and Insurance Concepts		L, E	x	s	s	se
J. Regulatory Laws (FCPA, etc.)		S, L	x	x	x	x
K. Personnel Security		S, L	x	x	x	x
L. Human Communications		S, U, L	x	x	x	x
M. Audit Closing Procedures		E, S	x	x	x	se
N. Audit Work Papers		E, L	x	x	x	x
O. Principles of Testing With EDP*		S, L	se	se	x	x

CODES: L, Literature; PC, Programmed Learning; S, Seminar; V, Vendor Training; U, College; E, Experience; se, some exposure; x, required or most desirable.

* This topic is dealt with in great detail in Part I.

sional training organizations and professional societies' seminars and conferences. Little is available in colleges and universities. This is because EDP audit and control disciplines are state of the art, and such constantly updated knowledge is not usually available from universities. The only other vehicle for acquiring information on the state of the art is through extensive reading of the literature which, unfortunately, is widely scattered in a variety of journals and publications and presents a serious upkeep problem to practicing professionals.

- *Training in conventional auditing and internal control concepts can be obtained to a good extent from university formal training in auditing* and by indoctrination in companies through assignments to conventional audit projects and a great deal of self-development and reading. We recommend that part of the training also include training in supporting subjects and in oral and written communications.

The type of training suggested explains why it takes so long to develop a proficient EDP audit/control specialist and why every organization with significant levels of computerization and attendant risks ought to have a viable if not *formal* training and development program on an ongoing basis. The training and development program is a good offset against loss of key personnel due to turnover and promotion or deliberate rotation of jobs.

Additional information on how and where to obtain training in EDP auditing and controls is provided later in this chapter, under the heading, "Suggested Training for a Non-Auditor in Auditing and for an Auditor in EDP-Related Experience."

Figure 10-6 provides a selected list of books and reference manuals that cover most of the topical subjects listed in Figure 10-4. It can be used to supplement the training of EDP audit personnel. Note that the list is only a partial compilation of books and reference manuals. The whole list of books related to the EDP audit and controls is now in the hundreds.

SKILLS REQUIRED TO AUDIT THE SYSTEM DEVELOPMENT CYCLE

Figures 10-4 and 10-5 summarized the types of training that should be present in the EDP audit group without making reference to the *grouping of skills required to conduct specific types of audits*. In this subsection, we summarize the sets of skills that would be required to conduct competent audits of

Figure 10-6
A Selected List of Books and Reference Materials With Useful Material to Supplement Staff Training

NAME OF BOOK OR REFERENCE MANUAL	USEFUL FOR ITEMS IN FIGURE 10-4	PUBLISHED BY
EDP FUNDAMENTALS		
• *Data Communications, Design, Security* J. F. Fitzgerald	15	John Wiley & Sons
• *An Introduction to Data Base Systems,* C. J. Date	21	Addison-Wesley
• *Distributed Processing & Data Communications,* D. R. McGlynn	27, 15	Wiley-Interscience
• *Operating Systems,* H. Lorin & H. M. Deitel	14	Addison-Wesley
• *Modern Methods for Computer Security and Privacy,* L. Hoffman	8	Prentice-Hall
• *Accuracy, Security and Privacy in Computer Systems,* J. Martin	6, 8, 22, 9	Prentice-Hall
EDP AUDIT AND CONTROLS		
• *EDP Risk Analysis and Controls Justification,* W. E. Perry & J. F. Kuong	25, 24, 26	Management Advisory Publications (book and seminar)
• *Audit and Control of Advanced/On-Line Systems,* J. F. Kuong (MAP-7)	29, 8, 15, 21, 23	Management Advisory Publications (book and seminar)

Figure 10-6
A Selected List of Books and Reference Materials With Useful Material to Supplement Staff Training (Continued)

NAME OF BOOK OR REFERENCE MANUAL	USEFUL FOR ITEMS IN FIGURE 10-4	PUBLISHED BY
• *Audit and Control of Computerized Systems,* J. F. Kuong (MAP-6)	11, 17, 19, 24	Management Advisory Publications (book and seminar)
• *Controls for Advanced/On-Line Data Base Systems* J. F. Kuong	15, 26, 29, 23	Management Advisory Publications
• *Checklists and Guidelines for Reviewing Computer Security and Installations* (MAP-4)	3, 5, 6, 7, 8, 9, 10, 12, 13	Management Advisory Publications (manual)
• *Computer Security, Auditing and Controls, Text and Readings,* J. F. Kuong (MAP-3)	3, 5, 6, 8, 9, 10, 11, 12, 13	Management Advisory Publications (book)
• *Advanced Tools and Techniques for Systems Auditing,* J. F. Kuong (MAP-8)	20, 24	Management Advisory Publications (manual)
• *Effective Computer Audit Practices Manual (ECAP),* W. E. Perry & J. F. Kuong (MAP-11)	11, 20, 24, 25	Management Advisory Publications (subscription manual in installments)
• *Generalized Computer Audit Software,* W. E. Perry & J. F. Kuong (MAP-14)	11	Management Advisory Publications (book)
• *Developing and Implementing an Integrated Test Facility to Test Computerized Systems,* W. E. Perry & J. F. Kuong (MAP-12)	20, 24	Management Advisory Publications (book)
• *Computer Auditing and Security Manual,* J. F. Kuong (MAP-5)	12, 11	Management Advisory Publications (manual)
• *Integrity and Recovery in Computer Systems,* T. Gibbons	22, 10	Hayden Book Co., Rochelle Park, N.J.
• *Data Control Guidelines,* J. R. Sharratt	6, 24	National Computing Centre, Manchester, U.K.
• *Organizing, Managing and Controlling the EDP Audit Function,* J. F. Kuong	17	Management Advisory Publications (seminar manual)
• *How to Test Internal Control and Integrity in Computerized Systems,* W. E. Perry & J. F. Kuong (MAP-15)	24	Management Advisory Publications (book and seminar)
• *Computer Control & Audit,* W. Mair, D. Wood and K. Davis	6, 12, 11	Institute of Internal Auditors
• *How To Prepare an EDP Contingency Plan for Business Continuity* (MAP-23), J. F. Kuong	10	Management Advisory Publications
• *Microcomputer Security, Auditability and Control,* (MAP-20), J. F. Kuong, G. Isaacson, C. Winters	28	Management Advisory Publications
• *ATM Controls, Audit and Security,* (MAP-22), C. M. Winters	29	Management Advisory Publications
• *How to Prepare Audit and Test Plans for EDP Systems,* J. F. Kuong	20, 26	Management Advisory Publications

the system development cycle; the next subsections list the skills required for testing EDP internal controls and for conducting data center audits.

Before we can structure a set of skills for the system development cycle, it is important to clarify the scope and the types of roles that the auditor or reviewer intends to accomplish. There are essentially three major roles that the auditor or quality assurance group can play in system development audits, namely:

1. *Conduct operational or functional audits of the system development process* along the lines of effectiveness and efficiency
2. *Conduct technical reviews of the design process insofar as its ability to support a sound system of internal controls* leading to a professional opinion on the security and system control aspects of a system
3. *Study the need for and specify the auditability provisions* to make the system auditable when it becomes operational

These are indeed three different roles which require different sets of skills. The predominance of skills to conduct the audits of the new system will also vary throughout the development cycle.

In order to clarify the above statements, refer to Figure 10-7 which shows three main phases of the development of a system:

- *Before* approval (feasibility phase)
- *During* the development process (technical phase)
- *After* the system is installed (postinstallation phase).

On this basis, Figure 10-7 shows that in the before-approval or feasibility phase and at the postinstallation review phase the skills that predominate are those of conventional operational auditing, or so-called "management issues." In the technical phase of development (during design) the more technical skills predominate. Here, the more technical EDP auditor skills are required, with a sound knowledge of controls design and various EDP audit techniques for testing the system and for auditability building. It is in the during-design phase, also, that technical skills on auditability building become quite important, with the auditor playing a user role.[2]

Figure 10-7 lists, in the form of a matrix, the type of skills required for the three main roles listed above. It is clear that the set of skills needed to perform all three roles in auditing a system development can be extensive and may not even all be present in a single individual. This figure also suggests that many of the conventional auditor's skills can be very handy with regard to the operational aspects of the audit of the system, which might suggest the need for both conventional and technical EDP auditors' becoming involved to complement each other's skills.

---

[2] See J. F. Kuong, *EDP System Auditability: Approaches and Techniques,* MAP-17 (Wellesley Hills, MA: Management Advisory Publications, 1985).

Figure 10-7
Audit Skills Required Depend Upon the Audit Role Played in System Development

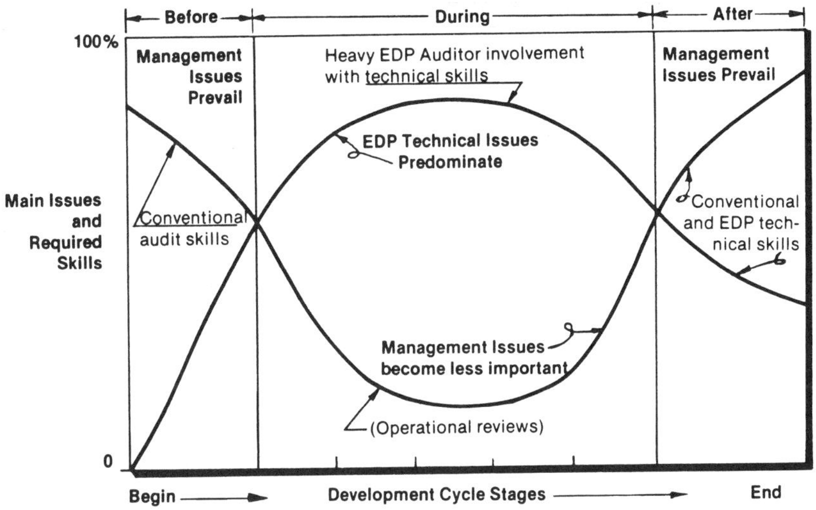

Adapted from *Audit and Control of Computerized Systems,* MAP-6 (Wellesley Hills, MA: Management Advisory Publications, 1980).

It is also apparent, from Figure 10-8, that the set of skills required for technical development reviews and auditability building is much greater than for auditing existing systems.

SKILLS NEEDED TO TEST EDP INTERNAL CONTROLS

Thirty EDP audit skills have been identified to help you assess and test EDP internal controls as discussed in Part I of this manual. These thirty skills, which you can possess at the basic or the advanced level, are explained in Figure 10-9.

Basic means that you learned the skill but are not proficient at using the skill. *Advanced* means that you are proficient at using the skill. For example, skill number 10 calls for knowledge of programming and program testing. A basic skill level would mean an individual understands the mechanics of preparing test data, but is not completely self-sufficient. The individual may not understand blocking factors, variable-length record implications, and other technical aspects of data which might require the individual to request aid from more highly skilled auditors. An advanced skill in preparing test data would enable that individual to develop test information for any computerized application under audit. The same distinction can be made for the other defined EDP audit skills.

Figure 10-8
Basic List of EDP Audit Skills Required to Audit Systems During the Development Cycle by Type of Audit Role Played

SKILL OR EXPERIENCE	TYPE OF AUDIT ROLE		
	Operational	Technical	Auditability Building
1. System analysis and design, including file structures and structured system design and programming	s	x	x
2. Knowledge of one or more programming languages	–	x	x
3. Knowledge or acquaintance with operating systems	–	x	x
4. Expertise in system controls (input, output, processing)	x	x	x
5. Knowledge of data protection and security procedures	x	x	x
6. File backup and recovery procedures	s	x	x
7. Cost/effectiveness methodology-alternative analysis	x	s	–
8. Project management and control standards	x	s	–
9. Program and system testing methods	s	x	x
10. Sound knowledge of EDP system analysis and programming standards	s	x	x
11. Design of auditability provisions	s	x	x
12. On-line/advanced systems, data communications, data base	if applicable		
13. Administrative and procedural controls	x	s	–
14. System and program conversion experience	s	x	x
15. Knowledge of system audit tools and techniques (test decks, audit software packages, parallel simulation, ITF, test software packages, tagging/tracing, dynamic (embedded) auditing, code checks)	s	s	x
16. Design and testing of internal controls	s	x	x
17. Prototyping	s	x	s

x, required; s, some knowledge; –, usually not needed.

Figure 10-9
Skills Needed to Test Controls in Computerized Systems

Type of Skill Required	Level of Knowledge	
	Basic	Advanced
1. Fundamental knowledge of EDP concepts		X
2. File design structures	X	
3. System testing approaches and methodologies		X
4. Audit test techniques (test decks, ITF, snapshot, parallel simulation, tracing, embedded data collection, etc.)		X
5. Generalized audit software		X
6. EDP risk analysis and threats to computer systems		X
7. Knowledge of file and record layouts		X
8. Knowledge of data center and operation controls		X
9. How to prepare detailed "test" objectives		X
10. Approaches to preparing, and types of, test data		X
11. Preparation of job control language	X	
12. System flowcharting and controls point flowcharting		X
13. Knowledge of one or more programming languages	X	
14. System analysis and design	X	
15. System maintenance methods	X	
16. System debugging methods	X	
17. System conversion methods	X	
18. Structured programming (if in use at the organization)	X	
19. Structured walk-through techniques	X	
20. Data base structures and data base integrity	X	
21. Prototyping	X	
22. Preparation and application of test files and data bases	X	
23. Use of test data generators		X
24. Understanding of operating systems	X	
25. Data base management systems (DBMS)	X	
26. Use of operating system utilities	X	
27. Knowledge of system requirements and specifications		X
28. Knowledge of sampling methods		X
29. Knowledge of testing methods and terminology		X
30. Various organization structures to test systems	X	

The skills needed by auditors to test internal controls in computerized applications have been indicated in the appropriate box in Figure 10-9. This shows which skills, at which level, are needed, as well as which skills of a basic level would suffice and which skills are not needed to test internal control. You will note from reviewing Figure 10-9 that internal control testing is one of the more technical aspects of auditing computerized applications. However, that should not discourage anyone with minimal skills from testing internal control. It does, however, raise a flag of caution that extreme care is needed to avoid making some erroneous decisions.

To test internal controls, you should have *basic* skills in the following areas:

- General computer room security and work flow (see Part III)
- Specifying simple extracts
- Programming audit software
- Conceptual understanding of computer operations
- Writing simple JCL (job control language) instructions
- Programming standard computer language
- Designing complex extracts
- Debugging systems
- Comprehending system maintenance implications

These basic skills provide the auditor with an understanding of how computerized applications are designed, implemented, and operated. While you do not need to program, operate computers, etc., it is important to have an appreciation of these skills in order to assess the implementation of controls in a computerized application.

To test internal control in computerized applications, you should have *advanced* skills in the following areas:

- Recognizing EDP terms and equipment
- EDP terminology
- EDP concepts
- EDP audit concerns (threats and risks)
- Reading record layouts
- EDP audit test approaches to operational systems
- Preparing test plans and data
- Understanding detailed systems flowcharts and recognizing control implications
- Various computerized tools and techniques

In addition, a knowledge of risk analysis concepts is very desirable. The advanced skills prepare you to identify control risks and pinpoint control points in computerized applications. This knowledge, coupled with the ability to prepare test plans and create test data, provides you with a good basis for testing the adequacy of internal controls in computerized applications.

SKILLS REQUIRED TO CONDUCT OPERATIONAL AUDITS OF DATA CENTERS

The set of skills required to conduct effective audits of the data processing department and its operations (data center) are considerably different from those required to audit application systems. The audit of data centers requires both very *conventional operational audit skills* as used for any functional audit of an organization's operations and *technical skills* to review the EDP aspects of the data center, as regards hardware, software, and EDP-related practices.

The operational or functional part of the audit is done along the traditional lines of evaluating resource management and application. That is to say, how is the data processing department being managed along the lines of the seven resources required to run any business, namely: *management, manpower, materials, money, machines, methods and standards, and management information for control.* (See Part III, Chapter 19.)

The technical part of the audit requires reviews of controls for the whole data center and for operating systems, data base administration, data base management systems, telecommunications system, and program libraries, etc.

Figure 10-10 lists some of the more important skills required as extracted from the list of total skills given in Figure 10-4.

Figure 10-10
Skills Required to Conduct Operational Audits of Data Centers*

1. Data Processing Fundamentals
   - Equipment characteristics
   - Elements of programming and programming languages
2. System Design and Programming Practices
3. Computer center operations and functions (scheduling, library functions, job assembly/disassembly, maintenance, environmental aspects, data preparation, report preparation, data control, etc.)
4. Organization and functional responsibilities of EDP.
5. EDP management principles (administration, management standards)
6. EDP system controls
7. EDP Risk analysis
8. Data, program and file protection techniques (privacy laws)
9. Computer complex physical security
10. Contingency planning, backup and recovery practices
11. Insurance, personnel practices, EDP contracts
12. Elements of operating systems
13. Data communications and on-line system technology
14. Data Base and file recovery approaches
15. Environmental software controls (operating systems, DBMS)
16. How to conduct operational audits of EDP
17. Familiarity with system utilities (SMF, job accounting)
18. System and hardware monitors and their operation
19. Cost allocation principles and algorithms
20. Project management and control
21. Measures of performance for data centers
22. Supporting disciplines (statistics, data reduction, data collection, etc.)
23. Data Collection methods and interviewing techniques.
24. Data processing contracts and clauses.
25. EDP Operations Standards

* Most of these topics are addressed in the checklists section of Part III of the manual

Data center audits can be quite challenging and can use a great deal of the EDP audit professional's previous background. Needless to say, you should be well skilled on how to present technical and technological findings and conclusions in plain managerial terms in order to communicate with management and cause action steps to take place. This is because senior management is often interested in the findings of a data processing department from an aggregate functional or operational view. Unless they understand the overall implications, they are not likely to take action steps to improve the situation.

SUGGESTED TRAINING FOR A NON-AUDITOR IN AUDITING AND FOR AN AUDITOR IN EDP-RELATED EXPERIENCE

Figure 10-5 clearly pointed out that no matter whether you start as an auditor or a data processing specialist, some degree of training will be required in the other skill. Figure 10-11 lists the types of training that should be provided to *non-auditor personnel* who come from the data processing camp, and the corresponding training (beyond desk-level or academic courses) that might be given to *conventional auditors* who join the new function on data processing-related matters. Providing some of this training will pay dividends in terms of familiarizing both groups with the kind of environment and the kind of thinking that prevails in each other's source environment.

This crosstraining will provide the trainees with fundamental concepts and terminology on auditing and on EDP in an almost working environment. For example, the EDP person will learn the meaning of:

- Compliance and substantive testing
- Concepts of materiality
- Internal control and the system of internal controls
- Compensating controls
- Audit risk
- Asset accounting
- Trial balance
- Consolidation, etc.
- Accounting rules and regulatory pronouncements

On the other hand, the auditor or accountant will learn firsthand:

- What an operating system does and how it functions
- How an application system is actually processed in the computer
- What a production and a test library are
- How jobs are scheduled in a data center
- What the function of JCL (job control language) is

Figure 10-11
Suggested Training of Non-Auditor and Auditor Personnel

TRAINING FOR A NON-AUDITOR, EDP TYPE PROFESSIONAL

In addition to the regular training in EDP auditing courses, the following would be helpful:

- A course in accounting and auditing
- Field training in accounting and auditing, such as for:
    - –Cash Count
    - –Physical Inventory
    - –Confirmation of Assets
    - –Physical Asset Verification
    - –Operations/Transaction Verification, Accounts Receivable, Billing, etc.
    - –Assignment to the General Accounting Group
        - –Follow document flows in a similar fashion to system analysis, using analytical flowcharting and functional analysis.
        - –Document entries to inventory, etc.
        - –Participate in statement consolidation preparation

TRAINING FOR AUDITOR TYPE PERSONNEL IN EDP

There is no substitute for some actual training or exposure to the real world of EDP. If a trained auditor with practical experience in auditing is selected, he/she should be able to understand the inner workings of EDP operations. It is somewhat unfair to the EDP group to have an auditor with only book knowledge and armed with voluminous checklists assess the intracacies of EDP. It is also awkward for the uninitiated auditor in EDP to be confronted with EDP people whose reference point can be how well the auditor understands EDP lingo, not the thoroughness of the auditor's checklist, EDP'ers will wonder has the auditor "been there"? If he was, I listen to him/her, otherwise, I shall ignore him/her.

- Spend some time in the EDP department, preferably observe the operation of the computer under guidance. Understand the various key functions of the EDP department. This is like sending the sales trainee to the manufacturing plant so he can get a better appreciation for how the product is made.
- Write a few sample programs with an audit utility, or regular programming language.
- Spend time within the Data Control Group. Understand its function and appreciate their usual weaknesses. Do some tasks there, such as: Librarian, Expediter (micro-scheduling), Job Assembly (JCL Procedures), Disassembly, Quality Control.
- Witness key sensitive functions in an EDP Department:
    - –Program change, Initiation, Change, Authorization
    - –New Program Cataloging to Production Library and Procedures used for such and by whom.
    - –Review the off-site storage
    - –Observe the check processing steps, become familiar with a contingency plan, etc.

- What the operations group means by an ABEND (abnormal end-job interruption)
- The functions of the librarian, of scheduling, etc

Keep in mind that terminology and lingo are an important part of the communication process and of developing rapport with the two sides of EDP and auditing.

SOURCES OF TRAINING AND KEY JOURNALS TO KEEP ABREAST OF DEVELOPMENTS

Since EDP audit and control is in a constant state of evolution, it is very important that both the newcomer and the seasoned professional try to keep abreast of new developments, approaches, and techniques being proposed by practitioners in the conduct of EDP auditing and control. This subsection presents selected sources of training for EDP audit, security, and controls. It also lists some professional organizations that are most active in promoting programs or publications in these fields.

Most of the constantly evolving information in the field is also published in a number of journals. Accordingly, those journals which most frequently publish information on EDP audit and controls are listed here for your convenience.

Basic Training and Seminars

Most of the initial training in EDP audit and controls can be obtained via these main sources:

- Seminars offered by professional training organizations
- Professional society conferences
- University continuing education with some occasional regular curriculum courses in accounting and business degree programs

Seminars

Seminars run by professional training organizations are by far the most common route to obtaining information on the basic and advanced concepts of EDP auditing and controls. This is because most of the information in new fields is usually at the state of the art which is practiced primarily by in-company personnel and consultants. The great majority of seminars are taught by professionals and practicing consultants as opposed to college professors. Universities offer relatively little of practical value in these fields, except in conventional courses on EDP internal controls or perhaps on the use of audit software packages. Also, their training seems to be geared more toward the needs of the external auditor as opposed to the needs of those inside companies. In selecting seminars offered by various training organizations, you face a problem in determining what best fits your overall training objectives and in discerning which are quality and qualified programs. Here are some guidelines and considerations to keep in mind in selecting organizations and courses:

1. *Investigate the reputation of the organization and its degree of concentration in the field.* There are reputable organizations, and then there are others who enter the market just because the person in charge knows methods of direct mass mailing.

2. *Many organizations offer a huge variety of subject matters in their professional training program.* Because of this they are likely to offer one or at the most two very general courses on the subject of EDP audit and controls. This means that, at most, the participant will be able to get an extensive vademecum of new technical terms with some in-depth deliberations, but not much by way of concentrated substance. The one- or two-course approach was adequate for the early seventies when most people were interested in a general introduction to the subject. Today's working professional needs substantive and detailed coverage of the subject, which can be accomplished only through a *series of logically* interlinked courses (a curriculum) or a single multiweek course (not usually available very often because of its high cost).
3. *Beware of short courses taught either by working professionals or by unknown specialists* who may teach one or two courses during their vacation or a respite from work. Even if the knowledge of the instructor is not questionable, the instructor who teaches infrequently may lack didactical capabilities and, for lack of commitment to training, might have inadequate course materials or texts to support the course. Also, when a seminar uses published books, you are sure to obtain information that is at least five years old as it takes from three to five years before a book is produced and known.
4. *Assess the credentials of the instructor who is to teach the course.* Be aware of his reputation in the field and make sure that the sponsoring organization does not use a front-end name for advertisement purposes, but an inadequate or inexperienced instructor to actually teach the course. In state-of-the-art courses, the instructor makes the whole difference. Oftentimes, even two good instructors may have widely different philosophies or viewpoints on the same fundamental issues. Having unqualified substitute instructors to boot is the height of folly. Beware also of individuals presented as experts who may be "between jobs" or who may be providing training in the professional market as a means of gaining credentials to later get into the field.
5. *When in real doubt, request references and names of individuals who have attended the advertised seminars* so that you may inquire about the course contents and its orientation. The reputable organizations should not have any difficulty in this regard.
6. *Prefer the organization that offers you the following characteristics:*
   a. *A well-conceived and well-structured curriculum* that enables you to obtain more *in-depth coverage* of a topical area (say, data center audits) as opposed to "all about the subject in two days."
   b. *A good deal of concentration in the field of EDP audit and controls as opposed to the "supermarket approach"* (offering anything from secretarial skills to the rheological properties of plastics, or

other esoteric topics unrelated to EDP controls). The administrators of these hugely broad programs are most likely unable to discern a qualified expert from an opportunist.

c. *An integrated and logical curriculum that enables you to progress from the more basic concepts to advanced topics,* such as on-line system audits, etc.

d. *Continuing education credits for the Certified Internal System Auditor or other equivalent credits.* Although this should not be a "must" criterion it helps in keeping the accreditation of your people.

7. *Beware of organizations that offer you primarily data processing courses disguised in the form of EDP audit and control courses.* With a shortage of specialists in this field, the temptation is great to take advantage of the market demand. If your need is for EDP fundamentals, such as data processing fundamentals, concepts of data base systems, etc., you should be able to obtain all this information from any of the regular data processing courses for *all types* of professionals.

8. *Be sure that you do not end up attending courses in computer security which are advertised as auditing and control courses.* Although the audit professional does need to know about computer security as part of his/her development, realize that courses taught by data security experts will not provide you with the information you need to audit and review controls in computerized systems. For example, if the subject is EDP risk analysis for security—since risk analysis methodologies are common to both professions, a course on risk analysis for security will satisfy some of your needs. Most likely, however, this course, taught by computer security experts, will not cover how to evaluate risks in a business computerized system application. The data security risk analysis course will be heavily oriented toward risks due to fire, water damage, and contingency planning and recovery—but this is only a small portion of the knowledge spectrum required by the auditor and control specialist in dealing with the whole issue of risks in EDP audit and controls.

9. *Prefer an organization that does not have a reputation for packing huge numbers of people into each seminar.*

An example of a curriculum-oriented training program is shown in Figure 10-12.

Professional Society Conferences

Unlike the seminar approach, the conference approach, usually sponsored by professional organizations such as The Institute of Internal Auditors and the EDP Auditors Association, seeks to gather many specialists for the presentation of papers on a broad range of subjects. Of late, these conferences have opted for presenting a number of "tutorials" or mini-seminars, usually

Figure 10-12
Example of a Seminar Curriculum for EDP Audit and Controls

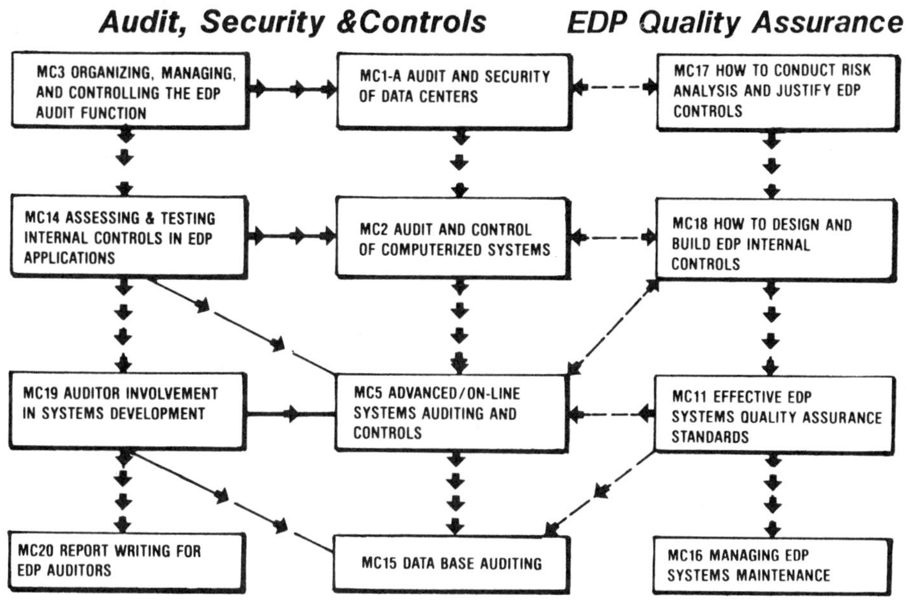

presented by the same people who also teach the full version as publicly advertised seminars. Keep in mind that these tutorials are a condensed version of the full seminar version and thus the information conveyance level or amount of detail provided will not be the same as when attending a regularly scheduled seminar.

The value of attending conferences lies in:

- The exposure to a wide array of subject matter
- Obtaining an indication of what many organizations are doing in the field
- Obtaining professional and social contacts
- Obtaining professional exposure to a large audience, if you should happen to be a speaker
- Having a variety of diverse topical areas to choose from on the basis of current interests
- Obtaining information on specialized topics which would not normally be found in a seminar because of the high degree of specificity (for example, a new technique for production library analysis).

Conferences definitely have a value for the continuing education of the EDP audit and control professional but are no substitute for in-depth circumscribed training via the seminar route.

From the viewpoint of economics and coverage in conferences, the better known and attended conference is the Annual Conference on Computer Audit, Controls, and Security, currently organized by Automation Training Center and co-sponsored by the EDP Auditors Association. The Institute of Internal Auditors is also very active and sponsors a number of regional and annual conferences which cover EDP audit topics of interest to all audit and control professionals.

For your reference, a list of professional societies of interest to the audit and control professional is presented in Figure 10-13.

Figure 10-13
A Selected List of Organizations and Publications That Offer Information and Articles on EDP Audit, Security, and Controls

AUDITING ORGANIZATIONS

The Institute of Internal Auditors, 249 Maitland Ave., Box 1119, Altamonte Springs, FL 32701. (International Association).

EDP Auditors Association, 373 S. Schmale Rd., Carol Stream, IL 60187 (International Association for EDP Auditors)

American Institute of Certified Public Accountants, AICPA, 1211 Ave. of the Americas, New York, NY 10036 (External auditors' view)

NIVRA, Nederlandse Institute voor Register Accountants, P. O. Box 7984, Amsterdam, Holland (Active on EDP audit matters)

Canadian Institute of Chartered Accountants, 250 Bloor St., Toronto M4W 1G5.

CHARTERED ACCOUNTANCY SOCIETIES exist in most countries with heavy use of computers. Many sponsor conferences and education programs and each publishes a journal. Among the better known societies are:
The Chartered Accountants Society in England and Wales
The Chartered Accountants Society in Scotland
The Chartered Accountants Society in Australia.

OTHER ORGANIZATIONS OF INTEREST

The British Computer Society, 13 Mansfield St., London W1M OBP. This society publishes *The Computer Journal,* and it has a "Special Interest Group in Auditing by Computer." *The Computer Journal* has very sporadic articles on EDP control.

National Computer Centre (NCC), Oxford Rd., Manchester M1 7ED, England. This is a non-profit institution devoted to EDP security and controls. A series of publications is issued from time to time on EDP security matters.

Data Processing Management Association (DPMA), 508 Busse Highway, Park Ridge, IL 60068. This association is devoted to the management of EDP and thus covers topics related to security and controls, including the legal aspects of EDP. They publish *Data Management,* which increasingly is featuring papers on EDP audit and controls.

Association for Systems Management, 25587 Bagley Rd., Cleveland, OH 55138. This society is devoted to matters related to systems administration and control. It publishes *The Journal of Systems Management.*

University Courses

Universities offer continuing education courses which are similar to seminars. Unfortunately, the "array" of courses they offer is usually limited to one or two. For the general exposure, three-day course some university offerings are comparable to those given by private seminar organizations.

When it comes to formal college courses taught by regular faculty, there are essentially not many courses offered. Some universities offer a basic overview Computer Control and Audit course for undergraduates which concentrates mostly on input, output, and processing controls, and controls testing from the viewpoint of the external auditor. The general observation is that university instruction in EDP auditing and controls is basic, not at the state of the art, and not very practical at present. Several universities are making good progress to improve the situation. Within the next five years, it is anticipated that university coverage of the field will improve. Meanwhile, public seminars and conferences are the best current route to obtaining applied education in EDP audit and controls.

User Groups

For certain products, usually software, the vendors organize so-called user groups which meet on some schedule. The information shared in these can be of value as regards the very specifics of problems encountered in the process of using the products in question. This kind of information, if needed, must be obtained on the basis of sharing and would not be obtainable through courses and seminars. If your organization has unique software products with unique problems, then the users' knowledge-sharing groups would be the avenue to acquiring this information. GUIDE and SHARE are well-known knowledge-sharing user organizations for software/hardware products.

Key Journals for EDP Audit and Controls

Figure 10-14 lists the journals that feature information in the fields of EDP audit, security, and controls most often. The main emphasis of the journal is given to assist you in selecting the journals that best meet your knowledge gathering and upkeep objectives. It is very likely that no single journal will provide all the information desired and that several may be required, at least at the departmental level, to satisfy the needs of your group.

Recommended Journals for Your Working Library

To help you keep up with technical and literature developments, your working bookshelf would benefit from subscriptions to several journals. Figure 10-15 lists suggested journals along with the nature of their contents and benefits.

Figure 10-14
Journals With Information on EDP Audit and Controls

Accountancy, Institute of Chartered Accountants in England and Wales, monthly. 56-66 Goswell Rd., London EC1, England.

COM-SAC, Computer Security, Auditing and Controls, Management Advisory Publications, semiannual, P. O. Box 151, Wellesley Hills, MA 02181.

COM-AND, Computer Audit News & Developments, every other month, Management Advisory Publications, P. O. Box 151, Wellesley Hills, MA 02181

Chartered Accountant, CA, Canadian Institute of Chartered Accountants, 250 Bloor St., Toronto, Ontario M4W 1G5.

CPA Journal (New York), New York Certified Public Accountants, 600 3rd Ave., New York, NY 10016, monthly.

EDPACS Newsletter, Automation Training Center, 11250 Roger Bacon Dr., Suite 17, Reston, VA 22090, monthly.

The EDP Auditor, EDP Auditors Association, 373 S. Schmale Rd., Carol Stream IL 60187, quarterly.

The Internal Auditor, Institute of Internal Auditors, 249 Maitland Ave., Box 1119, Altamonte Springs, FL 32701, bimonthly.

Journal of Accountancy, American Institute of Certified Public Accountants, 1211 Ave. of the Americas, New York, NY 10036, monthly.

Journal of Systems Management, Association for Systems Management, 24587 Bagley Rd., Cleveland, OH 44138, monthly.

MIS Quarterly, Society for Management Information Systems, 269 19th Ave., University of Minnesota, Minneapolis, MN 55455.

The Journal of Bank Administration, 301 S. Northwest Highway, Park Ridge, IL 60068, monthly.

There are over one hundred other journals which feature occasional papers on EDP audit and security.

There are approximately one-hundred journals on EDP, accounting, management, security, data base, as well as industry-related journals which touch in some way on matters of interest to the audit and control specialist. Since it is not economical to subscribe to all, nor is it possible for the staff to search through a multitude of journals, many of which may feature just one article every two years, the better alternative is to subscribe to an abstract service. Once a paper or book is spotted, the reader may go to the source for details.

For data processing developments, the staff would also benefit from the availability of data processing trade journals. The recommended journals are: *Datamation, Infosystems, Data Management, Computer Decisions, Computerworld* and *Software News*. These are more likely to contain hardware/software developments and security topics, with occasional references to EDP controls.

Figure 10-15
Recommended Journals for Your Working Library

JOURNAL	FREQUENCY	BENEFITS
COM-SAC, Computer Security, Auditing and Controls	Semiannual	• Complete review of all literature worldwide on the subjects with digests designed to save time and assist staff in searching for information. Practical articles and tutorials are also included.
COM-AND, Computer Audit News & Developments	Bimonthly	• Concentrates on key audit and control issues stemming from changes in EDP technology. Presents new audit ideas and audit guidelines in a practical and pragmatic manner with recommendations for action.
EDPACS Newsletter	Monthly	• Best known newsletter with monthly articles on EDP auditing and short stories on computer mishaps, fraud, etc.
EDP Auditor	Quarterly	• Articles written by members of the EDP Auditors Association, including academicians. Many papers are professionally oriented.
The Internal Auditor	Bimonthly	• Material covers the whole field of internal auditing. It would be useful for the general education of the EDP controls person on internal control. It has one or two papers on EDP auditing per issue.
Chartered Accountant, CA	Monthly	• If budget permits.
Journal of Systems Management	Monthly	• If budget permits.
The Journal of Bank Administration	Monthly	• Oriented to the banking industry, it features occasional papers on EDP auditing and controls from banking.

THE COST OF TRAINING AND DEVELOPING EDP AUDIT PROFESSIONALS

Our discussion on training and development would not be complete without considering the approximate cost of developing professional staff in EDP audit and control. This subsection provides guidelines for estimating the cost of training an individual (assuming he/she comes from another field) and for estimating the cost of maintaining or upgrading his/her skills on an ongoing basis. These are important elements in providing competent professional staff. If the reader disagrees with the magnitude of the costs because of particular local or company conditions, the information provided is still valuable in identifying the cost components of training and developing personnel.

Initial and Recurring Training Cost

The cost of developing a new EDP audit/controls professional can vary depending upon the level of experience of the individual being trained. We will compare three cases: (a) an EDP-trained person, (b) a trainee fresh out of school, and (c) an experienced senior EDP auditor/control specialist. The reader can make whatever adjustments that may be necessary to reflect his/her organizational environment and local costs.

The basic premises and assumptions for the three cases selected are summarized in Figure 10-16.

Total Cost of Training

The total cost of training per year for any of the categories selected can be obtained from the following equation:

$$TCT = OHF \times YS \times (1 - EF) + SD \times CPSD + OTC$$

Equation 10-1

where:

TCT is Total Cost for Training, \$/year
OHF is Overhead Factor as percentage of basic salary
YS is Yearly basic Salary, \$/year
EF is Effectiveness or Utilization Factor
SD is Number of Seminar-Days per year
CPSD is Cost Per Seminar-Day, \$
OTC is One-Time Costs, \$ (e.g., recruiting fee)

From the above figures we can construct a table or graph of cumulative expenses showing the relative costs. Figure 10-17 shows cumulative figures for both the training costs and the total cost of having the person on the payroll (including the full amount of salary and overhead). Figure 10-18 shows the graphical picture for training costs only. As one would anticipate, the cumulative cost of training and developing the new audit and control professional is

Figure 10-16
Basic Premises and Assumptions for Training Cost Comparison

CASE	A) EDP Specialist	B) Trainee	C) Experienced EDP Auditor
1. Background	EDP specialist, 5-6 years experience in systems/programming.	Trainee out of school, business or accounting.	Experienced EDP Auditor, 5-7 years.
2. Salary	$27,000/yr.	$18,000/yr.	$40,000/yr.
3. Overhead Factor, including all fringe benefits and cost of keeping the person employed (office, parking, etc.).	1.75	1.65	1.75
4. Estimated time to become fully proficient	3 yrs.	5 yrs.	1 yr.
5. Effectiveness or utilization Factor (percent of time the individual is providing useful value to the organization)[1]			
Year 1	.40	.10	.90
Year 2	.60	.25	.95
Year 3	.90	.50	1.00
Year 4	1.00	.75	1.00
Year 5	1.00	.90	1.00
Year 6	1.00	1.00	1.00
6. Number of seminar days of outside training			
a) EDP Audit	15	15	15
b) Auditing, other	10	15	
Total	25	30	15
7. Cost of outside training per seminar day	$500	$500	$500
8. Other costs— Hiring cost, one time			$10,000
9. Cost of skills upkeep, seminar days per year (recurring after acquiring proficiency)[2]	15	15	15
10. Inflation and merit raises	Overlooked for consistency in all three cases.		

[1] Because the new professional will be doing some constructive work, the actual cost would not be the full amount of their salary plus training as the organization will be deriving benefits from his/her EDP expertise. However, the payroll cost component is still by far the higher of the two cost components. The percent utilization factors are estimates for each type of personnel.

[2] Because of the dynamic state of affairs in EDP, it is imperative that the new professional receive continuing education. Studies also indicate that organizations that provide upkeep education for their staff experience less turnover than those that do not. Professionals in dynamic fields of endeavor fear obsolescence. A suggested schedule for maintenance of skills of 15 training days per year is recommended for a total cost of upkeep of $500 × 15 = $7,500 per year.

Figure 10-17
Cumulative Training Costs—With and Without Full Salary—for Three Staffing Alternatives

CUMULATIVE COST IN DOLLARS

CASE	A		B		C	
YEAR	Training Cost[1]	Total[2] including full salary	Training Cost[1]	Total[2] including full salary	Training Cost[1]	Total[2] including full salary
1	40,850	59,750	41,730	44,700	24,000	87,500
2	67,250	119,500	71,505	89,450	35,500	165,000
3	79,475	179,250	93,855	134,150	43,000	242,500
4	86,975	232,000	108,780	178,850	50,500	320,000
5	94,475	288,750	116,280	223,500	58,000	397,500

[1] Calculated using equation 10-1, page 142
[2] Calculated using a value of 0 for EF, effectiveness factor in equation 10-1 for all cases and years

highest for the trainee, followed by the cost for the EDP-trained person, and lowest for the experienced and already-trained professional, based on the premises used in the comparison. If one were to take the total costs, including full salaries for the first five years, the total dollars invested would, of course, be in exactly reverse order. Nevertheless, what we are concerned with here is the cost of training before achieving full proficiency and the time before the prospective professional is able to operate on his/her own in the more complex areas of EDP audit and controls.

This analysis would suggest that when faced with the need to produce credible results in a hurry, the best route to take, from both training *costs* and *time limitations* points of view, is to acquire the senior experienced EDP audit/control professional. This would be the case if only one person is allocated to the new group and that one needs to produce acceptable results immediately. When there is no time to train a new person, the manager must simply opt for the acquisition of ready-made personnel. The higher salary paid initially may be looked at as the "cost of expediting results."

If several individuals are allocated to form the new group, the better long-range strategy is probably to acquire a mix of senior and junior staff. This is the case because it may be difficult to hire and retain all senior, ready-trained personnel. Also, a mix of personnel should provide room for promotions and permit the use of senior staff to guide and train the less experienced staff.

The above analysis is not intended to suggest that one is always ahead using ready-trained personnel any more than that it is cheaper in the long haul, salarywise, to train inexperienced people. It is mainly intended to give you an idea of the relative costs of training, new personnel vs. acquiring ready-trained personnel. Organizations will always need to train new personnel and should do so for reasons explained in the previous paragraph.

Figure 10-18
Comparative Cumulative Costs for Training of Three Staffing Alternatives

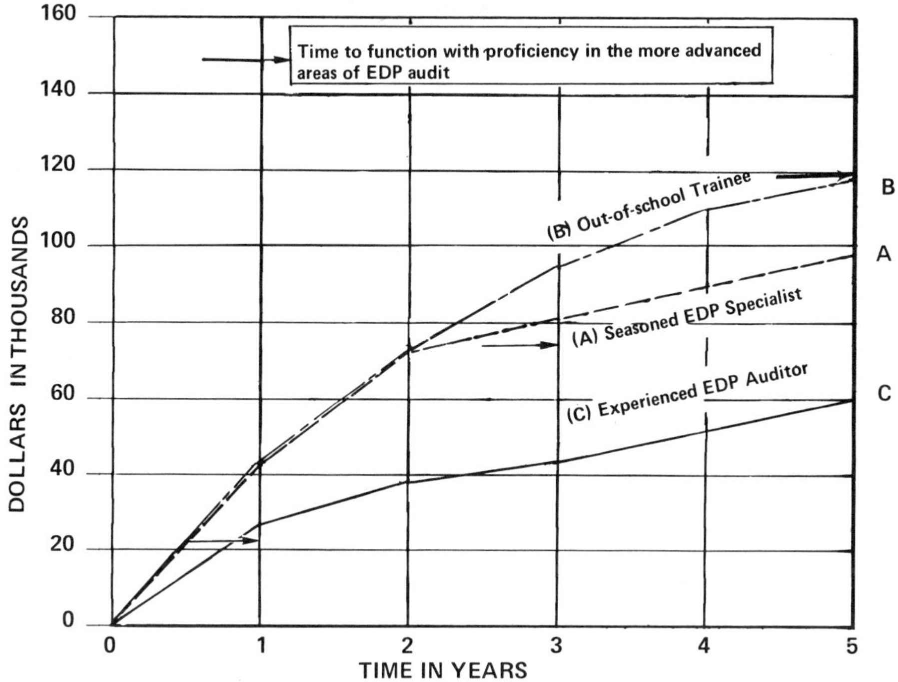

Example calculation:

Case A, Senior EDP specialist without EDP audit experience

Obtain figures and values from Figure 10-16

$TCT_1 = 1.75 \times 27{,}000\ (1. - 0.40) + 25 \times 500 =$ *\$40,850/yr.* First year

$TCT_2 = 1.75 \times 27{,}000\ (1. - 0.60) + 15 \times 500 =$ *\$26,400/yr.* Second year

$TCT_3 = 1.75 \times 27{,}000\ (1. - 0.90) + 15 \times 500 =$ *\$12,225/yr.* Third year

Case B, Trainee fresh out of school

$TCT_1 = 1.65 \times 18{,}000\ (1. - 0.10) + 30 \times 500 =$ *\$41,730* First year

$TCT_2 = 1.65 \times 18{,}000\ (1. - 0.25) + 15 \times 500 =$ *\$29,775* Second year

$TCT_3 = 1.65 \times 18{,}000\ (1. - 0.50) + 15 \times 500 =$ *\$22,350* Third year

$TCT_4 = 1.65 \times 18{,}000\ (1. - 0.75) + 15 \times 500 =$ *\$14,925* Fourth year

$TCT_5 = 1.65 \times 18{,}000\ (1. - 0.90) + 15 \times 500 =$ *\$10,470* Fifth year

Case C, Experienced EDP auditor

$TCT_1 = 1.75 \times 40{,}000\ (1. - 0.90) + 10{,}000 + 7{,}500 =$ *\$24,500* First year

$TCT_2 = 1.75 \times 40{,}000\ (1. - 0.95) + 7{,}500 =$ *\$11,000* Second Year

11

Future Needs in the Training and Development of EDP Audit and Control Personnel

THE NEED FOR MORE AND BETTER-TRAINED EDP AUDIT/CONTROL SPECIALISTS

In previous chapters, we have provided guidelines that you can follow in developing more and better trained EDP audit and control specialists. As we foresee continued change in the EDP revolution, we forecast that even more will have to be done by all concerned professionals.

This chapter presents an analysis of new developments in EDP technology with which you need to be familiar. From these anticipated developments, suggestions are given as to what needs to be done and how to cope with the unavoidable changes to come in EDP technology. The following topics are discussed:

- EDP technology trends and the new skills required
- Organizational changes derived from technological change
- New audit approaches and techniques
- The need to plan for the development of competent personnel

EDP TECHNOLOGY TRENDS AND THE NEW SKILLS REQUIRED

From stand-alone, small and clumsy computers in the sixties, to centralized and powerful multiprocessing computers of the seventies—EDP technology has now given rise to three important developments:

- A plethora of mini- and microcomputers within the reach of virtually everyone
- The new reality of distributed data processing (DDP) or "network" systems

- A revolution in office automation and the virtual linkage of word processing and minicomputers to networks of computers via increasingly sophisticated data communications capabilities.

All these have already brought and will continue to bring major changes in the set of skills that the modern EDP audit and controls professional must become familiar with. It will also bring corresponding new approaches and techniques for auditing and controlling the EDP complex.

Some of the implications of these technologies are as follows:

- Distributed computer power to every potential user.
- A proliferation of hardware/software acquisition by users in the most recondite locations of the organization which will be difficult to manage and control.
- The potential for very remote users to access corporate and divisional data and data bases on an almost worldwide basis.
- Proliferation and dispersion of vital company data in many distributed data bases.
- An extremely dynamic environment for hardware and software modifications unparalleled in the industry. Company procedures could be changed by the minute throughout the organization. Some changes may not even be in the form of software but so-called "firmware" (chips with predesigned logic that could be added or replaced in minicomputers).
- Proliferation of user-developed system applications at many locations without the disciplines of standards and documentation that are at least somewhat possible in larger, well-controlled computer systems.
- Dispersion of the control function to every desk that uses microcomputer power.
- Problems associated with the maintenance of reliable and up-to-date data for corporate accounting and planning purposes.
- Massive data and physical security problems and exposure.
- A great diversity of vendors operating software and utilities with so many variations of equipment.
- Organizational changes in the data processing department, user areas, and control groups.
- Auditing problems in terms of a great diversity of equipment software and locations to cover. As EDP becomes distributed, the audit and controls functions may have to follow a similar pattern, unless audit approaches can be found to be able to audit from fewer and select locations.
- Problems associated with testing networks and EFT systems.

ORGANIZATIONAL CHANGES DERIVED FROM TECHNOLOGICAL CHANGE

Changes in organization will most likely occur in the following areas:

- Data processing department
- Data management and control functions
- Auditing
- User areas

Data Processing Department

With the proliferation of data processing power now taking place, undoubtedly both structural and functional responsibility changes will occur in the way the data processing manager conducts his/her functions. System and programming capabilities will surface in many locations thus reducing the total number of systems/programmers at corporate locations. On the other hand, to offset this situation, the data processing manager may have to spend more of his/her resources in standards and guidelines development and in corporate or regional consultancy capabilities advising local users who may lack the expertise to implement and control their EDP operations. This is already taking place in the form of the "Information Resource Center." More effort in surveillance may need to be instituted to police the great proliferation of EDP equipment and systems. Auditability and controllability features may have to be built into system applications and data base management systems to permit ongoing audit and monitoring of remote locations. Backup and recovery practices are sure to change and become vital.

Data Management and Control Functions

The operation of data management and control functions presently under EDP or user departments will also undergo change. From the centralized concept of the data base administrator and security function, means will have to be developed to distribute the data management and control functions. Since it is infeasible and uneconomical to have data base administration, security administration, and quality assurance in every conceivable location, ways to distribute and deputize these important functions must be found. The forms this may take range from standards development and dissemination with reviews of compliance, to deputizing local user administration for enforcement, to development of advanced methods of surveillance at corporate level of the operations in remote sites. The possibility of using microcomputers to check mainframe computers is not out of the question.

Auditing

The question of the relative roles of auditing and the control functions mentioned above comes up. One possible scheme of organization for the future is shown in Figure 11-1. Here we show the *strategic* nature of auditing, the *tactical* functions of data administration, data security, and quality assurance, and the *operational* nature of data control functions operating in a properly correlated fashion. In the example shown, in order to control the great complexity of advanced and distributed systems, the audit and control functions would build audit and control features in major systems which produce audit and control information for ongoing evaluation of developments in all remote locations (or in a single centralized system, if no dispersion takes place). The information then produced could go to the various levels of audit and control in proportion to their ability (staff and accountability) to review performance and compliance to controls. Under such an arrangement, corporate or divisional auditing would concentrate some of its efforts in reviews of compliance via batch inspection of audit and control reports or by using audit terminals or minicomputers to examine the complex system (on-line) or network (if distributed). Audit would then rely on the control structures built into the systems in question during the development cycle. The development and building of such mechanisms would best be done by joint design and agreement between the audit and control functions (to be later operated by the users) and data process-

Figure 11-1
Sample Security, Audit, and Controls (S.A.C.) Organization

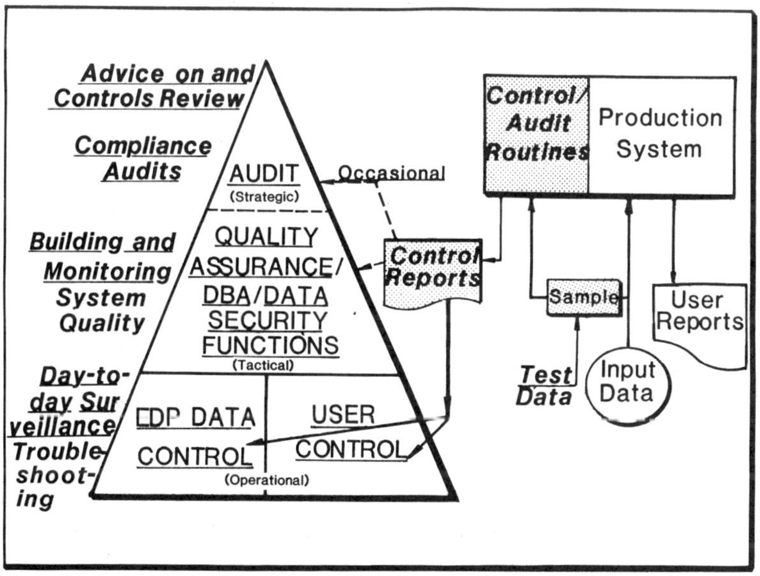

ing groups, and monitored by audit and the control functions. An approach such as is depicted here would be one way to offset the proliferation of data processing power that is likely to come in the future.

User Areas

With the advent of advanced on-line systems and distributed data processing systems, many of the data control functions performed at the central site are redistributed or dispersed back to users. On the other hand, distributing microcomputer units throughout the organization or in network form makes for very lean staffs and poor separation of duties. Good training, compensating controls, and procedural standards need to be provided for users. Supervisory levels must be drawn into the control process to provide some degree of duties separation.

If the systems have security implications, the need to deputize data security functions from the corporate security office down to the local level is evident. Built-in monitoring routines might be added to the systems to notify supervisors or other monitoring offices of any erroneous or abnormal transactions.

Corporate or divisional data processing groups may have to provide consulting and monitoring capabilities to inspect local site operations and review enforcement of standards. Audit of local operations may have to be enhanced by independent audit groups. This can be an expensive proposition in view of the numerous possible locations. Advanced audit approaches using remote microcomputers for audit may be required as explained in the following section.

NEW AUDIT APPROACHES AND TECHNIQUES

New and more sophisticated audit techniques are sure to be needed to deal with the new technological scenarios of advanced on-line data base systems, distributed data processing, and data communication networks. In terms of audit and control resources, this means that audit and control departments will have to devote more resources to the development and implementation of new audit approaches, tools, and techniques than has been the case heretofore. Some of this research should probably be conducted by the professional societies under industry sponsorship. However, even in this case, each organization will need to devote more manpower to the adaptation of whatever methodologies may be developed to the specifics of their own organization.

Figure 11-2 lists some of the topical areas for the manager and audit and control technologist to explore. Dwelling on each of them is outside the intent of this book; each could require at least a monograph to handle. Please see References 6, 23, 24, and 40 listed in the Bibliography, Part II, for more information on this topic.

Figure 11-2
New Audit Approaches and Techniques for the Future

A. AUDIT APPROACHES

- *The traditional snapshot periodic audit cycle approach may see a revision in favor of forms of "continuous auditing" approaches,* whereby the auditor collects audit evidence on an ongoing basis through advanced auditability methods implanted during the design of the system. This information can then be audited on a batch or continuous basis. The dynamics of future systems and the coming of the "auditor of record" and the need for auditors' opinions being based on events that occur through the year, as opposed to on a fixed point in time, may bring about the need for these new approaches. These concepts are discussed in References 16 and 23 in the Bibliography, Part II.[1]
- *System testing approaches may gravitate from the conventional batch, after-the-fact, snapshot approach to in-line, interactive approaches* in the same software and hardware environment as that under which the system operates. (See References 23 and 24.)
- *For some highly sensitive systems, the concept of parallel system logic to audit the operational system may be desirable and economical.* In the parallel system approach, the system of internal controls is always being audited or monitored. (Reference 23)
- *The use of audit microcomputers to audit other minicomputers or maxicomputers is becoming a reality.* The audit microcomputer can reside in the auditor's office and be connected to the other minicomputers in a network or to a central computer with complex activity. In this way transactions could be intercepted for audit analysis or data from the data base extracted for audit analysis in the minicomputer. The microcomputer can be further used to automate many of the traditional functions, tasks and reporting done by conventional manual methods even today. When coupled with word processing capabilities, the author sees the potential for automating even audit report writing capabilities other than the audit analysis. Audit test plans can also be stored, retrieved, and updated at the auditor's convenience.
- *The possibility exists of using audit chips that can perform audit functions* and are embedded in micro- or minicomputers to monitor or check processing activity or collect relevant information.

B. AUDIT TOOLS AND TECHNIQUES

A number of new audit techniques will derive from the above audit approaches, many of which will not be apparent until the above approaches materialize. We see, however, increased use for some of the following techniques:

- *Integrated test facility.*
- *Embedded audit data collection methods.*
- *Programmed snapshots.*
- *Automated embedded testing routines.*
- *Parallel audit logic* for select sensitive functions.
- *Auditor's data base segments* built into the data base.
- *Interactive audit software packages,* using terminals and even minicomputers.
- *Data base audit logs.*
- *Complex multicondition analysis routines or transaction conflict matrices* embedded in the edit routines package.

(Continued)

Figure 11-2
New Audit Approaches and Techniques for the Future (Continued)

- *Audits of data base systems in a virtual test mode* (running the data base system in a separate partition, much as an EDP colleague goes about testing a system, to avoid interference with production data bases). See Figure 8-2 in Part I.
- *Embedded audit analytical routines to do the data collection* and the analysis, thus leaving only the function of interpretation for the auditor. Even the reporting could be automated via microcomputers and office automation methods.
- *Increased use of audit microcomputers connected to other micros and mainframe computers.*
- *Use of fourth generation user-friendly languages* to write audit programs.
- *Use of the capabilities of personal computers to "automate"* many presently tedious and time-consuming review tasks.
- *Use of "expert systems"* (based on artificial intelligence concepts) to conduct evaluation of internal control and audit programs.
- *Use of "audit computer monitors"* to do auditing and control on a dedicated and ongoing basis.[2]
- *Use of "prototyping" methods to review controls* in developing systems.

[1] See also, J. F. Kuong, *EDP System Auditability: Approaches and Techniques* (Wellesley Hills, MA: Management Advisory Publications, 1985).

[2] C. Riddle and J. Austin, "Updating Security, Auditing and Quality Assurance—The Dedicated On-Line Computer Security Monitor," *COM-SAC, Computer Security, Auditing and Controls,* Vol. 13, No. 1, 1986.

THE NEED TO PLAN THE DEVELOPMENT OF COMPETENT PERSONNEL

Organizations contemplating increasingly complex systems using new emerging technologies should start now to develop plans for the training and development of competent personnel. Since most organizations use their audit and control staff in pressing and current audit projects, this means that very seldom is any staff set aside to devote time to their self-development in the new skills that will be required to audit and control new and complex technologies. When the technologies are here, managers will be faced with the same vicious circle of retraining their staff on an after-the-fact basis. Most of all, they would be unable to provide *timely* and necessary *strategic* audit and control input *while the technology is being selected,* which should increasingly be a responsibility of the audit and control groups.

Steps that responsible individuals should consider in the training of future audit and control professionals are as follows:

1. *Identify the potential EDP technology planned for adoption.* This can be accomplished by keeping in close contact with EDP groups responsible for technology assessment and technology introduction and plan-

ning. If possible, someone in audit and control should become a guest participant in the key presentation sessions of these groups.

2. *Entrust someone in the audit and control group with the responsibility of developing the audit and control implications of the new technology or technology changes,* as regards controls likely to be needed, new or modified audit approaches, and the training program for personnel in the audit and control group. A most likely place for this kind of activity would be the audit research and development function within EDP audit and control.
3. *Develop the specifics of training and development down to types of courses, sources of training, and individuals who should take the training program.*
4. *Obtain approval and implement.*

When considering the training program, it is well to point out that training considerations should also involve the training of regular auditors and the users and designers of systems. If the audit group develops audit and control guidelines for the new technologies, these should be shared with users and designers of the new systems under the new technologies.

The difference between success and failure of audit efforts may very well rest on the diligent anticipation of staff preparation to handle the future tasks. This is more important in today's EDP environment because the lead time required to produce results is much longer in EDP systems than it was for manual systems, when procedures could be modified after-the-fact and on a spot basis without great detriment to controls.

The forward-looking and aggressive EDP audit and control professional and manager will take the necessary steps and will succeed. To these audit and control pioneers go best wishes for success.

PART III

Checklists and Guidelines for Evaluating Computer Installations Controls and Security

Preface to Part III

The advent of the computer and computerized systems has given rise to a number of threats and has rendered organizations which use computers quite vulnerable to physical damage, potential disruption of data processing services vital to company operations, perpetration of fraud and theft of funds and data, and unauthorized access to or accidental disclosure of critical information.

These conditions have created the imperative need for better safeguards. Because of the many potentially costly implications, there is a great need for organizations to review the security of and the controls used for protecting their computer installations, and also, the need to audit computerized systems, in order to safeguard the integrity of data and improve the system of internal controls.

When confronted with the task of auditing the computer complex, it would be quite helpful to be able to conduct the audit with reference to a set of standards by which EDP activities are supposed to operate. Where a set of standards does exist, the auditor's or reviewer's task would consist of determining: (a) how good the standards are, (b) are the standards being followed, and (c) how can they be improved upon. Unfortunately, it is quite common to find that such standards are either too meager or are virtually nonexistent in most installations. In the majority of these cases, therefore, one must resort to other tools to facilitate the conduct of the audit.

One of the important tools in conducting audits of computer activities is a set of checklists and guidelines. These checklists and guidelines are, in fact, supposed to be derived from a set of standards used for operating a computer complex. This section of the manual provides checklists and guidelines which should be a part of every auditor's, EDP department's, and security office's set of working tools and an integral part of the internal audit program for the firm. They are based on many years of actual experience in conducting intensive and extensive reviews of data processing installations both in the U.S. and abroad, and supplemented by extensive research on the subject of EDP auditing, security, and controls evaluation.

The guidelines are quite useful in the detailed review of EDP centers and serve to pinpoint what to look for in the EDP review. It is well to point out, however, that the checklists by themselves are not a substitute for experience and the use of the appropriate procedures and approaches.

The key objective of this section of the manual is to provide you with a comprehensive, ready-to-apply set of review guidelines and checklists which you can use in the review of the whole EDP complex. Unlike the previous two sections that concentrated on two main topical areas, this section covers review guidelines for *all* aspects of the data center and EDP systems development.

One key feature of this section is that it first provides some background on the area being discussed, then presents a review checklist. This is intended to provide you with sufficient understanding of the topic being covered so that you will more readily understand the meaning of the questionnaires and guidelines. Most often, checklists manuals available in the literature provide you with a list of questions without any previous explanation of what is involved. This has at least these disadvantages: (a) it causes the reader to apply questionnaires mechanically without a fundamental understanding of what is involved, and (b) it tends to provide a superficial coverage of the area under review without any reference to cause and effect relationships. This makes it more difficult for the user of the information to arrive at constructive recommendations and solutions to weaknesses in control. Also, when employing junior personnel to assist in audits of the EDP complex, the use of checklists alone without a suitable explanation can often create many ambiguous and misleading impressions.

These checklists and guidelines will prove of value to you and to all members of the audit security, EDP and EDP standards professions, as well as to managers who must deal with the question of computer audit and control.

12

Using Checklists and Guidelines Effectively

DEFINITION

An audit checklist is one of the tools used by auditors or reviewers to test the existence of controls and for measuring standard practices or performance. It consists of a set of criteria, expressed in the form of statements or questionnaires, based on standards of acceptance or sound practice. They enable the auditor or examiner to pinpoint conditions by asking questions concerning if, how, when, where, with what, and by whom, something is done, and to determine existing conditions. On the basis of these answers, one can obtain a good idea of the status of the operation under review. One could even establish a point rating and rate the operation according to such a point system.

Actually, the set of criteria or questions contained in a checklist stem directly, or are a reflection of, a set of management and operating standards—if such exist—which apply to the particular installation. In other words, one can, in fact, consider a checklist as an extraction of the criteria or accepted procedures from the standards manual, if one exists, for use in evaluating the EDP center's activities and performance. Conversely, if a standards manual does not exist, one can use a set of checklists as a means for inferring how well the computer operation is being run, and as a means of establishing areas of weakness in control.

SCOPE AND LIMITATIONS

As can be expected, checklists can vary in scope and level of detail and applicability, depending upon the size and complexity of the installation being reviewed. Thus, in using generalized checklists, adjustments are sometimes necessary to make them applicable to a given specific situation. Also, judgment should be exercised in their application. Although a very useful tool, checklists must be used with due caution and should not be used indiscriminately by totally inexperienced personnel, without some guidance and indoctrination by someone well versed in their use. Most of all, they should not be used as a substitute for other important basic knowledge of auditing and good common sense.

USE OF CHECKLISTS BY AUDITORS, EDP PROFESSIONALS, AND MANAGERS

Sometime during their professional formation, EDP professionals, auditors, and examiners have been confronted with the problem of where to begin and what to look for in an EDP center audit. Those who have not had the benefit of extensive experience in computer operations and who have attempted to make sense of the complexities of EDP, appreciate the value of good checklists during the inquiry and data gathering phase of an audit. The audit checklists presented in this manual can serve as an invaluable aid to both seasoned and inexperienced analysts in auditing computer installations. As mentioned in the Preface, the use of checklists does not obviate the need for judgment and common sense on the part of the auditor. However, they provide a useful guide and serve as a reminder of the areas that the auditor should look into. If a ''no'' answer is obtained to a question or group of questions, it is not absolute evidence that a weakness in internal control exists. Instead, such evidence should be evaluated in the light of the total system of internal controls and the presence of any other compensating controls. When evaluating a particular system, the auditor should look into the nature, scope and capabilities of the particular system. In order to obtain this knowledge, the auditor should review also the set of flowcharts, input and output layouts, the set of system internal controls contained in the system documentation. In addition, he should inspect the computer operations, hold interviews with users of the systems as well as EDP personnel and computer vendors, and he should refer to the reference manuals and system documentation. The approaches and procedures for conducting this type of review are discussed in books on EDP operational auditing.[1]

The checklists presented here assume a reasonable knowledge of data processing fundamentals. The checklists apply to a number of situations and attempt to cover various types of arrangements. In this sense they are generalized. The auditor will, therefore, need to modify certain aspects of the checklists to adapt them to a particular set of conditions, equipment configuration, and operating mode (batch, on-line, service bureau, etc.). Some of the checklists may prove to be more elaborate than required for less sophisticated installations. Adjustments will be required for such situations.

CHECKLISTS AND GUIDELINES ORGANIZATION

Organization

There are a number of ways in which audit checklists could be organized, depending upon the scope of auditor involvement and the emphasis that is

[1] See, for example, Chapter 7 of *Computer Operations and Systems Auditing* (Wellesley Hills, MA: Management Advisory Publications, 1978).

placed on the various areas of EDP auditing. The following approaches have been used:

1. Audit checklists which follow the system from initiation through installation and operational phases, including:
   a. The "before" system development phase
   b. The "during" the development phase
   c. The "operational" phase (data center operational audits)
2. Audit checklists can be detailed by key work station or by important areas of control in data processing activities. For example, File Library Questionnaires, Input/Output Control. These types of guidelines are useful in evaluating a given important component of the EDP complex or in designing controls by area. These individual areas can be treated as control points.

The approach used in this section includes features from the above two approaches. However, its organization focuses on the key areas which are a factor in EDP security, or the main areas of EDP management control, required to provide total protection and control for EDP. In other words, it is organized along the lines of key and well-accepted areas of security and protection programs in a computerized environment.

Format

The question of format is a moot one. Some prefer the "yes" or "no" questionnaire list. Although this approach lends itself to a worksheet approach, it has limitations. Ambiguity is a problem. For instance, it is not readily apparent from these lists whether yes or no is the desirable thing to find. Although most checklist questionnaires are designed to suggest that a "no" condition is undesirable, they provide no background information and no fundamental basis for interpreting the goodness or badness of the condition. This could be dangerous for the uninformed or the uninitiated. For example, the question:

Is the Computer Center near or adjacent to an elevator shaft?
Yes ☐ No ☐

Does a "no" answer mean that this is good because ready access and withdrawal by a would-be intruder would not be easy, or does it mean that it is bad in the event that evacuation of personnel is required, in an emergency, and there is no handy exit? Or does it mean also that such a condition is bad because remoteness to an elevator means awkward access to heavy forms, equipment, and parts (which may be located on other floors), or difficult removal of heavy reports to wherever they are needed, from an operational convenience standpoint?

Others prefer to use a rating system opposite the yes-no answers. This is fine if all questions are relevant, so that the totals for the rating are not invalidated when only a few are applicable.

Figure 12-1
Relationship Between EDP Objectives, EDP Activities, Standards, Measures of Performance, and Audit Checklists

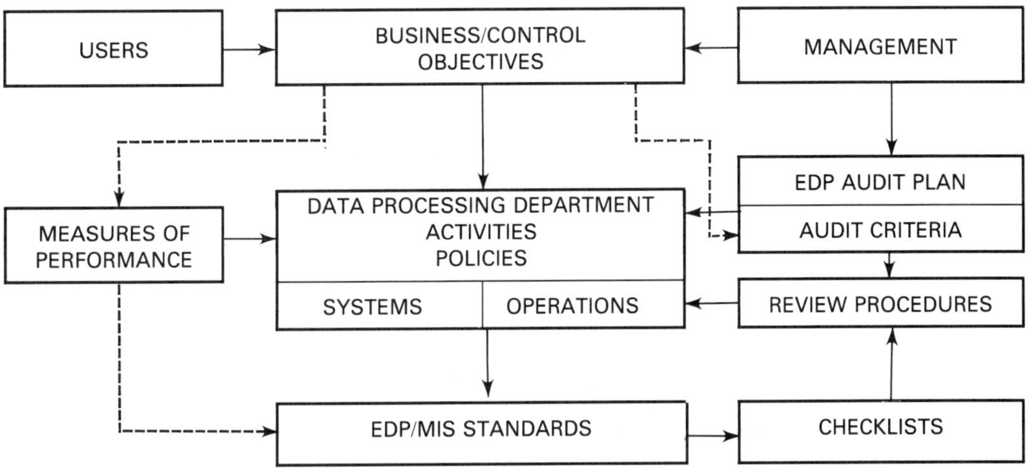

This picture depicts the interrelationship between EDP and control objectives as defined by users and management, EDP activities resulting from these objectives, and the EDP/MIS standards. It also shows that the checklists ideally derive from the standards, which are then used to assist in the audit of EDP activities.

The approach used here consists of the following, in most cases:

- First, a statement of the objectives for each main guideline.
- Second, a narrative description or a general background section on the topic. This is intended to help the user comprehend what is involved before getting into the checklists or questionnaires.
- Third, the relevant questionnaires listed in question or statement form.

We have refrained from offering a point rating system, since this is highly subjective. On the other hand the checklists can be assigned a point and weight value to suit individual preference.

The checklists are practical in nature. In using them, keep in mind that every checklist is somehow related to a policy or accepted practice that presumably should exist. They represent, in fact, audit or performance criteria and should be relatable to the selected criteria for evaluation. (See Figure 12-1.)

In using this section, refer to the descriptive portion first for some general background and then proceed to study the checklists and questionnaires. Those who are well-trained in the fundamentals, may proceed directly to the checklists.

13

Organization and Management Control of EDP

OBJECTIVES

This section is devoted to checklists and questionnaires for the manager and the executive, looking at the EDP complex from an overall management viewpoint. It deals with questions related to the administrative control of EDP as a function and its organizational structure. It emphasizes questions related to policies, objectives, administrative procedures, and standards which are necessary for EDP to function properly and to serve the objectives of the organization. A basis for aggregate measurement of EDP performance by management is also offered.

Besides being a good tool for auditors or reviewers, in relating their findings to management, this review checklist should be of value to management in general and to those executives to whom the EDP function reports. It should also be of value to EDP managers in gaining an appreciation of how their activities are likely to be viewed by managers and auditors, so that they prepare to meet the challenge of their responsibilities.

The topics covered here are:

1. Objectives
2. EDP Management Standards
3. EDP Department Organization—Charter of Responsibilities and Separation of Functions
4. Measures of Effectiveness (Measurement Criteria)
5. Vital Records Program
6. A Generalized Checklist for Executives

Other administrative guidelines, safeguards, and controls which are also obviously important and related to administrative controls, such as personnel security, legal protection, and insurance protection, are covered in Chapter 20.

The standards manual for a given organization should, therefore, contain a written record of all policies, procedures, and techniques which are to be used throughout the data processing organization. Such a manual facilitates communications among programmers, helps in the training of new personnel,

Figure 13-1
EDP Complex Review Areas and Guide to Audit Guidelines and Controls

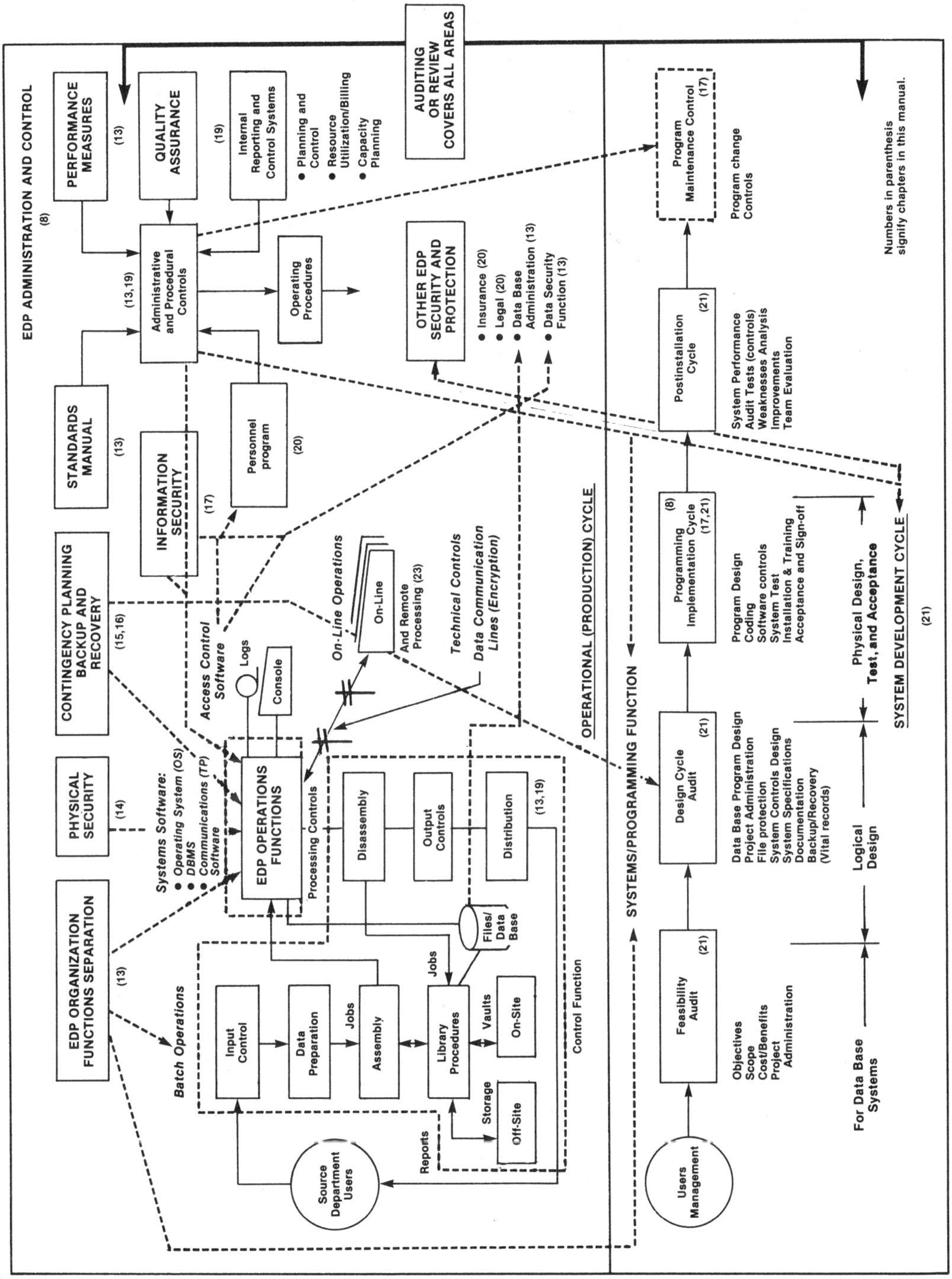

and prevents the development of conflicting procedures or widely different products. Also, in case of personnel changes or turnover, it eases the transition when a new individual takes over a project.

Figure 13-1 shows in aggregate form most of the management and control areas required in EDP in relation to a number of the EDP management standards listed above.

EDP MANAGEMENT STANDARDS

It is often argued that the whole aspect of EDP and EDP systems is an art and, therefore, less subject to pragmatic control than other well-established disciplines. Likewise, for this reason, some advocate that it is not possible to establish standards and basic ground rules for EDP. This is a weak argument indeed. Concerning development activities, when planning and managing the "man on the moon" program, there was no previous history or hard data to rely on, yet the program was achieved within the boundaries of the initial goals. Certainly it is desirable, if not mandatory, to have standards and methods for planning, operating, and controlling EDP programs and operations. Standards are needed to help in the day-to-day management process, to aid in coordinating programs, to help exercise control during system development, during the processing cycle, and to help in the training of new personnel within EDP. In the case of EDP center operations, standards are even more important to provide the framework for effective, secure, and efficient operations.

The Role of EDP Management Standards

Ideally conceived, a computer department should be managed by a set of soundly established and enforceable standards. Many aspects of EDP activities and tasks can be, and ought to be, standardized. For example, although each computer program is unique in its purpose, there are many programming techniques and procedures which are common to all programs. It is desirable that these techniques and procedures be standardized and set forth in a programming standards manual. This is also true of various departmental policies and guidelines particular to each company, concerning such things as maximum program size, use of decision tables, standardizing on given languages, etc.

Programming Standards Checklist

1. Is there a standard format for the program file which should be assembled for each program?
2. Are flowcharts and block diagram symbols and procedures standardized?
3. Are program techniques standardized for the following?

a. Table look-up or search methods
b. Use of program switches
c. Initialization routines
d. Tape record blocking
e. Use of table-driven mechanisms

4. Are program testing procedures well established? Do they include program as well as system tests?
5. Are means for specifying logical and/or decision rules standardized, such as by use of decision tables or other charting techniques?
6. Are halt addresses standardized as to location and use?
7. Are symbolic programming labels or tags standardized?
8. Is there a separate section devoted to controls and classed as: system, procedural, data protection, administrative, or other controls?
9. Have all standardized procedures been compiled in a programming manual and is the manual current?
10. Are advanced techniques, such as structured programming, used and standardized?

Areas Subject to Standards

Examples of areas that can be standardized are:

- Charter of organization and functional structure, outlining responsibilities and separation of functions in EDP.
- Programming approaches, procedures, and languages.
- Project planning and control procedures. How projects are initiated, approved, reviewed by all concerned (including auditors), documented at given control points, and how they are implemented, accepted, and signed off upon installation. How manpower and key skills are allocated and leveled (balancing demand/supply over time).
- Procedures for introducing system and program changes.
- Procedures for data control, error management, and quality control, including forms.
- Standards for transfer of developmental projects from systems to operational status, including standards for testing programs during development.
- Standards for the vital records program of the company with particular reference to the upkeep of the EDP portion of the program.
- Standards for maintenance of equipment and environmental support facilities.
- Personnel standards, including hire/fire; career path, development and promotion; security clearance, and background check.

- Documentation standards for the system development and installation cycles and for future program changes. The latter is referred to as "maintainability provisions."
- Standards for security procedures to be followed by EDP.
- Contingency and emergency preparedness procedures to include backup and recovery procedures. These should include "checkpoint and restart" provisions.
- Standards for program and systems testing.
- Standards for computer operations practices (production, testing, reruns, library, shifts, personnel, equipment breakdowns, etc.).
- Standards for EDP management planning and control, and reporting of activity against preestablished criteria. This includes procedures on what data to collect at what point, by whom, and in what forms. Also, what data reduction procedures are to be used to generate what performance reports.
- Standards for control provisions and statistics on printed reports. Namely, control summaries produced upon report completion, indicating report code, what programs are used to generate report, what file labels are used, batch balancing, etc.

Organization and Elements of an EDP Management Standard

What Is a Management Standard?

A management standard is designed to provide a sound "approved" basis for the conduct, management, and control of a given phase of the operation of the EDP complex. It also serves as a basis for evaluating performance or compliance with established practice. Last, but not least, it is an important training tool.

A standard contains essentially three hierarchical components, as follows:

- Management policies or guidelines. These are at the "strategic level."
- Operating standards, performance guidelines, or capacity ratings. These are "tactical" in nature.
- Operating procedures or detailed instructions. These are "operational" in nature.

Management policies, as defined in this part of the manual, refer to all those basic statements of position which are spelled out by management, concerning how they expect the EDP complex to operate. They represent fundamental postures and principles by which the conduct of the data processing department should be guided. They relate to ways and means by which EDP is to serve the firm's objectives, how resources are to be used and the scope of the EDP department activities.

Operating standards and procedures should obviously be instituted with due regard and being subjugated to the main policy guidelines. These consist normally of a series of working guidelines and detailed operating procedures, performance ratings and techniques required to operate the particular phase of the complex or a given organizational unit, according to sound and previously measured or accepted practices. The emphasis here is on specific and detailed instructions.

Every data processing department should begin by defining the main policies first, (which should be compatible with corporate policies). In addition, they should not be in conflict with other departmental or division policies of which EDP is a department. This may have a bearing on the level and location of EDP.

The policies are likely to depend upon:

- The industry the EDP department serves, e.g. banking, industry, retail, service industries, nonprofit institutions or government
- Whether or not the center serves the needs of only internal or external functions, or both
- Whether the organization of the firm is centralized or decentralized, and whether EDP serves all departments, or is primarily the tool of only one department (engineering, accounting, etc.)
- The manner in which EDP is justified and costed out and whether its services are absorbed by corporate overhead or billed to each user

In order for a standards manual to be complete, it should first specify overall policy. A sample statement of overall policy would be:

> It shall be the policy of the EDP department to have a formal maintenance function for all equipment. This shall include preventive and corrective maintenance provisions. It shall be the responsibility of the Machine Operations Supervisor to plan and execute this program.

Next, the functional charter of responsibilities for that particular function should be described, indicating functions, responsibilities and activities to be discharged. The next phase may consist of a number of guidelines and procedures to be followed, along with reference tables, rated capacity standards, reference points, operating limits. At each step, the standards should state the objectives and give clear references as to who or what position description is to perform what, to pinpoint accountability and provide a basis for performance measurement.

The standards should also include the position descriptions of all the functions affected or involved. Where possible, detailed documented examples of how the standards and procedures were applied to a particular case or problem should be included, for ease in understanding. Other data pertaining to who approved the standard, the date of issue, version it supersedes, etc., should also be shown. Finally, the necessary forms, formats, and data logging and reporting procedures should be clearly spelled out.

As can be readily appreciated, the process of developing and implementing standards is quite sizable and should not be taken lightly, if good results are to be obtained. Furthermore, it is an ongoing and dynamic process to accommodate changes in the EDP environment.

Guidelines for Basic Documentation and for Checking the Existence of Standards

In a properly managed data center, a minimum of basic documentation and standards should be readily available. The EDP manager should be in a position to produce copies of this documentation merely for the asking, in a fashion similar to the documentation available for operating an important industrial plant. If this information is not readily available, it is, in fact, an initial indication that the EDP installation is not properly organized, managed, and documented.

A basic useful list of documentation is as follows.

EDP Organization Chart. This illustrates the structure of the EDP department broken down into individual functions, their reporting level and the staffing head count of the department. See the material below, under "EDP Department Organization," for examples.

EDP Functional Charters. Written documents which outline the key generic responsibilities assigned to each and every functional unit within EDP. These charters are function/responsibility-oriented and not man- or job-oriented. They are a statement of the group's key functions. It is the document through which the scope of the function is specified and the key responsibilities delegated. A charter is also referred to as a "mission statement."

Position Descriptions. These are written descriptions of the duties of each position in the organization chart. Although, at times, there may be a position description for every functional charter, this one-to-one correspondence may not always occur. For instance, there may be several position descriptions within a charter operating at various levels. Also, the position description is man- or job-oriented. It serves two purposes: (a) to outline for the incumbent the responsibilities of his job, thus providing a basis for measuring his performance, and (b) to provide a means for specifying skills required, guide recruiting efforts, and help in establishing salary and wage administration parameters by personnel groups.

Personnel Files. These are a series of folders with detailed information on each present or past employee of the department, containing: date of hiring, background information (resumé), job and salary progression, performance evaluation sheets, along with observations, re promotability, need for training, or glaring deficiencies or defects. Factors related to security should be included here also. For example, clearance level, "nondisclosure" agreements, etc.

Personnel Indoctrination and Development. This is a statement of approved procedures for initiating new personnel. It includes initiation programs, indoctrination on official standards, specification of limits of access to information, career path, and personal development data. An outline of the department's training program and policies regarding secrecy agreement sheets, publication of reports bearing on company activities, and instructions for eligibility to attend colleges or special courses, are clearly specified here.

EDP Department Plans and Planning Process. This is a document, often called the strategic EDP plan, outlining the department's plans over the next, usually three to five years, and a form or instruction sheet describing how plans are prepared and approved. Since EDP can be looked on as a minicompany, with both staff and line responsibilities, serving many departments, plans should be along the lines of projects in the staff area and operational control in the computer operations and control areas of activity. Further, the plans should be along the lines of allocation and management of the seven key resources common to most organizations: manpower, materials, machines, methods, money, information and management processes. (See Chapter 19 for details.) Naturally, these plans should show the relationship of activity or programs to the firm's overall plans and objectives, even if this is accomplished indirectly through the users EDP serves, by virtue of the services rendered. The sheet on planning procedures simply describes the planning cycle, the timing, and the process of obtaining approval and endorsement by management. It should of course describe how users are made to participate in the planning process for new projects.

EDP Management and Operational Reports. This includes a number of periodic or semiperiodic documents and reports related to the recording, reporting, and controlling of EDP activities. Among others:

- Copies of monthly cost reports for a period of time.
- Copies of periodic (usually monthly) activity reports showing:
  - –Level of activity (hours, shifts, staff complement)
  - –Relative utilization (equipment and personnel)
  - –Trend charts relative to either utilization or departure from historical standards
  - –Project activity (systems and operations) reports according to preestablished reporting norms for each system, user development project, internal development projects.
  - –Special reports relative to key areas, such as systems and equipment maintenance, report errors and reruns, and the like.

Actions taken should also be logged and reported.

Other Reports and Statistics. This comprises records of all assets and resources under EDP custody, to include:

- Equipment inventory, configurations, capacities, and characteristics.
- Rentals and/or depreciation schedule (if owned).
- Equipment billing from vendors, including overtime.
- Contractual agreements on hardware, software, services, (bureaus, leases [building or equipment]), maintenance agreements, replacement clauses, etc.

Operating Systems—version in effect, history of changes, modifications, and problems. If acquired from other than regular vendor, the appropriate data should be recorded.

A Detailed Inventory of All Hardware—listing models, number or units, vendor, etc.

Auxiliary Equipment—such as buildings, air conditioning, detection and security equipment, etc.

Documentation of Other Data Center Elements.

- *File Library Inventory and Logs*—stating number of tapes, disks and other file sources, serial numbers, scratch disks, etc.
- *Equipment Meter Logs*—for the last few years, including vendor adjustments.
- *Customer Complaint Logs and Files*—outlining the history of problems with users relative to quality, quantity, and timeliness.
- *Due-In and Due-Out Dates and Time*—agreed upon with users for data to EDP center and reports to users.
- *Official Distribution List for Reports.*
- *An Official List of All Systems Programs and Reports*—run by the EDP center and users.
- *Copies of Important Reports or Studies*—related to the department's operations, equipment proposals, and justifications.
- *Console and Rerun Logs*—indicating run and operator actions.
- *Program Changes Log*—tracing every change made to a program, by systems and programming.
- *Inventory of Forms*—used in the EDP area with key emphasis on sensitive forms (checks, authorizations).
- *Method Used for Billing or Allocating EDP Department Services*—should include samples of charge distributions.
- *Samples of the strategic data processing plan.*
- *Samples of requirements plan (usually monthly, identifies demand) and facilities schedules* showing day-to-day operations runs.
- *Samples of current correspondence* related to systems, problems, and other departmental activity.

- *Samples of job or application runs* showing detailed operating procedures.
- *Samples of data entry, data preparation, and data control procedures.*
- *Samples of control unit operating procedures* concerning logging, batching, quality control, dispatching, job assembly/disassembly, report binding and distribution procedures, and disposal of excess copies.
- *Outline of housekeeping rules* and samples of housekeeping surprise audits.
- *Outline of security procedures and security logs and activities.*
- *Copy of the contingency planning and recovery plan.*

Audit Master Chart and Index to Standards and Guidelines

The scope and complexity of EDP is such that it is easy to become confused in the process of planning and conducting an audit or to lose perspective as to what to cover, depending on the situation at hand. It is equally easy to overlook important areas of audit significance. To assist the auditor or examiner in grasping a clear understanding of the total scope of EDP control, Figure 13-1 gives an overview of the important areas of review. This chart can be used to:

- Define the elements of review and the scope of the EDP complex audit.
- Illustrate the variety of organizational units involved, the stages and the work stations at which controls are required, and the types of controls and procedures required to run an EDP complex.
- Provide a handy reference as to where to find the detailed coverage of the guidelines and checklists, pertaining to each area, in the manual.

Upon inspecting this chart, the user will immediately realize the wealth of standards, controls, and information that are required to: (a) manage and control an EDP complex, and (b) audit EDP activities in a thorough fashion. In fact, from a control viewpoint, the audit should be a mirror image view of how the EDP complex operates. It is also clear that a thorough and professional audit of the EDP complex can be very encompassing and involved, depending upon the objectives, the approach, and scope of the audit.

EDP DEPARTMENT ORGANIZATION—CHARTER OF RESPONSIBILITIES AND SEPARATION OF FUNCTIONS

General

Assuming that we have competent people, an important element in the success of an organization is how well the people in any given function are grouped and what their assigned responsibilities are.

Further, from a control and security viewpoint, it is important to ensure that the proper level of separation of functions is established. In the precomputer days—and even before—when punched card equipment dominated the scene, separation of functions was practiced at the individual level. There was a great degree of subdivision of tasks. Therefore, for fraud to occur, collusion of some form, involving several individuals (internal or external), was required. With today's increasingly centralized, computerized, and integrated systems, we have reached a high degree of concentration of data. Also, company procedures are "precaptured" into a series of computer programs, even "in advance" of any transactions being processed by them. In other words, computer programs have replaced manual procedures and approvals through the preauthorized logic imbedded in the now computerized application. What is more, many computer programs actually invalidate traditional "separation of functions" provisions, by initiating a series of transactions and authorizing corresponding actions (decisions), which were previously performed by different individuals, all within the same given program or set of programs, without any interim human intervention. Some way of counter-arresting this condition must therefore be found. This implies that separation of duties in the traditional sense and at the individual level can no longer be practiced. The procedures and controls of the past have been replaced by certain new data processing functions involving different skills and a series of computer programs. An evaluation of the EDP organization and its various functions is therefore very important to the security of the business organization and is an essential part of the review of the internal controls of the firm.

Objectives of a Sound EDP Organization

The objectives of a soundly conceived organization are two-fold:

1. To promote efficiency, effectiveness, and economy of operations
2. To protect the accuracy, integrity, and security of data

In the past, primary consideration was given only to the efficiency, effectiveness, and economy side of EDP. When one considers the security and control requirements, EDP organizations will often take a different structure. Such modified structures may even cause, at times, certain inefficiencies in the way EDP must operate—at least in the views of EDP personnel. However they are necessary to the restoration of an adequate level of controls within EDP. The basic question for those who object is: Do we wish to continue driving a three-wheeled car for lack of good controls?

Basic Elements

We need to consider three basic elements when analyzing the EDP organization:

1. The level of the function (reporting level)
2. The structure (the grouping and separation of functions)
3. The functional characteristics of each group (individual or unit responsibilities)

The level of the function has to do with the level at which the EDP activity reports within the organization. This indicates the lines of communication to management and to other important related functions. The structure has to do with the break-down of functions into groups, for purposes of delegation of responsibilities, for reasons of balancing, and to ensure separation of duties is practiced. The functional characteristics refer to the individual responsibilities of each subfunction. They outline each function's mission. The latter is often called the charter of responsibilities.

Organizing for Separation of Functions

Among one of the important administrative controls is the structuring of a proper organization for EDP, which provides for an effective separation of functions. A very important characteristic of administrative controls is that, once established, they are permanent until they are changed. Unlike technical individual audits, such as audit software tests, administrative controls operate continuously. Individual technical audits may have a limited time duration. Individual audit findings may tend to be overlooked or become obsolete because they are after-the-fact and static in nature by design. That is to say, they are snapshots of conditions at the time they are conducted.

In order to explain separation of functions, we will begin with the most elementary case; that of very small organizations, where separation of functions cannot be effectively practiced. We will then build up to the more complicated cases with multiple functions, where effective separation of duties can and must be exercised.

EDP Function Location

One of the first points to be considered in the analysis of the EDP organization is its location within the company. In fact, the location of the function represents the first level of separation of functions. For example, does the function to which it reports use a great deal of EDP services, such that objectivity in the use and allocation of EDP resources can be impaired?

Viewed from the traditional standpoint of operating, custody, and accounting functions, the data processing department is performing an accounting function and should therefore be independent of operating and custodial departments. Logically, it should function as a service organization. It could report to an executive responsible for more than one line department, or to any person independent of organizational units being served, such as a vice-president of administrative services. In addition, this concept would specifically require that data processing employees have no other accounting duties and not be required to originate source documents. Oftentimes, where the importance of the EDP function is deemed paramount to the organization (such as in banks), the function may report to the chief operating officer or president, to provide it with the status and leverage it deserves, and to avoid possible conflict of interests. Although a high reporting level is not necessarily a guarantee that the results will be better, in general, a high reporting level coupled with a sound EDP manager, will probably result in a better arrangement than if EDP reports at a low level or to a specific user department. It will also tend to avoid conflicts resulting from any other function, to which it reports, applying self-serving practices. Experience also shows that, from a return on the EDP dollar viewpoint, a high reporting level may make it more possible for EDP resources to be allocated to the most fruitful areas of the business, as a result of proper access to senior management, and hence overall direction.

EDP Functional Structure

Our discussion on structure is from the viewpoint of security and controls. Because structure is bound to change with the size or complexity of the DP installation, we describe EDP structure from the most primitive to the most complete; from the ridiculous to the sublime.

Within the data processing area, an ideal arrangement of duties would provide for at least the separation of these three basic functions:

- Systems development and programming
- Control (handling of input, quality control, output distribution, and data custody)
- Operation of data processing equipment

Since these are basic functions, a number of EDP installations are organized along these lines. In actual practice, however, strict adherence to these principles is not always easy to accomplish. For example, only computer operators should be allowed to operate the data processing equipment and load magnetic tapes. To make this effective, programmers should not be allowed to process their own test runs. Program testing should be done on a scheduled, remote-test, basis by computer operators, subject to a suitable authorization sheet logged in with the control group. When using TSO (time sharing option) whereby testing is done from terminals, testing of systems by programmers should never be done on "live" but rather on "test" files.

As another example, computer operators should not have access to block diagrams and program listings. This restriction implies detailed "halt instructions" for the computer operator that would cover only mechanical operations. They should not be instructed to change data or programs. Furthermore, someone other than computer operators should review and investigate such output items as record counts, control totals, out-of-balance batches, editing rejects, computer detected errors, and the console typewriter logs. The latter is normally done by the control function. There are very few EDP installations that adhere to this complete segregation of functions, but good organization is fundamental to good control. With regard to system programmers, a good control practice is that the latter should not have access to applications documentation.

Description of Functions and Separation of Functions

One-Man EDP Organization

The most elementary, and certainly undesirable, EDP organiztion is that of the "one-man" EDP function. It is often encountered in extremely small and unsophisticated installations. Here, essentially, one man performs all the data processing functions of systems, programming, machine operations, data preparation, and data control. In addition, he acts as the supervisor.

This arrangement is fraught with potential problems. The first and most serious situation is the firm's exposure to: (a) losing operational continuity, in the event something were to happen to the key man and (b) possible fraud or covering up of errors, in the absence of control. In the one-man arrangement, it is quite likely for systems to be poorly designed and poorly documented. Standards are probably nonexistent, and the lack of separation of functions can lead to plain lack of control. Besides lack of time, the reason why this happens is the fact that one man cannot possibly possess all the required knowledge.

Other than not ever allowing yourself to get into such a situation, about the only thing that management and auditors can do, is to make sure that at least some form of control desk is established at each of the data-source and report-recipient departments, to check and validate their data. This is particularly true when it comes to interface with the accounting department. Figure 13-2 illustrates this arrangement.

Organization for Small Installations

The minimum desirable separation of functions is shown in Figure 13-3. In addition to the EDP supervisor or manager, the three traditional separate functions of control, machine operations, and systems/programming are shown. Under this basic arrangement, systems/programming is responsible for the development of new systems but not for their operation. Operators do not have access to and do not change programs. The control function serves to coordi-

Figure 13-2
One-Person EDP Organization
(No Separation of Duties)

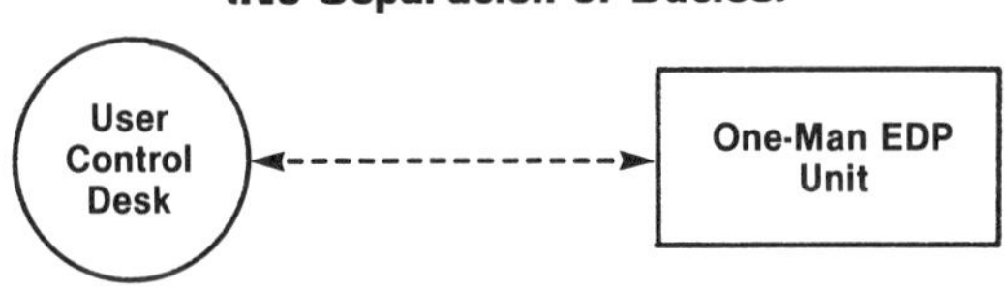

Figure 13-3
Minimum Desirable Separation of Functions—Small Installation

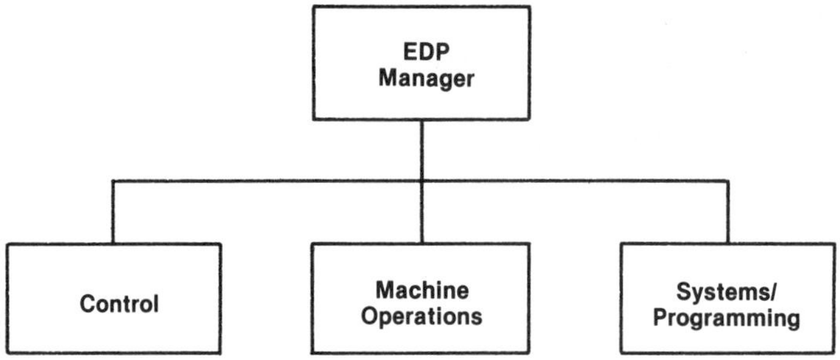

nate and control the daily flow of work into and out of the EDP center. All key administrative functions are performed by the department manager.

Organization and Separation of Functions in a Large Installation

In a large installation it is not only possible but absolutely necessary that the EDP organization be structured for a greater degree of separation of functions. This is shown in Figure 13-4.

In the development function it is possible, and desirable, to separate the systems analysis and design function from the program design and programming function. Ideally, this is desirable because better systems result from such a functional separation. The systems analysis and design personnel are oriented towards the needs of the business or the user department and think in terms of what should or could versus what should not be computerized. Theirs is essentially the problem-definition and problem-solving phase, by considering a number of computer or noncomputer viable alternatives. The provision of sound controls is also their responsibility. The programming function is oriented towards the machine-implementation phase. Their emphasis is on how best to utilize the hardware/software capabilities.

Managing this delicate balance between how much is accomplished at the analysis and design phase, versus how much one tries to accomplish "by default" at the programming phase through countless subsequent changes for failure to define the system well, is one of the secrets for success in developing good systems. One should try to do all the necessary wheelspining at the analysis and design level, long before any programming activity commences. The mechanism for communication between the analysis/design phase and the programming phase should be the "set of system specifications," which reflect the needs of the business. Even where a mixed systems/programming function exists, the analyst/programmer should be made responsible for the generation of a set of detailed specifications for documentation purposes, even if he were to also handle the programming phase himself. In this manner, proper documentation is ensured for the future.

Figure 13-4
Organization and Separation of Functions—Large Installation

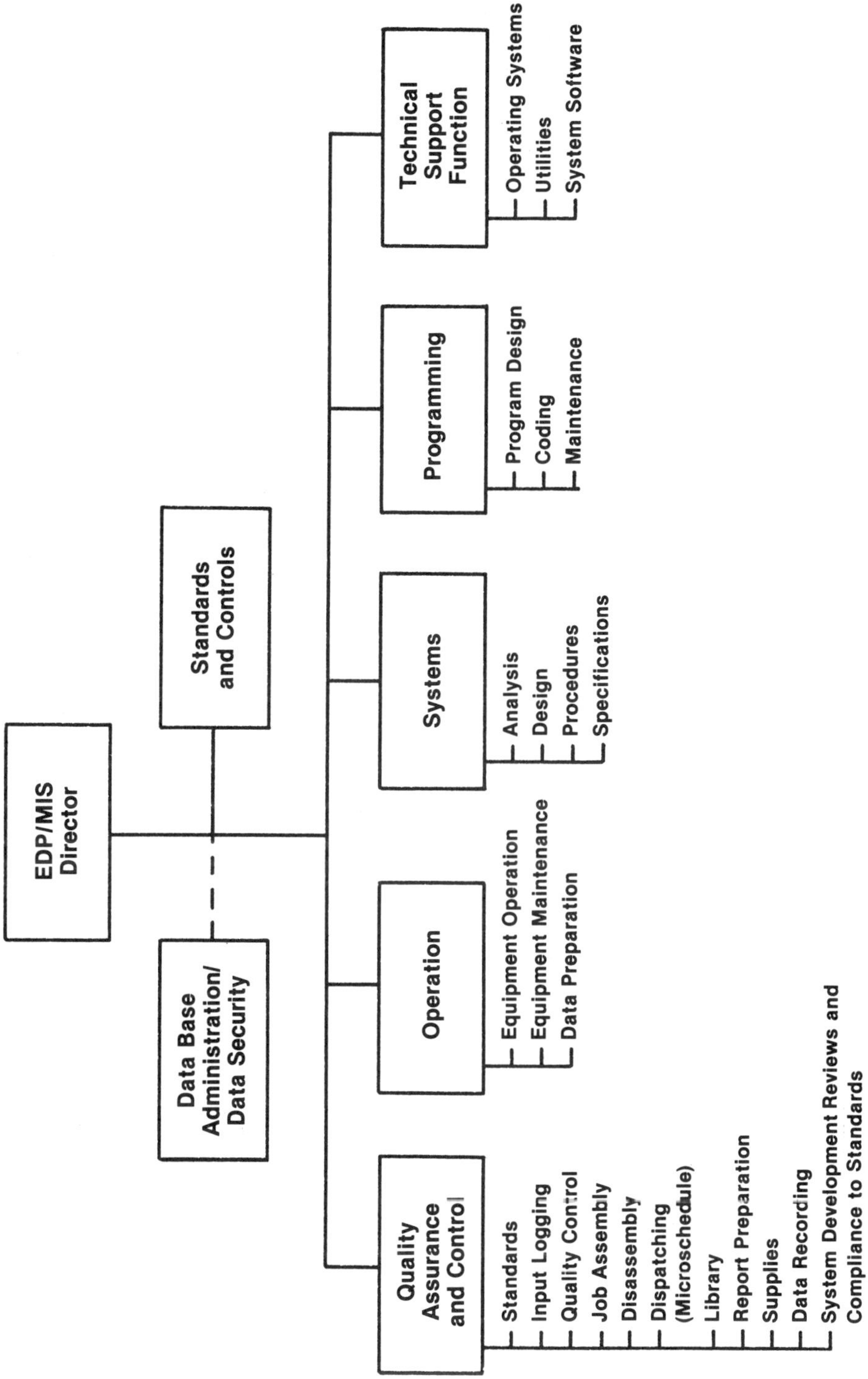

There is at least another reason why this functional separation should exist. In many instances, programmers do not make good analysts, even after extensive training. Those who have experienced such phenomenon, have been known to say, "In a desire to promote programmers into systems, I gained a very poor analyst and lost an excellent programmer."

The other important element in the development phase is the use of a system project manager and a sound project management and control system to control project progress and to smooth the communications flow among the various project participants.

The machine operations function should be responsible for only two functions: (a) to operate EDP equipment, and (b) to maintain the assigned equipment. This function is refrained from having access to detailed system/program documentation, except insofar as it relates to how to operate the system. They are likewise forbidden from changing program logic or program code. Their duties are guided by a set of operating standards and procedures, either provided at design time or developed by the user, or within the EDP department, to ensure proper operability and accountability.

The data preparation function provides another level of separation of duties. Although often included as part of the machine operations function, it is best set as a separate unit. In this manner, all communications are between data preparations personnel and control function personnel, who are responsible for delivering, scheduling, and receiving data. No communications should exist between data preparation personnel and either user (or source data) and machine operations personnel. By having data preparation separate from machine operations, one minimizes the possibility of collusion between these two groups or of errors made by either group being concealed or glossed over.

Technical support functions comprise a series of technical functions necessary to the operation of modern and advanced systems. Discharging these functions may require a part-time person in small organizations or a sizable group in large and technically complex organizations. This function deals with the technical and administrative aspects of what can be termed "environmental" software required to run the computer hardware and which surrounds and impinges upon the applications systems software. This group of functions consists of the capability to support the operating system, the data communications software, and the data base management systems. Together, these three main software packages are responsible for job and resource management (the operating system), communications message management (the data communications software), and data management (the data base management system). Generally, the personnel responsible for this system software are among the most technically skilled, and thus they represent a significant risk and source of exposure in terms of concentration of knowledge and overdependence on this knowledge. It thus requires you to develop and provide an adequate set of standards and controls measures to safeguard the integrity of the system environment.

The data base administration program encompasses a series of important functions and tasks vital to the design, operation, maintenance, and security of the corporate data, the data resident in the data base, and information stemming from the data base. This function is most instrumental in developing or coordinating standards and practices for data management. This function is also normally responsible for managing key aspects of the selection, acquisition, and maintenance of the data base management systems (DBMS) and the data dictionary system (DDS), if one is used to help manage data.

The data security administration function is primarily charged with the responsibility for the logical access security and the privacy and confidentiality aspects of the company's information systems. This relatively new function goes beyond the more traditional *padlock and physical access security* boundaries of the past. In smaller organizations, it is not unusual to see data base and data security activities combined under one single function. This is acceptable as long as the important aspects of these two types of activities are in fact taken care of. When they are separate, the data security administration function may be more concerned with the selection, implementation, and administration of the data security access programs. The data base administration function on the other hand may deal more with the DBMS and data dictionary software related to data management and with managing the "quality" integrity of data in the data base.

Another distinguishing feature between these two functions is that whereas data base administration concentrates on provisions for the recovery aspects of the data base, the data security function may be more concerned with the total or overall aspects of contingency planning and recovery and is a driving force behind the elaboration of a "total" contingency and recovery plan for the whole data center and all business systems.[1]

The quality assurance and control function is an important component of the EDP organization. Traditionally, it has been grossly neglected, poorly structured, and often staffed with substandard personnel. This function is quite important from both an efficiency and from a controls and data security viewpoint. For the EDP manager, it constitutes a good investment in effective EDP. For the auditor, its presence represents a powerful ally and the means by which the *day-to-day controls* which were established to process any application, are in fact practiced, recorded, and monitored. This function is also an excellent source of control information, when the auditor needs to conduct a system or operational audit, assuming it is well-structured. Most of all, the existence of this function means that the auditor can play less of a day-to-day monitoring role in EDP, and can concentrate on other more important tasks of greater impact to the firm.

Because of its significance to control, this function will be described in

[1] For more information on this point, see the book by J. F. Kuong and G. I. Isaacson, *How to Prepare an EDP Contingency Plan for Business Continuity* (Wellesley Hills, MA: Management Advisory Publications, 1986).

greater detail. The control function provides a single central control point for all data and procedures flowing into and out of data processing. This function provides the communications channel between all users or data source departments and EDP and among EDP functions. For example, even new versions of a changed program should be routed through control.

The chief functions of the control group are as follows:

- Input and output control (logging)
- Quality control and product monitoring
- Job assembly/disassembly
- Job dispatching and job microscheduling (not planning)
- File Library functions (including off-site backup)
- Report preparation and distribution
- Supplies management
- Data recording and internal EDP control
- Coordinating QA and EDP standards and overseeing adherence to them.

The QA function is also vitally instrumental in developing standards for new systems and reviewing compliance to these standards in the system development cycle.

The input/output task is concerned with the logging of all data, materials, documents, and reports which enter and/or leave the EDP department. Through this function, it is possible to centralize the flow of all materials into and out of EDP. It is common to keep a central log showing precisely what was received, at what time, from whom, by whom, in what quantities, and with what authorizing document, letter, or request form. This central log provides a permanent document of all activity into and out of the EDP department.

The quality control and product monitoring function is concerned with the accuracy and timeliness of jobs processed throughout the data center. This includes batch balancing, comparison of output with expected results to detect unusual or abnormal items and to initiate corrective action by EDP or the responsible or affected user or data source organizational unit outside EDP. In order to operate well, this section must follow the set of standard practices and procedures developed for each system application or job being processed.

The job assembly/disassembly task consists of the preparation of jobs to be run by EDP, by gathering all the data, procedure, and file elements necessary to process a given job. In doing so, the control individual consults with posted schedules, job run sheets, or layouts and procures the necessary master files, work files, and job control language cards from storage sites. In some EDP departments these functions may be integrated with the librarian's functions.

Job dispatching and job (micro) scheduling is another important control function. Here the control unit helps by performing a coordinating function across EDP functions (not EDP machines alone). Based on the available due-in and due-out tables for data and reports and the posted schedules, their mission is one of providing microscheduling of all steps required to get a job done to minimize delays and possible errors. An important tool of this group is to develop a table or matrix of all due-in and due-out dates by job and by work station to enable the scheduling of key punching, assembly/disassembly, and expediting of all jobs through the whole processing cycle. In very complex installations the schedule matrix with job routes can be computerized to aid in control. An example of the due-in/out and route sheet is shown in Figure 13-5.

The file library function is responsible for all matters related to receipt, storage, retrieval, and custody of all files, especially those recorded on magnetic media (tapes, disks). The file librarian keeps a detailed log of all tapes and disks in use, describing contents, dates when generated, serial numbers, etc. He is also responsible for the actual storage, retrieval, and custody of all files and for monitoring their activity and use. Likewise, the librarian keeps track of all file retention cycles and issues scratch tapes when the scratch dates are reached or exceeded. For more details of the librarian functions see Chapter 18. The file librarian is also responsible for custody over and updating of files in

Figure 13-5
Due-In/Due-Out Control Sheet
to Monitor Timeliness

System/Application ________ Department ________

Log In			Data Prepar.	Report Distribution	Log Out		
Due-In	Actual	Diff.			Due-Out	Actual	Diff.

the off-site backup facility. This is a key security function in view of the high concentration of records and knowledge in off-site storage facilities.

The report preparation and distribution unit has for a function the preparation of all processed reports received from the librarian, disassembly, or quality control units, in terms of decarbonation, bursting, collating, and building. This group has a key custody function in that they must distribute the right report to the right user according to a key authorization table, which is supposed to be kept up-to-date. Any excess copies are shredded or incinerated. All carbons are disposed of to prevent disclosure through browsing or theft of copies.

Supplies management is concerned with inventory, storage, and custody of all key supplies for EDP operations, including paper, cards, and forms. Special forms, such as for checks and invoices are kept under special control. Periodic counts and analysis of usage of key forms is important. This function also sees to it that no excessive amounts of combustible paper and trash are present in the computer room to minimize the danger of fire.

Data recording and internal EDP control functions consist of a number of tasks related to operational performance, such as: logging, equipment utilization, analysis of break-downs, errors, maintenance, job reruns, and quality and timeliness statistics. This group shall be concerned also with the maintenance of due-in dates for data and due-out dates for reports with data-source and report-user departments.

This group accumulates data and provides analysis for purposes of performance analysis, isolation of variances, analysis of trends, and development of performance standards or rated capacities for all units within EDP. In performing their duties, they are instrumental in developing or instituting new data collection forms, and in establishing quality control charts to detect undesirable trends. The data accumulated by this group also serves as a basis for preparing monthly or other periodic reports by EDP for management. They are also an excellent source of control data for auditors when auditing EDP.

Coordination and development of standards is another key function of the quality assurance and control function. The QA function may either develop many of the standards or coordinate the development or acquisition of standards from available sources. QA and control is often also instrumental in conducting the ongoing review of compliance to approved standards and reporting violations to the chief data processing executive. Other tasks that have been assigned to QA in recent years are overseeing the preparation of sound system test plans, reviews of new system development projects at key milestones, and, even, assisting in the building of internal controls in systems and overseeing that sound contingency plans are developed or implemented.

Strengthening of the QA and Control Functions

There are various approaches to organizational strengthening of the control function. The first alternative, of course, is to take it away from under machine operations and have it report in parallel with machine operations. In this sense, it can be viewed as a "separate" quality control and assurance unit.

A second alternative is to create an all-encompassing QA and control function with systems and staff control functions and with operations control capabilities. This section head would report in parallel to systems and operations and directly to the EDP executive. Under this arrangement, the operations control portion performs all the tasks previously described, whereas the systems and staff control unit would concentrate on such things as: management and operations improvement, developing of new standards, reviewing systems before they are adopted as operational, making sure that the standards re documentation, ensuring thorough testing of systems, etc., are upheld. This unit can also perform internal or surprise audits of EDP to improve effectiveness and security and as a basis for performance improvement and enforcing adherance to approved standards.

A third alternative consists of setting up the control function completely separate from EDP and making it a part of another department, which acts in effect as an audit group for all EDP activities. This approach is favored by some where there is reason to feel that a more objective control and stronger monitoring of EDP can be accomplished from outside EDP. The advantages from a control and separation of functions is obvious. However, it is natural to expect that when a third party is introduced, it can make communications between users, EDP, and the separate control group somewhat lengthier and awkward. It should work, however, when properly set up and assuming clear agreements are established and in the presence of well-established standards for all of EDP.

EDP Organization Checklist

Review Procedure—Separation of Functions

1. Obtain an organization chart of the EDP department. Determine position titles, reporting levels, job descriptions, and names of persons in each key position. Determine the personnel count and compare it to the budgeted complement. Update the organization chart to reflect present conditions. Use it as a basis for determining who should be interviewed. Get the descriptive charters of organization as a basis for subsequent analysis of functions.
   a. Is there a current standards manual for the department?
   b. Are the organization charts (a) available, and (b) current?
2. How removed from top management is the data processing manager and why?
   a. To which function does EDP report?
   b. Is the EDP department independent of all operating units for which it performs data processing functions?

3. Is there segregation of duties? Are the following work units physically as well as organizationally separate: (a) computer center, (b) control unit (including program and tape library), and (c) systems and programming units.
   a. System design and programming are separate from computer operations.
   b. Programmers do not operate the computer for live processing runs with actual files. Likewise, they do not test programs with production files.
   c. Computer operators do not have access to data and program information beyond that needed for performing their assigned task.
   d. The employees in data processing do not initiate transactions and originate requests for changes to the master files.
   e. Programmers do not catalog programs. Program cataloging and loading is done only by operators via authorization forms for cataloging programs, and possibly, through the use of librarian packages which provide an audit trail.
   f. Are the operators assigned to individual application runs rotated periodically?
   g. Are the computer operators required to take vacations?
   h. Is supervision of operators sufficient to verify operators' adherence to prescribed operating procedures?
   i. Are there adequate logs to record operator activity?
   j. Are there surprise audits to verify adherence to established practices?

Administrative Practices and Controls

1. Is there a systems and procedures manual for the activities of the EDP department?
   a. Is there a programming standards manual?
   b. Are program and console run-books adequately documented for each computer program?
   c. Are file retention procedures adhered to?
   d. Are master files stored under reasonable protective custody?
2. Is there an annual procedure for evaluating and defining project priorities for new automated applications?
3. Is there a formal system for evaluating and reviewing all computer requests for services?
4. Is there a written plan for future systems and/or changes to be made to systems?
5. Is approval for each application supported by a cost/benefit study?
6. Is a schedule of implementation prepared showing actual versus projected progress?

7. Is there a formal checkpoint and control procedure for every EDP project?
8. Is there a formal sign-off procedure for the acceptance of new systems by operations personnel from the systems group?
   a. Before becoming operational, new systems should be approved by:

      –User departments.

      –EDP manager

      –Senior executive

   b. System changes should follow similar procedures. Users should be advised of changes.
   c. Auditors should "endorse" the internal controls if the system was audited during development.
9. Is there a postimplementation review procedure for all installed systems?
10. Is there an allocation or charge-back procedure (or billing algorithm) to determine accountability for the use of EDP resources and as a means to help both users and executive management determine the worth of the EDP services being rendered?
11. Does data processing control costs, overtime, and other budgeted items?
12. Is there control of equipment and other resources utilization? Are reruns analyzed and all corrective actions documented pinpointing responsibility or reasons for reruns?
13. Is there an internal (within EDP) information and control system to gather data on project and operations activity, analyze facts and reporting of EDP activities, that paves the way to corrective steps?
14. Does the EDP department's charter of responsibilities include a section outlining their accountability for planning, implementing, and securing systems and computer operations as well as data under their custody? Are the appropriate standards reflected in the standards manual?
15. Is there a "current" inventory of all hardware indicating its characteristics, vendor code, date of acquisition, and whether it is purchased or leased?
16. Are there any measures of performance for the EDP complex and corresponding reporting mechanisms to gauge data center performance against these measures?
17. When equipment is eliminated or removed, is there a procedure to adjust the inventory and are provisions made for asset accounting, tax, and other considerations to be taken care of?

MEASURES OF EFFECTIVENESS
(Measurement Criteria)

General

The EDP complex is an important company activity. It consumes company resources. Therefore, it should be subject to as much scrutiny and measurement as any other company function. Management should be interested in at least the following three main viewpoints to ensure complete grasp of control of EDP.

1. How is it administered and how efficiently does it run?
2. How well does it serve the various user departments?
3. How securely does it operate?

The first viewpoint is concerned with the responsibility every executive has to see that a given function is operated effectively and is accountable. The second viewpoint considers the user's (client's) viewpoint. (Under point one EDP may meet budgets but do they serve the needs of the users well?) The third viewpoint has, at long last, received the recognition it deserves, in view of the many fiascos and breaches of systems and data security that have occurred, plus the fact that processing data through EDP has created a massive problem of risk concentration and, therefore, vulnerability to operations discontinuity.

Measures of Performance

In order to evaluate EDP performance, we must first establish some fundamental norms or criteria for measurement. To date, this area has been avoided by management or auditors, in the belief that, because EDP is a high-technology activity, the performance criteria should be highly technical and complex. Nothing could be further from the truth. If we look for "aggregate" measures of performance, the same principles and criteria of measurement that apply to any other business operation apply also to EDP. If we focus our attention on individual system components or take a limited view of EDP performance, naturally, technical measurement criteria do apply. Such is the case, for example, when we analyze CPU processing speed, communications channel utilization, file structure and utilization, or when we perform benchmarks tests to measure relative speed of equipment to process a program or relative efficiency of several programs to perform equal tasks in the same machine. This is the province of technical EDP reviews. But we also agree that these are not representative nor are they an overall measure of how the EDP function performs, such as management is concerned with.

We must establish some basic premises, as follows:

- EDP is a service function set up to satisfy users' needs, not the other way around.
- EDP has development and operational activities.

With these in mind, we can apply conventional measurement criteria that apply to a service-oriented function and to project and operational activities.

Four main categories or measures of performance are proposed:

1. Quality of Services (quantity is implied)
2. Timeliness (Punctuality) of Services
3. Resource Utilization Effectiveness
4. Adequacy of Security and Controls

These basic criteria can be applied to both EDP development projects and to EDP center operations. Differences are a matter of procedure and tools. Many additional categories of measurement can be added, if one wishes. But we can essentially say that most of these other criteria can be made a subset or component of the four main criteria listed above. The administrator or auditor may add such semiintangible factors as: EDP manager personality, morale, personnel turnover, organizational make-up. These can be added as additional "opinion" criteria of measurement. However the above four are subject to factual measurement and are indicative of the soundness of operation of the EDP department and are, therefore, recommended.

As an example of how various operating factors can be related to the four measures of performance, the sketch below illustrates a cause-and-effect type of relationship for data centers.

Quality of Services

- Error frequency and error management
- Data quality and data management program
- Accuracy of systems
- Service-minded and responsive to user
- Reliability of information services
- User-data center liaison and public relations program
- Quality of programs in relation to user needs
- Operating standards and documentation
- Organizational structure for designing systems
- Quality of EDP control unit
- Quality of personnel (systems, maintenance)
- Quality of supervisory personnel
- Involvement of users during design
- Systems flexibility

- Capacity (bottlenecks, equipment/personnel)
- Reasonableness of data due-in and report due-out times (too many concurrent due-times)
- Requirements planning and job scheduling

Timeliness of Services

- Work load profiles (high seasonality through the day and through the month)
- Too much processing centralization (everything done in one machine with attendant creation of queues and loss in flexibility)
- Poor equipment reliability or poor maintenance practices by EDP or vendors
- Data source departments not on time with source data
- Lack of adequate data center operating standards
- Inadequate and/or poorly-trained operations personnel
- Information facility uptime (on-stream factor, mean-time between failures, mean-time-to-repair factors)

Resource Utilization

- Excessive idle capacity
- Inefficiency of programmed systems
- Inadequate work-leveling programs
- Inadequate capacity balancing programs (equipment bottlenecks)
- Lack of good equipment balance
- Lack of EDP resource utilization information system
- Poor scheduling practices
- Control function inadequately set up
- Lack of cost control and charge-out procedures
- Lack of priority rules for allocation of equipment and personnel resources
- Improper use of operating system
- Inadequate use of primary memory and peripherals
- Poorly designed systems
- Inadequate operating procedures and/or personnel training
- Frequent report reruns
- Ineffective job stream management (poor use of buffering, spooling, etc.)

- Inadequate organization structure and separation of duties
- Lack of management standards
- Lack of physical protection program
- Inadequate data/software protection and backup and recovery provisions
- Inadequate administrative, procedural, and processing controls
- Insufficient system-programmed controls

Security and Controls

- Insufficient or lack of EDP audits
- Lack of vital records program
- Inadequate user/EDP interface controls
- Inadequate contingency planning and recovery provisions
- Unavailable or inadequate data and resource access control program (lack of access software provisions to control the profile of information accessibility, password management, etc.)
- Inadequate libraries management standards and controls
- Inadequate management of system software versions
- Inadequate privacy and confidentiality management (concealment and encryption and key management program)
- Inadequate network management and security provisions
- Insufficient application system controls
- Lack of internal control-building methodologies and risk analysis programs.
- Inadequate data base administration program and data base integrity management
- Poor quality assurance and data control program

In the case of measuring EDP system project performance, the tools are somewhat different but the concepts do not change. Here the most important control tool becomes the application of a project management and control system. Refer to Chapter 21 for other details.

VITAL RECORDS PROGRAM

General

Every organization is required to keep some form of a vital records program by virtue of regulatory agency requirements, as a means of protecting the confidentiality of company information, protecting stockholders' records and interests, and to protect the very continuity of the organization.

The objectives of a vital records program may include such things as:

- Protecting records crucial to company operability.
- Protecting records on employees, ownership, and customers. This may include safeguarding insurance, pension plan, and other confidential records.
- Keeping backup records required by the income tax (IRS) or other regulatory bodies (SEC, comptroller of the currency for banks, etc.)

Note that the vital records program is all-encompassing. It involves the identification, classification, and protection of all records relevant to the vital records objectives outlined above. This includes both computerized and non-computerized records. The reason for including a discussion on vital records is that increasing amounts of company records are now stored in computerized or magnetic media. Therefore, increasing emphasis must be given to EDP records.

Developing the Vital Records Program

There are some very basic questions to be considered, as follows:

- What is vital and what are the vital records?
- What are the types and levels of disaster that can affect the vital records?
- What are the most suitable protection methods to be used?

The first question involves the process of identification of what is vital and what is not. It also involves a classification process to determine "levels" of vitalness. Many records thought to be vital may only rank very low in the list of what is functionally needed in case of disaster. In some respects, actually the chain of what leads to the ultimate vital records may be more important. A number of classifications exist for determining vitalness. These can be along the lines of confidentiality or along the lines of vitalness; both concepts must be kept in mind. One must also consider computerized records kept outside EDP. Records may be classified as vital, important, backup, and useful.

When determining the types of catastrophes one must think in terms of types of threats: fire, water damage, earthquake; humanly inflicted threats, such as bombs and theft; and accidental sources of threats, such as may stem from equipment malfunction and operator errors (file obliteration). See also Chapters 14, 15, and 16, especially concerning protection and storage of duplicate records in off-site premises.

Testing the Vital Records Program

It is a good idea to validate the vital records backup program. See Chapter 15 for additional checklists on this.

Vital Records Checklist

1. What are key functions of the company?
2. How are these functions supported by records?
3. What are the key functions that must be reconstructed?
   a. Employee records?
   b. Stockholders' records?
   c. Customer records (receivables)?

4. What information is required by vital functions?
5. How is such information captured, recorded, stored?
6. Is information stored in several forms?
7. What information is in EDP form?
8. Which files, records are critical?
9. How are they generated and by whom?
10. What hard-copy documents exist? Are there duplicates?
11. Are there records dispersed among many locations or individuals?
12. What IRS regulations affect your record retention program?
13. What regulatory agencies require special records retention and which are these?
14. Are there any contracts requiring records backup, such as government contracts?
15. What are regulatory agency audit requirements? (Comptroller of the currency for national banks, etc.)
16. Are there clearly defined vital records retention cycles? Schedules?
17. Who is responsible for the vital records program and for its maintenance?
18. Has the record retention program been tested? See "Testing the Recovery Program" in Chapter 16.
19. Are there adequate facilities for retrieval of records and reconversion to readable form, if in machine-readable form?
20. Is there a formal document describing the vital records program? Is this document properly backed up and limited in circulation to those duly authorized?
21. Is the vital records program monitored and audited?

A Generalized Checklist for Executives

As a first guide for executives and managers, the generalized checklist given below can be used to obtain an overall feeling for the soundness (or lack thereof) of the operation of their EDP complex. A high percentage of "no" answers may be indicative of problems which may call for further studies and special attention.

1. Have you issued a formal document stating key "management control objectives" for EDP systems?
2. Are EDP objectives identified in relation to company goals?
3. Are key priorities established for computer applications?
4. Is the EDP function reporting at a high level and is it properly structured?

5. Are there short-term and long-term plans for EDP systems?
6. Are feasibility studies conducted for every new system, and are projects properly justified?
7. Are there clearly defined measures of performance for EDP?
8. Are results forthcoming on time and with professional quality?
9. Are the users satisfied with the services they receive?
10. Are systems cost-effective?
11. Are systems timely?
12. Are systems well-protected?
13. Do systems have sound systems of internal control built in during the development phase?
14. Is the EDP manager management-oriented as opposed to technically-oriented?
15. Are systems personnel of broad caliber?
16. Is turnover relatively low?
17. Are users involved in systems development?
18. Are users properly educated in EDP and indoctrinated in the EDP systems?
19. Are projects completed on time?
20. Are systems well-tested before they are declared operational?
21. Are systems and programs changed frequently; if so, why?
22. Are changes substantiated, approved, and well-documented and reviewed by auditors?
23. Are physical and data security procedures adequate?
24. Do you review EDP activities at least once a year?
25. Is there a strong internal audit function for EDP?
26. Are operations reviewed constantly?
27. Is a postaudit of EDP system projects conducted for every major system?
28. Do you have a good overall feeling for the EDP function and its problem areas?
29. Are there clearly defined policies and a manual of standard practices for EDP?
30. Are there adequate backup and recovery procedures?
31. Is there a sound vital records program, and are you aware of its contents?

14

Physical Protection

PURPOSE

The purpose of the physical protection program for EDP is to safeguard corporate assets by lessening the chances that damage can occur to the computer complex, data and information, and personnel, as a result of hazards to which the organization may be exposed. Physical security embodies a whole range of elements when one considers the viewpoint of the total organization's needs. Since the emphasis of this manual is on EDP-related protection, the guidelines presented here are concerned primarily with the security of the EDP complex. Many other general security practices used for protecting other areas of the firm, also enhance EDP protection. These usually fall within the province of the security officer of a firm.

HAZARDS WHICH PHYSICAL SECURITY COULD HELP PREVENT

A small sample of case histories which a sound physical security program could have helped prevent or, at least, minimized, are quoted from a variety of newspapers.

> "A member of an antiestablishment group invaded the computer center and unloaded a revolver into the brain of the computer hoping to damage the total system. Fortunately for the company, the attacker did not know any better. Had he decided to ruin the file library, the damage might have been more serious."
>
> "A discontented employee stole the company's master file of more than 2 million customer names and sold them to an eager competitor. Estimated loss to the firm was $3 million."
>
> "A bitter employee of a West Coast electronics firm man aged to destroy virtually every one of the company's computer files and programs."
>
> "It seems almost incredible how easily a computer tape can be destroyed. At one company, an employee inadvertently attached his magnetic flashlight to the side of a tape cabinet

while cleaning the interior. Result: The company lost six full days of computer time while it reconstructed the data the magnet had erased from the tapes. Another computer service man forgot he had a magnet in his toolbox while working near tapes. His oversight destroyed some 80,000 of a credit company's customer records, which had to be re-created from hard-copy files at a cost of $10,000."

PHYSICAL PROTECTION PROGRAM ELEMENTS

The physical protection program must be concerned with a number of elements, each requiring careful thought and diversified skills in the preparation and execution. The classification into the seven components given below, although somewhat arbitrary, is designed to show the main areas of concern to EDP physical protection. It also provides for a finer, easier-to-use, breakdown of the checklists than if all factors were grouped in one single grand list:

1. Access Control
2. EDP Center Location
3. Construction and Building Considerations
4. Environmental Support
5. Fire Protection
6. Protected Storage (Vaults)
7. Housekeeping and Maintenance Program

ACCESS CONTROL

Objectives

- To limit the approach, admittance, and actual access of personnel to the EDP complex to those duly authorized on a "need to be there" basis.
- To detect unauthorized or illegal entry into the EDP security perimeter.

General

Access control is an important part of any security system and represents the first line of defense. Industrial security people say that one must thwart the craving often created by a simple availability. The EDP security system must prevent unnecessary availability by using any combination of the following and other procedures:

- Security perimeter.
- Fenced areas, locked doors, and alarm systems.

- Armed guards and canine patrols.
- Television monitors.
- Personnel identifications and use of access devices. (Visual, voiceprint, fingerprint, badge, password, etc.)

The first line of defense is to set a security perimeter. There should, if possible, be only one entrance used into the building, with a guard stationed there at all times. All windows and doors should have alarm devices. Any attempt to get into the building by other than the main door should trigger an alarm to the guard and to a central point. The guard should inspect all packages into and out of the complex to ensure against explosives or firearms being carried into the building or to prevent valuable data from leaving the premises. A checklist of do's and don'ts should be provided to security guards and personnel for searching, if necessary.

Access to the computer facility should be limited to those whose presence is needed. The day of the computer as a showpiece is gone. Visitors should be limited and always accompanied by a supervisor or duly authorized escort. Security equipment detailed under "Construction and Building Considerations" should be used. Employees should wear color-coded badges. One color would enable the wearer to go into all parts of the data processing department, except the computer room. Another color would provide entry to the computer room. Despite card colors, moreover, face recognition or introduction of a new employee by the supervisor, helps control unwanted visitors. Also, a log of all visitors should be kept. Any visitor permitted to take anything from the computer room or tape vault should be required to sign a receipt, after prior inspection of the item. Auditors may want to crash the access security barriers by attempting to gain admission or remove objects from the EDP center, in an effort to test the access control system. (See the material on housekeeping later in this chapter.)

Access Control Checklist

1. Do you have an access control, zone security, and intrusion detection program?
2. Is access to the computer area restricted to selected personnel having a legitimate mission there?
3. No one should have unrestricted access to all areas.
4. There should be a roster of personnel authorized to enter the security perimeter, and it should be kept "current."
5. Some steps or provisions to be considered in protecting computer security are:
   a. Closed circuit television surveillance, plus electronic devices for detecting magnets in possession of personnel entering data processing areas.

b. Establishing guards at the entrances to computer centers and requiring identification badges to be worn by personnel having access to such areas.
c. Inspecting packages brought into or out of the centers.
d. More stringent security checks on personnel, particularly those who work on second and third shifts, even night cleaning crews (usually outsiders).
e. Limiting areas to which visitors have access. Only personnel with a "need to know" or "need to be there" are permitted in the computer center. It will often be wise to extend this provision to restrict critical-area visiting within the computer center.
f. Are personnel trained to challenge improperly identified visitors?
g. Can an individual gain access to the data center during off-shift hours without the knowledge of a security guard or another employee?
h. Do you utilize keys, cipher locks, and other security devices to control access?
i. Protection during working hours includes multilevel access control means (redundancy principle), as follows:
–Receptionist at entrance to area.
–Log-in and log-out procedure. (Use of badge-key system for limited access.)
–Guard service.
–Badge system.
–Electric locks (double doors).
–Restricted entry policy.
–A pass procedure for taking in or taking out packages.
–Devices which detect unauthorized removal of tapes and discs or the bringing in of magnets.
–Sanitation area (a prescreening room prior to actual entry to the data center, at which checks for ID, magnets, objects, takes place).
j. Protection against entry after working hours includes:
–Guard service (log-in and log-out).
–Door alarms installed and periodically tested.
–Door locks secure and in use.
–Authorization pass for after-hours work.
–Roster of authorized personnel and schedules for regular off-hours personnel and special permission for occasional personnel.
–Set of clearance provisions for equipment and software vendor personnel.
k. Do you discourage advertising the location of your computer?
l. Is the computer room screened so that it is not visible from the street?

6. Discouraging militant groups calls for protection methods which stress

lower visibility of the center. Directories should be less available. Reduce general publicity. Data center phones should be restricted.

a. Where applicable, install bulletproof glass and riot doors and reduce exposure of equipment and files to window walls.

EDP CENTER LOCATION

Objective

- To reduce the risk of hazards by selecting the best physical location for the computer center.

General

Judicious choice of the "outer location" might avert a computer catastrophe. If choice of building location is possible, one should consider possible catastrophes. If the area is subject to hurricanes and/or floods, don't build on the waterfront. Select a higher and protected location instead. Don't build over a fault. There might not be an earthquake, but if there is one, damage normally is much greater over the fault. Select or erect a strong fireproof building in a safe location. It would, for example, be foolish to have such a building at the end of a busy airport runway or next to an explosives plant. Similarly, sharing a building with a firm housing volatile materials would increase the danger of a catastrophic fire. Do not locate the center at the end of a road intersection.

Location *within the building* should also be considered. The safest location is as close to the center of the building as possible, and on the lower floors. In a multibasement building it may be on the first floor below the street level. This would provide the best protection from sabotage and against radar. Of course, if it were necessary to put the computer in a building close to a waterfront subject to floods, a second or third floor location may be preferable. The lower in the building the computer is, the less will be the danger of earthquake damage. Aside from these precautions, one should select a location away from the regular stream of pedestrians, out of sight, and not contiguous to danger areas. For example, the computer center should not be next to the Selective Service office or munitions manufacturing offices or unattractive areas of town, since these may be often the objects of protests. In such protests your data center may become a target.

Everything being the same, the computer should be located above ground floor level, although such an arrangement may cost somewhat more from a support viewpoint. When leasing part of a multitenant building, contiguous floors above and below should be inspected for structural soundness and fire/flood/drainage problems. Contiguous areas on the same floor should also be reviewed for the absence of combustibles, incompatible operations (e.g., film development laboratory on the floor above). Briefly, in selecting the location inspect the north, south, east, west, above and below contiguous areas, for safety as well as the neighborhood's location.

EDP Center Location Checklist

1. What is the physical location of the computer?
   a. The computer area should be located away from explosive manufacturing or processing plants, centers of magnetic or radar activity, stairwells, storage depots, receiving docks, gas mains, flammable fluids, and major sources of vibration.
2. Is the computer center subject to possible damage through flooding or water seepage?
3. Do you have adequate drainage provisions under the raised floor? The floor above?
4. Are overhead pipes for water, steam, and gas forbidden except for the sprinkler piping system?
5. Are provisions for drainage of contiguous areas adequate to prevent water overflow from above floors or from neighboring areas?
6. Have you inspected the quality of foundations and drainage provisions of the floors above the center?
7. Is the data center located away from main highways, airline flight paths, and roads feeding perpendicular to the center itself?
8. Does the center have a window showcase for public display near the street?
9. Is the center located in an undesirable high-crime area?
10. If the center is located in a basement floor, are flood drainage capabilities and evacuation paths provided for?
11. If located in an old building, have the electrical, sewage, and water systems been reviewed for safety?
12. Is the center located away from elevator shafts to avert intruders' access (this chould permit the possibility of an intruder throwing a bomb at the center and making a quick get-away).

    (See also the material under "Environmental Support" in this chapter.)

CONSTRUCTION AND BUILDING CONSIDERATIONS

Objective

- To ensure that the building and construction requirements for the EDP complex are sound and meet good code or standard practices of safety and security.

General

Considering that fire and water damage contribute most frequently to EDP damage, they should be considered in construction design.

Fireproof, computer sites constructed in fireproof buildings provide the best protection against fire. To prevent damage from leaks, no wet pipes should be in the computer installation. Carbon dioxide fire extinguishers could be dangerous to people. Sprinkler systems can damage the computer severely. Halon 1301 is a less destructive fire extinguisher but costs more than carbon dioxide or water.

Most sprinkler systems have wet pipes, which have the ever-present danger of leakage. There is, however, a dry pipe sprinkler system (also called "on-and-off" and "on-again," systems). If the temperature below the sprinkler rises to 140°F a solenoid allows water to flow into the pipe. If the temperature below the sprinkler approaches 212°F water is released. When the temperature drops below 140° the sprinkler turns off.

Faraday cages or RF shielding provide the best protection against emanations from external sources for very sensitive data centers. These precautions, however, are costly. Grounding will help dispel the energies of such emanations.

The use of window baffles can keep radar beams from destroying records. Better, do not have magnetic files exposed to windows.

A voltage regulator with a fly-wheel should keep power fluctuations within the plus or minus 10 percent range. In case of power stoppage it will enable a "slow stop," thus preserving data. Temperature and humidity controls will prevent many computer malfunctions.

Carpeting on the floor normally should be avoided. Carpets cause static electricity to build up when the humidity is low. Cases of trouble with programs failing because of static electricity generated from plastic-covered chairs and from carts being pushed near the computer have occurred.

Locked, maximum-security doors provide the best protection against undesired intrusion. A plain lock, which can be opened easily from inside the installation is preferable. Under normal conditions, locks opened by specially treated cards work very well. If for any reason, such as fire, the electricity is cut off, these locks do not work. Optional means also are available,so that people can get in or out of the installation. In an Air Force base with a tube computer, a card identification lock was used. A power failure shut down the computer and the air conditioning system. Personnel could not get out for hours. Had the power been cut by fire, a tragedy might have resulted. Special doors must be used for data centers requiring shielding protection against emanation of sensitive data. In the 1970 California earthquake, the door to a computer room could be opened only by the guard outside. He fled, leaving the computer operator imprisoned in the computer room.

To protect against both unwarranted intrusion and the carrying of metals to the computer room, a double door system or "sanitizing area" with a scanning zone between might be used. The first door, opened by a key, must be closed and locked before the person entering is able to pass through the electronic metal scanner. He then can open the inside door if he passes inspection. If not, an authorized person must clear his access or admission.

For protection against theft, unauthorized use of the computer, and sabotage during off-hours, closed circuit TV provides comparatively inexpensive protection. A continuous picture of the computer installation can be relayed to the guard's station. If the danger is great enough an ultrasonic or infrared detector system, with alarms to both the guard and a central point, will supply added protection.

There should be a minimum of outside windows. This can help avoid outside radar interference and water condensation on cold days. Also, this can minimize the danger of unauthorized entry, when the intruder cannot penetrate the main access door.

Construction and Building Checklist

Computer Room Access

1. Limit the number of entrances. Have them where inspection can be practiced.
2. Limit night entrance to only one.

Prevention Measures

1. Building design which provides protection against fires, floods, etc.
2. Radio-interference shielding. Installing baffles in windows to deflect radiation waves.
3. Computer room shielding against electromagnetic emanation and electronic eavesdropping.
4. A good system of fire prevention, detection, and fighting measures which should be periodically reviewed by insurance, building, and fire department inspectors.
5. Emergency power shutoff.
6. Emergency pumps.
7. Fire drill procedures and practice drills.
8. Consider discussing requirements from a fire insurance costs viewpoint.
9. Raised flooring is made of noncombustible material.
10. Ceiling and floor of computer area is constructed of a noncombustible, watertight material.
11. Generators or transformers are located outside of computer area.

12. The building's water and steam pipes do not pass through the computer area.
13. Machine cables or wiring does not pass through an area containing combustible material.
14. Backup battery or generator lighting is available.
15. Drainage facilities are adequate.
16. False flooring supports are constructed of noncombustible materials.
17. False floor removal tools are available and their location is clearly identified.
18. Openings in the false floor are properly screened to prevent debris entrance.
19. Power and communication lines are underground if possible.
20. All machine electrical power lines are double faced.
21. The room's lighting power supply is separated from the computer and air conditioning power supply.
22. Separate computer air conditioning and lighting emergency power off switches are located near exit ways. Power and air conditioning switches should be linked. (In case of fire, the air conditioning system may induce the fire to penetrate through ducts or carry combustion products out of the fire source and into other areas.)
23. All emergency power off switches and their locations should be clearly marked.
24. Wire mesh cages should be installed on the emergency switches to avoid accidental power shut off.
25. Electrical wiring should not be located near air ducts or other serviceable objects.
26. Recording and control instruments for monitoring environmental conditions should be checked regularly.
27. Air conditioning system should be properly filtered and filters checked regularly.
28. Oil should not be used to increase air filter efficiency.
29. Fresh air intake should be located above ground floor level and away from smoke stacks, sources of combustion, or dust.
30. Air intake outside building should be screened with ¼-inch mesh.
31. Windows should be constructed of wire mesh base material.
32. Fire dampers should be installed in air conditioning ducts.
33. Fire curtains or window shutters should be on all openings.
34. Curtains, paint, and wallpaper should be of the flame retardant variety.

35. Computer installation furniture and ornaments should be of the non-combustible or non-fire-supporting type.
36. Fire-rated walls from floor to ceiling should preferably be used.
37. There should be no "hot spots" in the computer room due to improper distribution of air flow.
38. Use fire dampers in air conditioners which are actuated when the temperature rises.
39. Make sure emergency power shut-off controls are easily accesible and near exit points.
40. Power for emergency lighting should be provided via battery-powered equipment at key areas of the computer room. Test these occasionally.
41. Have smoke detectors and test them periodically.
42. Use doors with overlaps at the adjoining ends to prevent data emanation through door cracks.

ENVIRONMENTAL SUPPORT

Objective

- To minimize detrimental effects to the EDP equipment and data stored in various media through the observation of sound practices for EDP environmental support equipment operation.

General

Some experts claim that failure of the environmental control equipment is more likely to occur than failure of the EDP equipment. Environmental failure can cause temporary damage to data files. Air conditioning failure can cause cards, tapes, and disks to become temporarily unreadable. Often, it is necessary to restore the media to the appropriate levels of temperature and humidity through reconditioning by exposing the media to the prescribed conditions over a period of 12 to 24 hours. This is why manufacturers recommend conditioning of media stored in remote storage units by storing them in the computer area for a period of time before processing. Unusual power failures may also cause some processing problems, such as is the case with power brownouts, although the possibility of damage to the file itself is somewhat remote.

The control and maintenance of computer facilities at precise levels of temperature and humidity are prime prerequisites for trouble-free operation. Although the many spec sheets issued by EDP equipment manufacturers claim that hardware may function at temperatures ranging from 50° to 95°F and a relative humidity (RH) of 20% to 90%, actual computer room site-requirements for the major mainframes are much more stringent. A computer "comfort index'' of 72°F + 2° and an RH level of 50% + 5% is the norm. Deviations above or below these critical values are bound to cause malfunctions in system operations.

Environmental Problems

Afflictions which plague many computer installations with inadequate or improperly designed environmental conditioning systems involve the following:

Poor temperature control and air distribution—Most computer equipment is cooled internally by air drawn in from floor-level vents. Cooling air is forced past heat-producing circuitry or components, heated, and then discharged upward toward the ceiling. Improper distribution or delivery of cooling air to the computer intake vent, or an overall lack of cooling system capacity, results in higher operating temperatures and increased component failure.

High relative humidity levels—Moisture-laden air with an RH in excess of 80 percent corrodes electrical contacts, causing equipment malfunction or total failure. High humidity levels can also affect the operation of paper-handling EDP devices (card/paper tape readers and punches, OCR readers, printers). Paper expands in excessive RH environments, resulting in an increased incidence of card jams, forms misfeeds, etc.

Low relative humidity levels—Static electricity associated with low RH affects the operation of magnetic tape or disk, and paper-handling peripherals. Static discharge disrupts read-write operations for tapes and disks, and the presence of static charges on paper surfaces brings on jams or misfeeds due to paper sticking.

Considerations in Minimizing Air Quality Problems

The first step in preventing environmental problems is to isolate the computer room from external heat/humidity sources and sinks.

Site selection and preparation—The preferred location for a computer room is in an interior building area free of windows and adjacent to conditioned office or factory space. Where an external site location is mandatory (exposure to an outside building wall or to adjacent unconditioned areas), windows should be partitioned-over to thermopane glass installed. Doors that access outdoor or unconditioned areas should be gasketed. Double-door configurations should also be considered where traffic in and out of the computer room is high.

The computer room site should be insulated and vaporproofed. Vaporproofing is a must, even for sites adjacent to conditioned areas. Building or office air conditioning operates at RH (relative humidity) ranges of 20% to 30%; maintaining a computer room at 50% RH with an inadequate vapor barrier is almost impossible—even with an over-capacity computer air conditioning unit.

Fresh air input (makeup air) for ventilation of computer facilities should be filtered to remove dust particles. For large installations—those requiring over 200 CFM of ventilation or over 7000 square feet in area—or smaller facilities fed from an unconditioned area, a separate makeup air system is required. This system filters/heats/cools, and controls the humidity of ventilation air to rough tolerances, not necessarily equal to those required by the computer room.

Packaged computer air/environmental conditioners—Simple comfort air conditioning units or systems built for human consumers cannot meet the critical conditioning requirements of computer equipment. Besides differences in relative humidity levels (20% to 30% RH for humans versus 45% to 55% for computers), other variations in conditioning are encountered. A typical office, 1000 square feet in area, requires from 2.5 to 6.5 tons of conditioning; an equal size computer room needs from 10 to 20 tons. Likewise, cool air circulation for this same office area is at rates of 1000 to 2500 CFM; the computer facility would require from 4000 to 10,000 CFM. Most computer facilities also experience periodic changes in equipment placement, brought about by system expansion or site relocation. The air conditioning system must, therefore, be flexible enough to allow for such rearrangements of processing equipment with a minimum expenditure of time, labor, and money.

Packaged air/environmental air conditioning systems have been designed to meet the varied needs of computer operations. These packaged systems come complete with internal cooling, heating, and humidification modules, and sensitive, fast-response controls to maintain temperature and RH within critical computer limits. They are configured with high efficiency air filters and fan assemblies which ensure the flow of clean conditioned air in the computer room. Packaged units are mobile. They can be moved within an existing site or to a new location. They are also very flexible when employed with raised floor computer installations. Using the raised floor area as a plenum, packaged conditioners can deliver cool air directly to floor-level equipment intake vents via strategically placed and adjustable floor grill panels. New equipment arrangements can be easily accommodated by simply moving grill panels.

Packaged computer room conditioners come in capacities that allow dedicating individual units to the separate components of an EDP system. This modularity provides a means of eliminating temperature and humidity "hot" spots that may exist in a large computer room, especially sites supplied by ceiling cool air ducts. Operating (electric power) costs will be reduced since only those conditioners servicing an active or heat-producing room area are providing cooling; other units will be on idle status. Modularity also provides for cooling system redundancy. A computer facility requiring 20 tons of conditioning may be supported by three 10-ton units; continuous operation is ensured even if one of the conditioners is out of service. Finally, the availability of packaged systems rated at capacities lower than 10 tons allows the economical conditioning of small computer systems; cooling power can be configured to the needs of the small system user.

Where possible, conditions leading to static electricity, dust and particulate material, smoke and vibration should be avoided. For example check sorters reading checks at a high rate can shed a great deal of paper lint.

Cooling Loads

Figure 14-1 presents the cooling load factors to be considered when calculating the needs of a computer facility. When the computer room is located in an interior area surrounded by conditioned space, only those factors relating to lighting, personnel, makeup air ventilation and computer equipment need be considered. Depending on the type of packaged conditioning system employed (air-, water-, glycol- or chilled water-cooled) and system operational levels, one ton of air conditioning capacity equals from 11,000 to 14,000 BTU/hr.

Environmental Support Checklist

Air Conditioning

1. Are air conditioning facilities adequate?

Figure 14-1
Cooling Load Calculation Guide

Unit/Component	BTU per Hour Load
Exterior Wall Areas excluding windows	5 to 11 BTU/hr per square foot dependent on exposure to sun
Thermopane Window Areas clear glass-no protection	27 to 77 BTU/hr per square foot dependent on exposure to sun
Thermopane Window Areas glass with shades, blinds, tint	21 to 51 BTU/hr per square foot dependent on exposure to sun
Roof Areas with ceiling underneath	4 to 7 BTU/hr per square foot dependent on insulation in roof
Interior Wall Areas exposed to unconditioned areas	8 to 14 BTU/hr per square foot dependent on partition material
Ceiling Areas exposed to unconditioned areas	4 BTU/hr per square foot
Floor Areas exposed to unconditioned areas	5 to 9 BTU/hr per square foot dependent on office/factory environment
Lighting	3.4 BTU/hr per watt
Personnel	500 BTU/hr per person
Fresh Air Ventilation @ 15CPM per person	340 to 825 BTU/hr per person dependent on conditioning of incoming air
Computer & Peripheral Equipment	3.4 BTU/hr per watt
Growth & Safety Factor	30% of Total BTU/hr calculated
Total Cooling Load	130% of Total BTU/hr calculated
Minimum Sensible Cooling	85% of Total Cooling Load

2. Is the air conditioning system for the EDP complex separate from that for the building?
3. Is there a backup air conditioning capability?
4. Does the system operate within the design requirements and limits?
5. Is it reliable?
6. What maintenance arrangements are available, especially in the summer?
7. Is the air intake in an adequate location so as not to pose air quality problems and dust?
8. Is the system designed for backup, i.e., several smaller units rather than a single large one?
9. How is the system set up? Does it shut down if the main power off switch is shut off?
10. Are there adequate temperature and humidity recording and controls?
11. What type of filters are used? How often are they changed and how effective are they?
12. Are there automatic dampers installed in the duct system (such as at fire walls) to prevent smoke from being blown into other areas or into the EDP room?

Power

1. Is the system equipped with voltage regulators to reduce transients?
2. Are there any provisions for brownouts (voltage reductions)?
3. Are there specific procedures for handling blackouts resulting from power failures or power disconnection from the utility company?
4. Are there alternative power source connections from the utility company or emergency generating equipment?
5. In critical installations, is there an uninterruptible power supply (UPS)?
6. What procedures are available for monitoring the quality of the power supply and for ensuring its correction?
7. How is the power line system connected to other vital parts of the total system? The air conditioning system?
8. Are power shut-off boxes located at strategic points in the EDP complex?
9. Are devices used to measure the quality of the line output, recorders, galvanometers, line voltage recorder, especially in areas subject to brownouts?

Telecommunications

1. Is protection for telecommunications and line failures adequate?
2. Are there alternative transmission means? Extra lines?
3. Are the lines monitored for errors, noise, and other failures?
4. Is there a procedure set for dealing with data communications problems which usually involve multisupplier conflicts?
5. Is the telephone switch room locked and protected?
6. Are telephone company employees properly cleared and authenticated?
7. Are "port"protection devices installed if unauthorized entry by "hackers" is expected through dial-up lines?
8. Are modem telephone numbers kept secret?

FIRE PROTECTION

Objective

- To prevent, minimize (contain), and combat conditions leading to possible damage of the EDP equipment and computerized data stored in various media.

General

Fire, along with water, ranks very high in the statistics of reasons for data processing equipment and data destruction. Fires can occur from accidental reasons resulting from poor or defective design or carelessness in the handling of materials of a combustible nature. For example, IBM experienced a serious fire in their Program Distribution Center in White Plains, NY, which was ascribed to personnel leaving packaging cartons and materials within the EDP processing area. The Volkswagen Parts Distribution Center in San Antonio likewise suffered a major fire in their EDP center a few years ago. The Pentagon lost a large number of tape files containing manpower information, as a result of a fire that originated from overheating of a supposedly noncombustible ceiling in the file library, caused by an overheated light bulb. Although one seeks to develop procedures and install measures to try to prevent fires in EDP, one must also consider measures to protect the data in case a fire did occur, or at least the capability to re-create or regenerate the data in the event of a catastrophe. (See Chapter 16.)

Some facts and opinions of fire damage to data media are as follows:

- Actual complete destruction of computer equipment is relatively rare. EDP equipment is made of fire-retardant materials. At high temperatures, the equipment will of course burn or fuse. The computer does not support combustion by itself.

- Cables are usually not a source of fire but under intense surrounding or building fire they will deform or burn.
- Tapes and disks are vulnerable to temperature. At a temperature of 150°F, a tape can be damaged if exposed for a period of time. At 250°F tapes can become damaged within 5 to 10 minutes. A tape will burn at a temperature of 1000°F or over. The point is, however, that before this high temperature level is reached, the tape can be damaged.
- Disk packs are quite delicate. At 180° or over data can be distorted. Because of this vulnerability, magnetically recorded media should be stored in fire-resistant vaults. Which files to protect are a topic for the vital records and backup and recovery programs to determine.
- Card files are subject to combustion if exposed to enough heat for a good period of time. When stored in tight decks in card files, cards have been known to survive fires, except for damage to edges and the attendant problems of removing them from files. Fire retardant card files for critical decks would be desirable. If not deformed, cards can often be reproduced.

Fire Protection of Computers

Although the frequency of incidence is low, insurance underwriters recognize fire as the greatest single cause of a maximum foreseeable loss. Electronic equipment can be replaced and stored data can be duplicated in time, but business interruption caused by a fire could be the beginning of the end for a small company. Even larger firms could experience severe losses from manufacturing downtime; lost customer goodwill; additional expenses incurred in renting or securing facilities—usually on an overtime basis.

Protection of High Value Density Areas

A drastic change in the traditional guidelines for the design of fire protection systems is necessary. Characterized as high value density, electronic equipment can be worth considerably more than the room or building that houses it. An effective means of minimizing equipment loss and, of even greater importance, eliminating downtime must be provided. Fire protection systems must be capable of:

- Detecting a fire at its incipient stage
- Providing early warning or alarm to enable personnel to attempt hand extinguishment
- Automatic (or manual) releasing of extinguishing agent when hand extinguishment fails or when the protected areas are unattended

- Utilizing an extinguishing agent that provides rapid extinguishment of the fire, that will not damage electronic equipment, and that is safe for people
- Providing additional functions, such as signaling the local fire department, shutting down equipment, closing fire dampers—all on an automatic basis

In the past, sprinkler systems have provided the main line of defense. Local building and fire codes and insurance companies have dictated that these systems be used for extinguishing building materials and paper products fires. A valve in the sprinkler head releases the water when high temperature (160°–180°F) melts a fusible link. But before a ceiling temperature of 160°F is reached, a fire could be well advanced and cause considerable damage. In addition, if the fire occurs within equipment, water cannot readily find its way into the cabinet. Although water will not generally cause permanent damage to electronic equipment, a thorough drying must be accomplished before repowering. Conductive sediments in some local water supplies can also cause problems by inducing additional short circuit paths.

Water will extinguish or contain the fire, but the time required for "clean-up" should be seriously considered by data processing managers when evaluating possible fire protection systems.

Total flooding systems using a gas as the extinguishing agent are ideal for electronic equipment and stored media. The gas rapidly disperses into all areas of the protected environment. There is no residual damage and no permanent damage to the equipment from gaseous extinguishing agents. Unless there has been fire damage to the equipment, immediate start-up is possible.

Until recently only carbon dioxide (CO_2) was available as a gaseous extinguishing agent. But the disadvantage of CO_2 was its danger to personnel. In the concentrations required to extinguish a fire, CO_2 can suffocate a person. A delay in agent discharge is, therefore, required to permit the safe evacuation of personnel from the area. This delay in extinguishment can cause additional fire damage to equipment and facilities.

In May, 1970, the National Fire Protection Association (NFPA) issued a new standard (12A) officially recognizing Halon 1301 as an extinguishing agent and setting forth recommendations for its application. Since then both Factory Mutual and Underwriter Laboratories have tested and approved fire suppression equipment designed specifically for use with Halon 1301. Here was a gaseous extinguishing agent that was ideal for high value density areas. Unlike CO_2, Halon 1301 does not extinguish a fire by oxygen displacement; it produces a chemical "chain-breaking" reaction on the combustion process itself. It is a colorless, odorless, electrically nonconductive gas that is relatively safe for people.

Despite the fact that Halon 1301 is more costly that water and CO_2, it provides the means for total damage control to high value density areas. Fire damage, water damage, clean-up, and numerous other factors are additive. An automatic fire suppression system using Halon 1301 can provide protection against property damage, business interruption, additional operating expense, and, least recoverable, lost customers.

Fire Protection Checklist

1. Make a survey of the fire-prevention steps that have been taken.
   a. Is the computer housed in a building which is constructed of fire-resistant and noncombustible materials?
   b. Is the computer room separated from adjacent areas by noncombustible fire-resistant partitions, walls, and doors? The tape library should be separate.
   c. Have the following provisions been made?
      –Smoke or fire detectors are installed in the room, false floor area, and air supply system.
      –Fire detectors are properly located.
      –A fire extinguishing system is installed in the room, and in the false floor area.
      –If a carbon dioxide fire extinguishing system is used, gas masks are available and their location clearly marked.
      –If a sprinkler system is installed, watertight plastic or metal equipment covers are available.
      –Fire protective walls around the computer area do not contain windows.
      –Fire doors are installed in all computer area access ways.
      –A separate computer area air conditioning system is installed.
      –Each individual computer system is separated by a fire partition.
      –Watertight sills are installed on all fire door tracks.
   d. Are portable fire extinguishers available?
      –Portable fire extinguishers should be available and their location clearly marked using obvious marks, circles, different paint colors.
   e. Is the computer area protected by:
      –Automatic carbon dioxide?
      –Halogenated extinguisher (Halon 1301)?
      –Water? (sprinkler system)
   f. Are safety precautions on the use of these well-known?
   g. Are there any potential fire hazards in areas contiguous to the computer and library? In floors above or below?
   h. Are auxiliary equipment, furniture, cabinets noncombustible?
   i. Is there fire detection equipment?
      –In file library?
      –Under raised floor?
      –In the ceiling?
      –In the air ducts?

j. Are there smoke detectors for the previous items?
k. Are there fire alarm boxes in key areas?

2. Initiate or strengthen the following prevention practices.
   a. Is smoking banned in the computer area?
      –Smoking should be prohibited in the computer area, without exceptions.
   b. Are paper and other supplies stored outside the computer area?
      –Combustible waste should be immediately disposed of. Cartons, packaging material should not be allowed in the EDP area.
      –The tape cleaning solvent is immediately removed from the EDP area after use.
      –Supplies should not be unpacked in the EDP room.
   c. Are operators trained periodically in firefighting techniques and individual responsibilities clearly spelled out in case of fire?
      –Personnel must be trained in firefighting, evacuation, and first aid.
      –A manual fire alarm device is located in room.
      –Fire department and Civil Defense telephone numbers are posted.
      –An emergency procedure plan is posted (See Chapter 15.)
      –Operators should be trained on the following:
      - Location of emergency power shut off and air conditioning
      - Use of emergency fire extinguishers and under what conditions to use them
      - What precaution to take (toxicity, ventilation)
      - Where are key storage areas, cabinets and their keys
      - How to brief supervisors in case of fire

      –Operating procedures for all fire extinguishing equipment should be available.
      –Emergency shut-down switches are clearly marked. Emergency power shut-off should shut down air conditioning.
   d. Are good housekeeping practices observed? (See the housekeeping section in this chapter.)
      –Space under floors is cleaned frequently for combustibles.
      –Emergency lighting is checked.
      –Hand extinguishers are checked.
      –Smoke detectors are checked.
   e. Are emergency access and evacuation exits functioning properly? If electrically operated, does battery emergency system work?
   f. Do the fire alarms register or sound in areas outside the EDP complex where personnel are available 24 hours a day?
   g. Can firefighting stations be called from key areas?
   h. Is fire insurance protection available?
   i. Is firefighting equipment inspected regularly?
   j. Are key files stored in fire-protected vaults, preferably outside the EDP room?

k. Are fire walls built from ceiling to floor?
l. Are critical areas rated for the number of protection hours (2,4), and are protection walls provided for them (e.g. tape library)?
m. Are other key storage areas fire-protected, such as the off-site records and files storage?

PROTECTED STORAGE (VAULTS)

Objectives

- To provide protected storage facilities for the safekeeping of data and records against possible permanent destruction from fire and water damage.
- To minimize the danger of intentional destruction by denying access to key files to all but authorized personnel. (Access to protected storage applies to both internal and off-premises personnel, especially at off-hours and on holidays.)

General

Protected storage comprises primarily three types of data or asset-protective shelters:

- Safes and special containers
- Vaults
- Protected rooms

A detailed account of these is beyond the scope of this manual. Reference manuals on security and fire protection should be consulted for more details, such as those listed at the end of this section. For information on heat damage to tapes and other media see the material on "Fire Protection" earlier in this chapter.

Most of the protected storage devices or facilities are designed to protect contents against robbery and/or fire. Fire resisting containers are classified by the Underwriters' Laboratories. (See Reference 2 following.) They are listed as Classes A,B,C,D,E, and 150; a brief description of each follows.

Class A — Good for 4 hours with the temperature reaching 2000°F. The interior temperature one inch from the walls is not to exceed 300°F.

Class B — Good for 2 hours with temperatures reaching 1850°. Interior temperature one inch from the wall not to exceed 350°F.

Class C — Good for 1 hour with temperatures approaching 1700°F. Interior temperature same as for Class B.

Class D — Same as for Class C. The interior temperature at the center of the container or 7½ inches from any wall is not to exceed 350°F.

Class E Good for ½ hour with temperatures approaching 1550°F. Interior temperature limits same as for Class D.

Class 150 Good for containers in which the temperature must not exceed 150°F. A Class 150, one-hour container is capable of maintaining the temperature from rising above 150°F for one hour. These are used for protecting disks, tapes, and cards.

Storage rooms are containers constructed for the storage of records where the storage volume required is larger than for safes or vaults. The Department of Defense has guidelines for the construction of such enclosures. (See Reference 7 following.)

Reference Guidelines

Safes

1. Underwriters' Laboratories, Inc., "Burglary Resistant Safes," UL 687. 333 Pfingsten, Rd., Northbrook, IL 60062.
2. Underwriters' Laboratories, Inc., "Fire Resistant Classification of Record Protection Equipment," No. 72.
3. Underwriters' Laboratories, Inc., "Security File Containers," UL 505.

Vaults

4. National Fire Protection Association, "Standards for Protection of Records," Pamphlet 232, Battery March Park, Quincy, MA 02269.
5. Underwriters' Laboratories, Inc., "Fire Resistance Classification of Vault and Fire Storage Room Doors," UL 155 and UL 669.
6. U.S. Department of Defense, Office of Civil Defense, "Protection of Vital Records," FG-F 3.7, Superintendent of Documents, Washington, DC 22161.
7. U.S. Department of Defense, "Industrial Security Manual for Safeguarding Classified Information," DOD5220.22-M, Appendix IV, "Outline Construction Specifications for Storage Vaults," Superintendent of Documents, Washington, DC 22161.
8. General Services Administration Interim Federal Specification AA-D-00600a (GSA-FSS), "Door, Vault, Security," Superintendent of Documents, Washington, DC 22161.
9. U.S. Atomic Energy Commission, "AEC Security Manual," Superintendent of Documents, Washington, DC 22161.

Protected Storage Checklist

1. Is there a formal procedure for protected storage administration and review?

2. Are the responsibilities for protected storage procedures clearly assigned?
3. How does the protected storage program fit in with the overall vital records program? With the tape/disk library procedures?
4. Has a security perimeter been established for the storage of key records and for the location of the key protected storage facilities (safes, vaults)?
5. Is there a map showing the protected storage areas and a detailed list or inventory of what is kept where and why?
6. Is there a fire-resistant vault to store all key files, operating systems? (A Class 150 safe can be used to protect magnetic tapes which can be damaged above temperatures of 150°F.)
7. Are adequate fire-resistive ratings provided for various types of protected storage, such as, two-hour, four-hour, six-hour vaults according to records being stored?
8. Are burglary and fire-protection capabilities considered for protecting vital records?
9. Have manufacturers' specifications for magnetic tape protection been observed?
10. Are appropriate protective canisters used for the transportation of key tape files to and from the off-site storage facility?
11. If government documents and data are under custody, are their specifications for record protection being followed?
12. When changes in personnel with access to confidential information occur, is a debriefing procedure followed? Is the security officer or person in charge notified of such changes to ensure locks are changed, passwords modified, combinations protected, storage devices monitored?

HOUSEKEEPING AND MAINTENANCE PROGRAM

Objectives

- To ensure that proper housekeeping and maintenance practices are observed in the EDP center.
- To ensure that appropriate safeguards for fire protection, humidity controls, and temperature control are enforced.

General

Insisting on immaculate housekeeping methods is an important part of the physical security program. Regular maintenance by qualified engineers is also an integral part of assuring continued computer performance and good accuracy. The reviewer should inform himself of maintenance and other requirements applicable to the computer system and equipment under review. A set of rules should be developed concerning what constitutes good housekeeping and maintenance practices, and they should be monitored via periodic or surprise audits. Ground rules should be established relative to handling of supplies, maintenance equipment (magnet, diagnostic equipment, other tools), flammables, conditions and operability of admission and exit pathways, utilization of doors (normal use and emergency), routine clearing procedures for personnel admission and strangers' clearing, amount of processing supplies to be allowed within the computer area (paper, forms, etc.), disposition of packing and packaging materials (card boxes, wrappings, fillers), earmarking of areas for unpacking materials (never in the computer room), etc.

An effective way of ensuring that the adopted measures are in fact followed is to institute a housekeeping audit group. This team, which should include the auditor, should first establish a detailed checklist of all the approved procedures and practices, and develop a detailed procedure of the audit steps for surprise reviews of the EDP complex. Such a procedure might even include a check of the access security system, trying to penetrate key areas, such as the tape library and attempting to break established rules. The computer operations supervisor should be included in the team. One way to do this, and yet conduct the audit on a surprise basis, is to notify the operations supervisor of the audit only a few minutes before the team appears on the scene and have him join the review team. The team, which can be subdivided into subteams, then goes over the detailed audit procedure along with the EDP supervisor, and even additional EDP operators if necessary. This is an important part of the involvement process. By working together, the affected groups are in a position to acknowledge the findings and the shortcomings of their existing practices. This makes agreement on correction of bad practices a great deal easier to implement.

Housekeeping and Maintenance Checklist[1]

1. Has a policy been established regarding visitors, neatness, smoking, etc., in the computer center?
2. Are housekeeping policies well-established and clearly made known?
3. Is the hardware serviced by qualified engineers on a regular basis?
4. Are manufacturer's cleaning recommendations for the computer center strictly followed?
5. Are manufacturer's temperature and humidity requirements maintained?

[1]See also the material under "Fire Protection" earlier in this chapter.

6. Is the maintenance department cleaning the room carefully so as not to raise dust?
7. Are filters changed regularly?
8. Are all furniture and drapes noncombustible?
9. The following routine practices should be observed:
   a. There should be at least two persons present when power is "on" in the computer.
   b. There should be frequent removal of all waste material from the computer center area.
   c. There should not be loose cards, containers full of trash, and other miscellaneous supplies stored around the computer center.
   d. Supervisors' desks should not be used as interim or semipermanent storage or work tables for incoming data or processed reports (work tables should be used).
   e. Floors and corridors should be clear and not cluttered with documents, boxes, cards, or empty boxes. In addition to exposure, they could make evacuation difficult.
   f. Storage of paper, punched cards, and other combustible supplies should not be permitted in the operating area.
   g. Each operator should be made responsible for the cleanliness of his own equipment and work area, and for turning over a clean work area to the operator on the next shift.
   h. Operators under medication or inebriated should not be allowed to operate equipment.
   i. Dust conditions should be kept at a minimum, especially in areas where machine-readable records are kept, machine processing areas, and the file library.
   j. Specific procedures should be observed for the proper handling of tapes and disks.
   k. Equipment that produces dust and lint (such as check sorters) should not be near dust sensitive equipment such as disk and tape drives.
   l. Specific procedures should be enforced for starting up and shutting down the computer and all related auxiliaries. A more detailed procedure should be followed when shutting down for weekends, including checks of the temperature indicators and key alarms.

15

Emergency Preparedness Procedures

OBJECTIVE

The objective of emergency preparedness is to provide procedures for handling emergency conditions in the immediate aftermath of a catastrophe or major threat, in order to protect personnel, minimize the possibility of damage to the EDP installation, and reduce the magnitude of the service interruption. Emergency procedures *apply to conditions before or shortly after a serious catastrophe* and are meant to take care of unusual emergency conditions. They are temporary in nature.

GENERAL CONCEPTS

A set of emergency procedures is a very important component of the overall computer security program. The emergency procedures are usually contained in a document which spells out, in clear terms, the policies and detailed procedures to be followed in the event of a catastrophe or a major service interruption, whatever its cause.

Another important aspect of the emergency procedures is, of course, to specify the organizational structure which outlines who is responsible for initiating the necessary steps that must be taken in an emergency situation, the people who are to be informed of the events, and the authority vested in certain individuals for initiating such important tasks as notifying police and other authorities and authorizing evacuation procedures, should the latter become necessary.

As a minimum, the emergency plan and procedures should contain the following components:

1. Guidelines to determine the nature and criticalness of the catastrophe, (in other words, classification criteria), its level of seriousness, and the directions for and the types or classes of procedures to be followed.
2. A table of authorized personnel and individuals responsible for taking action in an emergency, as well as a list of the people who should be notified immediately upon the occurrence of an emergency. This should include a list of coordinators responsible for centralization and

dissemination of information during an emergency (press releases, etc.). The persons to be notified may depend on the type of emergency.

3. A communication channel to disseminate the evacuation signals to all personnel.
4. A procedure for the immediate securing of all tapes, programs, and other valuables. It may be advisable to consider the placement of certain critical tapes into fire insulated safes.
5. Designation of safe evacuation routes.
6. Designation of wardens to assist in evacuation.
7. Primary and alternate transportation routes in the event that it becomes necessary to send employees home.
8. A provision for medical assistance.
9. A procedure to request police and fire assistance.
10. A procedure to store grandfather backup tapes and data base dumps in a location separate and apart from a computer center.
11. A procedure for activating backup equipment.
12. A set of complete instructions should be provided for the following:
    - Designating an emergency headquarters where key people will operate during the emergency period
    - Locating emergency procedures as well as locations where these are available or stored
    - List of emergency telephones and key executives, such as: security officer, administrative executives, public relations, police, fire, ambulance, hospitals, data base administrator (if any) in large installations
    - Defining criteria for evacuation in the event that the proper authority cannot be reached
    - Evacuation plans and alternate plans in case of fire, bomb, or explosion
    - Handling bomb threats by mail, phone, or other methods
    - Roster of personnel and alternate personnel with specific training to handle important duties in the absence of regular staff
    - Emergency work stations or alternate facilities
    - Priority work and jobs that can be deferred
    - Minimizing damage to key files and equipment
    - Detailing emergency work, emergency pay, and extra expense compensation
    - Obtaining emergency services or processing special processing runs and acquisition of materials

- Guidelines for arranging special transportation
- Initiating the recovery procedures and beginning restoration of data processing services
- Developing a list of equipment, records, and areas to be protected with the highest priority
- Ways of estimating the most probable duration of the interruption by type of emergency
- Fire, flood, and bomb reporting and evacuation procedures
- Scheduling the testing or review of contingency plan components

RESPONSIBILITY

Management should assign the responsibility for establishing specific emergency procedures. If more than one group is involved, their respective responsibilities should be spelled out. The procedures should be posted at various locations in the computer complex. Typically the responsibility lies with the administrative services department, the security officer (if one exists) and the data processing personnel. For ease in reference, the key procedures could be printed on wallet-size cards and distributed to all affected personnel. These cards should contain items described above, such as telephone numbers for police, fire department, medical services and hospitals and the names of authorized members of management with responsibility over any adverse event.

EMERGENCY PROCEDURE TRAINING

Personnel should be trained on key emergency procedures and on the use of ad hoc equipment. One of the most common aspects of emergency training is to hold fire drills as well as indoctrination sessions on how to handle such things as telephone and bomb threats. Training may include such things as:

- How to determine the magnitude of the emergency
- When to call the appropriate authorities, fire department, and police and in what order
- How to evacuate personnel in case of emergency (including how to determine when evacuation procedures should be authorized and by whom)
- What prevention steps could be taken before evacuation, such as removal of records, key tapes and disks, vital data (and their storage in vaults)
- How to shut down electrical power switches and learning what other units are affected by the power-off (such as air conditioning)

- What procedures to initiate as soon as the emergency situation has subsided

EMERGENCY SYSTEMS TESTING

The only way to ensure that the security and protection systems are working is by actually testing them. Testing may include:

- Periodic test of the alarm systems
- Start-up of alternative facilities for power, air conditioning (see Chapter 16 for backup details)
- Testing employees with oral or written exams
- Involving the firm's auditor in evaluating the soundness of the emergency procedures before they are needed, not after it is too late

A checklist of emergency provisions follows.

Emergency Procedures and Preparedness Checklist

Emergency Procedures

1. Do you have a set of emergency assessment guidelines to be used in determining the severity of a hazard or emergency?
2. Are there specific emergency procedures to handle: natural disasters, accidental fires, bombings, outside intrusion, riots, national emergencies and, also, temporary inconveniences due to weather, flood, strike, or power failure?
3. Are the guidelines designed to meet short-term, intermediate, and long-term operations interruption?
4. Based on such guidelines, you may consider the following:
   a. Determine nature and criticalness of impending disaster.
   b. Notify management and operating personnel.
   c. Notify fire department or other responsible organizations by telephone or fire alarm.
   d. If time allows, obtain checkpoint restart data of in-process computer programs.
   e. Turn off electrical machine power.
   f. Dismount and store all magnetic tapes, disk packs, paper cards, and documentation.
   g. Close all safes, vaults, and file cabinets.
   h. Turn off room air conditioning or heating system.
   i. Cover all equipment.

   j. Release or place all window shutters and fire curtains.
   k. Activate or place all firefighting apparatus into ready status.
   l. Close all doors, windows, or other room openings.
   m. Dispose of all exposed combustible material.
   n. Place backup battery lighting, generator, and water pump into ready status.
   o. If small fire, attempt to extinguish with portable fire extinguishers.
   p. Evacuate all personnel.
   q. Verify that all fire doors and fire dampers have been released.
5. Do computer personnel know emergency procedures? Are drills held often?
6. Are security and operations personnel briefed on how to react to civil disturbances?
7. Are they familiar with local regulations or laws concerning civil disorders?
8. Do you have a working liaison program with fire, civil defense, law enforcement, and emergency units in your locality?
9. Do your personnel know how to handle telephone bomb threats? (See the procedure given later in this chapter.)
10. Can guards or other advance post individuals communicate with others under emergency conditions (two-way radios, private phone, intercom, etc.)?
11. If the catastrophe is of major proportions and you have to start anew, do you have information on the following:
   a. Equipment listing, layouts, and specifications
   b. Procurement of equipment
   c. Acquisition of supporting equipment (air conditioning, power)
   d. Manpower sources
   e. Alternate locations or existing buildings
   f. Ancillary equipment, files, cabinets, tapes, disk packs
   g. Priority list for jobs to be done along with their associated cost for delays
   h. List of service bureaus that may serve your needs
   i. Vital records list and vital records program (backup records)
   j. Mode of transportation to haul jobs back and forth to a new location
   k. Travel and possible lodging accommodations
   l. Key materials and supplies needed to operate
   m. Operating manuals
12. Are there bomb suppression blankets in the vicinity of the EDP area for use by qualified personnel?

13. Do you have a list of all key high-record concentration areas (such as the tape library) for periodic review?
14. Are there emergency lights in the tape library or vault area to enable personnel to store key files and lock the storage devices in case of emergency?
15. The plan for emergency and backup procedures (contingency plan) constitutes a key document in itself. Are copies stored in other safe locations under lock? In the off-site storage area?
16. Do emergency procedures provide guidelines for determining whether a real emergency condition exists (for example, in a fire situation calling someone else in the vicinity or looking for other signals)?
17. Is the emergency program reviewed periodically?
18. Is there formal reporting of various emergency conditions that arise indicating the nature of the emergency, the steps that were taken, their effectiveness and by whom they were exercised?
19. Are the emergency procedures kept up-to-date and copies sent to all affected and responsible parties?
20. Do internal telephone directories specify what numbers to call for various emergencies?
21. When plant additions or expansions are planned, are they checked for security and emergency procedure implications?
22. Have provisions been made to bypass certain security provisions, such as double doors, badge-operated locks, and other devices in case of serious emergencies or evacuation needs?

Emergency Preparedness

Testing for emergency preparedness should include the points listed below.

1. Fire protection checks include:
   a. Number of charged fire extinguishers throughout area.
   b. Periodic fire extinguisher inspection, and dates recorded.
   c. Location of all fire extinguishers clearly marked.
   d. Periodic tests of fire and smoke detection system are performed and dates are recorded.
   e. Emergency power/air conditioning shutoff are checked for accessibility and should be clearly marked.
   f. Inspect area beneath false floor for trash, water, cigarette butts, combustibles, etc.
   g. Ensure that all personnel exits are clearly marked.
   h. Review compliance with "no smoking" rule.

2. Water damage (leaking roof, broken water pipes above site, sprinkler system operation) protection methods check should include:
   a. Air conditioning, sprinkler system, and building water shutoff valves should be clearly marked and accessible.
   b. Emergency equipment covers should be available and locations clearly marked.
   c. They must be noninflammable.
3. Building adequacy for protection against damage from external events (hurricane, windstorm, riot) should include:
   a. Building designed with no exterior windows.
   b. If there are exterior windows, secure window shutters must be available; possibly iron grills in windows.
4. Electrical power supply alternatives should include the following:
   a. Variable supply transformer, for adjusting to changes of power supply voltage.
   b. Uninterrupted power source (UPS) such as in-house power generation.
   c. Standy motor-generator facility.
   d. Backup power from another source.
   e. Separate dual power input line.
5. Other areas to be checked include:
   a. Review of the backup storage areas where vital records are stored.
   b. Alarm devices tested periodically.
   c. Alternate facilities verified for operability and compatibility.
   d. Auditors should participate in the evaluation of the soundness and completeness of emergency procedures.
   e. A test of the viability of the vital records program is also useful. See the test procedure for vital records in the next chapter.

HANDLING AND REPORTING A TELEPHONE BOMB THREAT

In today's environment when terrorist acts are not uncommon, it is possible for organizations to be subject to a bomb threat. A well-prepared organization should have a procedure for handling telephone bomb threats. The persons who are most likely to receive such threats first should be properly indoctrinated in the procedure. These individuals may include telephone operators, secretaries, the head of computer operations, the shift supervisor, the control group supervisor and quite often high-level executives. It is also desirable to designate a specific telephone number to call to request specific and detailed instructions. It is advisable to have coordinators who may be contacted and who are properly indoctrinated and experienced in the administration of previously established emergency procedures. One should avoid a situation where those contacted may approach an unprepared person, who may likely become panic-stricken, to disseminate the news and to provide emergency instructions. A set of guidelines for handling telephone bomb threats follows.

Checklist for Handling a Telephone Bomb Threat

How to Proceed During the Bomb Threat

1. First of all, do not panic.
2. Listen intently to what the individual says.
3. Write down what the caller has to say. Pay attention to what he or she demands. *Do not* antagonize the caller.
4. Try to determine whether the caller is a male or a female.
5. Try to detect his/her accent and if possible the group that he/she claims to be associated with.
6. Try to detect other peculiarities of the person, such as voice pitch, inflection, degree of coherence in speech, and his/her general state of mind.
7. Activate a tape recorder if your area or installation has provided one for this type of situation.
8. If circumstances permit, you may ask the motive for the bomb and whether he/she is willing to disclose in which building, location within the building, and the time frame for the bomb to activate. Ask if you will receive additional signals or communications from the attacker.
9. After the verbal session, notify the appropriate person of the bomb threat so that the proper emergency and evacuation procedures can be implemented.
10. Set a meeting place to immediately brief the security coordinator on the information received and collaborate with him in every way possible.

How to Proceed After the Bomb Threat

1. Quickly evaluate the situation and make a decision on the emergency procedure to be followed.
2. Notify the police, and other authorities if deemed necessary (fire department, ambulances, etc.).
3. Establish communication with all coordinators or deputized persons in each area or floor to begin the implementation of emergency procedures. These may include evacuation of personnel, shutting down key

equipment, removal of vital processing runs (if time permits). Notify those areas that are most likely to be targets first.

4. Notify the building and engineering personnel and the maintenance personnel.
5. If the situation permits, organize the search parties with well-qualified personnel or the authorities when they arrive. Be sure to have emergency communications equipment other than the telephone, in case telephone service is disabled.
6. Put into effect any "preplanned emergency procedures" for the protection of life and vital data processing assets.

Notifying Employees of the Threat

1. When possible summon all employees and brief them about the bomb threat in a swift and calm manner.
2. Depending on the nature of the threat, you may ask them to look for suspicious packages or devices. Ask them *not* to touch or attempt to disable anything, simply report the findings.
3. Instruct them to stay calm and where they are or summon them to a previously designated safe place or shelter waiting for instructions on evacuation. Designate the evacuation routes carefully. Do not exit personnel through the exit where a bomb has exploded for fear that the structures may have weakened.
4. Stay in designated areas.
5. On evacuation, keep in mind the following:
   a. If the bomb is imminent, evacuate first.
   b. Do not use elevators (lifts) for fear that they may become inoperable or disabled on power loss.
   c. The handicapped should follow the handicapped access ways. A service elevator may be an alternative.
   d. Do not use the phone unless absolutely necessary. Too many calls may only jam the system beyond use.

How to Conduct the Search for the Bomb

Considering the seriousness of the problem, there is no single proven procedure for this task. Some guidelines follow:

1. Enlist the help of duly "trained" employees to conduct the search if there is time. Even better, engage the services of specialized SWAT police teams.
2. In addition to checking desks and obvious places, check halls, bathrooms, closets, trash containers, ashtrays in hallways, equipment in halls and vending machines, etc.

3. Have search parties report the progress of the search by expeditious communications equipment (walkie-talkies, etc.).
4. Report the areas that were searched.
5. If you see suspicious individuals, conditions, or objects, report them immediately to the appropriately designated person. Do not attempt to disarm any object or bomb. This should be done by specialized personnel.

16

Backup and Recovery Program

OBJECTIVES

The objectives of the backup and recovery program are: (a) to enable the organization to spring back to normal operating conditions in the event of temporary or permanent damage to EDP equipment or computerized data, and (b) to permit full recovery of files, and restoration of operating capability of the data processing complex, in case of a major and unavoidable disaster.

GENERAL CONCEPTS

This section has to do with the measures that should be provided to deal with a business interruption or catastrophe, after it has happened and the adverse consequences have materialized. From a planning and anticipation viewpoint, the preparation of a sound backup and recovery program for EDP can be looked at as a preventive measure. However, from the viewpoint of applying such measures in the event of a catastrophe, the procedures take place very much on an after-the-fact basis. The backup and recovery program is designed based on the premise that Murphy's Law will hold: "If it can happen . . . it will."

Backup and recovery implies a great deal more than mere equipment backup provisions. Backup and recovery embraces the following aspects:

- Provisions for short- and long-term interruptions of service
- Equipment and auxiliary equipment backup
- Data, file, and software backup and recovery (reconstruction) procedures
- Ancillary facilities, supplies, and procedures (know-how) backup
- Trained personnel backup

The need for all these elements is predicated on the concept that "the chain is no stronger than the weakest link." It is hardly consolation to have provided for equipment alternatives and not have adequate file and software (programs) backup, or to have an alternate facility but lack the up-to-date procedures properly backed up to be used when needed. It is likewise very foolish not to anticipate the need for trained personnel to operate the alternate facility, in case a disaster occurs (regular personnel may not be reachable), or in case of a general union strike; or even worse, in case your own data processing employees are unionized. In the latter case, one may have to plan for the training of supervisory nonunion personnel to operate the facility to keep service continuity.

There are essentially two main sides to backup and recovery in EDP. "Backup" is concerned with providing the necessary alternate facilities for equipment, duplicate documentation or duplicate copies of files of data, and standby trained personnel to operate the systems. "Recovery" concentrates on the very process of initiating and conducting the recovery or reconstruction process. It is procedural in nature or, at least, it is provided in the form of procedures. Both, together, have the ultimate mission of restoring operational normalcy as soon as possible.

NATURE AND TYPES OF SERVICE INTERRUPTION

Short- and Long-Term Service Interruptions

It is clear that one should distinguish between short-term (power brownouts, sporadic equipment failures, occasional unexplained processing errors, missing data, very partial destruction of a tape or disk, etc.) and long-term data center disability (stemming from storm, fire, earthquake, flood, civil disorder attacks). Some short-term interruptions might be handled routinely through backup and recovery procedures. For example, in a batch system, if a tape is destroyed or cannot be read, one could resort to the standard grandfather, father, son procedure and re-create (update) the affected file by withdrawing the backup file from the remote backup storage site and updating the transactions that were added since the last version. In an on-line system, standard file recovery procedures might be used which are usually part of the off-line reconciliation night run. This may involve the withdrawal of the latest data base dump (a copy of the data base as of the latest scheduled dump period) from the file library under protected storage and then setting up a run whereby the transactions recorded in the transaction logs (which contain the before and after images of transactions) are added to the backup dump to restore the data base to its most current status.

Long-term disability of the EDP center, on the other hand, calls for the application of more elaborate and numerous procedures which cover what it is to be done immediately after (see Chapter 15 on emergency procedures) and the application of after-the-fact measures for recovery. As part of the recovery procedures, and as mentioned in Chapter 15, criteria should be developed to assist in determining the severity of the interruption or catastrophe. These suggest the type of recovery measures that ought to be followed, which may involve a complete physical reconstruction of the whole data center.

Service Interruption Sources

The most commonly known sources of EDP service interruption, their possible consequences, and the backup/recovery means that apply are summarized in Figure 16-1. There are two main considerations connected with recovery: business interruptions resulting from data processing service interruptions and damage to or complete destruction of records and physical facilities and equipment. You may classify these into the following: temporary interruption, temporary inaccessibility, hardware damage, software loss, repairable damage, and catastrophic destruction. Each of these affects data processing services in various ways.

The common denominator of all these sources of trouble is processing delays and/or loss of valuable data or equipment. However, various classes of rules must be developed to deal with the recovery of each set of conditions.

THE AUDITOR'S ROLE

The auditor has essentially two roles to play. He should participate during the development phase of any catastrophe planning and recovery program *before* events happen. He can offer a useful service by playing the devil's advocate role, reviewing and suggesting ways to improve such a program. After the fact, the auditor can often attempt to help in the reconstruction program, but, more often, he may be asked to conduct a postmortem audit as to why things occurred or failed and what the firm could do to prevent recurrence of the event or to provide more adequate recovery provisions in the face of the inevitable. Naturally, the first role, although less glorious, is the more important. Another most important role is to instigate and participate in the periodic testing of the adequacy and workability of the contingency plan and backup and recovery provisions and issue recommendations for improvement.

HARDWARE AND AUXILIARY EQUIPMENT BACKUP

Since equipment is one of the key components of the data processing complex, backup of some sort is important. This includes temporary backup, via an alternate or duplicate unit (tape, printer) to full and long-term backup in case of major disaster. Provision should be made in advance for hardware failure, which is inevitable in the operation of any computer installation. The procedures to be followed when these failures occur will vary by type of equipment and its use in the installation. But the planning approach should include appraisal of each piece of equipment and the effects of its failure on the overall

Figure 16-1
Potential Sources of Service Interruption in EDP

SOURCE OF FAILURE OR HAZARD	ELEMENT AFFECTED	REQUIRED FOR CORRECTION
HUMAN		
• Errors (frequent)		
-Data	Files, results, delays	Reruns
-Programs	"	"
-Operator	"	"
-Control totals	"	"
• Poor instructions		
• Deliberate attacks: vandalism, riot, overt destruction	Data destruction, delays, equipment damage	Backup and recovery
• Personnel unavailable: union strike, sickness, area not accessible, transportation or communications breakdown	Delays, business disruption	Personnel backup, alternate facility
EQUIPMENT (relatively frequent)		
• Magnetic tape/disk drives	File destruction	File and data backup and recovery procedures, sound maintenance, alternate drives.
• Equipment breakdowns (various)	Lost time, reduced response time in on-line systems, possible data errors	Rerun and recovery procedures, use of alternate equipment units or graceful degradation, good maintenance practices and parts availability
• Sporadic processing errors	Lost or erroneous data	Equipment monitoring, maintenance.
• Power interruption (brownouts), power fluctuations	Lost data and time	Reruns, checkpoint and restart procedures for recovery
• Environmental support equipment (air conditioning, humidity, etc.)	Lost time, possible erroneous results	Same as item above.
• Data communications lines and equipment	Data and data base errors and results, lost transactions	File backup and recovery, off-line update runs, backup lines, alternate dial-up lines, maintenance
• Environment surrounding EDP (dirt, dust, smoke, gases)	Files and equipment may be affected	Filters, good maintenance and proper location of equipment
FREAK ACCIDENTS		
• Vehicle crashes, radar, magnets, gas explosions, and other	Business interruption, possible destruction of data and equipment	Full gamut of backup and recovery procedures depending on situation

Figure 16-1
Potential Sources of Service Interruption in EDP (Continued)

SOURCE OF FAILURE OR HAZARD	ELEMENT AFFECTED	REQUIRED FOR CORRECTION
OPERATING SOFTWARE • Software failures (relatively infrequent but do happen) • System software failures or aberrations	Data or programs in error, wrong results Lost processing time	Reruns or file recovery procedures Strong systems programming internal capability or vendor support
MISCELLANEOUS • Close-out, lockout of premises, such as when a service bureau goes bankrupt	Business interruption	Full backup and recovery program in alternate facilities
ACTS OF GOD AND NATURE • Earthquake, flood, wind, storm (ice, snow), war	Business interruption and possible data and facility destruction	Emergency provision and backup and recovery program at large

processing system. There should be a determination of the consequences of each component's failure and a plan laid out for alternate methods of processing. For example, you might tolerate a printer failure for four hours, but you might have to use a comparable installation for off-line printing if the failure lasted longer. A job priority list, based on critical applications, should also be made.

These are several possible failure situations and solutions:

Central Processor

1. Revert to planned "fallback" manual operations.
   a. Develop procedures to update files from time of failure with ensuing transactions.
   b. Train people to run manual operations for critical output. For example, send orders directly to warehouse where a computer is used for order processing system. (Manual fallback)
2. Transfer to backup facility.
   a. Determine that backup facility has same configuration.
   b. Determine effects on your company of use of a different shift.
   c. Define logistical procedures for transfer of files and programs and for transporting key personnel.

Peripheral Units

1. Substitute output units. For example, a tape drive may be substituted for an on-line printer. However, efficient substitution requires that this alternative be documented as part of operations procedures, and that full compatibility exists.
2. Transfer to backup facility.
3. Switch to alternative peripheral unit of same type. For example, an application that requires three tape drives for running should probably have a fourth backup unit, as part of the configuration as protection against failure. A computer feasibility study should provide for protection against failure of critical units within the confines of financial reality.
4. Operate in downgraded mode. This amounts to operation with less than full capacity, such as when part of primary memory fails, or a few drives falter. The defective portions of the system are blocked out while repairs take place. This is also called operating in a graceful degradation mode. Processing speed is affected, the number or size of jobs may suffer. In an on-line system, response time usually slows down. However, the whole operation does not stop.

Alternatives for Full Equipment Backup

There are several alternatives for providing equipment backup, as follows:

–*Using another data center within your own organization but at another location* if you have multiple and compatible installations.

–*Resorting to the "mutual aid partner" alternative* whereby arrangements are made with another organization to serve as backup via a formal contractual agreement.

–*Contracting "third-party, hot-site" facilities* from organizations devoted to selling this service under contract. A hot-site facility has equipment and system software facilities to permit a group of affected organizations to run their system applications for a predetermined period of time until they rebuild their own.

–*Using a service bureau* for some or most of the critical applications, under preagreed terms, if one can be found that can support your installation.

–*Using your computer vendor's customer test installation* on an interim basis. This might be possible when you are in a remote area where the only compatible facility available is the vendor's installation.

–*Using computer networks* where other units in the network can serve as backup units for the affected unit. This arrangement has the advantage that the transport of data is facilitated via telecommunications. It can be a viable alternative for advanced/on-line systems.

–*Combinations of the above alternatives* to house the various critical applications of your company. For example payroll may go to the service bureau and other more unique applications to compatible equipment alternatives.

–*Using the "empty shell" arrangement.* In this alternative, the organization has a data center building facility at another location with ready power, air conditioning, etc., to support a new computer system. At the same time specific agreements and arrangements are made with the computer equipment vendor to supply, on a priority basis, new equipment of the same configuration, as soon after the catastrophe as possible. Arrangements for survival during this reinstallation period must be provided to continue business operations, even by manual fallback means.

No single alternative is best for all organizations. A study and analysis of all the possibilities seeking to match your situation to the appropriate alternative backup solution must be made. For more details on this important topic, consult a book devoted solely to contingency planning, such as *How to Prepare an EDP Contingency Plan for Business Continuity,* (Wellesley Hills, MA: Management Advisory Publications, 1986).

ON-LINE SYSTEMS BACKUP

Concerning on-line systems, it can be stated that seldom does equipment backup have a real meaning. The reasons for this are very apparent. First, it is highly unlikely that any one potential backup organization would have the array of equipment and peripherals required to fully back up an on-line system of your particular configuration down to the remote terminals. Second, even if a replica "mutual-aid partner" installation were to be found, it is very unlikely that it could have the capacity to absorb a "second" installation at precisely the same operating time without sacrificing response time and even be able to host two on-line systems. The only kind to back up for on-line systems usually turns out to be: (a) design for high reliability (redundancy in some files and equipment), (b) operation in a downgraded mode under graceful degradation (slower processing of the most urgent jobs), and (c) in case of total destruction of hardware facilities and/or building, the only real backup amounts to agreements with the vendor to replenish the desired configuration on some other premise within a preagreed time period, or the use of *network* backup, if available, until your own installation is rebuilt. The key element of backup here becomes then, the contract agreement with the vendor and the file and records backup through the off-site storage facility. The net result in the interim can amount to a real business disruption, temporary manual mode of operation (if at all feasible) or processing of a few key reports in a batch mode in a service bureau (usually not very much). The net conclusion is that backup for on-line systems must be carefully planned as part of the design of the system. The ideal full backup alternative is the use of twin data center installations which is affordable only by the very few (NASA, some banks, extremely EDP-dependent organizations).

DATA, FILE, AND SOFTWARE BACKUP

Provision for data, procedures, and software backup is an absolute must. In fact, one can reason that equipment can always be replaced in the ultimate sense. Data that is destroyed *without backup* provisions could be lost forever. In this section we are concerned primarily with physical backup. Data protection and recovery procedures are also discussed in Chapter 17. The most common measure to provide records backup is to store them in an off-site location. Possibilities for off-site storage locations include the following:

1. Another branch of the company. This is a step in the right direction but, if adopted, involves a number of potential problems and inadequacies. These include:
   a. Lack of direct supervision by data processing people directly concerned with and knowledgeable on the sensitivity of the backup records
   b. A lower level of security prevailing at an informal storage area compared to an off-site facility designed for protection of EDP records
   c. Possible unavailability of the records when needed, if the host who has the access keys is not available or nowhere to be found
   d. Possibility that the informal off-site facility's insurance provisions may not cover data processing media
   e. Possibility that the informal backup facility may not be adequately fire-protected
2. A reciprocal arrangement between two companies close to each other, whereby each stores the other's backup. The premises must be far enough apart, however, so that a major disaster cannot destroy both of them.
3. Bank facilities offer a good arrangement from the security aspect, but the big drawback to this type of storage is the limited hours of access.
4. The facilities provided by a professional vital records storage center. Companies that provide this service tend to do so in an efficient manner because this is their business. There is no slackening of security as is the tendency in most on-site systems and, in many cases, the amount

saved in lower insurance rates will more than pay for the cost of space rental. Determining which of these alternatives should be adopted requires an evaluation of individual and local conditions.

5. Your own, specially designed, off-site backup facility. This is the best alternative.

For a list of data to be backed up see also Chapter 17.

PERSONNEL BACKUP

Personnel may become unavailable for one of the following reasons: sickness, accident, breakdown in communications, becoming stranded or as a result of transportation disruptions. Increasingly, in these days of unionized labor groups, employees may become unavailable because of a strike. Whatever the reason, personnel backup is very necessary. The following are approaches to personnel backup.

- A job rotation program
- Crosstraining
- Agreements with a host computer or backup organization re use of their personnel
- Training of supervisory level personnel to operate the facilities in case of strike
- In extreme cases, possibly equipment vendor personnel or temporary personnel services, if available

OTHER ELEMENTS AND PROCEDURES

A number of other elements need to be backed up, such as procedure manuals and special forms. These are listed in the backup checklist and in Chapter 17.

Testing the Recovery Program for Vital Records

Once the program is established, it is essential to test it. Having a test team exercise the backup provisions is a good idea and can help solve actual operational problems. Auditors should also be asked to participate in the test process.

Testing the recovery program and using the stored vital records accomplishes two things:

- Management is assured that the program does work and can take corrective action if it doesn't.
- Through participation in a test, people get involved with the program and cooperate better in helping carry out its mission.

Checklist for Testing the Vital Records Recovery Program

The following items should be considered and typical questions answered when testing the recovery program.

1. Determine who, if anyone, is missing in the disaster; find replacements.
2. Reconstruct the ledger to prepare statements as of latest possible date.
3. Prepare the next scheduled payroll for mailing to all employees paid by this location. For each employee, reconstruct the following information:
   a. Year-to-date earnings
   b. Year-to-date "sickness and accident" benefits paid
   c. Basic salary rate
   d. Balance in stock purchase plan
   e. Balance in savings bond program
4. Prepare a detailed list of assets destroyed, showing gross asset value, reserve for depreciation, and net book value. Include serial number, description of asset, capitalization date, expiration, and account code.
5. Demonstrate ability to produce all information necessary to reestablish manufacturing facilities for production of the following units:
   Product ABC
   Product QRS
   Product XYZ
6. What is the cash position as of latest possible date, including:
   a. A breakdown of cash balances by bank?
   b. The status of all working funds?
7. What purchase orders are open for material supporting manufacturing operations?
8. What is the current status of accounts payable files, including accounts payable for all materials which have been processed through receiving inspection?
9. Identify the suppliers who serve this location. Identify their addresses and the commodities they furnish.
10. For use in possible rebuilding of the destroyed location—What information is available on structure, utility lines, etc.?
11. To make temporary reassignments, determine how many employees are available in essential categories; for example:
    a. Senior associate manufacturing engineer
    b. Staff engineer
    c. Staff programmer

   d. Lab specialist
   e. Senior associate programmer
   f. Tool and model maker
   g. Test engineer
   h. Project engineer
12. Establish the position of customer orders placed with this location.
13. Produce the latest level of document drawings and/or logic for the following development projects:
    Development Project A
    Development Project B
14. Produce the latest level of programming documentation on the following development project:
    Program Development XXX
15. What arrangements have been made for backup data processing, microfilm, and reproduction equipment? Is there a written plan for use?
16. Produce copies of the recovery plan for this location.
17. Determine what insurance coverage would apply.
18. How well does the alternate backup facility respond to the anticipated needs?

Backup Checklist

Overall Backup Checklist

Does the backup and recovery program include the following?

1. Equipment and Auxiliaries.
   a. Backup arrangements should be defined. Agreements should be made with other companies with "compatible" equipment to be used as an alternate. For on-line systems, dual systems or standby extra units or a network backup provision may be needed.
   b. Environmental support equipment: with provisions for (a) emergency power supply, (b) air conditioning
   c. Appropriate alternate building facilities
2. Data, File, and Software. Duplicate copies of up-to-date program source decks, listing:
   a. Key master files
   b. Working transaction files to update master files
   c. Systems and program documentation
   d. Compatible operating system
3. Auxiliary Facilities, Supplies, and Procedures.
   a. Operations run manuals (input/output, user interface, etc.)

   b. Inventory of key forms, check blanks, printer bands
   c. Cabinets, special storage canisters
   d. Maintenance of key spare-parts inventory
   e. Assurance of prompt and competent repair service with vendors
   f. Preagreed maintenance and equipment replenishment clauses with the vendor in the contract, in case of catastrophe
4. Backup Off-Site Storage.
   a. One of various backup storage arrangements in companies with multiple data centers; swapping arrangements are possible. (See Data, File, and Software backup earlier in this chapter)
5. Manpower Backup.
   a. Availability of trained personnel
   b. Crosstraining of personnel in key areas (job rotation)
   c. Roster of alternate personnel with appropriate training, including addresses, and telephone numbers
   d. Contract personnel sources

Records Backup

1. Is there a vital records program for the whole firm?
2. Is there off-site storage installation to keep backup records?
3. Is there a detailed procedure for the operation of the backup facility?
4. Is access to the off-site location restricted to only a few authorized persons?
5. Are people who handle files and the records storage well-trained and experienced?
6. Are magnetic tapes and microfilm files stored in adequately safe storage conditions?
7. Are storage facilities engineered for appropriate environmental conditions of temperature and humidity?

General Practices

1. If you have unionized EDP employees, can professional nonunion staff run the installation?
2. If you were to use alternate backup facilities, will their people or yours operate the facilities? If only theirs, are you in a position to provide accurate and clear operating procedures for their use?
3. Are agreements with the backup facility clear concerning such things as: (a) clearance for your personnel, (b) permission to operate their equipment or instructions you will supply for them to operate your systems, (c) priority scheduling or block time agreements, (d) safe storage of files, (e) work areas, (f) costs?

4. Are the backup facilities and backup storage subject to similar physical protection measures as the primary facilities? (See Chapter 14.)
5. Do you have a detailed contingency operating plan to enable your staff (systems, programming, operations, library, and control) to operate under handicapped conditions or at off-site locations?
6. Is there a detailed inventory, specifications and layout for existing equipment and facilities?
7. Are there special canisters or containers to transport key records in card or tape form?
8. Have provisions been made for communications and transportation facilities and arrangements when operating on a backup mode?
9. Are all key system jobs structured so as to permit immediate running in the backup facilities without major modifications relative to hardware features, peripherals, and operating system versions?
10. Are applications changes kept up-to-date for backup?
11. Do you have a streamlined roster of critical applications and a production schedule for the trimmed-down list of critical jobs?
12. Have you received the physical and data security procedures at your backup facility to ensure they meet with your minimum standards?
13. Have you anticipated how you want the backup personnel to handle your confidential data, runs, and programs, in case the alternative backup organization must operate your systems (such as in a service bureau environment)?
14. Is there a set of relaxed security rules during the emergency period?
15. Do you have a good contractual agreement with your backup partner? Has it passed legal review?
16. Do you test for compatibility and operability at least once a year?
17. Is your backup partner at least equally as serious about backup, recovery, and security as you are?
18. Do they really have the capacity to handle your key applications?
19. Are their key personnel aware of your contingency plan and under what conditions they are to support you?
20. Do you have an implementation plan for the use of backup installation?
21. Do you have a written contingency plan? Is it updated constantly to reflect the latest conditions?
22. If an alternative building (the empty shell approach) is to be used in case of major disaster and a new computer is to be installed (cases of serious fire), does it have space and provisions for:
    a. Computer hardware
    b. Decollating, bursting, and distribution

c. Data preparation
d. Data files
e. Program files
f. Tape files
g. Programming functions
h. Administrative functions
i. Safe locked storage
j. Power
k. Telecommunications
l. Environmental support (air conditioning, etc.)
m. Protection against the elements (fire, water, snow, etc.)
n. Minimum security

Recovery Procedures Checklist

(Refer also to the data security information in Chapter 17.)

Processing Interruptions

1. Do you have checkpoint and restart procedures for short-term processing interruptions?
2. Are they incorporated in all key systems?
3. For batch systems, are there well-defined file reconstruction procedures based on backup files?
4. For on-line/data base systems, are file dumps and transaction logs provisions available?
5. Are file labels used and well kept?
6. Are file and vital record retention cycles well specified and maintained?
7. Are all program changes fully documented and controlled, and backup versions kept up-to-date?
8. Are system recovery instructions for every key system properly developed and documented?
9. Are these part of the backup records in the off-site facility?
10. Has the file backup system been checked regularly?
11. Are all operating manuals checked by computer operations regularly?
12. Do you review backup documentation regularly to ensure it is current and applicable?
13. Have you simulated major recovery procedures to ensure they are workable?
14. Do you have guidelines for transferability and portability of jobs to an

alternate facility, especially if your program library may have to be modified to fit the host computer operating system?

15. Are personnel teams for operating the backup facility defined, and do they include operators, control, and programming personnel?
16. Is there a detailed recovery procedure for each type of catastrophe or disruption?

Other Considerations for the Recovery Process

1. Determine if the room construction structures will support entering personnel.
2. Provide adequate lighting.
3. Determine that no fire still exists.
4. Determine if it is safe to turn on electrical power.
5. Have an authorized person certify the condition of the installation site before attempting any recovery steps.
6. Clear debris.
7. Determine if air conditioning system is operable.
8. Determine if all computer components are operable.
9. Place all environmental monitoring and fire detecting systems on operational status.
10. Put all fire dampers, fire doors, and fire curtains into normal position.
11. Shut off sprinkler system if it is still active and replace fusable heads.
12. Determine if all master file and processing programs are serviceable.
13. Obtain the latest duplicate file for all master files.
14. Update all master files with later transactions and adjust destroyed data.
15. Obtain duplicate copies of tape library processing programs.
16. Duplicate all master files and processing programs before operations begin.
17. Perform some pilot runs of a few test applications.
18. Draw up a new roster of priorities for critical applications restart.
19. Have procedures for notifying users concerning what and when their system applications will be available and when they should discontinue operating in the emergency interim user fallback mode.
20. Have provisions and adjustment procedures to reconcile the status of master files and transactions to avoid so-called transaction overlaps or transaction gaps.
21. Start a reindoctrination program for all concerned if the recon-

structed and recovered facility causes changes from the modus operandi before the initial facility was destroyed.

22. Involve the accounting and auditing groups in making sure that asset integrity has not been affected and that the appropriate authorized accounting adjustments are made.
23. Have auditors audit the contents of sensitive files and test the internal controls in the recovered mode.
24. Gradually restore the security standards to the normal mode.
25. Gradually restart the less critical application systems which had to take a back seat to the critical ones.

17

Data and Program Protection

OBJECTIVE AND SCOPE

The objective of the data and software security program is to provide adequate measures for the protection of data, recorded information, programs, and all other records which are vital to the survival and operational capability of the EDP complex and, hence, the organizations it serves. This program is often labeled the "data and logical" protection program to distinguish it from the "physical" protection program dealt with in Chapter 14.

The scope of this program includes the following important aspects:

1. Physical protection for data
2. Data and file protection measures and techniques (including logical access)
3. Administrative and procedural controls, such as:
   - Control of program changes
   - Systems documentation
   - Library procedures
   - Operational testing of software
   - Vital records program
4. Legal safeguards for data and programs and data privacy considerations
5. Control over the systems development cycle before systems become operational

Most of the items related to 1 were covered in Chapter 14. Item 2 is dealt with in this section and also in Chapter 18. Items 4 and 5 are dealt with later in Chapters 20 and 21 of this manual. The reason for not covering all aspects in this chapter is that almost every aspect of security does in fact affect data protection. Also, if all topics were handled in this chapter, it would make for a disproportionate coverage of subjects all in one chapter. When we refer to data protection we mean data in every form, hard-copy, magnetically recorded, programs and procedures. Because so much of an organization's data is computerized these days, the emphasis is naturally on data in EDP readable form.

GENERAL ASPECTS

The Need for Data Protection

The protection of EDP data stored on tape and disk forms and on other media and the need to protect the software and programs that operate on data is of paramount importance. There are two reasons for this: (a) the actual asset value, or investment of the data in question or the cost of regenerating such data, and/or (b) the intrinsic value of the particular data to the firm. Further, equipment for processing data, although expensive, if lost or damaged, can be replaced in kind (vendor contracts usually specify the period within which the client can expect new equipment to be replaced, in the event of destruction by accidental sources). On the other hand, if data or information were lost, it may in some cases, never be replaced, yet its unavailability may spell disaster for the user organization.

To illustrate the difference, a few years ago, a dissident attacked an "establishment" computer in the Los Angeles area. He emptied the contents of a revolver into the "guts" of the computer hoping to do considerable damage. His approach was naive. Had he penetrated the file and program library area, the impact of his intended damage would have been much greater and, perhaps, irreparable, if adequate backup measures were not in existence at the victim's installation.

Protection of software and programs is likewise very important for at least the following reasons:

- They represent official policies and procedures of the organization which are encapsulated in the form of programs. They are often of a confidential nature.
- They represent an asset of the organization in the sense that many man-years of effort may have gone into the development of these programs. They could be a target for theft by interested parties for various reasons, a common one being to save the development cost.
- They can be subject to unauthorized alteration or fraudulent manipulation in order to change assets, issue illicit payments, change contents of files, or even destroy someone's character by changing what is recorded about a given individual.
- Once computerized, many businesses depend upon the availability of these programs to operate their businesses. If these programs were destroyed, and no backup provided, a major business disruption could result.

Types of Data Damage and Their Impact

Data or information may be lost or damaged by one or combinations of the following routes:

- Destruction or obliteration
- Modification
- Disclosure

These may occur through:

- Accidental destruction, modification, or disclosure
- Intentional destruction, modification, or disclosure
- Processing errors resulting from human error or improper procedures
- Hardware and/or software-induced errors or data destruction

Currently, destruction and modification are of greater concern to all users of EDP. Disclosure is of increasing concern in view of prevailing practices in industrial intelligence which affect both private and governmental circles. Disclosure has also taken new dimensions of importance in the public sector in connection with the individual privacy problem and legislation to eventually regulate data banks containing personal information. The U.S. Privacy Act of 1974 already applies to government. In many European countries, data banks are already subject to regulation (Sweden, Britain, Germany) and many others are working on data privacy acts. Most states in the U.S. have various forms of privacy protection statutes.

The damages resulting from the above can range from minor losses to complete loss of operability of the EDP complex and the organization being served by it. Punitive fines or legal actions apply for privacy violations. In all cases, one should look into the following strategies to try to protect data:

TYPE OF PROTECTION STRATEGY	NATURE OF PROTECTION MEASURE	
1. Physical protection and logical access control	Preventive	Strategies
2. Prevention		
3. Detection		
4. Ameliorative or containment measures		
5. Monitoring and tracing		
6. Backup and recovery	Remedial	
7. Audit of systems	Preventive and Remedial	
8. Redundancy		

The strategy or combination of strategies to use naturally depends upon the type of situation encountered and the type of data involved. Preventive measures are always important. However, in situations that are unavoidable the only recourse may be to anticipate and install "backup and recovery" measures to prevent complete collapse of the system or complete loss of the ability to recover. Backup and recovery procedures to be used in case of a major physical or file obliteration catastrophe are a good example of such a situation. These were discussed in Chapter 16.

Types of Protection Depend on EDP Alternative Used or Depth of Protection Sought

Data protection methods may vary considerably depending upon the method used for obtaining data processing power. Basically the following are the main types of data processing alternatives:

- In-house batch installation
- In-house on-line installation serving internal needs
- Time-sharing or on-line installation serving many different organizations via terminals
- Small or minicomputer installation
- Service bureau arrangement with courier service
- Combinations of the above
- Small or microcomputer installation
- Data processing networks

The procedures and techniques for protecting data in greater depth can vary significantly as would the cost of achieving such protection. For example, a number of control strategies could be applied to achieving protection. One can protect data at the very entry point by a combination of a preventive strategy, such as access control, and also by establishing a high-security area (a form of a containment strategy), whereby only duly authorized personnel, under guard, can be admitted to the secured terminal area. If you wanted to use a multilevel access control strategy (which is a form of the redundancy strategy), you could use passwords and even so-called physiological or biometric identifiers (such as signature systems, retina and voice identifiers, etc.) to enable the terminal user to access the system. Once you gain initial access to the system, if protection were needed to access various functions and data in the system, you may need to resort to mechanisms that match a given profile of authorization to the profile authorized for each individual in order to distinguish among individuals with different authorization profiles. To accomplish this, it is possible to use control mechanisms that provide access on the basis of a "mapping" of what the individual is allowed to "see or do." This can be accomplished by one or several of these mechanisms:

1. Providing *authorization tables* depicting user profiles of access, such as you can read but not change, you can read but not copy, etc., in the form of a matrix of individuals (or programs) and actions.

2. Installing *access control security software packages,* commercially available, designed to provide access profile management.
3. Using *specially programmed provisions* in the application system designed to provide specific authorization upon recognition of special codes.
4. Using the *delimiting provisions of the data base management system,* if one is used, to restrict access through such mechanisms as programmed control blocks (PCBs in IMS), whereby an individual is given access to certain programs. However, in turn, a given program may access only data elements A, B, and C, but not D. On the other hand another program may be given access to data elements A, C, and D, but not B.
5. *Dial-back and communications port control devices* which verify if the caller's telephone number is authorized before connecting the line to the central processor. This applies to the control of hackers.

At present, alternatives 1 and 3 may require a considerable amount of extra programming so that many organizations are resorting to the use of security access packages of the type mentioned above. The method mentioned in alternative 4, can be implemented in connection with the design of the data base system. Alternative 5 applies to controlling access by common dial-up telephone lines.

In summary, it is clear that security protection can be provided at varying depths, such as at the file, record, field, and event character-within-a-field level. The deeper the level of protection, the more expensive the protection process is likely to become. Providing cost-effective protection requires that you conduct a risk analysis and cost-benefit analysis. A detailed knowledge of the various technical controls is also very desirable.

Differences in Approach for Data Security and Backup and Recovery Procedures

There are some important differences between data/software protection procedures covered here and the emphasis placed by the backup and recovery program discussed in Chapter 16. *Data protection* is concerned with protection, access control, and preventive measures required to preserve the integrity of data. It also seeks to minimize the possibility of errors in data and any potential accidental or intentional destruction or modification of data. *Backup* and *recovery* measures for data, on the other hand, relate to the threat of data destruction and are concerned primarily with how to restore operability and operational normalcy in the event that a catastrophe were to occur.

Another difference is that data protection concentrates on protection against manipulation of data and prevention or identification of fraudulent schemes. Recovery from a potential fraud situation would be considered more of an administrative problem.

PHYSICAL PROTECTION FOR DATA

Objectives

The purpose of the physical protection measures for data is essentially the same as those discussed in Chapter 14 for physical protection in general, except insofar as they apply to data, as opposed to buildings or equipment.

Elements

The physical protection program for data includes:

- *Access control*—Limiting the number of people who have access to the computer facility and to the physical files (see library function).
- *Physical security*—Protective measures, such as those discussed in Chapter 14, to safeguard data: fire prevention, fire control, water damage control, environmental control.
- *Safes and protected storage*—Protection against theft and fire/water damage.
- *Data transportation*—Protection of data while being transported between the data center and other locations: use of appropriate courier service, use of tape, card canisters, etc.
- *All the other elements* discussed in Chapter 14, such as location, environmental control, and housekeeping practices, also contribute to data protection.
- A new element of protection is the *data integrity program* under the data base administration function.

Data Physical Protection Checklist

(Refer also to Chapter 14, "Physical Protection," for more information.)

1. Are the same physical safeguards used to protect the EDP complex and hardware applied to protect data and files and programs?
2. Are key record, file, and program storage areas protected against fire through fireproof vaults or safes? (See "Fire Protection," and "Protected Storage" in Chapter 14.)
3. Are key record and files storage units burglar proof?
4. Is there a set of access control measures used to protect access to data and programs, similar to that used for access to the computer complex itself? Access should be on a "need to know" basis and only by approved rosters, according to specific time schedules (See "Access Control" in Chapter 14.)

5. Are environmental conditions of humidity and temperature control adequate? (See "Environmental Support" in Chapter 14.)
6. Is there protection against power fluctuation and power failures? (See "Environmental Support" in Chapter 14.)
7. Is the data center in a safe location? (See "EDP Center Location" in Chapter 14.)
8. Do you use lock-and-key containers for confidential tapes and disk packs, at the data center and when transporting sensitive data?

DATA, FILE, AND SOFTWARE PROTECTION

Objective

The objective of this portion of the program is to safeguard data, files, and software against destruction, erroneous entries, and modification of contents. Another objective is to devise the means to prevent unauthorized access to data and file contents, and to preserve data integrity and privacy.

General

The second major aspect of data, file, and program security is to protect these against unauthorized access, erroneous creation and processing of data, and potential accidental or intentional destruction or modification of data, whether this may stem from equipment and software malfunctions, human intervention, or even defective procedures and standards. Reconstruction of data is naturally also involved, although this aspect was discussed in Chapter 16 under backup and recovery.

Briefly, the major present threats to data, files, and programs originate from the following sources:

- Accidental destruction from defective equipment or software.
- Erroneous entries from data source departments caused by human error, poor procedures, or erroneous accounting totals.
- Potential manipulation of files and programs. These could be intentional for personal gain or the result of unintentional or unanticipated alterations in the process of trying to implement a legitimate change (program change) or in the process of trying to correct a processing step.
- Outright data or program theft.
- Electronic eavesdropping whereby interlopers pick up the emanations from data transmissions or equipment.

Figure 16-1 illustrates, in more detail, various causes of data and file errors and destruction which fall under one or several of the above sources.

Approaches to Protection

There are several approaches to protecting data/files and software against the above threats. The approaches depend upon the nature of the threat or the type of controls one must resort to to achieve protection. Basically, these approaches can be classified into the following five:

- Administrative controls
- Processing controls
- Systems controls (imbedded in the system)
- Special hardware/software additions
- Technical controls (mostly for advanced on-line systems)

To achieve the desired level of control and protection, it is obvious that one may have to resort to a combination of the above. Seldom will just one type of control provide total protection. A brief description of each of these types of controls is given below.

Administrative Controls

Administrative controls include a number of organization, policy, and procedural matters required to protect data and software. Assuming that they are properly established and implemented, these controls can be very powerful and effective. Most of all, they may be instituted without a great deal of expense and without the need to have an in-depth knowledge of data processing. One of the nice things about administrative controls of this type is that, once established, they operate on a continuous basis in the area they are supposed to protect, unlike individual audits of systems conducted one at a time, whereby snapshot results and protection are obtained. No protection applies until the next audit. A good example of this situation is when one conducts a system audit using audit software. After the audit, we learn a number of things about the files or programs as of that moment. It does not tell us anything about the next day or the next computer run. Administrative controls have a continuing effect.

A list of some of the most important types of administrative controls follows:

1. Adequate organization structure and good separation of functions. (This was covered under "EDP Department Organization" in Chapter 13.)
2. Data processing standards for all important areas of the EDP complex. (Discussed in the "Objectives" section of Chapter 13.) Of specific value to data protection, the following standards are important:
   –Backup and recovery procedures (discussed in Chapter 16)
   –Program change control procedures (see "Data, File, and Software Protection" in Chapter 17)

–File and program library procedures (Chapter 18)
–EDP operations activities accounting and monitoring (Chapter 19)
–Equipment maintenance practices (Chapter 19)
–Sound systems and program testing procedures before promotion to operational status (Chapter 21)
–Sound and complete documentation standards (Chapter 18)
–Viable vital records program (see "Vital Records Program" in Chapter 13)
–Legal safeguards and insurance protection (Chapter 20)
–Standards for controlled "sysgening" of operating system versions

Processing Controls

Processing controls for data protection refer to a number of operating procedures that should be observed in the data processing complex, controls programmed into the systems to safeguard data, and, also, the operating system features provided with the equipment which are addressed at protecting data and keeping errors and illegal operations to a minimum.

Some controls of this type are:

- Edit controls between runs
- Batch-to-batch and run-to-run controls
- Computer center operating procedures and appropriate run books
- Features of the operating system designed to control processing, such as console messages and reports, supervisor overrides, special no-dump features to prevent dumping of files or programs, automatic copying of key data before file updating or before program blanking out.

Systems Controls

Systems controls for data protection refer to a number of control techniques used to accomplish one or several of the following objectives:

- Verification of data correctness
- Control over completeness of data
- Control over correctness of processing and calculations
- Processing of rejected data
- Providing adequate audit trails

The important characteristic of these types of systems controls is that they are planned at the design stage and are *imbedded* in the system itself. The list of internal systems controls is too long to enumerate in this manual. The reader should refer to Chapter 18 for further details on these controls, as well as to texts on data processing and data security. (See references 4, 24, 26, and 33 in the Bibliography, Part I.) Examples of the types of controls included in this type of system controls are: edit controls (valid character, field, size, sign); check digit tests; valid transaction tests; limit or reasonableness tests and sequence checks; error reject lists; suspense file items; control totals crossfooting; run-to-run and batch-to-batch tests, etc. (For other suggestions, see "Checklist of Test Conditions Commonly Used for Test Decks" in Chapter 21.)

Special Hardware/Software Additions

Security techniques have progressed to the point where there are commercially available a number of hardware devices or software packages that can be added to the system to enhance security for data. This is particularly more prevalent in the advanced and sophisticated systems, such as time-shared, multiprogramming, and on-line systems. A list of some of these follows:

Hardware Type

- Memory protect feature
- Memory bounds
- Hardware monitoring devices to check the operating soundness of the systems

Software Type

- Threat monitoring packages (monitoring system operability and reliability, monitoring unsuccessful access attempts to passwords and files, etc.)
- Special routines developed to prevent access by unauthorized personnel to privileged areas of a system
- Special programs written to manage access to various files according to various levels of authorization, according to so-called authorization tables.
- Special packages designed to log and record any version of a program and channel program cataloging in such a way that all program changes are made through the software package
- Software packages designed to check the proper functioning of complex systems (so-called software/hardware monitors)
- General purpose access software packages

Technical Controls

These types of controls are directly associated with the more advanced systems. They are controls that were not known and required for simple batch systems, but are rather the product of the more advanced technology brought about by multiprocessing, multiaccess, on-line systems and data communication networks. These systems have brought about at least the following needs for data and file protection:

- How to protect the files from being accessed by unauthorized individuals (password systems).
- If a person has gained legitimate access to the file, how to keep him from accessing those portions of the file that do not concern him, and how to restrain the type of operations he can perform on the system or file. For example: read a file only, limit the ability to change records, prevent a program or portion of a file from being dumped (authorization tables).
- In a file that is being accessed simultaneously by various individuals, how to prevent a record from being destroyed through simultaneous updates or changes to the file by several users (the concurrency problem).
- How to preserve the audit trail in a dynamic environment.
- If someone managed to obtain a physical tape of disk file, how to prevent him from being able to read its contents, or if someone managed to tap or intercept (eavesdrop) the communications lines, how to protect the contents of the data being transmitted (encrypting methods for data).
- How to plug the leaks in today's security-deficient operating systems (possible modifications to the operating system).
- How to protect the system against the unauthorized intruder (hacker) who uses common carrier direct dial-up lines to penetrate a system.

This field constitutes a specialty in itself and is highly complex and technical in nature. For details on these controls, further reading is suggested.[1]

As examples of technical controls, consider the following:

Hardware Controls

- Read/write protection
- Memory compartmentalization
- Volume (file) mount protection
- Lock-and-key features for terminals
- Magnetic stripe card access for authentication
- Cryptographic hardware at terminals and encryption systems for telephone lines

---

[1] See also, J. F. Kuong, *Controls for Advanced/On-line/Data Base Systems,* (Wellesley Hills, MA: Management Advisory Publications, 1985), vols. 1 and 2.

- Data communication port control and call-back devices[2]

Software Controls

- The use of access control software packages
- Identification, authentication, and authorization techniques, such as:
  - –Passwords to clear access to the system
  - –Authorization tables for various levels of access (read only, compute, update, etc.)
- Audit trails of file access and reporting system to determine accountability and access trends
- Monitoring and surveillance to detect deviations or to watch ongoing events
- Operating system modifications to strengthen security
- Use of monitoring terminal under the security officer's control

A REVIEW OF SOME ADMINISTRATIVE CONTROLS OF IMPORTANCE TO DATA AND SOFTWARE PROTECTION

Scope and Coverage

In dealing with the subject of data and software security, one always encounters the problem of where to include the discussion on a given protection control. In preparing this manual I have opted for covering as much relevant material as near as possible to the main section topic, while trying to avoid an unnecessary level of duplication. With this in mind I have covered some of the useful and valuable techniques for data protection here while many of the others which are also related to the field, are covered elsewhere in the manual, particularly in Chapter 18, on procedural controls. Backup and recovery, which is very relevant to data protection, is discussed separately, in Chapter 16, because of its importance, and is therefore not covered again in this section. This section is devoted primarily to program change control.

A list of other administrative procedural controls which have a direct bearing on data security were listed earlier in this chapter, under "Approaches to Protection," indicating where they are covered in this manual.

Control of Program Changes

Many installations spend between 40 and 70 percent of their programming energy on program and system maintenance. By "maintenance" we mean any

---

[2] J. F. Kuong, et al, *Microcomputer Security, Auditability and Controls* (Wellesley Hills, MA: Management Advisory Publications, 1985) Chaps. 9 and 10. See also E. F. Troy, *Security for Dial-Up Lines* (Washington, DC: Superintendent of Documents, Pubn. NBS-500-137, 1986).

change to a system from the time it is installed until it is abandoned. Maintenance may be of the "crash" variety because something didn't run properly. (This should be minimized through good systems design.) Very often, the maintenance change is required as a result of a legitimate need for change originated by the changing nature of the business.

Since program changes are a necessity of the business and are bound to occur, a great deal of care must be exercised in securing computer programs from accidental or deliberate tampering. Changes to programs should be performed in a controlled and formalized manner so that the proper changes are in fact made, a complete audit trail of the change is produced, and the change is tested and documented. Quite often program modifications can have far-reaching effects. They can invalidate previously approved controls or they can affect other programs downstream. A formal written authorization and a formal procedure is a sound operating practice even if it must create some inconveniences, at times, in terms of so-called expedience. Together with a good separation of functions scheme, program change control can be a very powerful fraud control procedure. If a programmer is able to make the desired manipulation on paper, but he is never allowed to actually process the change without an authorization procedure, and further, as part of the control procedure, he cannot catalog the program in the program library himself—it must be done by means of a cataloging authorization sheet, which is registered with the control group, and the actual cataloging of the program is done by the operator, not the programmer—there is very little chance that the official version of the program can be altered. Further, if the programmer is not allowed to operate the newly changed program with "live" files, there is even greater assurance that the fraudulent condition cannot materialize, since, in most cases, live files are needed to produce a special payment. Another very important control is to have a separate development and testing group so that programmers do not test or approve the results of testing.

Another important aspect of program change control requires a bi- and often a tripartite approval of the change; namely: the user, the EDP manager, and some other executive or the auditor. After acceptance of the program for the production phase, change authorization, no matter how insignificant, should be controlled by a change control committee that includes the user, the EDP manager, the operations supervisor (for operability) and the auditor or some other executive. At this time a review could be made of the formal procedure via a checklist to verify whether all the steps were met.

If more stringent control is required, one can use program change control software packages. These are available in the market to assist in providing program security and in maintaining program maintenance records. A number of source language and test data files can be stored via these programs to produce an audit trail of all changes. Often all changes must go through the software package, which, in fact, becomes a modification of the operating system. These procedures keep accurate records of when each update occured, giving data on last update and modification numbers. They will also print out a change report, giving an audit trail for all revisions; and, finally, these packages make available the use of keywords for controlling access to the program documentation and all changes made to it. Likewise, the programs can be encrypted upon loading, or upon dumping, to preserve their confidentiality. A number of programs are available for this purpose.

Program Change Control Questionnaire

1. Is there a formal procedure for handling program changes? Does it include the following:
   - Program change policies and classifications to determine what constitutes a program change.
   - Are program changes submitted by the requesting authority via a formal request for change form? Is the form logged in the control group?
   - Are specified changes cleared through persons of authority other than by the systems/programming personnel involved?
   - Is the program change reviewed and approved by user management, EDP management, and, where required, the auditor?
   - Upon authorization is the assigned person responsible for: (a) stating the reason for and the objective of the change, (b) assessing the effect of the change on the existing system on other related programs and on existing controls, and (c) developing and presenting a change plan for review and approval by user and EDP management and for independent review by the auditor?
2. Are changed programs tested in the same manner as new programs? Are potentially affected programs upstream and downstream reviewed for impact, concerning data and controls? (This the ''regression'' type of test discussed in part I, Chapter 2.)
3. Are changed programs documented following a standard procedure, which includes:
   - Application summary, reason for and effect of change and adjustments required?
   - Logic diagrams, source, and object decks?
   - Updated run and operator manuals?
   - Adjustment to files and library procedures, if any, such as retention cycles, cutoff dates?
   - Test procedures used?
4. Are changed and programmer-tested programs subject to auditor review and independent testing? Is there agreement as to when auditor review is needed and when auditor review is to be done after the program becomes operational?

5. Are all the backup copies of the program and its documentation brought up to date at the off-site location?
6. Is there a checklist and review procedure for the whole program change cycle?
7. Are changes to a program made only on a copy of the original program version without affecting the original source deck?
8. Is there a procedure for logging and numbering program change versions?
9. Is there an audit of documentation of changed programs?

Data, File, and Software Protection Checklist

Administrative Controls

1. Is the EDP complex properly organized according to sound separation of functions? (See organization checklist, Chapter 13.)
2. Is there a complete set of management standards to promote data security?
3. See Chapter 18 for other checklists on administrative and procedural controls, including library procedures.
4. Is there control over programmers and operations personnel?
   a. Are programmers not allowed to retain copies of operating programs or test files containing important data?
   b. Who assigns, reviews, and approves programs written by programming personnel and by what procedure?
   c. Do programmers have access to live data files, especially for sensitive systems, such as payroll and others?
   d. If you use outside programming resources, are there stringent procedures available to sign materials and manuals in to outsiders and a procedure to debrief them upon job completion? Are they made to sign secrecy and confidentiality agreements?
   e. Do computer operators have systems and program documentation, including logic and listings?
   f. Are all tests for systems changes by programmers logged as to the purpose of the test and are tests routed to operations through the control section?
   g. Are programmers forbidden to operate computers, especially with live files?
   h. Are operators forbidden to write program modifications and to effect supervisor overrides (direct changes from the console)?
   i. Are program patches banned?

Application Programs

1. Are there program test standards (see Chapter 21)?
2. Are programs subject to rigorous testing before receiving operational status?
3. Do you have standards for application programs? As regards structure, size, and programming techniques to be used?
4. Do you have guidelines to define what constitutes a high-security program?
5. Do you have a program approval or certification standard which all key programs must pass?
6. Does the certification standard include documentation standards, efficiency and security standards?
7. Do you have a comprehensive checklist to be used at system acceptance time during certification?
8. Does the internal auditor participate in or conduct an independent certification of new programs? Also program changes?
9. Is there a list of the most important systems and programs which are subject to independent audit by: (a) user departments, (b) auditors, (c) outside examiners?
10. Is there a clear procedure to communicate with and inform all concerned of systems review for changes and certification?
11. Is there a formal procedure for the transfer of programming product from the systems and programming group to computer operations?

Program Changes and Fraud Control

1. When files are updated or maintained is every record change registered indicating time and date of change? (For example, using program hash totals and time/date stamps.)
2. Do you have a standard procedure for verifying that backup copies of important programs are identical to operating (library) copies, such as by reviewing a random sample of programs at random intervals for very sensitive programs?
3. Do you forbid program changes at the object level such that all programs must be changed at source level following an established program change procedure with certification before use and documentation audit trail?
4. When developing programs to handle confidential files, do you have a security procedure for testing the programs using simulated data rather than live data? (For example, when testing authorization tables, payroll rates, security codes, etc.)

5. When performing live file tests, do you have an authorized team in charge to supervise tests and certify the system?
6. Do you have special procedures for handling data and programs which affect individuals who program and maintain the system? (One such procedure may be to have a separate group processing manual payroll or checking accounts [in a bank] for EDP personnel, or a special run separate from the mainstream of the payroll to enable quick monitoring.)
7. On authorized tables (account rates, pay rates, etc.) are these hash-totaled or somehow monitored for changes, before, during, and after processing?
8. On key formulas and algorithms, do you have audit routines built-in and external (to EDP) procedures for checking their proper functioning during processing and at random intervals? (This is a form of ITF-integrated test facility. Examples are checking interest formulas, complex decision tables for inventories, pricing, etc.)
9. Do you perform analysis of file updates for correctness and integrity, such as by taking random samples? (Accounts payable, payroll, etc.)

Technical Controls and Advanced Systems

Access Control

1. Is access to key programs assigned on a need-to-know basis?
2. Do you use keyword or password protection for files? Do you use a password system for the use of TSO?
3. What provisions do you have to safeguard the confidentiality of passwords? Use of one or several of the following is desirable:
   a. Frequent change of passwords in critical areas on a nonperiodic basis.
   b. Limit number of password trials.
   c. Avoid printing the password on the printer or console. Variations are to scramble the password before printing, print several rows of random digits before printing the password on the console.
   d. Passwords assigned to terminated or transferred personnel should be changed immediately.
   e. System should cancel inquiry or access after two or three unsuccessful password tries.
   f. Password table should be kept under lock by the security officer.
4. For highly sensitive applications where line tapping is a problem do you use algorithms? (The user is asked to compute an answer based on some numbers issued by the computer; the password algorithm does not travel over the communications lines.)

5. Do you maintain logs of accesses to data banks or any sensitive files? Are they reviewed?
6. Do you use security routines to monitor attempts to access sensitive files by unauthorized users?
7. Does the routine notify the operator via the on-line console?
8. Does the routine provide a record of all attempts via a printout at given intervals?
9. Does the security officer use this data to develop patterns to track down suspects who have unauthorized access to data by terminal?
10. Do you use multilevel access control to your data files:
    a. By various levels of security classification?
    b. By read only, write only, update, etc?
    c. By file segmentation according to privacy needs?

Authorization

11. When using authorization tables (discriminatory access: read only, change only, etc.), do you have guidelines for the design of these procedures and means of monitoring changes to the authorization program or the authorization table? (One way is for the access program to be written as a separate module that can be verified readily. The authorization table is subject to random audits, especially concerning table authorization changes due to maintenance requirements.)
12. Do you regularly check the security software utilities and tables of access codes against approved ones?
13. On proprietory or confidential programs, are provisions made through code and other administrative procedures such that a terminal user cannot request program dumping in any form? If an operator is authorized to dump the program, there should be a number of procedures that record program dumping and produce an audit trail. (Example: console messages, automatic copy on tape of portions copied and reporting of such as part of the system controls. The ultimate is modification of the operating system to prevent program dump.) Tables of passwords could be encrypted in case of accidental dumping.
14. On highly confidential programs, do you have routines built in for automatic erase of memory contents after program use?

Monitoring

15. Do you have specific procedures for program monitoring before and during execution, during and after by computer?

16. Are your programs and systems designed to keep statistics on their operation which relate to monitoring of changes or abnormal conditions? Example: percent of memory or disk allocation, unused memory, running time, ratios, percent of transactions that actually were accepted for file updates, error rates, etc.). Use of the job accounting packages provided by vendors of equipment gives this information.
17. On data base systems, do you have file contents monitoring routines to check the reliability of data base contents, missing codes, addresses, and plot or tabulate these during processing? Occasional random validation of actual physical count vs. on-file figures is a useful tool. This can be performed by a control or data base monitoring group operating from a console/terminal and by using data base inventory integrity software packages that keep track of the physical inventory of data elements in the data base.
18. Are terminal users allowed only high-level languages to prevent access to machine coding?
19. Are there standards developed for key sensitive systems on running times for given transaction volumes from actual production runs?
20. Are significant variations from normal running time explained and accounted for?

Recovery

21. What recovery procedures have been planned for the on-line system?
22. How fast can it be recovered in the event of a failure?
23. With the advent of "telecommuting," whereby programmers and users can work from the comfort of their homes and interact with the company's mainframe computer using terminals and microcomputers, is there a set of formal rules and standards for the use of remote processing, especially regarding access to programs, files, and testing of programs on a remote basis?[3]
24. Are there controls to prevent duplications of processing when a system returns to a checkpoint in case of interruption and rerun?

Operating System

1. How is your operating system rated concerning security relative to other operating systems? (The Department of Defense [DOD] Security Institute periodically rates operating systems for security worthiness.)

[3] J. F. Kuong et al. *Microcomputer Security, Auditability and Control* (Wellesley Hills, MA: Management Advisory Publications, 1985) Chap. 5.

2. Do your operating systems have protection to prevent the bypassing of security utilities and the unauthorized access to data bases?
3. Do you control operating system version changes and certify them after ensuring that they do not affect important systems?
4. Have you checked your operating system to ensure it does not dump valuable data, password and file access authorization tables? Have you determined under what circumstances such may occur?
5. Are memory bounds tested following maintenance, initial program load, and each restart?
6. When loading highly confidential data through data decks, are there special security procedures in force? Is it done in the presence of data owners? Is it processed immediately? Are source data tapes returned under security procedures for safe storage along with any listings?
7. Have you invalidated any console instructions that can access sensitive files or tables, such as authorization tables and password lists?
8. Have you made an inventory of operating system loopholes that may compromise the security of your system?
9. If yes, have you outlined the alternatives for closing the loopholes through: (a) manual administrative procedures, (b) possible modifications to the operating system with vendor help, (c) warning routines to let you know of occurrences when they do occur? Have you set up special monitoring procedures to watch for such loophole conditions?
10. Can programs which violate the operating system be identified in source or object form?
11. If authorization tables are stored in mass memory and disks, what provisions have you made to ensure they are not copied? Have you provided for a security file log to record all important statistics relative to inquiries, access frequency by terminal and by user? Is there a program designed to analyze the statistics and produce summary and analyzed reports for the security officer and the auditor on an off-line basis at the end of a given period?
12. Do you have software audit routines that attempt to violate a number of security provisions, such as:
    a. Dump critical priviledged data/files?
    b. Read out of its operating area and violate memory bounds?
    c. Adjust memory bounds during processing to include unauthorized areas?
    d. Read a file beyond its assigned extents?
    e. Write into memory beyond its assigned area?
13. Have you tested the authorization system and logic to ensure it works as planned? (This applies to the implementation and operation of the access software package used by your installation.)

14. Upon violations to system security procedure, does the operating system: (a) record all statistics before shutting the system down, and (b) report violations on the console or by other means?
15. If an authorization system exists, does the security administrator have a main security terminal from which authorization tables can be changed? Is the use of privileged instructions for the operating system and data base management system restricted?
16. Is your operating system certified by a systems programmer after a new version is generated? Is it tested with some applications before it is released for production work?
17. Have you tested to ensure that a user cannot get out of his allocated space and violate another user's programs or tamper with the operating systems?
18. Do changes to operating systems and system software follow change standards?
19. Is a log kept of all operating system changes?
20. Can operators tamper with the operating system from the console without appropriate messages appearing on the console log?
21. Is your system programmed to test memory bound and other hardware security features before transferring control to the application program?
22. When security rules are violated are jobs automatically cancelled and messages written on the console and the security master console?
23. Are checkpoint and restart provisions available? Is the checkpoint information disposed of when no longer needed?
24. Are user "exits" from the application systems to the operating system and in the operating system itself properly controlled at design time and at the operational phases?

18

Procedural and System Controls

PURPOSE

This section covers a number of so-called procedural and system application controls. But before we deal with them in detail, we will classify them into three important groups, namely:

1. Administrative (related to organization and policy)
2. Input/output procedural controls (related to transaction flow)
   - Input (source) controls
   - Processing (programmed) controls
   - Output (quality) controls
3. Operating practices and standards (see Chapter 19 for other related areas) such as:
   - Library procedures
   - Program change controls
   - Error management and rerun control
   - File update control
   - Documentation

Administrative and policy controls are related to organizational provisions, structure, and separation of functions. They are an important element of planning for and enforcing security and controls. These were discussed in Chapter 13 of this manual. Management has a great deal to do with instituting these controls. The auditor should make sure that these controls exist and are observed at all times. The external auditor makes a point to review them as well.

Input/output controls and procedural controls and operating standards, on the other hand, have to do with official or accepted good practices (''modus operandi''). Through careful specification, enforcement, and review for compliance of these controls, the organization ensures that sound protective measures are provided at all levels of the EDP complex. Input/output controls deal with the practices and procedures required to ensure that data and transactions are entered, processed, or posted accurately and completely. This includes provisions to ensure the transaction is normal, accurate, complete, and acceptable.

These controls are oriented toward the control of the proper flow and processing of data. They deal with what happens to the data or transaction and their intrinsic value.

Operating practices and standards deal with approved procedures relating to the proper operation of the data center itself and its work stations. They are concerned with work initiation, authorization, and flow, to ensure proper and authorized "processing" of EDP action steps. These controls are oriented to processing tasks rather than to the contents or the form of the transactions themselves.

All three types of controls are fundamental to a sound and secured operation of the data center and of application systems.

SCOPE

The scope of this section is limited to the review of practices and procedures that have a bearing on how the system applications and computerized data are handled by the various operational and functional groups of the data center. By inference, therefore, we are concerned with the existence of basic controls and with how good these controls are. When reviewing data center practices and controls, the emphasis is on how these controls work for **all applications** or processing activities. We do not delve into the specific built-in controls as they apply to each **individual** system application. This matter is covered when the auditor examines specific system applications. To clarify further, in this review we examine, for example, the existence of and quality of the library procedures as they affect **all** jobs processed in the data center. When we look at input controls or output balancing procedures we seek to establish whether these controls exist for all applications, and we are also interested in how the data center handles the specific controls built into each system for batch balancing. We are less concerned, for example, with the determination of whether application "X" should have more intrinsic controls, such as limit tests, check digits, range tests, and a host of other system controls which could apply to that particular system. This is the mission of the system application audit, which may be conducted either during the development cycle (see Chapter 23) or when reviewing a specific operational system application.

Another important point to bear in mind is that the emphasis is on soundness of controls from the viewpoint of accuracy, quality control, and security. We are less concerned with costs, effectiveness, and efficiency of resource utilization. This is the thrust of Chapter 19. Of course, it is the combination of the points of view in this chapter and in Chapter 19 that gives us a more complete assessment of the total effectiveness of the operations of the EDP complex.

THE CONTROL FUNCTION

Purpose

The normal cycle in the processing of data or transactions in batch EDP involves: (a) receipt of source data from data originating or source departments, (b) processing of the same in the various work stations within EDP, and (c) control of quality and delivery of processed results or reports to the end-user. This involves a number of human and mechanized steps requiring detailed flow coordination and control through the data center. It also creates the need for interface procedures and controls between users and EDP and between the various work stations within EDP, including liaison between programming and operations. In order to provide an effective interface most EDP centers usually have a control function, also called control unit or data control, which is responsible for a number of functions and tasks, as explained below. The key objectives of the control function are: (a) to provide a central point of liaison between outside and inside EDP activities, (b) to control the quality of results and to exercise custody over key data, and (c) to aid in promoting operational efficiency.

When dealing with advanced/on-line/real-time systems, many of the controls migrate to the on-line system itself, via compensating edit, and other integrity controls.

Main Responsibilities/Tasks of the Control Function

The most important responsibilities or functions of the control function were discussed in Chapter 13, page 179. Because of the importance of the control function in implementing many of the procedures of this section, these functions are listed again in Figure 18-1 and further expanded.

According to these objectives the control function becomes an extremely valuable function of the data center. It provides a central point for all communications between EDP and users, and within EDP functions. It also provides a mechanism for the day-to-day implementation of tasks and established controls for management, and a powerful ally for the auditor. In fact, the auditor's job can be simplified when an organization has a properly structured control function, which can be a good source of information about EDP operations.

ADMINISTRATIVE CONTROLS

These controls deal with the broad policy and organizational aspects of operating a data center. They stress such matters as reporting level, organization structure and separation of functions, and management directional guid-

Figure 18-1
Functions/Tasks of the Control Function

FUNCTIONS/TASK	COMMENTS
1. Input control	Logging of all incoming data, user requests, or new documentation on changes
2. Microscheduling/Dispatching	Coordination of job movement throughout data center
3. Job assembly/Disassembly	Job setup according to procedures
4. File library functions	Custody, management, and control of all data files and work files
5. Program library (including off-site storage)	Upkeep and custody
6. Report quality control (output)	Report balancing and review for compliance of standards
7. Report preparation and distribution	Report bursting, decollating, binding, and delivery per authorized roster
8. Error and discrepancy management	Perform exception detection and error handling procedures
9. Performance statistics	Logging of data on data center activities
10. Stock and supplies control	Self-explanatory
11. Client relations	Self-explanatory

ance and involvement (for example, the existence of a steering committee and its functioning). These types of controls were dealt with essentially in Chapter 13 of this manual.

Basic Questions

There are several questions to be answered about data processing controls. What are the objectives of controls? Who is responsible for them, how do we control the source data, how do we assure everyone that computer programs are reliable, how do we control the actual processing, how do we check the output, and how do we satisfy other interested groups, such as public accountants, federal tax authorities, etc., that information given to them is correct? Let us review some of these. In advanced data base environments, new questions arise concerning data ownership and responsibility for maintaining data elements and their integrity. These questions involve the data integrity program under the data base administration function.

General Objectives

The chief objective of data control is to ensure that only valid data is accepted and processed, that no invalid data is introduced during processing, and that the data is processed accurately and completely. Controls should prevent loss of information or incorrect processing of data. Loss of information might result from loss of a field in a record, loss of a whole record, loss of a reel of tape in a multireel file, or even loss of an entire file. Controls should also ensure the control accuracy of file contents to avoid financial integrity problems and erroneous decision making by users.

Control systems for computers have four major objectives:

- To ensure that all data are processed and processed consistently
- To ascertain that the correct data are processed
- To ensure accurate and timely processing of the data
- To assist in determining the cause of errors when inaccurate processing occurs

This chapter gives a guide for determining which controls are useful and appropriate for application to computer systems.

Audit Trails

Another important function of controls is the provision for audit trail. With data processing, audit trails can become lost in the collection and summarization of data. There are several ways to keep the audit trail alive in data processing, and they all involve essentially the same concept: keeping a detail file of the transactions as they occur. The detail file might be kept by printing daily proof listings of each day's transactions. It might be kept by printing a transactions journal showing opening balance, detailed transactions, and closing balance for each active account over a short period of time. Or it might be kept by assembling all transactions on a journal tape for on-line systems when there is no hard-copy evidence. This tape could then be the input for an audit program which would extract the transactions for selected accounts and print them in such a way that the accountant or auditor could trace the status of an account, transaction by transaction. Audit trails are best built into the systems during the development cycle. At review time, the reviewer can only ascertain whether there is an adequate trail and make suggestions for improvement.

Cost Effectiveness of Controls

The controls built into a system should be cost-effective.[1] You should balance the incremental cost of controls against the risk of loss that could result from the lack of controls. The cost resulting from lack of controls, which might consist of rerun time, a dissatisfied customer, an out-of-stock condition in inventory, and many other intangibles, is difficult to measure. The incremental

---

[1] W.E. Perry, and J.F. Kuong, *EDP Risk Analysis and Controls Justification* (Wellesley Hills, MA: Management Advisory Publications, 1981).

cost of controls is not difficult to measure, though some of it is involved in other functions and is, therefore, not essentially an out-of-pocket cost. Management, users, and EDP personnel are willing to invest in controls to avoid reruns, lost time, and other losses, if they know the impact of the losses. This impact is best arrived at using risk analysis methods to quantify the losses and balance them against the cost of the controls.

TYPES OF SYSTEM AND PROCEDURAL CONTROLS OR CONTROL PHASES

As mentioned above, procedural input-to-output controls are concerned with controls over the flow of data. Most books and the literature consider three types of controls for applications:

1. Input controls
2. Processing or throughput controls
3. Output controls

Although this classification is useful, it is often more educational to think in terms of the three main equivalent phases, namely

1. Input phase (source document control, preprocessing)
2. Processing phase
3. Output phase (output control-error control, distribution-user controls)

A schematic view of these phases and what they encompass is shown in Figure 18-2. The input phase generally encompasses both the source document and preprocessing stages. The processing phase deals with the actual transformation stages, and the output phase usually includes the data center output quality controls, and distribution procedures and user-end control procedures.

When viewed in this light, we obtain a more complete understanding of the whole transaction flow process from transaction initiation to the time when the end user receives the required information. Both processing steps and the associated controls are considered in this manner.

RESPONSIBILITY FOR EXECUTION OF VARIOUS CONTROL FUNCTIONS

It is useful to show which of the various functions or tasks belong to the input, processing, and output phases, and which data center units are responsible for execution of these steps. Figure 18-3 tabulates functions pertaining to the three main stages of transaction flow along with responsibility for execution. These basic functions are directly related to the processing of batch system applications. Figure 18-2 also shows some other data center internal

Figure 18-2
Transaction Flow in a System Application

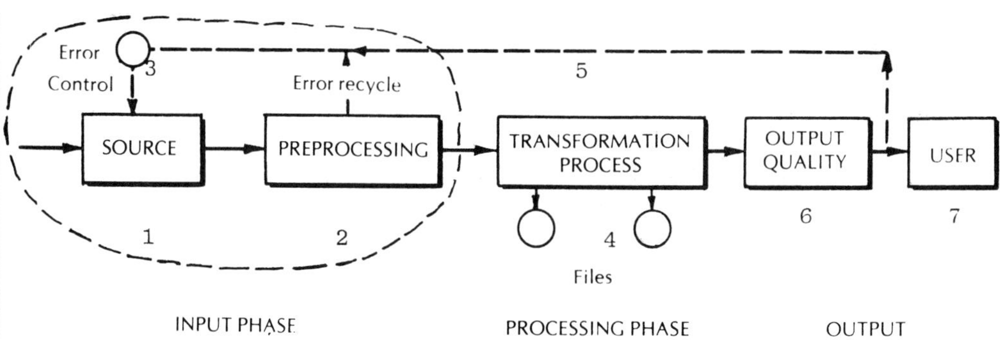

Transaction flow control consists of the following stages or points:

1. Input controls at source level
2. Preprocessing controls and standards before actual conversion
3. Recycle (error) controls and standards
4. File load and update controls
5. Processing controls for:
   - Logic decisions
   - Computations
   - Quality controls over 1, 2 and 3 (programmed into system)
6. Output quality controls
7. User end-use controls (quality, quantity, accuracy, timeliness, security, etc.).

Each of the above has a series of steps or sub-stages which must be considered on their own merits. For example, for the INPUT PHASE, we can distinguish the following important stages:

- I-1. Source data preparation (usually manual preparations, tickets)
- I-2. Data authorization
- I-3. Data conversion
- I-4. Data transmission
- I-5. Input validation
- I-6. Error correction and re-entry procedures

(I-3 to I-6:) These may be subject to both manual and computerized procedures.

administrative functions which are more directly concerned with operations control, such as performance statistics or stock control, which are not directly related to application processing. For this reason, they do not appear in Figure 18-3. These and other operating functions belong more appropriately in category C, **operating practices and standards.** For a more detailed discussion of these, refer to the section on "Data Center Operating Practices and Standards" in this chapter, and also to Chapter 19.

Figure 18-3
Application Control Phases in Relation to Functions Responsible for Execution

FUNCTION/TASK	APPLICATION CONTROL PHASE			PERFORMED BY
	INPUT	PROCESSING	OUTPUT	
Input control (Logging)	X			Users and control clerks
Microscheduling/ Dispatching	X			Control
Data preparation	X			Data preparation (preprocessing). In advanced systems, by on-line edit programs built into the system
Job assembly	X			Control
File library	X		X	Control–librarian
Processing functions		X		Machine operations
Job disassembly			X	Control
Report quality control			X	Control
Report finishing and distribution			X	Control
Error discrepancy and management	X		X	Control and users

INPUT PHASE CONTROLS

Definition and Objectives

Input phase controls constitute a set of procedures to ensure the proper authorization, validity of normality, and completeness of source documents and data to be processed. A large number of these procedures can be performed manually by the source and/or user department. Many can also be mechanized by programming them into the application system.

The objectives of input controls are:

1. To ascertain that all transactions have been properly recorded at the source level
2. To ensure that all transactions to be processed are accounted for at source level and at the preprocessing stages (e.g., keypunch)

3. To ensure proper authorization of transactions
4. To ensure that all transactions are transmitted from point of origin to point of processing
5. To ensure that error-reentry procedures are followed
6. To ensure that data batches are logged properly (signed in and out)

Types of Input Controls

The controls may apply at the source document level or at the data contents level, which includes the data itself and control over master file changes.

Computers follow instructions exactly. This requires that data entering the system be translated into machine language in correct form and content. If input is captured accurately and completely, the processing of data will be relatively simple once computer programs have been debugged. The development of formal procedures, written instructions, and the minimization of transactions requiring special treatment will increase input accuracy and strengthen internal control.

Control Over Source Documents

The need to provide controls over source documents and computer input is important. Prenumbered documents, document counts, and sequence checks could be used wherever possible, together with written approvals wherever appropriate. All transactions should originate outside the data processing department and a register should be maintained, or multiple copies provided. Document counts, dollar control totals, and control totals for other fields should be developed for each batch of documents sent to data processing. Regular deliveries should be scheduled and transmittal forms used with each request. For on-line systems, with random data entry, these controls are programmed into the system and on-line editing routines.

Special emphasis should be placed on the need for control over master file changes. Changes to these files can influence dollar answers. For instance, a vendor added to a master file of approved vendors might be the basis for approval of an invoice upon a match in the computer. In this situation, there is an obvious need for this vendor to be genuine and to be approved by authorized personnel. A written authorization for changes to master files is a good operating practice. In on-line data entry systems, the technical controls discussed in the previous chapter apply, such as logical access controls and authorization tables.

Many controls that contribute to improved validation of input data can be programmed into the computerized system to detect anomalies for subsequent corrections. These are dealt with in the next section. Figure 18-4 summarizes the types of transaction controls that can be used.

Figure 18-4
System Application Transaction (Data) Control Needs

Transaction controls are needed to ensure that:

1. The transaction is complete.
2. The transaction is normal (not anomalous). For example:
   Alpha instead of numeric
   Quantity larger than normal, etc.
3. All transactions in a group are transmitted and/or processed. Control totals in the control log to reconcile input controls with controls (totals) generated upon processing. Example:
   A batch control total on:
   A. Number of transactions per batch ensures that all clock cards in a payroll application (documents, checks, cards) are received. However, this is not good enough for accuracy of the amount. Therefore we use:
   B. A field total (say, hours worked). This can be used to validate the computer processed output against input controls received.

For Items 1 and 2, input validation techniques are available. They are listed in Figure 18-5.

PROCESSING PHASE CONTROLS

Definition and Objectives

Processing controls encompass a set of manual and mechanized procedures and techniques designed to help meet basic quality, accuracy, and regulatory requirements of information during the computer processing phase at the data center.

The basic objectives of processing controls are to:

1. Detect loss or nonprocessing of data
2. Determine if arithmetic or mathematical calculations were performed correctly
3. Determine whether all relevant transactions were posted to the proper record, file, or data base
4. Spot possible program deficiencies or errors and aid in their resolution
5. Ensure that proper files are loaded for a given job (procedural control)
6. Minimize operator errors or job assembly mistakes (procedural controls)

For items 5 and 6, see also the information under "Data Center Operating Practices and Standards" in this chapter.

The Nature of Processing Controls

Whereas input and data capturing controls are designed to ensure that the data entering the system is what is intended, processing controls, on the other hand, are intended to ensure that the data that did enter the system is processed correctly and completely and to ensure that the data and results are properly recorded in the files or data bases and not lost or destroyed.

The accuracy of processing will depend on a number of factors and control techniques, many of which are of the programmed variety, that is to say, the system designer and programmer have a definite input into this matter. As part of the cadre of processing controls, one should also remember that the vendors provide a number of control provisions and checks to ensure that the hardware performs its functions as intended, such as parity bits, bit counts, dual reads, file protection rings, hash totals, etc.

The more important controls are those which the designer and the auditor as a consultant on controls, are able to conceive, specify, and program during the design cycle of the system in question. In this regard, the ideal way to ensure that processing controls, and for that matter any system control, are incorporated in the system is to institute an *internal controls design methodology* during the system design cycle which should complement the system design methodology.

Programmed Controls

The number and variety of possible controls and checks that systems designers, auditors, and programmers can program into a system are indeed limitless and constrained only by the economics of adding controls relative to the potential loss of not having controls. Except for situations where there are regulatory reasons for adding the controls, you should add as many controls as the cost-benefit aspects of the situation permit. The economics of internal controls are discussed amply in the book: *EDP Risk Analysis and Controls Justification* (Wellesley Hills, MA: Management Advisory Publications, *1981*).

The following are some of the controls to consider. See also Figure 18-5.

- Batch totals and account balancing against predetermined amounts
- Record counts
- Hash totals (a total of a set of codes or items)
- Sequence checks
- Run-to-run totals
- Checking for valid code or valid data against master files or reference data
- Reasonableness checks
- Crossfooting
- Transaction numbering and sequence checks
- Downfooting

- Tolerance ranges
- Rounding algorithms to handle rounding error
- Sign checking
- Data composition checks
- Duplicate and complement arithmetic
- Reverse computation
- Subtracting back to zero
- Checks on program sequence and linkage validity
- Hash totals on programs
- Checks against reference table

Figure 18-5
System Application Controls for Input Validation

For data completeness and normality checks, it is common practice to use input validation control techniques.

Input validation should be practiced as soon as possible. This is usually done through computerized (programmed) edit controls (or filters) for the following needs or conditions:

1. Validity (transactions, codes, fields). Accept/reject type. Reject relative to:
   - Validity
   - Reasonableness
   - Limits

   Criteria can be against
   - Quantity
   - Amounts
   - Codes

   Relative to:
   - Values given
   - Tables of values
   - Actual master file accounts, items
   - Official values, rates, discounts, etc.
2. Completeness
3. Limits
4. Logical tests. Relationship to other things: Branch code, transaction code, teller no. terminal no. and assigned password, etc.
5. Control totals
6. Sequence
7. Self-checking digits
8. Ratio tests
9. Pattern analysis
10. Multicondition matrices, transaction conflict matrices, or decision tables
11. Data base or file scanning routines

File Controls

The above controls address processing of data. Controls that ensure the accuracy of updating and the accuracy of data in files are also necessary. These are programmed controls for files and data bases. These controls are addressed to the problems of accuracy in accessing the correct data, updating of the right record or data element, and of deleting the data that wasn't intended. Some of the controls for this area are:

- Tape and disk internal labels to ensure that the right file is used
- Record counts and run-to-run controls
- Redundancy checks, such as a code to identify the last name of an account
- Hash totals on a group of records
- Checks against reference values
- Checks for code and record validity
- Read back of record after updating
- File protection to prevent accidental file erasure
- Use of suspense files for erroneous accounts or unsuccessful update attempts
- Tests of data/record completeness
- Data base dumps at periodic intervals to serve as backup
- Use of transaction logs in on-line systems to permit data base reconstruction.
- Procedures to force the cleaning of suspense accounts and transaction
- Comparison of values to reference values
- Batch totals or groups of transactions totals to replace batch totals in on-line systems
- Setting control files with a summary of control information to permit balancing or reconciliations
- Data base administration data integrity program

OUTPUT PHASE CONTROLS

Objectives and Scope

The objectives of output phase controls are to:

1. Reconcile output data with input controls during processing
2. Determine reasonableness of the information produced
3. Check for normal format and quantity of information

4. Control rejected input data produced during processing and take the necessary steps to route it to the appropriate people for disposition
5. Review and control the distribution of output reports to authorized users according to established quality, quantity, timeliness, and security acceptance criteria

During the output phase, the control unit has the last opportunity to ensure that data processing output is correct, free of obvious abnormalities, and that, in fact, it reaches only authorized personnel.

Another set of output controls are those practiced by the originating or user group through review of abnormal items or conditions. This process is greatly aided by a combination of the programmed controls mentioned above and the use of exception report capabilities built into any one system, to warn the user of any possible anomalous situations.

Control Over Reports

Adequate control of reports and documents requires participation by departments outside of data processing. A sound system should include regular systematic review of output by these using departments to ascertain that established requirements are being met. Since most reports are used by someone, and in this use are subject to some scrutiny, it might be contended that this requirement is automatically fulfilled. The key to effectiveness of review, however, is the planned approach on a regular basis using such yardsticks as predetermined totals, appropriate budget amounts, reference quantities, standards of performance, results of prior periods, and other tests of reasonableness, along with exception reporting. It is also possible to relate present balances on a recent report to balances of previous reports for the previous period plus the net of new transactions for the new period. In other words, by conducting a period-to-period balancing.

Error Control and Resubmission of Corrections

One of the problem areas created by EDP is computer-detected errors. In most manual systems, and in some machine systems, many of these errors would go undetected or would be dismissed as immaterial. Unless told to do so, the computer cannot process even the slightest error. Many of these errors are due to carelessness in preparing the original source document, incomplete transactions, or an anomalous condition. A good system should provide information that can be used in improving performance of the data originators. Reducing the number of source document errors is one of the best ways to improve computer performance. For on-line, interactive systems, the best way to handle this problem is through the use of conversational or "dialog" edit and control provisions which enable the data entry operator to clean up his data before acceptance can take place or place it a suspense file.

Procedures should provide assurance that all error data are investigated, corrected, and resubmitted. Generally, all errors from a given application should be controlled by one department outside of data processing, with that department contacting others as required. This department should be provided with an error register and the applicable source documents should be filed in such a way as to allow the particular document in which the error exists to be located. Written approvals should be used for error correction, wherever appropriate, and further control is necessary to ensure that the error is corrected and resubmitted. This is normally done through the control section within EDP. Using a separate data reentry group tends to reduce fraudulent resubmission of data.

Input Phase Controls Checklist

Control Over Input and Output Data

Although the review of controls over input and output data must be done for each application eventually, general questions regarding these controls may be used to ascertain whether use of control procedures is evident.

1. Are source departments required to establish independent control over data submitted for processing (through the use of batch totals, document counts, record counts, hash totals, etc.)?
2. Is the number of basic types of input documents limited so as to facilitate control and processing efficiency?
3. Are all input documents prenumbered (in batch systems) or preprinted?
4. Are all numbered documents accounted for by the control unit?
5. Are data processed in serially numbered batches?
6. Are all source documents identified by batch number and canceled to prevent reprocessing?
7. Are data controlled by the number of documents processed and by hash totals as well as by dollar amount?
8. Does the control unit use a document register or other positive method of comparing machine run totals with control totals?
9. Is responsibility fixed, and are adequate procedures in effect, for tracing and correcting input errors?
10. Are corrections identified and recorded in such a manner that duplicate correction will not occur and subsequent audit will be possible?
11. Are all instructions to keypunch operators (or bookkeeping machine operators preparing paper tapes) written in clear, concise form?

12. If the computer writes checks or other negotiable instruments, are the requisition and use of blank stock closely controlled?
13. Are both master files and transaction files handled equally insofar as controls and verification is concerned?
14. Do source/user departments maintain independent control over master files?
15. Are all data batches clearly identified and preferably serially numbered?
16. Is each batch accompanied by a batch control document (ticket) created by the originating department? (A copy of the source document should be maintained by the control unit for verification purposes.) Does this ticket show: batch number, date, control totals by important field, transaction count, previous batch number?
17. Are sequence controls and quantity control totals used, such as hours, units, items?
18. For on-line systems, are sound edit and data cleaning controls provided for use at the terminal?

Error Management and Control

Error controls should ensure that rejections are corrected and reentered into the system. Sometimes rejection reports, cards, etc., are lost and the corrected data is never reentered. Good systems keep open files of rejections and clear them only when they are reentered correctly. Also, it is usually best to have rejections printed on separate reports rather than on reports containing other information. This makes them easier to isolate and correct. Sending copies of error reports to a third party or to supervisors encourages corrective actions. Preparation of routine error reports on data base elements by the data base administration function helps correct erroneous data in data bases.

Other error control procedures include:

1. Are batch contents listed for user review?
2. Is erroneous data captured in an error listing which accompanies each batch input printout?
3. Are there procedures for rejecting erroneous data? On-line edit checks in on-line systems?
4. Are errors which cause out-of-balance conditions spotted and rejected to keep the system in balance?
5. Are source documents cancelled to avoid reentry or reprocessing?
6. Are errors and rejected input managed by the control section, sent to orginating departments and records kept for reentry later?
7. Are errors removed preferably before final processing? It is prefera-

ble to catch errors, correct them, and then reenter them in a new batch.

8. Are corrections actually made by the source department rather than the control unit?
9. Are master files listed and purified at appropriate intervals to reduce error sources?
10. If error stems from master file contents, are there specific procedures to correct master files?
11. Does the control unit follow up reprocessing of rejected data?
12. Are all error corrections reviewed and approved by persons who are independent of the data processing department?
13. Are records maintained of errors occurring in the EDP system?
14. Are these error records periodically reviewed by someone independent of data processing?
15. Are anomalous conditions spotted by the data base scanning routines acted upon?

Data Preparation/Conversion

1. Are there up-to-date written procedures for all data preparation/conversion applications, including data formats, forms, and controls? Are on-line screens properly designed to minimize errors?
2. Are check digits used for account codes or item numbers, where appropriate?
3. Is there a manual which describes all card and screen applications, formats, and layouts, including special instructions?
4. Are there controls for data conversion to machine-readable form for all types of data conversion? (data entry keying, optical scanning, key-to-tape, using document counts, batch totals)
5. Are personnel properly trained on verification procedures and on handling of discrepancies?
6. Are there procedures to prevent reentry of cancelled documents?
7. Are records kept of transaction volume and number of errors made?
8. If data transmission is used, are there adequate transmission controls to determine correctness and completeness of transmission or message loss? (e.g., echo checks, beginning and end of transmission, etc.)
9. Are there sound retention procedures for documents for an appropriate time period to enable reprocessing in the event of magnetic file loss? Do retention cycles comply with regulatory agency and audit needs?

Processing Phase Controls Checklist

Processing Standards

1. Are operator's run manuals up-to-date giving run instructions and including:
   a. Complete job description
   b. Source, form, and condition (sorted) of input
   c. I/O files and which peripheral unit should be used
   d. Operating steps
   e. Console switch settings
   f. Halts and required operator action
   g. File labels
   h. Configurations required for on-line systems
   i. Job streams
   j. Journal logs
   k. Data base dumping
2. Are there rules on the use of utility programs to copy files or other media?
3. Are there procedures to print out program constants (rates, discounts, prices), and are these reviewed by authorized personnel? Are there stringent procedures to maintain contents of tables in table-driven systems?
4. Are there adequate procedures over use of the console by operators?
5. Are console listings reviewed by a group outside EDP? Are console logs for sensitive systems: (a) reviewed, and (b) stored for reference?

Programmed Control Over Processing

Programmed controls are usually evaluated in terms of each application. For further details on program processing review, refer to system application review questionnaires for system audits.

1. Are control totals used to check for completeness of processing? These may include trailer file labels, run-to-run totals, etc.
2. Are programmed edit controls used to test processing of significant items?
   a. Limit and reasonableness test
   b. Crossfooting test
3. Does the program check for improper switch settings (if sense switches are used)?
4. Do programs provide an adequate console printout of control information (switch settings, control violations, operator intervention, etc.)?

5. When a program is interrupted, are there adequate provisions for restart?
6. Are there adequate controls over the process of identifying, correcting, and reprocessing data rejected by the program?
7. Is the handling of unmatched transactions (no master record corresponding to transaction record) adequate?
   a. Reject and note on error log
   b. Reject and write on suspense record
   c. Other (notify appropriate person)
8. Does the system input data in such a manner as to minimize errors?
9. Has due consideration been given to the design of foolproof source documents and good screens?
10. Have checking procedures been set up, both manually and within the computer, to detect errors?

Output Phase Controls Checklist

Output controls are utilized to determine the accuracy of the processing system and to ensure that the output goes to the proper and authorized user.

Report Distribution

After a job has been processed, the output should be returned to the operations control area.

1. There the job should be logged out in the log book and the output or outputs routed to the authorized recipients.
2. Open output bins are not desirable.
3. All output should be maintained in a controlled environment until the courier can take them directly to the user.
4. It is useful to have a set of report distribution instructions. A checklist of control data that should be maintained for each important report is shown in Figure 18-6.
5. Are batch controls checked by the control unit: predetermined controls vs. printout of input?
6. Does the control unit compare source media against the printouts on a 100 percent or test basis? (100 percent at the start of any new system.)
7. Is the source media and a copy of the printout returned to the originating data preparation unit, which should perform its own checks for accuracy?
8. Are output reports and documents reviewed before distribution to ascertain the reasonableness of the output?

Figure 18-6
Report Distribution Control List

Report Specification Data
- Report name
- What is the report intended for (brief description)?
- Who is the report intended for and who will use it in the user group?
- Size of report (no. of pages)
- No. of copies and authorized roster for distribution
- Retention cycle (file copies, microfilm)?
- Sample copy of report or report format layout
- Schedules and due-out dates. Frequency of processing (daily, etc.)
- Specification of official programs used to generate report according to run book.
- Table of data elements or items printed in the report, including where these originate from, regarding data source and how arrived at in processing
- Special instructions for security and confidentiality and handling of excess reports

9. Are there adequate procedures for control over the distribution of reports?
10. Is there a control of usage of sensitive forms such as checks and the use of check signing devices by other than EDP personnel?
11. Do processing programs report errors or exceptions?
12. Are output totals balanced to the original input control totals?
13. Is there a record of errors from all sources maintained in report form and summarized periodically for review?
14. Are excess copies of reports shredded?
15. Is the list of report recipients updated regularly?

DATA CENTER OPERATING PRACTICES AND STANDARDS

This section lists a number of data center operations-related practices, standards, and controls. Although their existence and proper execution have a great deal to do with the quality, timeliness, processing effectiveness, and security of processed data, they are primarily operations-oriented and apply to all applications and not just to any one application. These controls were classed as the third type in the purpose section.

The areas for which checklists are included are:

- General practices (control section)
- Computer operations practices
- Control of job reruns
- File update and change
- Program change controls
- File library

Because of the importance of the library function, the discussion of file library practices and guidelines is treated as a separate heading further in this section. Included is the file library checklist as well as guidelines for protection and backup of tape reels and disk files.

Backup and recovery checklists were covered in Chapter 15. Testing belongs to the area of system development (Chapter 23), as does system documentation.

The review of these procedures is necessary to determine that financial and accounting procedures have been established and to assure that good operating controls exist in the data center.

Processing operations, as used here, includes all functions performed from the point at which the computer receives data in machine language to the final report. During this time the method of storing and transmitting data may change many times. The nature of data may be altered by other data already in storage or by factors built into programs. The auditor should be familiar with how data are processed, in what form, by which function, and with what results.

Data Center Operations Checklist

General Control Section Practices

1. Is there a person or group responsible for the control function in the data center? Review their responsibilities which should include:
   a. Control over receipt of input data and recording of control information
   b. Reconciliation of control information (batch control with computer control totals, run-to-run controls, etc.)
   c. Control over distribution of output
   d. Control over errors to ensure that they are reported, corrected, and reprocessed
   e. Review of console logs, error listings, and other evidence of error detection and control
2. Is the group responsible for control over processing by the data processing department independent from the group responsible for equipment operations?
3. Are there transaction count controls when batch controls are not available (such as for on-line systems)?
4. Is there a report distribution list? Is it checked at least quarterly?

General Practices

1. Are there data input and logging procedures to handle all kinds of requests (processing runs, master file updates, program tests, rerun requests)?

2. Is there a central log in the control section where all data, requests entering EDP are logged in?
3. Is access to control data restricted to employees of the control unit?
4. Is the control unit responsible for recording and expediting all data processed by the EDP section, including control over the number, due date, and distribution of reports?
5. Do routing documents have the necessary information for authorization and control?
6. Communications between the operating staff and the control unit should contain at least the following information:
   a. Name and department
   b. Project number or account number to which the run will be charged
   c. Time estimate of the job
   d. Instructions to the operator, including what tapes and disk packs are to be used, and any special run instructions
   e. Other instructions that will simplify processing
7. Is there a positive follow-up to determine if corrections are made on errors found by the machine?

Computer Operations Controls (See also Chapter 19)

1. Are the following control practices adhered to?
   a. Computer operations personnel should not have access to operational data or data authorization or preparation actions.
   b. Computer operators should not be responsible for input error corrections.
   c. Equipment should be operated only by operators.
   d. All unauthorized production or test runs should not be processed by operators unless properly routed, documented (run request), and received from the control unit. All jobs or revisions are supported by a written request.
   e. Computer operators do not initiate any transactions or change master files.
   f. There should be up-to-date clearly documented run books for every job or run including:
      –Specific equipment to be used
      –Purpose of run
      –Input and output specification
      –Set up
      –End of run
      –Manual switch settings
      –Details of all programmed machine halts and required action

–Action to be taken in the event of breakdowns, halts, rejected input
–Job control language (JCL) instruction

g. Supervisors should be present when running sensitive jobs.
h. Machine utilization records should be kept which account for all time used (see Chapter 19 for other details).

2. Are all instructions to operators in writing in clear and unequivocal language?
3. Are operators cautioned not to accept oral instructions and not to contact programmers directly when errors are detected?
4. Are all halts (except end-of-job) and errors recorded and the record retained for audit?
5. Is the use of external switches held to a minimum, and are the instructions for their use set forth in writing?
6. Are the situations whereby data may be inserted or extracted by the use of the console set forth in writing and limited to circumstances which cannot be handled through the stored program?
7. Are console printouts controlled and reviewed by persons (other than operators) who are familiar with the activity being performed?
8. Are console printouts labeled so as to be reasonably intelligible?
9. Are checkpoints provided in lengthy processing runs, and are program or external restart instructions provided in case a checkpoint fails to balance?
10. Is a schedule maintained of the reports and documents to be produced by each EDP system?
11. Other operating practices
    a. Printer carriage control tapes should be kept in good condition.
    b. Ribbon printers should be cleaned at least twice per month. Other printer types maintained by vendor recommendations.
    c. Old ribbons and carbons should be destroyed.
    d. Sensitive documents and extra copies of reports should be shredded. (The shredder should not be in the computer room itself to avoid dust.)
    e. Hardware errors should be checked by the operations manager and the maintenance engineer.
    f. Sound preventive and remedial maintenance procedures should exist.
    g. The control clerk or group is responsible for dispatching jobs to the computer room. He should record what machine the job is run on, what time the job is submitted, and what time it is completed. He can also inform users of the status of their jobs. In order to do this, he needs a set of due-in-due-out times, run sheets, and route

sheets. Where this is automated by job accounting packages, periodic reviews of job processing are desirable.

12. Controls for processing jobs
    a. Provisions should be made, where possible, to isolate debugging activity from production activity.
    b. The console log should be established to assure continuity of recording.
       –All unexplained stoppages or interruptions are to be accounted for.
       –A register of errors should be maintained, action taken, and a record kept of manual interruptions.
    c. Records should be kept of file maintenance updating, notifying point of issue to confirm updating.
    d. There should be a preauthorization for all overtime computer usage. This authorization should not pertain just to the computer, but also to:
       –Use of operator instructions for overtime computer usage
       –Programs
       –Tapes and disks
       –Usage of input data for overtime runs
    e. Special efforts should be made to ensure that important controls written into computer programs cannot be indiscriminately overridden. For example, in most accounts payable systems, audit programs ensure that for each invoice entered, there is a corresponding authorized purchase order on file. In addition, the audit programs test whether purchase order unit price agrees with invoice quantity, etc. Override routines are written in the programs which allow an invoice to be paid without going through the audit tests. The special override codes are used to avoid investigating errors; as a result, an organization may lose control. Exception procedures should receive the closest scrutiny.
13. Control over the console
    a. In large scale systems a console typewriter may be used and it would normally record all operating events where the only access to the computer to alter programs or stored data is through the typewriter. Analysis of the message and instructions entered into the machine would help in identifying troublesome programs and provide a means for detecting program alterations and unscheduled processing. Where such a device is used, it is a sound practice to prenumber console pages and account for their sequence. Where there is no console typewriter, output printers may be used to create the same effect when combined with programmed checks. Some computers can inhibit the console printing so that these may not be absolute controls.

b. It is a good practice to minimize operator-entered actions. A good operating program should not interrupt processing because of a discrepancy in data but rather the system should eliminate the record, adjust the trailer record control totals, and proceed. At the end of the processing, the eliminated records should be identified for possible manual correction. If this approach is not used, error action should be specified on the "halt" instructions, and proof of the action taken should be evident through the console typewriter or the input device.

c. For communication between shifts, as well as for diagnosing and recovering from nonrestartable system failures, it is important that a log recording all significant system events be kept at the console. The depth of detail in the log should be determined on the basis of the characteristics of the workload, and the availability of personnel to maintain the log. The following should all be listed:
–The console output should be considered to be the minimum operator's log. It should be kept for at least twenty-four hours, preferably for a week or so.
–Each end-of-job should be recorded, along with any unusual event during the run. If the job ran uneventfully and successfully, that should be noted.
–All "crashes," hardware and software, should be recorded, as should all loops and anything requiring a new IPL. The reason for the crash or re-IPL should be stated, along with the remedial action taken, whether a dump was made, and who made the entry. ABENDS (abnormal ends) should be logged.
–All mounted volumes should be identified.

Control of Job Reruns

It is a fact of data processing operations that a number of computer runs will require reprocessing, as a result of data, program, machine malfunction, software errors, procedure, or operator mistakes. When a job is reprocessed it is usually called a job rerun. These conditions require that the data center establish and observe sound procedures for job rerun control.

The objectives of rerun control are:

1. To eventually reduce the number of reruns
2. To help trace the cause of the reruns and establish the methodology to remedy the situation for all possible recurrences of the problem
3. To improve efficiency
4. To improve data and program security, since a possible defrauder may take advantage of frequent rerun and erroneous conditions to perpetrate his deed or disguise his purpose

Procedures should be in effect for rerun control through the use of a form or table which lists the reruns and possible sources of errors. A sample form is shown in Figure 18-7. This form was used in a client installation for purposes of recording and managing reruns.

In many data centers reruns are often not recorded. This is especially true where the control function is intermingled with the machine operations function, whereby, naturally, certain embarrassing situations are not likely to be reported by operators who may also serve as control clerks. This has been the case, in our experience with many consulting assignments, for both small and large installations. Provisions for recording reruns must be made and, most importantly, the mechanisms for **detecting** the underlying cause and the application of corrective measures should be instituted.

The following aspects, among others, should be investigated whenever a rerun is incurred:

1. What was the cause of the rerun?
2. Was it due to: program failure, data error (keypunch, etc.), defective control total, machine malfunction, maintenance problems, operator mistake (loading the wrong file), defective or insufficient procedures, console keying or remote terminal entry, or sporadic error connected with the operating system?
3. What action steps were taken and by whom?

This information, logged on a form similar to Figure 18-7, should provide the basis for a monthly report of rerun activity for costing purposes and for monitoring reruns. This report can be used by all concerned (data processing manager, users of systems, quality control unit, systems department, and auditor), as a basis for taking the necessary steps to minimize the number and the severity of reruns, and as a basis for **fixing responsibility** for current and future actions.

Figure 18-7
Sample Form for Recording Job Reruns

RERUN TYPE	DESCRIPTION EXTENT	COST	REASON FOR RERUN						ACTION TAKEN	PREVENTIVE MEASURE
			KP	Control	Prog.	Equip.	Oper.	O		

O, Other

File Update and Change

1. Is there a properly established procedure for file changes and change control through:
   a. A written request for change from authorized users
   b. Register of all changes which are reviewed by the initiating department
   c. Supervisory or multilevel review of changes
2. Do you have a master file change form with properly approved procedures?
3. Do changes to master files have proper approvals, especially for sensitive systems?
4. Are transaction items accurately posted to master files?
5. Are departments that initiate changes in master file data or program data factors furnished with notices or a register showing changes actually made? (Examples of such changes are changes in pay rates, selling prices, credit limits, and commission tables.)
6. Are master file changes or changes in program data factors authorized in writing by the initiating departments? For data base systems, are all data element changes routed through the data dictionary system?
7. Are key master files periodically printed out in detail, reviewed, screened, and purged by means of:
   1. A periodic listing and detailed review
   2. Periodic test against reference data
   3. Sampling tests or file scanning techniques
8. Is this done by a group outside computer operations? Is the data dictionary system used for data base systems?
9. In on-line systems, do you use file scanning techniques to check integrity, errors, or degree of file degradation?
10. Do you have specific procedures for dealing with erroneous master files entries which may have been rejected during update time through an error routine or exception routine which lists the errors in the suspense file? Do you have a periodic review procedure for all outstanding master file erroneous or questionable entries and is responsibility clearly assigned to the appropriate group to do these tasks? Is the data owner in data base systems responsible for data element error management?

Program Change Controls

1. Is approval and justification required before development of new programs within an established system?

2. Can changes be made to programs without the using department's knowledge and approval?
3. Are the following practices followed for controlling program changes?
   a. The management of using departments approves the programs before they become operational.
   b. All program changes should require review and approval.
   c. All program changes should be adequately tested under supervision.
   d. All program files and documentation should be periodically reviewed to determine that they are up-to-date and complete.
   e. All user departments should be advised of changes and determine that they are proper and approve them.
   f. Flowcharts and procedures should be standardized.
   g. There should be a standard format for each program file.
   h. Program labels and tags should be standardized.
   i. Program change documentation should be kept up to date.
   j. Program cataloging into the production or executable library should be done only by operators after suitable written approval from the control unit.
4. Are all program tests done on a "remote" basis (by operators with no hands-on testing by programmers)?
5. If not, are tests, program assemblies, and hands-on time properly controlled?
6. Is management able to determine whether programmers are making excessive tests and assemblies because of poor programming techniques?
7. Are targets established for reasonable "hands-on" time rerun because of operator or programmer error?
8. Do operators have access to program flowcharts, source decks, program listings?
9. Operators should not know program contents.
10. Is an operating log maintained to record any significant events and actions taken by the operator?
11. Is there a roster of all official and active programs, which includes a brief description of the functions performed by each program, their date of approval, and identification or code number?
12. Are approved copies of all computer programs and their documentation kept and maintained up-to-date in the program library? Are there strict procedures regarding authorization for release of copies?
13. Are master programs kept in a secure fireproof vault, along with documentation and operating manuals?

14. Is there a well-defined procedure to ensure that all programs affecting master files are kept current after any change, and is responsibility for such clearly assigned to one person such as the file librarian?
15. Are "print" or "display" programs controlled?

FILE LIBRARY PRACTICES AND PROCEDURES

Importance of File Library Review

Other than the programs themselves and the documentation of systems, the files contain a great deal of the organization's information on a permanent or semipermanent basis. A review of the file library function and its standards and procedures is therefore very important. This section contains both descriptive guidelines and checklists for auditing the library function. The auditor should first ascertain that proper operating practices exist and next, whether these practices are being followed in all shifts. These practices should be consistent for all three shifts where possible. Also, the communication procedures on library matters between shifts should be sound. Another important aspect related to file library protection is the matter of contingency plans and backup provisions for files. Although a great deal was said about this matter in Chapter 16, additional information is included in this section, as it applies specifically to files and to the library.

File Library Guidelines and Practices

- There should be a library function, preferably for every shift.
- The librarian should be independent of the operations and programming functions and should control the issuance of all files to these groups; normally only to computer operations or to the off-site storage locations.
- The library should have a complete record of all files on a dynamic basis.
- All tapes and disk files should be maintained in the library when not in use, not on desks or in programmers' offices.
- There should be clear standards and procedures to manage, secure, and operate the library function.
- The library should be manned and/or locked at all times. Access should be limited to only the librarian or duly authorized supervision at special times.
- Programmers, operators, and users do not have access to the library.

- All files should be clearly numbered and labeled by a given procedure which is part of library standards.
- Header and trailer labels should be used where indicated.
- There should be a list of personnel authorized to use certain key files.
- Sound storage facilities and procedures should exist to protect files against fire and other hazards.
- The library should not be in the computer room as a precaution against simultaneous damage to both computer and file library. It should not be near windows or areas neighboring the outside of the building to avoid the possibility of sabotage or vandalism.
- Tape logs should be maintained with a complete record of tape withdrawals, returns, times, purposes, and individuals involved. This enables verification of authorized use and keeping track of files.
- Tape retention dates for files should be carefully maintained.
- People coming near the library (such as maintenance personnel) should not carry magnets.
- Jobs accepted from programming cease to belong to programming; live files should not be issued to them unless properly authorized.
- Library tapes should all be ring-protected until, and if, they become scratch tapes (ring in).
- Tapes should be marked with "date obsolete" data.
- Defective tapes (spots or if tape was cut) should be noted. In the case of packs, defective tracks should be indicated.
- Scratch tapes should be tested periodically by a program which writes on the tape and reads back the contents. Tape testers may be used to advantage.
- An appropriate file backup and recovery procedure should exist.
- Duplicate copies of master files and vital data should exist and should be stored in a secured area (grandfather, father, son system) according to well-managed retention schedules.
- Copies of data base dumps and transaction logs for on-line systems should be kept.
- The courier service responsible for transporting files should be checked for reliability, or bonded.
- Data on tapes, disks, and cards should be periodically printed out as a checking mechanism and to avoid full dependence on existing media, especially for valuable files.
- The backup procedures should be audited periodically or on a surprise basis.
- There should be a formal tape cleaning system for tapes.

Protection for and Backup of Tape Reels and Disk Files

Needless to say, the information on magnetic files must be protected by safeguarding the magnetic media on which it is recorded, usually magnetic tape reels and magnetic disks. To this effect, there should be carefully planned and written standards for magnetic media protection, in case of destruction and to permit recovery and reconstruction.

In protecting information in media, you should consider standards for dealing with batch conventional systems and for on-line systems. *For batch conventional systems* the most common way to back up the files is using the so-called generation protection scheme: grandfather-father-son. This involves the storage of three generations of files according to a retention system of three cycles. As a new generation is created, the oldest generation is disposed of or "scratched." When the current generation gets destroyed, the installation requests the next or "father" backup generation. If the latter were also destroyed, one can resort to the "grandfather" generation for backup. Bear in mind that the data between generations should also be kept in retention to enable you to reconstruct the current version of the file by adding the information between generations.

In the event of massive destruction from whatever causes (physical damage, fire, water flooding, etc.), it is usually required that the installation make provisions for off-site or off-line storage on the principle that it would be much less likely that the two physical locations were destroyed. If storage of the files is done on-site, provisions should be made to provide "protected storage" in the computer room in the form of a library using fire-protected storage such as safes and fireproof vaults. Bear in mind that most vaults are designed only to retard the possibility of damage by maintaining the temperature of the media at an acceptable level for a given time period, usually expressed in the form of a rating, as discussed in Chapter 14 of this manual.

When the protected storage provisions are drawn up, please keep in mind that a set of carefully prepared standards and procedures must be in place to reduce the possibility of mishaps or illegal access, and to monitor adherence to the rules of protection. This is usually taken care of through a set of library procedures. The checklists that follow give you an inkling of the diversity and level of detail of the provisions that should be in place.

One important consideration when having off-site remote storage of backup files is the means and avenues by which these backup files are transported. This brings up the question of the safety and confidentiality with which the courier services operate and the protection of the backup files while in transit. Rules for the selection of couriers and for the handling of files must be in place. Also, when handling confidential files, provisions should be made to train the transportation people and even "bond" the selected personnel.

For on-line systems, backup procedures change considerably. In addition to the retention of father and grandfather files for the main master files (data bases in on-line systems), there is the need to capture the on-line data which arrives randomly, transaction by transaction, by means of so-called transaction logs. These logs must also be backed up and stored safely so that, if obliteration of the data base occurs, the data base or master file can be restored to its current state by adding the "before and after image" information (information on the data base before the change and after the change is made) captured in the transaction logs to the information in the last dump or copy of the data base at some period of time before. It is paramount that both the periodic dumps of the data base and the transaction logs be transported and stored in safe and protected off-site storage and custody.

Testing the Currency of Contingency Plans

In view of the importance of the contingency and recovery plan to the ability of a business to maintain continuity, it is very important to ensure that these plans remain current and reflect the latest status of the hardware, system software, application systems, and supporting documentation, and procedures. Both the business and the data processing environment are "dynamic." It is therefore very likely that the contingency plan that was developed at some period of time before will gradually become out of date. All the benefit derived from the effort in preparing the plan can be lost when and if one discovers, only too late, that the plan is inoperable.

The way to do this is by means of periodic or surprise audits of the status of the contingency plan. For a framework to use in auditing a contingency plan, the reader is referred to: "What to Look for When Auditing Your Company's EDP Contingency and Recovery Plan for Business Continuity," *COM-AND, Computer Audit News and Developments,* Sept-Oct. and Nov.-Dec., 1985.[2] With regard to file media backup, the audit of this plan should encompass at least these points:

1. Review the roster of all tapes and disks that are required to support the critical applications. Determine that all of these are kept in off-site protected storage. The documentation on the tapes' usage and movement in the form of a tape file history can serve as a basis for review. A tape file history records an account by type of tape, reel number, month, creation date, scratch date, a record of which job the tape was used for, the date when the tape left the library, and the date when it was returned. For a scratched file, the date when it was done should be recorded.
2. Determine if there are tapes lying around not in protected storage.

---

[2] *COM-AND, Computer Audit News and Developments,* is a bimonthly newsletter published by Management Advisory Publications, Wellesley Hills, MA 02181.

3. Determine and review all the programs, operating instructions, JCL (job control language), and documentation for all critical applications.
4. Review the structure of the contingency plan. Does it have all the key elements of a thorough plan:
   –Emergency preparedness
   –User standby (interim) provisions
   –Backup provisions (duplicate facilities and files)
   –Recovery procedures
   –Plan documentation
   –Updating procedures and plan testing
5. When testing the currency of the plan, select static and active testing methods. Static methods may require that you walk through portions of the plan. Active methods may require that you witness the system being run.
6. Inventory and review all the documentation and the backup elements that should be in the off-site storage facility.
7. Review the adequacy of the librarian function and the updating of the off-site stored media.
8. Review the mechanisms for updating changes in hardware and system software and application software.
9. Check the adequacy of the off-site storage facilities, the courier service system and the protection devices for these storage areas (fire extinguishers, drills, etc.)

If some of the above elements are faulty, your role as reviewer requires that you make the necessary recommendations for correction and that you instigate the mechanisms for implementing corrections.

File Library Checklist

Library Function and Standards

1. Is there a clearly defined file library function, with assigned manpower and physical resources, located in a carefully selected site away from hazardous materials and not easily accessible to unauthorized personnel?
2. Has the responsibility for the operation of the library been clearly assigned to a librarian in each shift, or if only one shift, have appropriate procedures been set up to cover the second and third shifts or weekends, when the day librarian is not present, such as having a supervisor control access?

3. Is there a standards manual covering library policies, functions, procedures, retention cycles (according to legal, regulatory, and other requirements), security rules, and responsibilities? If one is available, how good is it?
4. Is there an inventory kept of all tape and disk files at the data center and at the off-site storage location?
5. Are all important files stored in approved libraries and facilities and not dispersed all over the place or on individual's or programmers' desks?

Library Protection and Access Control

1. Is the library kept separate from the computer room with protected storage provisions?
2. Does the library reside in an approved fire-retardant vault according to approved ratings?
3. Is the area near the library maintained clean, free of combustibles, excessive traffic, dust and debris?
4. Is the library located away from glass windows, parking lots and in general, away from areas from which damage can be inflicted by vandals, terrorists, and outside attackers?
5. Is there a librarian with responsibility for strictly enforcing access rules?
6. Is there a detailed procedure for labeling, recording the movement of tapes, and storing and retrieving files? Is there a sign-in/sign-off log?
7. Is the library adequately protected against damage from fire and water? Is there a fire alarm system? Is there fire suppression equipment or a system available? Does it have an automatic discharge capability? Does it have a smoke alarm? Are there manually operated fire extinguishers and are these tested periodically for operability? Does the library have 24-hour fire surveillance?
8. Is the electrical wiring for lighting within the library vault properly designed and approved to prevent the possibility of electrical fires?
9. Is the equipment within the library made up of noncombustible or fire-retardant materials?
10. Are proper housekeeping practices strictly enforced in and around the library?
11. Is the library environment properly conditioned for temperature, humidity, and dust?
12. Are there rules for restricted access? Are they strictly enforced? Are vacation periods for librarians planned in advance and suitable backup personnel duly trained?

13. Is there a log of all movement of files in and out of the library?
14. Is there a computerized record of all files and their movements? Is it kept up to date?
15. Are library doors always kept locked and keys or combination codes carefully controlled?
16. Are computer operators and programmers kept out of the library?
17. Are system development programmers not authorized to handle production master files for testing purposes?
18. Are unapproved materials kept from being stored in the library? Are combustible materials kept to a minimum?

Library Operating Practices

1. Are library procedures duly documented?
2. Are all librarians duly trained in the handling of magnetic media and library procedures?
3. Is the librarians' access to the library after hours controlled?
4. Are procedures for managing and storing file generation backup (grandfather, father) clearly spelled out?
5. Are procedures for handling data base dumps and transaction logs for on-line systems clearly outlined and enforced?
6. Are procedures for handling tapes/disks retrieval, removal, and logging all spelled out?
7. Is there a roster of personnel authorized to receive critical files?
8. Is there a schedule for cleaning tapes and disks?
9. Is there a periodic testing of "critical" master files kept for long retention? Is there a periodic rotation of all tapes?
10. Is there a labeling system in place to record version, generation date, and expiration date?
11. Are there explicit procedures for "scratching" tapes whose retention date has expired?
12. Are there specifications for the use of only approved tape reels to store sensitive data or data for long storage periods?
13. Are there clear rules for long-term storage of reels and for gradual and proper reconditioning of reels that may have been stored at different temperatures to prevent "stretching" or "cinching"?
14. Are scratch tapes with "sensitive" information properly "sanitized" (degaussed) or destroyed if extremely sensitive data?
15. Are extremely sensitive tapes or disks encrypted and the keys properly managed to avoid interception or key loss?

16. Is there a detailed list of all "critical" tapes required for contingency planning to run critical applications in case of disaster?
17. Is there a procedure to ready tapes required for the next production period to avoid delays?
18. Is there a procedure to ensure that processed tapes are quickly put in protected storage rather than lying around in the data center?
19. Are tapes left in suspense for various reasons promptly identified, labeled, and processed to prevent the accumulation of unknown tapes?
20. Is there an adequate supply of new tape reels and scratch work tapes on hand?
21. Is there a procedure to account for tapes to be destroyed because of age or other reasons?
22. Are there emergency procedures available in case of power interruption, such as lighting, operation of alarm equipment, etc.?
23. Is the library located away from sources of magnetic, radar, electrical equipment disruptions, or disturbances?
24. Are there procedures on how to salvage tapes in case of smoke, water damage?
25. Are there specific procedures on how to label tapes and diskettes?

File Backup Procedures

1. Is a complete list of backup elements and files available to support the organization's critical applications?
2. Is there a list of all items that should be backed up for use in any eventual reconstruction following a disaster?
3. Are all the prescribed generations of files kept as intended?
4. Are dumps of key master files or data bases taken, properly labeled, and kept for the prescribed safety retention time? Are the expired dumps erased according to prescribed procedures to prevent file scavenging (illegal reading of contents)?
5. Are periodic checks made of vital master files for existence and for validity?
6. Are copies of all the prescribed lists of backup items stored in the off-site facility?
7. Are the means for transporting files to and from the data center sound? Are the couriers bonded if necessary? Are they trained in the handling of magnetic media? Are they briefed on security procedures? Are protection canisters used for file transportation?

8. Are procedures for transporting vital master files and tapes to a backup data center worked out and kept in ready form?
9. Is a copy of the contingency plan kept in safe storage?
10. If external vital record storage services are used, are the necessary procedures for interface with the service center and their personnel spelled out?

Handling of Magnetic Tape

In EDP, data processing activities are organized around files as opposed to functions as in most manual systems. For example, in the typical EDP installation the hash receipts processing function will be subordinated to the accounts receivable file maintenance. The proper control over, and maintenance of, these files is of major interest to the reviewer. Guidelines for the use and handling of disks and tapes are therefore important. Some relevant points are covered in the following list.

1. Are there physical controls to prevent inadvertent erasure of tapes?
2. Are there formal procedures for preventing premature reuse of tapes?
3. Do external tape labels contain the following?
   a. Reel or disk number
   b. Serial number
   c. Number of reels or disks in the file
   d. Program identification number
   e. Date created
   f. Retention date
   g. Density
   h. Drive number
   i. Criticality and confidentiality rating
4. Do header labels have the following data?
   a. Program identification number
   b. Reel number
   c. Date created
   d. Date obsolete
5. Are there specific procedures on the safe handling of magnetic tapes?
6. Do trailer labels have the following data?
   a. Block account
   b. Card count
   c. Document count
   d. Record count
   e. Hash totals
   f. End-of-reel or end-of-file designation
7. Do programs test for header and trailer labels each time a new tape is accessed or the end of the reel is sensed?

8. Has a policy been established for the retirement of tape reels which have excessive read or write errors? Are there purchasing specifications for acquisition of blank magnetic media for valuable files?
9. Are sound volume (disk, tape) handling procedures used?
   a. **Disks.** Do not attempt to slow or stop the pack manually while waiting to demount it. Cover the pack as soon as it is removed. Keep it as free as possible from dust and foreign objects (cards, labels, etc.). In the event of a select-lock, try the pack again on another drive. If that fails, the pack is probably at fault, and no further access attempts should be made. Units that have gone down should be labeled as such and turned off.
   b. **Tapes.** Unused tapes should be stored in cases in the library. Smoking should not be permitted around the tapes. Tapes should be stripped and reversed periodically, and they should be tested before initial use, either by a tape tester or a suitable program. Care should be taken not to place tapes on hot equipment. A log should be kept of all tape errors. All nonscratch tapes should be file-protected unless specified otherwise. All tapes should have internal labels which should be checked before writing. A sufficiently long leader should be used. An external labeling scheme, such as color coding to show sensitivity, should be used, and it should be the same as the labeling conventions for disk packs. Finally, all mounting/demounting should be done by properly trained personnel.
   c. **Tapes and disks** can suffer serious damage if subject to heat. If tape is exposed to a temperature of 150°F over a period of time, it will be damaged. At a temperature of 250°F, a tape will become unreadable in 5 to 10 minutes. At 1,000°F, a tape will burn. Disk packs can endure a heat of only 180°F before the top cover distorts. Files must be stored in a fire-resistant cabinet or vault if they are to be preserved and protected.
   d. Follow manufacturers' rules on safe handling of magnetic media.
10. Are there established procedures for the handling and storage of microcomputer diskettes? (Generally, diskettes have a wider tolerance range for temperature on storage; nevertheless, handling practices should be clearly stipulated and disseminated to users of personal computers.)

19

EDP Administration and Control

PURPOSE

The purpose of this section is to discuss the review of the data center from a management control viewpoint and to offer guidelines and checklists for reviewing this aspect of the total audit of EDP activities.

BASIC CONCEPTS AND SCOPE

The effectiveness of the EDP department can be reviewed from two fundamental points of view:

1. Evaluating EDP from a **procedural practices and controls** viewpoint
2. Reviewing the EDP department from a **management planning, administration, and control viewpoint**

Both viewpoints, taken together or separately, are important to obtaining a complete picture of EDP effectiveness.

Chapter 18, and other parts of this manual, dealt with issues and approaches related to the first viewpoint. This chapter is concerned with the second point of view. Although there can be a good deal of overlap regarding the areas of coverage, when reviewing the EDP activity areas from the viewpoint presented in this chapter, the emphasis is substantially different as is the information sought from this type of review.

To clarify further, when we conduct an ''administrative and management controls'' review of EDP we look at the EDP department in terms of how the seven basic resources of any business are managed and controlled by the EDP personnel. As will be explained later, an EDP function is quite similar to a manufacturing company. Accordingly, EDP has an equivalent set of resources which require managing just like in any other major business operation. For convenience, we shall define the seven major resources to be managed and controlled as being made up of the so-called six M's of business and the I for information, as follows:

1. **M**anpower (personnel)
2. **M**achines (equipment, buildings, etc.)
3. **M**anagement (direction and control)
4. **M**aterials (data and supplies)
5. **M**ethods (standards and procedures)
6. **M**oney (capital)
7. **I**nformation (both the product of EDP, and EDP's own internal information for administering the above six resources)

The review of EDP from the seven-resource point of view supplements those explained in Chapter 13 on "Organization and Management Control of EDP" and Chapter 18 "Procedural and System Controls." As mentioned before, most other chapters in this manual tend to emphasize aspects related to standards, procedures, and practices for a given area of EDP exposure or concern (for example, backup and recovery procedures). This chapter attempts to look at EDP as an aggregate organizational unit by itself and is concerned with the effectiveness and efficiency aspects of its activities, both developmental (systems/programming) and operational (the data center). Because a great deal of the recurring activity takes place in the computer operations department, this will receive more attention. Also, when conducting annual inspection reviews, internal and external auditors usually delve primarily into the computer center as a primary source of reports and as the repository and custodian of assets and information in files and associated processing procedures (existing programs).

The review of system/programming activities is usually conducted along the lines of operating standards, and project administration practices as well as the quality and quantity of the staff. (See "Systems and Programming Activities" in this chapter.)

EDP DEPARTMENT RESOURCES

In order to suggest evaluation guidelines for EDP resource administration, we should be more explicit and specific about the seven key business resources as they apply to EDP. A summary of key EDP resources, classified according to the basic seven, is shown in Figure 19-1.

The variety of resources described in Figure 19-1 provides a basis for the review and evaluation of the EDP department's effectiveness.

EVALUATION APPROACH—MEASUREMENT CRITERIA

Having clarified the audit viewpoint of this chapter, we need to define an audit approach and measurement criteria. In reviewing the EDP department's

Figure 19-1
Main EDP Resources Classified by Seven Basic Categories

1. Manpower
   Includes personnel for the following major functions:
   1. Systems planning and analysis
   2. Systems design
   3. Programming
   4. EDP operations
   5. Management standards and control section
   6. Scientific computing and management sciences
   7. Technology (operating systems, data base, communications)
   8. Data security, quality assurance

2. Machines and Auxiliaries
   1. EDP equipment (CPU, peripherals, etc.)
   2. Auxiliary equipment (Preprocessing: data entry and preparation; Postprocessing: burster, decollator, report preparation, shredders, cabinets, etc.)
   3. Buildings and ancillary facilities (power, air conditioning, off-site facilities, raised floors)
   4. Secured storage areas (on-site and off-site, such as safes, vaults, record storage rooms)
   5. Safety and security protection equipment
   6. Telecommunications equipment and lines

3. Management
   Comprises management personnel for:
   1. EDP administration
   2. Second level administration who are responsible for the key management functions of:
      a. Objectives and goal setting
      b. Management planning (MIS)
      c. Decision making
      d. Manpower planning, development, and administration
      e. Resource and project management and control
      f. Client relations

4. Materials
   This comprises mostly custody over input or source data (raw materials) and operating supplies required to operate EDP, such as:
   1. Input data in various forms
   2. Source documents (before and after processing)
   3. Error correction and recycle
   4. Supplies (paper, tapes, disks, consumables)

Figure 19-1
Main EDP Resources Classified by Seven Basic Categories
(Continued)

5. Methods or Standards
   This refers to the set of management and operating standards as well as practices and technical procedures required to operate an effective, efficient, and secure EDP activity. They include:
   1. The organization's policies and standards manual
   2. Operating guidelines and procedures
   3. Specific operating instructions
   4. Measures of performance (against given criteria)
   5. Methodology for effective resource utilization.
   6. Methodology for system development
   7. Methodology for internal controls building
   8. Data base design methodologies
   9. Programming methods

6. Money (Capital)
   This resource is implied in the other ones. Basically, money management is not a major function of EDP; however, custody over capital and working capital tied up in EDP resources is implied in the other six.

7. Information
   This embodies both the management of **information processing** and its **custody** by EDP. Elements of information are:
   1. Finished reports while under EDP's custody and retention
   2. Data files (master and transaction files)
   3. Data bases
   4. Software programs
      a. Operating systems, data base management systems, communications software, etc.
      b. Application programs (provided by the company or acquired)
   5. Documentation and know-how manuals, run books

It also encompasses the accumulation of data records and statistics on the actual operation of the EDP center in general and by individual work center.*

* A work center or station is a preidentified unit (with its set of resources and standards) capable of performing a set of definable functions. Example: data input, job assembly, quality control and batch balance, etc.

resources and how effectively they are managed, we may consider the following criteria.

1. A **review of their existence** (an inventory of the most important resources available).
2. A critical or **analytical review of their adequacy.** This immediately suggests a review of their quantity of supply or capacity in relation to demand (workload profiles through the day and throughout the month) and bottlenecks.

3. An analysis of the **utilization of available resources.** This suggests an analysis of how a given resource is utilized for (or consumed by) what type of activity or category. For example, production, downtime, rerun time, development or test time, idle time resulting from failures, delays in input, and excess capacity relative to actual demand, or due to lack of other resources (such as manpower and supplies or other limiting factors). Criteria to use may be upstream factor, mean-time between failures, mean-time-to-repair.
4. A review of **performance as a result of adequacy of standards** or procedures **or lack of compliance** with prescribed standards.
5. A review of **custody and protection practices** over key assets (information and equipment).
6. An analysis of resource **accountability** (who uses what resource, how much of it, and for what reason), **how resources are used** or **apportioned,** and what **accounting methods are used to cost and record usage,** and how they are depreciated. This may include an analysis of the allocation or billing algorithm to users of services.
7. An **analysis of strengths and weaknesses** as well as an identification of the key resource or work station bottlenecks and what could be done to overcome them. This includes human resources and the relative balance between manning and equipment.

Now, for each of the above categories and for each resource, it is necessary to establish clear and specific measures of performance in detail. In other words, some means of reference is needed, such as degree of user satisfaction, rated capacities, performance levels or comparative reference points based on what others are achieving, or on industry standards, if available, or on historical statistics.

Evaluation Approach

An aggregate picture of the evaluation approach is shown in Figure 19-2. It shows the data or input required and highlights the elements required to aid in the evaluation, such as measurement criteria, reference criteria, special tools, and analytical techniques, as well as the resulting product in the form of opinions and reports.

Which Resources Should Be Considered First

Generally speaking, the evaluation of resources is centered around hardware and personnel, since they usually account for the major portion of total expenditures. Often, it is best to measure them separately and later try to assess their interrelationships as if they constituted one system, considering how one depends upon the other. For example, which of the two is the limiting

Figure 19-2
Review Approach to EDP Center Performance

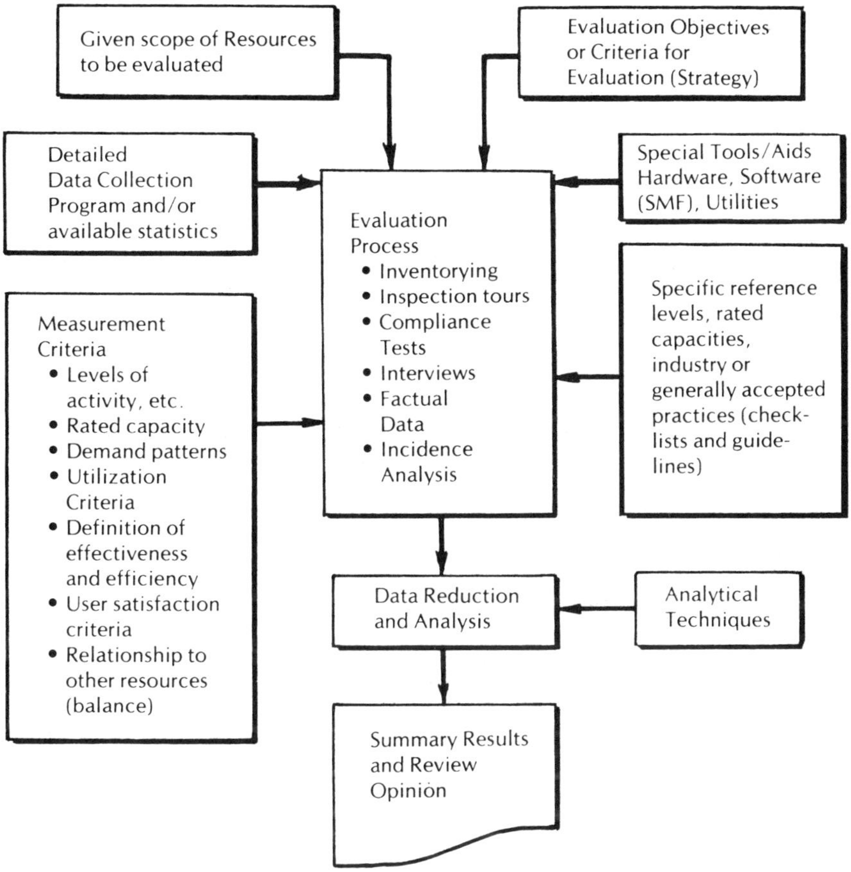

factor? Is one in larger supply with respect to the other? Are both in ample supply with respect to the demand pattern for them? As an illustration, given a demand for keypunch or data entry equipment, first, an analysis may be performed of whether equipment and personnel are in adequate supply to cope with the demand. Next, an analysis might be made to determine whether the level of equipment is in balance with respect to personnel to man it, or whether one is in excess over the other. If so, one can define whether savings can be accomplished.

SYMPTOMS SUGGESTING PROBLEM AREAS

In determining the need for further analysis or in grasping a feeling for the types of problems that might be encountered, it is useful to spot check and recognize some common prevailing symptoms in data centers. Some of these are listed below:

- Tense relationships between EDP and users. EDP personnel are in a defensive mood seeking ways to avoid or shift blame.
- There are no established criteria for measuring acceptable EDP performance by users (no agreements).
- Users complain about their share of the EDP services bill.
- There is regular or repeated lateness in delivering reports.
- There is an abnormal level of job reruns which affect users' and EDP schedules.
- There is significant unscheduled overtime for processing jobs.
- There are frequent or abnormal equipment breakdowns and associated delays.
- There is a disorderly appearance in the various work stations and poor housekeeping practices are observed.
- Layout and flow of work seem ineffective.
- Personnel assigned to various functions seem to perform tasks outside their normal functions by their own job descriptions or by industry standards.
- Personnel turnover in important areas is high, morale is low, and lack of career development is evident.
- Insufficient internal performance statistics and reports or statistics are collected. Otherwise data are available on irrelevant aspects and not on important facts (evidence of lack of performance measures or control mechanisms).
- All kinds of system/program changes are made without proper screening and authorization (no standards).
- High incidence of errors from various sources (keypunch, programs, operators). High job rerun rate.
- Key data is misplaced or intermingled with other unrelated data or reports (work flow problems and poor control procedures, no defined work stations).
- Cost and budget overruns. Ratio factors are out of line with industry equivalents.
- System shutdowns with attendant loss of records and productive time (maintenance problems).
- Lack of planning, scheduling, and administrative procedures and lack of accountability (poor standards, no control and reporting system).
- Uncontrolled and unpredictable requests for additional hardware or other supplies (no planning).

- Poor-quality systems, delivered late, suggesting possible lack of project planning and control procedures.
- Systems programmed before the system functions were clearly defined.
- Very high maintenance-to-development-efforts ratio.

BASIC FUNCTIONS OF THE DATA CENTER

In order to get a better understanding of the EDP center, it is appropriate to review some of its main functions and functional activites or tasks. These are summarized in Figure 19-3. Most of them were also described in Chapter 13.

The Nature of EDP Operations

The data center resembles in most respects the operations aspect of an industrial organization. It is like a manufacturing or processing company when

Figure 19-3
Operations and Control Functions in the Data Center

FUNCTIONS/TASK	UNIT OR GROUP RESPONSIBLE
1. Activity planning and scheduling	
a. Requirements plan	Planning and scheduling unit
b. Scheduling	(large organization)
c. Short-term (Interval)	Control section
d. Scheduling-Dispatching	
e. Long-range strategic planning	EDP manager and staff
2. Data flow and coordination and user relations	Control section/Staff or client relations
3. Data preparation	Machine operations/Users in on-line systems
4. Input/Output control	Control section/Clerks
5. Report balance/Quality control	Control section/Quality clerks
6. File library	Control section/Librarian
7. Job assembly/Disassembly	Control section/Librarian
8. Computer processing–(Production and remote tests)	Machine operations
9. Report preparation/Distribution	Control section/Clerks
10. Operations analysis and control	
a. Statistics	Control section/Staff
b. Costs	Control section/Staff
c. Reporting activities	Each section
11. Equipment maintenance	Machine operations
12. Operating software maintenance	Systems programmer (functionally under systems)
13. Operating systems	System software function

we exclude the research and development activities. The latter is equivalent to the systems planning, design, and programming functions in EDP.

The data center has essentially the following missions:

1. Receiving approved source data from source or user departments through the control function
2. Transforming (processing) these data according to approved procedures and technology
3. Returning processed results through the control function to users in batch systems or by displaying on-line response to user terminals in a satisfactory time

In order to achieve the data transformation process, two organizationally **separate** functions are required within EDP:

- Machine operations
  –Data preparation
  –Computer operations
- The data control function

The specific subfunctions or work stations performed by each of these units were explained in Chapter 13, Figure 13-3, and also Figure 13-4. Thus they will not be repeated here. A few additional words are warranted on the activities planning and scheduling function because of its importance to good and timely operations.

The **planning and scheduling function** comprises a number of policies, standards, and manual or mechanized procedures required to organize and process the flow of jobs/tasks and to allocate resources to jobs according to given priority rules. The levels of scheduling are:

- **Requirements planning.** This is a long-term anticipated schedule of jobs workload, and the resource requirements to process these jobs. It may be prepared monthly covering a quarter's or semester's activity. This plan enables data center management and the control group to anticipate workloads and possible resource shortage or problem areas so that steps can be taken in advance. The requirements plan takes into account all types of jobs: regular production, special jobs, estimated test time workload, maintenance, downtime, and an allowance for unanticipated work. The requirements plan is usually based on average historical run times for established jobs and on best estimates for nonproduction work. Many EDP centers do not follow this practice.
- **Daily Schedule** (short-term). This is a detailed outline of work to be processed daily, down to time of day and given machine system (if more than one). It is based on due-in and due-out times for each job. This is the only type of schedule normally encountered in EDP centers.
- **Microscheduling** (or short-interval scheduling). This refers to the detailed procedures for scheduling and dispatching jobs between and

across work centers in the control function and the machine operations center. It is normally done by the control group staff, particularly the assembly/disassembly people and the tape librarian. This function is very important to a smooth flow of tasks from source or user department, through EDP and back to the user, and can produce important gains in efficiency.

- **Long-range strategic planning.** This is the province of the EDP manager and may be done with the assistance of the EDP administrative and technical support group (if one is available), and referring to any corporate strategic and directional plans issued by senior management. The objective of long-range EDP planning is to enable data processing to respond to corporate goals. The chief function here is to evaluate capacity and acquire new technology.

In large EDP installations, requirements planning and scheduling are prepared regularly by an "activities scheduling group" especially chartered for these functions. In smaller shops, the control function develops these schedules in joint cooperation with machine operations. Its importance cannot be overemphasized.

AGGREGATE MEASURES OF PERFORMANCE—DATA CENTER

There are a number of ways to look at EDP performance. The various measures suggested throughout this chapter can be applied to a detailed audit of EDP when a major audit is conducted. However, the data center should have a set of practical, everyday measures of performance to gauge how operations are proceeding.

Since, the EDP center is a service organization, the same criteria used for evaluating services should apply, namely:

1. Quality (quantity, accuracy) of services (errors, reruns, etc.)
2. Timeliness of service (by due-out dates, response time in on-line systems)
3. Costs
4. Compliance with security and controls

The DP manager should attempt to develop a set of daily measures of performance of his own.

SYSTEMS AND PROGRAMMING ACTIVITIES

Introduction

The other major area of responsibility in EDP is the development function. Typically, this function is carried out by the systems planning and analysis, systems design, and programming groups, which may or may not constitute separate units, depending upon organization size, or the organization's approach to systems development.

Contrary to the data center functions, which are of a recurring or production nature, most of the systems/programming functions are nonrepetitive and discharged on a project-by-project basis. This area functions primarily on the basis of discrete and identifiable projects. This is even the case with the program maintenance function, which is charged with the task of correcting, amending, or improving existing systems.

Key Aspects of Management Control

By the nature of the systems/programming function, the key resources involved in the management control of systems activities are: manpower, methods (standards), management, and information. Materials and machines are not a normal responsibility of systems. Therefore the central issues of control revolve around methodology and procedures to manage these resources, as follows:

1. Personnel administration and performance
2. Project administration and control
3. Systems/programming standards (including documentation)
4. Quality of the systems produced

Personnel Administration and Performance

This is a whole subject unto itself for those directly responsible for managing systems personnel. In many respects, a number of issues are not resolved, especially concerning how to measure systems analysts' and programmers' productivity.

From a review viewpoint, as emphasized in this manual, the audit process has to be tempered with these present limitations. Therefore, review findings and conclusions usually involve a combination of judgment and verification of whether or not certain basic guidelines or accepted practices are in force, via checklists and questionnaires, and through observation and interviews of EDP staff and affected users. See Chapter 20 for some review points related to personnel.

Project Administration and Control

Most of the activities of the systems/programming department revolve around a project. Therefore, it is imperative that the reviewer concentrate on the various aspects of project planning, administration, and control. This whole area encompasses a review of:

- **How systems activities are planned.** This involves the question of project selection in relation to the number of possible projects competing for limited resources (the resource allocation problem).
- **Project organization and staffing.** This could involve a review of project structure and also, a review of whether the skills required by a project do in fact exist in the project team. This may lead to the question of staffing, skills profile, and structure to determine whether the number of systems analysts, senior level programmers, and junior staff are available in the proper proportion and in relation to the aggregate demand for the department's project load. Imbalance between demand for given levels of skills and availability is quite often encountered. Through determining this possible imbalance, the reviewer can assist management in considering the alternatives of either (a) acquiring skills in short supply, (b) switching project priorities (or curtailing projects) and reshuffling staff to bring about a better balance, or (c) engaging outside professional services where deemed necessary and feasible.

Resolving issues in this area can pave the way to the completion of projects of quality and on time.

Systems/Programming Standards

In order to have an orderly and uniform approach to systems development, it is imperative that a basic minimum of standards should exist. A review of this area is very necessary indeed. Often, however, the auditor will find that this area and project administration and control are virtually nonexistent or terribly neglected. When asked whether EDP has standards, they will reply without hestitation that they do. What is available often boils down to only a few procedures for flowcharting and a few working forms. Most of all, what is available is not only incomplete but outdated as well. The reviewer should ascertain whether there is a set of standards covering the whole system development cycle, standards for designing internal controls, data base standards, programming productivity methods, etc.

Quality of the Systems Produced

The ultimate product of the systems department is a workable system that is acceptable to the user because it meets: (a) the objectives and goals set out at the feasibility stage and as spelled out in the "user functional specifications" and the "internal control specifications or control objectives," and (b) the "certification" or "acceptance criteria" spelled out by the systems acceptance committee, usually established for every major project.

This whole area of measuring the quality of systems and their acceptance embodies a whole array of considerations beyond the scope of this manual. For the mechanics of system development, the reviewer should consult texts on the subject.[1]

Management control and audits of developmental systems usually cover at least three major stages:

1. **Before** commitment of resources, at the feasibility stage
2. **During** the development/design cycle
3. **After** the system is installed (postinstallation audit)

For guidelines on system acceptance criteria, the reader can apply the same general criteria used for data center evaluation, except using different subdivisions that apply to the particular system at hand. The set of user system specifications and the set of control objectives provide detailed criteria for acceptance.

1. Quality (accuracy, meeting user needs)
2. Timeliness
3. Costs
4. Security and control requirements

The checklists for this section are oriented toward the management, effectiveness, and control aspects of the systems/programming department, in keeping with the scope of this chapter. Guidelines and checklists for individual system applications and their controls are presented in Chapter 18 and in Chapter 17 for data security. See also Chapter 21.

AUDIT RESULTS SUMMARY

A large number of the findings in the review of this chapter on EDP complex administration can lead to important cost and other improvements in effectiveness. Therefore, management will be interested in the findings. Also, the findings deal with common sense elements related to resource management and control with which general executives are usually quite familiar.

Results should therefore be presented in a manner so that management can quickly grasp the meaning of the findings. The question of presentation is a manner of personal style. The same concept of relating findings to the basic seven resources explained earlier can often be useful. Findings can also be summarized as follows:

1. Establishing existence, level, and status of condition

[1] On matters related to **how to audit** the system development cycle, see Chapter 21. For additional assistance on this subject, the reader is referred to J. F., Kuong, *Audit and Control of Computerized Systems,* available from Management Advisory Publications as publication MAP-6 and W. E. Perry, *Auditor Participation in System Development,* also available from Management Advisory Publications.

2. Compliance with existing standards for management policies, established plans, budgets, schedules, accepted practices and procedures, and resource utilization statistics
3. Development programs in the systems/programming department and their status
4. Major strengths and weaknesses
5. Areas in need of immediate (short-term) attention, intermediate, and long-term situations
6. A general judgment of the situation encountered (relative to acceptable industry norms) with reference to these main issues:
   - Management control and planning efforts
   - Resource utilization and control (costs)
   - Standards and practices
   - Proper use of technology
   - Adequacy and competence of manpower
7. A suggested milestone action plan indicating who are the natural functions/individuals to be responsible for problem resolution, in a proper order of priority and according to payoff or noneconomic need (must-type projects) criteria

EDP Administration and Control Checklist

Depending upon the scope assigned to this part of the review, this section could encompass a large number of questionnaires, many of which were already included in the other sections of this manual. Accordingly, this section will present questionnaires related only to the **effectiveness, technical efficiency,** and **management control** aspects of the data processing department, in keeping with the intent of this section. They are classified into the following four categories:

1. Planning and Administrative Control
2. Resource Utilization and Control Reporting
3. Management Standards and Practices
4. Systems/Programming Activities (along the same criteria)

Planning and Administrative Control Procedures

This checklist refers to broad administrative issues related to management control of EDP.

1. Is there a charter of responsibilities for the EDP function including objectives and goals?

2. Is there a long-range plan for EDP data center resources which includes a quantitative exposition of existing capacity, current utilization level, and projected requirements based on transaction volume growth and new system additions?
3. Is the planning procedure explicit and is the long-range plan capable of being evaluated?
4. Are future requirements projected in a manner that enables management to review the components of growth, such as:
   a. Expected volume changes
   b. New system applications
   c. Alternative ways of increasing capacity
5. Are strategies outlined for resource (equipment and personnel) increase in orderly steps in relation to anticipated demand? (capacity planning)
6. Are there strategies established for stop-gap capacity increase without major system additions via bottleneck removal, possible system improvements, outside resources?
7. Are system and equipment reviews conducted at least annually as a basis for plan reviews?
8. Are utilization reports generated monthly as outlined in the next checklist, and are they used by management to review and monitor efficiency of operations?
9. Are management control reports tied in to management control objectives and key measures of performance?
10. Are key overall measures of performance clearly established for quality, timeliness, costs, and security, and are these fully understood by management and EDP?
11. Is there a formal procedure for proposing and justifying new resource additions, which considers fundamental alternatives, lease-buy considerations, and cost-effectiveness methodology?
12. Is there a corporate policy for use and charge-out of EDP services?
13. Are EDP services charged to users? If so, are users fully cognizant of the basis for billing EDP services, and do they understand the nature of the charges?
14. Is there a procedure for charging out idle (excess) capacity or is it absorbed as corporate (unused capacity) overhead?
15. Have cost centers and standards been developed for each important work center? Are fixed and variable costs well-defined?
16. Is there an overall management standards manual for EDP which outlines the above, among other things?

Resource Utilization and Control Reporting

The EDP center is a production operation. Information on its activities should be collected just as any industrial operation does for purposes of record-keeping, analysis of deviations, and detection of trends. Also, these statistics are needed to prepare periodic reports of activity against prescribed measures of performance. A lack of this information is evidence of poor management control by the EDP department.

In many areas, the tools of cost accounting, industrial engineering, and quality control apply equally as well.

Resource Inventory and Background

This checklist is designed to establish basic facts and obtain information useful in subsequent reviews of various data center areas. Following is a detailed checklist of typical EDP resources (use Figure 19-1 as a basic guide):

1. Make a detailed inventory of the existing EDP resources along the lines of the seven key resource categories with emphasis on equipment/software and personnel. If possible, reconcile this inventory against previous resource inventory, if available, or against source documents, agreements, leases, rental contracts, or vendor purchase agreements.
2. Analyze time of acquisition, commitment periods, and conditions or limiting clauses.
3. Review responsibilities assumed by your organization regarding payments, penalties, overcharges, shift overtime, legal and/or insurance protection coverage by vendor and to be furnished by the user organization.
4. Review disengagement clauses, if pertinent (see Chapter 20 on insurance and legal protection).
5. Is there a documented and detailed inventory of all important resources of the EDP center? Is it complete? Is it updated?
6. Are physical inventories of resources taken periodically and reconciled to resource rentals (equipment), purchase costs, previous inventory plus additions or deletions?
7. If discrepancies occur, are there specific procedures for dealing with differences and is action taken with vendors or within the organization?
8. Are meter usages and those on vendor bills spot checked? Are there procedures for dealing with discrepancies? Are vendor time credits for machine failure spot checked?

9. If equipment is returned to vendors for reasons of overcapacity or replacement for another unit, are vendor invoices checked to ensure proper credits or adjustments have been made?
10. Are periodic checks made of inventories and consumption of sensitive supplies and forms (payroll, payables, disbursements)?
11. Is the manning table kept up-to-date down to position level by number, and are key associated data current concerning grades and pay rates?

Physical Layout

Review the data center layout.

1. Where are the data center and the computers located? (See Chapter 14, "EDP Center Location," for other detailed factors.)
2. Is the layout sensible?
3. Is the supervisor's (main operator's) console or desk located logically with respect to key control areas?
4. Is the operator's location such that he can see key aspects of system resources (peripherals, tape drives) operation?
5. Are vital control points within quick access (power-off, switches, emergency lights)?
6. Is the machine room logically located with respect to supervisor's offices, file library, etc.?
7. Are partitions logically set up to isolate key areas?
8. Is the overall equipment layout conducive to avoiding operator fatigue? Is it overcrowded?
9. Is the layout properly designed for good flow of work? (Follow a few sample job routes.)
10. Are there adequate facilities (work tables) to hold to-be-processed assembled jobs **separately** from processed jobs (for disassembly) to avoid mixups?
11. Are the physical space and boundaries for key work stations properly set up to avoid intrusion and mixups?
12. Is the physical security perimeter well-defined? (See Chapter 14 for details.)

Resource Allocation and Scheduling

1. Do EDP center personnel fully understand the elements of resource allocation and scheduling?
2. Are short-term resource requirement plans prepared periodically? For example, a short-term requirements plan may consist of a projec-

tion of resources needed every month for a six-month period, with greater emphasis on the current month, and good anticipation of future quarter-end or semiannual periods and peak periods.

3. Are daily scheduling procedures prepared by system, by key work center, and by job?
4. Are these correlated with the resource requirements plan?
5. Is there a table of priorities for important jobs to help resolve priority conflicts in case of equipment shutdown, lost time, or job backlog?
6. Is there a set procedure for authorizing schedule changes by assigned individuals?
7. Do schedules take into account the "limiting" resource or unit?
8. Is there a procedure for authorizing overtime as a result of schedule overflows or lost time? Are these logged?
9. Is a log of job backlogs kept and is the backlog held to manageable levels?
10. Are there provisions for managing peak loads?

Resource Utilization Logging, Analysis, and Reporting

Logging

1. Are there recording procedures for logging machine and personnel utilization?
   a. Manual?
   b. Computerized?
   c. Both?
2. Is the information collected adequate and relevant to the criteria by which performance is measured and controlled?
3. Is a software package or utility used for logging resource utilization?
   a. If yes, is it a vendor system or other?
   b. How is the utilization package used?
   c. Is the utilization package equipment-utilization-oriented by system (unit) resource? By application/job? Or both?
   d. Does it produce machine utilization reports for:
      –Equipment utilization usage
      –Billing purposes by job?
   e. If billing of services is practiced, is the allocation algorithm on which the software package is based in agreement with the distribution or billing method adopted for users?
   f. Are adjustments necessary?
4. How are the utilization statistics used? Are they used for:
   a. Resource utilization accounting?
   b. Billing purposes?

c. Security monitoring purposes?
d. Auditing purposes (watching unauthorized actions, file utilization patterns)?
e. Resource planning purposes (additions/deletions)?
f. Adjustment of scheduling procedures to improve utilization and processing time?
g. An aid in planning and reviewing justification for continued use of equipment? (This may be done in conjunction with periodic reviews with users as to whether reports serve a useful purpose.)
h. Developing usage distribution patterns for subsequent adjustments to billing algorithm or distributions?

5. Do equipment statistics reflect usage by the following categories?
   a. Production time
   b. Data conversion time
   c. Job set-up time
   d. Rerun time, frequency, and cause, by
      –Machine error (malfunction)
      –Operator error
      –Program error
      –Source data
      –Batch or control total error
   e. Test time
      –Development (new)
      –Maintenance (existing)
   f. Software—operating system
      –Library maintenance
      –Generation
   g. Downtime
      –Scheduled maintenance
      –Breakdown (unscheduled) (specify source—machine or power)
   h. Miscellaneous
      –Demonstrations
      –Training
   i. Idle time
      –Power off
      –Excess capacity

Analysis and Reporting

An elaborate collection of good statistics is next to worthless unless it is properly digested and analyzed.

1. Are collected statistics and historical events analyzed periodically and compared against reference levels or standards for all important categories (reruns, downtime, idle time)?

2. Are deviations analyzed for meaning/causes, and are action steps postulated for correction?
3. Are these statistics used for future planning purposes?
4. Are quality control techniques used for monitoring trends against acceptable or tolerance limits or against budgeted cost or usage?
5. Are these control charts followed and are action steps taken in time to correct defective situations? Examples: percent of check rejects in a sorter is above tolerable limit, cumulative costs or usage to date is above forecast line, frequency of downtime is above historical average, rerun time is ahead of acceptable limits, schedule changes are too frequent, and a host of other important control conditions.
6. Is responsibility clearly assigned to specific groups and individuals for the data collection and analysis and recommendations process?
   a. Typically, in most EDP centers, the responsibility for data collection is assigned to the **control function.** Responsibility for analysis may be assigned to the **management standards and control section,** which operates at a higher level. This section may work in liaison with the technology group, in large installations, to detect anomalies of a highly technical nature (operating systems, data communications, security breaches).
7. Is the responsibility for the actual preparation of reports of activities clearly established and assigned to given groups within EDP?
8. Is there a review meeting after activities reports are issued to determine action steps, and is there a formal action program set up, assigned and reviewed for progress at the next period's review meeting, with explanations for failure to perform?
9. Are there statistics on maintenance?

Resource Costing and Utilization Analysis

1. Does the installation have an annual budget that shows a breakdown by quarters and by main cost categories, such as equipment, personnel, supplies, outside purchased services, software rentals, and other accounting elements?
2. Does the installation have standard costs or cost centers established for each major work station?
3. Does the organization have an approximate breakdown of the use profile of the installation resources by user or client area?
4. Does the installation bill out for services and is there a clearly established billing algorithm?
5. Are there standards or throughput rates established for each work center (data entry, report preparation, etc.)?

6. Is there a variance analysis system in place and are costs compared to cost standards with variances explained?
7. If there are job accounting packages for the installation, are they used to analyze system utilization to improve throughput or system utilization?

Management Standards and Practices

These checklists deal with the review of some specific standards, practices, and procedures, related to effectiveness and efficiency only, which every well-run data center should observe or have. Previous checklists in this chapter, and the balance of the manual, cover a great number of those checkpoints outside the scope of this section, and should be consulted for specific details.

Generic to All Functional Units

1. Is there a charter of organization for all functional units clearly spelled out, indicating functional structure, separation of tasks, performance goals and incentives?
2. Are communications procedures between functional units clear?
3. Is there a standards manual for each section?
4. Is there a clear understanding of equipment and personnel resources capacity and availability?
5. Are there good statistics on workload profiles through the day and throughout the month?
6. Is there a complete set of timeliness, quality, and cost criteria of performance (due-in and due-out times, priorities, etc.), and report distribution lists?
7. Is there a detailed housekeeping program in force?
8. Are personnel, training, and administration programs and procedures sound?
9. Are the procedures for collecting and reporting management planning and control statistics set up properly?

Control Function

1. Are there good data control procedures? (See Chapter 18.)
2. Are library (tape/disk) functions well-organized? (See Chapter 18.)

Scheduling

1. Are there detailed statistics for jobs and job streams (run times, job dependency, data sets, memory requirements, I/O devices, due-in/due-out times, job assembly/disassembly instructions)?

2. Is there a monitoring procedure to check job timeliness and accuracy?
3. Are there lists of I/O and CPU bound jobs to aid in scheduling and avoiding conflicts? (This should be done with the resource utilization software package that may be in use at the installation, to help determine job mixes.) These statistics should consider the various workload profiles throughout the day and the month.
4. Console sheets should be reviewed to locate system bottlenecks, including resources under contention, I/O devices.

Data Preparation

1. Data control procedures should be enforced.
2. An accountability procedure should exist for all jobs received from and returned to the control unit.
3. Verification procedures should be clearly spelled out for each job.
4. Data entry instruction manuals should be available and up-to-date for each job.
5. Data entry standards should be available for operators in strokes-per-minute and as a function of card column count. Statistics should be kept to refine standards.
6. There should be appropriate forms for data preparation to avoid operator fatigue and minimize errors.

Machine Operations

1. Personnel practices should be clearly spelled out.
2. Procedures for logging work in and out should exist.
3. Up-to-date run books should exist by job describing how the job is to run and what to do when halts occur, as well as when to proceed with the next job. A backup copy should exist.
4. Console logs should exist, should include time of day for IPL's, downtime, reasons for downtime, rerun statistics, security messages, etc. Copies should be sent to appropriate agents (auditor, security officer, supervisors). Console sheets should be numbered.
5. Operators are not allowed to perform program changes and supervisor overrides.
6. Manning statistics should be kept.
7. There should be a carefully structured preventive maintenance program and clearly spelled out procedures for handling remedial maintenance with vendors.
   a. Tape drives should be cleaned at least once a shift and after incurring data checks.
   b. Tape usage records should be kept.

8. There should be a follow-up procedure for scheduled maintenance each month, with special procedures to reach higher levels of vendor and EDP management when results are not forthcoming.
9. CPU meter times should be checked against wall clock time and checked against billing.
10. Logs should be kept of downtime, jobs aborted, re-IPL's, and reruns along with their reasons.
11. Approved security procedures should be in force.
12. Running of sensitive jobs should be recorded in a log, and should include specific remarks about actions taken during the run, such as on passwords, disk labels, etc.
13. Procedures for sensitive operations should be enforced, such as for program change cataloging, copying files, updating master files.

For checklists on other functions in the EDP Center, such as librarian, input/output control, distribution control, see Chapter 18 of this manual.

Systems/Programming Activities

1. Is there an organization charter for systems and programming activities? Review its structure, manning, and the ratio of analysis to programming resources.
2. Are systems analysis functions separate from programming functions?
3. Is there a long-range or master plan for the system suggesting business-needs-oriented priorities and interrelationships between systems? Possibly approved by an EDP steering committee?
4. Is the skills requirement in balance with skills demand profile?
5. Is this plan related to the equipment long-range plan?
6. Does management review and approve the long-range plan? (The vehicle may be the EDP steering committee.)
7. Is each system in the plan reviewed with user management prior to authorization of resource commitment and before work on the system project commences?
8. Is there a sound project management and control procedure which governs projects throughout the development cycle? Does this procedure include:
   a. Initiation (authorization)
   b. Objectives and goals (benefits) setting
   c. Justification analysis and methodology (return on investment, alternative analysis, cost-benefit/trade off analysis, etc.)
   d. Project organization and staffing

e. Project control procedures at key milestones
f. Project progress reporting
g. Procedures for measuring accomplishments at each control point.
h. Procedures for handling deviations from plan (change management)
i. Project documentation
j. System certification and sign-off
k. Time and cost control
l. Postimplementation review procedures

9. Is there a systems/programming standards manual covering all phases of the development process and accepted methodology, documentation, and involvement procedures with management users, auditors, and EDP operations (control/unit)? Does it include design of controls?
10. Are testing policies and procedures clearly established for remote-testing, remote job testing (TSO), other?
11. Are there formalized procedures for system user acceptance and certification and audit review?
12. Are relations between systems development and systems programming (operating systems technology), and data base administration well-established?
13. Are there standard cost rates available for each functional category or level within systems?
14. Is there a procedure for staff plus overhead costs distribution by project categories (including nonbillable internal development or research)?
15. Are project charge-out procedures to users properly understood by recipients of services?
16. Are there housekeeping and security procedures to safeguard programs, data, files documentation?
17. Are statistics collected on system/programmers activity, by project, by program? Are utilization figures compiled periodically?
18. Are personnel time-recording procedures well-established?
19. Are these statistics analyzed for trends and for future setting of productivity standards?
20. Are procedures for system/program maintenance properly established?
21. Are procedures for transferring documentation and procedures from systems to the data center well structured?

20

Minimizing Insurance, Personnel, and Legal Problems

PART A: INSURANCE PROTECTION

Objectives

The objectives of the insurance protection program are to provide the organization with the ability to **recover** from potential financial loss resulting from the variety of threats and risks that beset computer operations and computerized assets. Many of the programs covered before were addressed to provide anticipatory or "preventive" protection of some sort, seeking to minimize the chance of undesirable events happening. Insurance protection, like backup and recovery procedures, (Chapter 16), is designed to provide financial protection in the event that other preventive mechanisms fail, and Murphy's Law takes place.

Insurance Considerations

Insurance should be provided to reduce financial loss in the event that preventive measures do not forestall a mishap in the computer system (Murphy's Law at work). Most of the current literature relating to EDP operations concentrates on the processing of data, rather than on the protection of data or facilities.

As early as the 1950s managers were warned of the dangers when the insurance industry announced that policies especially tailored for computer systems were available. Electronic data processing equipment is expensive, all its associated software often costs even more; consequently, insurance premiums may be costly, but as with other assets, the businessman must trade the risk of loss against the cost of insurance protection.

Not all businesses can afford, or even need, a very elaborate and expensive insurance program. Each manager must determine the value of his EDP operations. He must decide which areas are sensitive and require protection.

Whether it is a small operation or a giant organization, the security of the EDP complex must be reviewed from an insurance point of view.

Concerning records protection, it is conceivable that neither on-site nor off-site backup storage facilities are sufficient to ensure the security of a company's vital records. Insurance may be required to recover from potential financial loss in case of record damage. The manager must strike a good balance between protective measures discussed earlier and insurance coverage. This balance is related to two factors: (a) what is available vs. what can be done better through protective measures, and (b) the associated cost.

It takes quite a bit of effort to determine what the data processing risk is for your organization; the required coverage may run into many tens of thousands of dollars. It is "all-risk" insurance that we should be concerned with, since one cannot anticipate all the possible risks which may afflict computer installations. Policies are usually written with a significant amount deductible, resulting in reduced protection costs.

Time sharing and digital data transmission may have their own peculiar insurance considerations. Insurance counsel should be sought to review your entire EDP operation where deemed necessary. Exercise care to determine what coverage the equipment lessor provides and what your organization will need to provide. This should be determined at the time the lease is negotiated and reviewed periodically, when changes in configuration occur.

Types of Insurance Coverage

There are a number of areas that may require protection depending on the nature of the organization and its specific requirements. The most common types of insurance coverage needs are listed below.

- Protection of all hardware and auxiliary equipment at replacement or purchase price, whichever is greater. In case of leased or rented equipment, protection for those areas for which the user is responsible should be investigated. For example, even though the lessor may have protection insurance to cover his equipment, the lessee may be liable for damage sustained by the lessor's equipment on account of events that happened within the lessee's premises, which are not covered under the lessor's policies. This is a form of liability for rented equipment.
- Loss of raw media—physical tapes, disk packs, etc.—whose inventory can cost hundreds of thousands of dollars.
- Reconstruction of programs and data. This may take many people, temporary facilities, rental of computer time, transportation, lodging, etc.
- Loss of accounts receivable and other valuable papers and records.
- Loss of earnings resulting from major interruption of computer operations.
- Errors and omissions resulting from the provision of data processing services to others. This is particularly important for service bureaus, facility management arrangements, and, often, banks which process other banks' data.

- Protection of data at other than the computer center location; for example, record protection at the off-site facility. If a protected off-site storage service is used, their coverage of your data should be investigated.
- Special bonding coverage against employee dishonesty or special employees.
- Insurance for building and accessories.

A new type of risk that is becoming evident is that of EDP disruptions because of a union strike. It may be that this area will be troublesome enough to warrant the possibility of this coverage in the future. In a recent article, the case was mentioned of a company having switched to a facilities management arrangement to avoid the threat of interruptions by an employee strike, since the facilities management staff was not unionized.

Insurance Review Checklist

1. Determine who in the organization is responsible for insurance protection (treasurer's office, corporate insurance office, administration)?
2. Prepare a detailed list of areas of coverage singling out those that seem most important, via a risk analysis.
3. Review the "existing" insurance provisions with appropriate personnel and compare it against what would be desirable. Question those areas of potential exposure mentioned earlier under "Types of Insurance Coverage."
4. Inquire if the organization has a documented estimate of cost or value for all important EDP assets and value of files (if reconstruction is needed).
5. Are your records properly covered with insurance against loss or damage, while in storage (off-site) and in transit?
6. Does coverage include the physical cost of the tape or disk pack, plus the cost of re-creation?
7. Do the provisions cover data programs and documentation belonging to outside or contract organizations while in the EDP premises?
8. Are there clear provisions for coverage of errors and omissions either for defense purposes (if services are provided to others) or for purposes of litigation? Are all factors considered (machine, operator, clerical)?
9. Is responsibility for EDP insurance clearly established and is there a program for EDP insurance protection?
10. Has your conventional or corporate insurance program been checked for EDP coverage recently?

11. Does your insurance program consider the following elements?
    a. Fire
    b. Water damage
    c. Crime protection (vandalism, etc.)
    d. Business interruption
    e. Damage to EDP facilities
    f. Natural disasters
    g. Fraud, dishonest employees
    h. Extra expenses
    i. Errors and omissions (if a service bureau)
    j. Insurance against power failure
12. Do you have a specific EDP policy which covers:
    a. Equipment and auxiliaries
    b. Media, tapes, disks, other
    c. Extra expenses
    d. Business interruptions
13. Does your insurance cover the loss of accounts receivable or other records due to a computer system error or from loss of records?
14. Are you responsible for those portions of insurance on the equipment which are not covered by the lessor, if leased or rented?
15. Are input and output media covered?
16. Does insurance cover both replacement cost of the media plus the cost of data (contents) reconstruction (keypunch, machine time, extra expenses, and wages)?
17. Are programs covered?
18. Are the employee dishonesty coverage provisions adequate? What form is used (fidelity bond, blanket crime policy or dishonesty-disappearance-destruction)? What are the provisions for theft, burglary, embezzlement, etc.?
19. Is liability protection against personal damage adequately covered?
20. On business interruption insurance, are all conditions of coverage explicit (equipment failure, flood, fire, strike, etc.)? Are the provisions for cash in-flow disruption well spelled out as regards length of time or interruption period?
21. If you use external records custody services (in a mountain, underground storage), have their insurance protection clauses been defined as to how they would cover your data? How are "in-transit" records covered?
22. Is there a corporate (overall) insurance policy, which also covers EDP, or a separate "EDP package policy" in force?
23. Have the relative merits of either been evaluated?

24. If a corporate policy only, are there any specific elements of protection for EDP that have been left out, or are amounts sufficient?
25. Has the company taken advantage of all possible means to reduce premiums, such as through:
    a. Installation of security programs
    b. Use of detection and prevention equipment
    c. Use of sound housekeeping program?
26. Are insurance needs reviewed periodically and is this responsibility assigned to a specific person or group?

PART B: PERSONNEL SECURITY

Objectives

The purpose of the personnel security program is to set an environment conducive to minimizing the possibility of threats and risks that might stem from personnel-related factors. Through a sound personnel security program, it is also possible to establish and implement policies, standards, and procedures which should guide the conduct of EDP activities for both internal and external personnel. When auditing this area, therefore, the purpose is to evaluate both the security atmosphere and the prevailing rules and standards.

Considerations in Personnel Security

EDP threats and risks come from three main sources: (a) acts of God or nature, (b) accidents, and (c) human sources. In the human sources category we can distinguish two subclassifications: intentional and unintentional. This chapter deals with factors that can contribute significantly to preventing or minimizing threats resulting from intentional human sources. Other programs designed to counter the human threat problem are, of course, the internal audit and fraud control programs of the company. The auditor can also play an important role in reviewing the subject of employee bonding to provide recovery for losses caused by dishonest employees. Remember that regardless of how good a security system is, undependable employees can negate it. Computer department employees should be checked carefully before employment. Furthermore, a dual employee coverage system should be used. There must never be only one person in the computer room, especially during odd shifts or when on-site supervision is at a low point (evenings and weekends).

The personnel security program consists of:

- Personnel security standards and policies
- Policies and procedures to implement personnel security in the DP center
- Guidelines for dealing with situations after they happen

Personnel Development

Attitude plays a major factor in obtaining sound performance and security-minded employees. Incentives, career path, and employee development may tend to minimize sources of employee unhappiness. One should start with the matter of career path. An old myth in the EDP business is that personnel should move along a career path from operations to programming and then to systems design. In the process many fine operations personnel have been converted into marginal programmers, and good programmers lost only to gain bad analysts.

The computer operations function is sufficiently critical that it should have a career path of its own, made attractive by the same status, policy, and incentive considerations given to other skills groups. This does not mean salary incentives or escalations alone; almost never have salaries been the only cause of general complaint. It does mean establishing methods of recognition, reward, and motivation.

Many data centers also tend to underestimate the importance of the control group. This group is often ill- and understaffed. These weaknesses should be noted and recommendations issued to improve the situation.

Preventive and Remedial Personnel Measures

Most of the personnel security provisions are addressed to help prevent or minimize security threats from personnel. The personnel security program should also anticipate how to deal with unpleasant situations in the event that these occur. For example, if the organization were subject to a threat of attack, an actual attack or a fraud, personnel procedures should anticipate how to cope with these situations and should consider the involvement of other important company functions in consultation, such as, legal, public relations, and insurance.

Another common mistake is to have standards for handling internal personnel matters and paying no attention to outside personnel potential threats.

Personnel Security Checklist

General and Corporate Standards

1. Is there a formal personnel security program in the organization which involves EDP, personnel, and other management functions (legal, insurance)?
2. Is there a set of personnel security guidelines?
3. Are there procedures on how to deal with employee fraud or attack?

4. Are employees made fully aware of security rules and attendant penalties for failure to observe the rules?
5. Are employees required to sign an agreement or contract regarding development of new knowledge and programs, and disclosure limitations? Are they made aware of corporate ethics rules on nondisclosure, nonduplication or misuse of proprietary acquired or leased software (software piracy problem)?
6. Do employment forms request authorization to contact previous employers?
7. Are credit and background checks performed on all new employees?
8. Does employment application include the following?
   a. Employee's nicknames
   b. Names of relatives working in the company
   c. Disclosure of past habits (arrests, convictions, drinking, drugs, gambling, etc.)
   d. Whether employee has ever been refused a surety bond
   e. Birthdate and place
9. Are employee references checked?
10. Are educational data checked for accuracy?
11. Are gaps in employment history reviewed with candidate and investigated if to be hired?
12. For certain positions, such as operators and those working at odd shifts, is a record of medication needs while working checked?
13. Are medical tests comprehensive to determine possible drug abuse by special tests?
14. For sensitive jobs are clearance procedures followed? Citizenship requirements?
15. If previously cleared, is a check made of previous clearances?
16. If permissible, are checks made with law enforcement agencies in employee's residence area? (The privacy law may negate this possibility in the future.)
17. Are photographs and fingerprints used for personnel records?
18. Are identification documents (cards, ID badges, etc.) issued to new employees or employees changing employment categories? Do these include photographs and signature?
19. Is a declaration of possible conflicts of interest issued periodically?
20. Are there any relatives in jobs creating possible break of confidentiality or conflict of interest?
21. Is a background review made upon transferring or promoting personnel to responsible or sensitive positions?

22. Is employee advised of this step to prevent subsequent ill feelings?
23. Are personnel aware of the new provisions on the handling of personal data for privacy reasons according to the Privacy Act of 1974 and other regulatory agency statutes?
24. Are procedures set up to deal with employees' intrusion into confidential data?
25. Is the payroll for data processing employees handled in a special way (manual, noncomputerized, checked at random; if in a bank, checking accounts may not be permissible for EDP employees)?
26. Do service center personnel have access to client assets (charge accounts and bank accounts)?
27. Does the same person who studies the problem also program it?
28. Are there procedures governing authorization for employees to take documentation and data home or to other locations, overnight or on weekends?
29. Are rules governing clearance and behavior of employees outside working hours well-defined and enforced?
30. Are clearance procedures to have an employee admit a friend or colleague to the EDP premises well-defined and enforced?
31. Do your supervisors advise you of a possibly disgruntled employee?
32. Do your personnel policies allow for containment or immediate dismissal of employees who may constitute a threat to your installation?
33. Do your supervisors know their people well enough to detect changes in their living habits?
34. Are computer center employees, who are fired or resign, immediately relieved of all duties if they were employed in sensitive areas?
35. Upon an employee's giving notice or being laid off, do you immediately assign an escort or replacement to begin the debriefing process?
36. Do you debrief departing employees, retrieve all keys, passes, card identifiers, change important locks, passwords, authorization tables in the computer, notify the security officer of the change?
37. Do you send a circular announcing changes when it is useful to do so?
38. Is a leaving or discharged employee asked to return all copies of documentation according to a checklist or inventory of what was issued to him over time (manuals, programs, tapes, instruction sheets, materials)?

Division of Responsibilities

1. Are the following measures used to enhance security and stress separation of functions?

   a. Bonding (key personnel, couriers, librarian, etc.)
   b. Job rotation (for backup purposes and to induce change)
   c. Crosstraining
   d. Insistence on employees taking vacations and having someone take over their regular duties
2. Do programmers retain copies of operating programs?
3. Are changes to active programs approved and reviewed?
4. Do programmers have access to "live" data? If so, why?
5. Do operators have program listings?
6. Do outside software or consulting firms now write any of your production programs?
7. Are program maintenance jobs rotated in sensitive systems to prevent one man from having continuous access to the system?
8. Are there firm and enforced procedures for initiating, authorizing, and executing program changes and file changes?
9. Are penalties for unauthorized program or master file changes well known?
10. Is program testing regulated by standard testing procedures?
11. Is machine usage by programmers controlled through supervisors and the control unit?
12. Are programmers never allowed to execute production runs?
13. Are tests of sensitive lists, passwords, authorization tables, payroll rates, closely supervised?

Personnel Training and Morale

1. Is there a formal personnel development program for all categories of systems and operations employees?
2. Are there career paths? Do these career paths take into account possible problems of separation of duties in the future?
3. Is there a relatively high rate of personnel turnover in systems, operations, or control functions? Are reasons analyzed?
4. Are salary scales properly structured relative to the industry?
5. Do you have a continuing personnel education program in computer security matters?
6. Do your computer personnel receive good technical support and training?
7. Do you find it easy to hire competent technical people with the appro-

priate experience and to retain them by giving them challenging work and responsibility?

8. Do you recruit DP personnel from within your organization?
9. Do promotion opportunities to positions outside the computer center exist for computer center personnel, and are they aware of these opportunities?
10. Are outside hirings explained to EDP staff?
11. Are exit interviews conducted to determine the real reasons for an employee's leaving?

Outside Contractors

1. Are outside services or contractors used for:
   a. Systems/programming
   b. Office duties
   c. Building cleaning and maintenance
2. Are outside contractors checked?
3. What are the security agreements? Have they been briefed on security rules?
4. Are janitorial services properly screened?
5. Are computer service personnel subject to screening? Have their perimeters of operation and their restricted areas been defined?
6. Are contract employees asked to sign for any important items received?
7. On systems/programming contracts, are participants made to sign a secrecy and right-to-new-knowledge agreement?
8. Are contract programming and other personnel debriefed upon leaving (return of manuals, codes, keys, and other documentation and confidential information)?
9. Are procedures and practices clearly established for authorization and coverage of outside personnel working at night and weekend hours?
10. Are computer vendor personnel (salesmen, systems support, maintenance) properly indoctrinated on security procedures and have their areas of accessibility been outlined and restricted? Is a background summary requested from the vendor?
11. Are miscellaneous service groups (telephone repair, plumbers, etc.) properly escorted when working in sensitive areas?
12. Are outsiders employed in sensitive jobs bonded?

PART C: LEGAL PROTECTION[1]

Objectives

The objectives of the legal protection provisions for EDP are to: (a) minimize the possibility of exposure from poorly structured contract and agreements, (b) reduce the chance of loss on areas related to personnel, and (c) provide the necessary guidelines to enable an organization to be ready in the event of legal complications or exposure.

Areas With Legal Implications

There are a number of areas of interest to the EDP reviewer, which have legal implications. Among others:

1. EDP hardware/software contracts, agreements, or leases
2. Contracts for the purchase of services (time sharing, service bureaus) or furnishing of services (facilities management, correspondent bank arrangements)
3. Regulatory agency rules
4. Employee contracts or various agreements (confidentiality, nondisclosure)
5. Failure to perform services (errors and omissions policies)
6. Suits against suppliers for failure of hardware or software to perform by original specifications
7. Use of outside contract personnel
8. Proprietary knowledge agreements with employees or with outside programming companies
9. Liability of officers and directors of an organization
10. Compliance with privacy provisions of the Privacy Act of 1974
11. Legal restrictions on the use and copying of licensed software

Many other areas could be mentioned. Of the above, one area of frequent importance is that of equipment and software contracts or leases. Before signing agreements these should be reviewed for possible legal implications or limitations. Whenever changes in configuration or service policy occur, they should be likewise updated. Another area of common occurrence is service bureau or service contracts. The auditor should, as part of the total security

---

[1] This section is intended only as a guide to review existing legal provisions. It does not represent legal advice in a legal sense. If legal advice or other expert assistance is required, the services of a competent professional should be sought.

audit, review the high points of any agreement and contract for possible inflexibility or vulnerability.

It is expected that many governmental and, eventually, private sector organizations will have to consider the legal implications of the Privacy Act. Auditors may have to review existing practices and ensure compliance with the new rules.

If the organization performs services to governmental agencies under contract, the associated penalty and incentive provisions should be reviewed to ensure compliance with rules by responsible parties.

Legal Protection Checklist

1. Has the officers' and directors' liability for EDP been established and reviewed, and are they aware of it?
2. Were all contracts reviewed by competent legal authority upon acquisition of hardware/software or services?
3. Are all contracts in force or is your organization operating under expired agreements?
4. Do you have a secrecy agreement for EDP employees?
5. Do you have rules governing dealings with outside EDP services and use of manpower?
6. Are responsibility clauses in contracts clear for multiparty participant contracts (EDP, communication lines, terminals, software)?
7. Is your installation safe, from a legal viewpoint?
8. Aside from liability protection for damage and fire, have you anticipated possible suits for nonperformance, against loss of vital records, or mishandling of confidential information, either personal or stockholders'?
9. Have the legal responsibilities of officers and directors been checked with respect to EDP operations?
10. Is your organization in compliance with any recent new regulations by IRS, SEC, other governmental and regulatory agencies at the federal and state level?
11. Do you have any databanks storing private information of individuals or, if in a service providing computer services, do you handle or process such for one of your clients?
12. Have you studied, defined, and established what the liability is for handling these and the attendant responsibility for possible leaks, losses, or inaccuracies and misrepresentation, as indicated by the Privacy Act of 1974?

13. Is the organization EDP contract bound with a contract that limits flexibility?
14. Has a general legal review been made recently?

If you are a CPA firm advising clients on EDP matters, consider the following:

15. Have you checked into the nature of the EDP-related or advisory services you render?
    a. Do you advise clients on the selection of vendors and service bureaus?
    b. Do you assist or recommend the use of audit software or other software packages? If so, are you liable for any possible ill effects?
    c. Have you developed a policy for dealing with these potential problems and do you discuss them with the client upon engaging in an assignment?
    d. Have you defined the boundaries of responsibility when assisting clients in the design of systems with impact on operations and financial statements?
16. Does your organization have a clear set of policies, rules, and practices on how to handle the use of outside proprietory knowledge, software, and confidential information. For example, a corporate policy may be in effect that dictates the code of conduct by employees on the use and application of proprietary knowledge. This may include the need for "employee nondisclosure" agreements at time of employment or when assigned to certain responsible positions or access to sensitive information.

21

Systems Development Phase Review

PURPOSE

The purpose of this section is to provide review guidelines and checklists for the system development cycle. They apply to the process of creating new systems prior to the operational phase (Part A), and to the postinstallation review (see Part B).

PART A: PREINSTALLATION REVIEW

Scope

Most of the guidelines and checklists contained in the preceding chapters of this manual were addressed to the review of computer center installations and the processing of existing system applications. This chapter is devoted to a general review of the procedures used in the development of systems. The emphasis is on the approaches used and the impact that procedures used during the development cycle have upon the processing of information in the data center when the new systems become operational. Details and guidelines for the audit of an individual system application are beyond the scope of this manual. The reviewer is referred to texts and guidelines manuals on system development and systems auditing.[1]

This section covers the following:

1. The Need to Audit the System Development Phase
2. System Development Phases and Stages
3. Feasibility/Proposal Phase Review
4. System Development and Implementation Phase
5. Project Management and Control and System Development Standards

---

[1] In this regard, see "*Audit and Control of Computerized Systems,*" MAP 6 (Wellesley Hills, MA: Management Advisory Publications).

6. Testing Procedures
7. System Documentation

The postimplementation review phase, usually, conducted sometime after the system is installed, is covered in Part B of this chapter.

The Need to Audit the System Development Phase

Many of the problems and difficulties associated with the processing of data stem from the manner in which the system was controlled and designed at the development stage. This involves both administrative control procedures and technical know-how considerations. Poorly designed and inadequately controlled systems give birth to countless sources of problems, user/customer dissatisfaction, and loss of revenues and time on the part of users or operations personnel. When a system has inherent deficiencies and is converted to an operational level, the "built-in" mistakes are "automated." It is therefore absolutely necessary that some form of audit or review of the system development phase be carried out, either by the auditor, a systems quality assurance group within EDP, or preferably, both. Of course, it could be argued that whatever the deficiencies or mistakes, they could be "fixed" later when the system is operational. This is an undesirable and unwise practice because (a) the cost of mending the system can be prohibitive (it costs one hundred times more to mend than to do the correct design at development time) and thus is often never done, and (b) deficiencies that were not detected because no development review was conducted might go unnoticed for years at great cost to the organization. Another reason for system development reviews is that they improve the chances of sound administrative project control practices being enforced, and of system development standards and procedures being followed (documentation and testing, for example). In summary, the old adage of "an ounce of prevention is worth a pound of cure" was never more true than when it comes to system development reviews.

System Development Phases and Stages

We can conceive three main system cycle phases, namely:

1. Feasibility (conception, definition/proposal)
2. Design and implementation
3. Postimplementation review (see Part B)

Each of these phases can be thought of as being made up of several identifiable stages or steps for purposes of management control and review. These stages are logical points at which management control can be exercised and decisions made. Also, they are points at which audit or review can take place to ascertain whether the system project is on a sound course. Figure 21-1 presents a schematic view of the main phases and their corresponding stages.

Figure 21-1
System Development Cycle—Main Phases and Stages

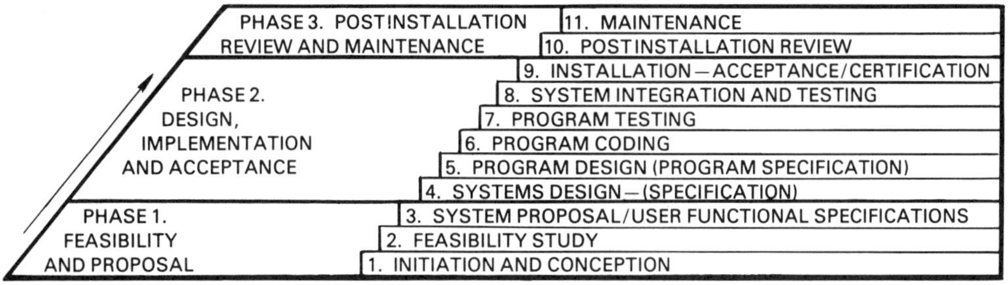

Feasibility/Proposal Phase Review

Long before actual design work begins, a number of steps should take place. Known by various names, this main phase comprises the feasibility and system proposal stages of Figure 21-1. The purpose of reviewing this phase is to:

- Set the foundation for future review steps during the development phase
- Provide an "independent" opinion concerning the merits of the project **before** management approves a major commitment of resources and authorizes the process of change that the new system would bring about
- Evaluate the various alternatives to and the economics or justification for the project
- Set the criteria of performance by which the resultant system will be measured
- Review user/sponsor requirements and their agreements with EDP concerning the new system (user specification)
- Enable the audit or review group to anticipate matters related to system controls and formulate audit plans for the development cycle

System Development and Implementation Phase

Objectives

This phase covers the actual process of designing and implementing the system. It consists of stages 4 to 9 in Figure 21-1. Its purpose is to provide a monitoring review of the whole development process to ensure that:

- Adequate controls are built in the system for accuracy, integrity, security, and reliability

- The project is properly managed and controlled
- System standards and documentation requirements are met
- The system is auditable
- The system meets user specifications

These elements are encapsulated in the "Key Goals for Sound Systems" section as follows.

Key Goals for Sound Systems

From a management vantage point, when you are entrusted with the vital task of developing a "sound" business system, it should exhibit **E.E.S.A.C.** properties. An E.E.S.A.C. system stands for the following:

EFFECTIVE	• The system serves the organization's and hence the user's functional needs. It responds to the intended user functional specifications which permit them to discharge their business functions.
EFFICIENT	• The system is tightly and efficiently designed with "no waste of resources" but subject to: (a) the functional effectiveness considerations mentioned above, and (b) the minimum level of cost effective *security, auditability, and control considerations* mentioned below.
SECURE	• The system has the required data, system, and access security requirements, and meets stated regulatory provisions and management policies on privacy and confidentiality and statutory rules. It also has well-conceived provisions to safeguard its continuity against loss or destruction of any nature.
AUDITABLE	• The system has the necessary provisions for auditability (ease of auditing), monitorability, and surveillance capabilities, and includes provisions for legal, regulatory, and auditing trails (as may be required by such agencies as IRS, SEC, comptroller of the currency, etc.)
CONTROLLABLE	• The system has all the necessary and cost-effective provisions that make for accurate, complete, consistent processing of data and for sound environment in terms of systems software and people, and sound provisions for error management and control to minimize systems data corruption and erosion and maintain a high-level of data/asset integrity.

The above is quite a "tall order" for organizations that lack the necessary standards and methodologies to achieve the fundamental goals of developing E.E.S.A.C. systems. You should realize, however, that building systems upon which the very activities and assets of your organization are to rely is not so trivial a matter and very costly, indeed, if improperly done. Further, sound management and economics dictate that an investment in E.E.S.A.C. is indeed a profitable venture in terms of reduced losses, increased profits, compliance with regulatory mandates, and protection of stockholders' assets. This ought to be the case, lest you are willing to accept the proverbial: "I will not pay now, but prefer to pay a great deal more later." Or if you are willing to live with the very costly philosophy of retrofitting controls and amendments, which in most cases is prohibitively expensive.

Approaches and Guidelines

A detailed discussion of the whole development process and its audit would take many chapters to cover adequately and is beyond the intended scope of this manual, which is on the "data processing" aspects of EDP installations. With regard to individual systems, generally speaking, the reviewer faces two kinds of system reviews:

1. Development system reviews
2. Existing or operational system reviews

The scope, approaches, and procedures differ to some extent for these two reviews. In the first type, the audit is progressive and cumulative in nature. The reviewer evaluates the system at each of the various stages shown in Figure 21-1, which become review points. It is usually a more encompassing type of review and requires a good deal of effort. The second type of review is conducted on an aggregate basis since the information is available all at one time and, by nature, it is after-the-fact.[2]

System Controls

Besides being concerned with how the system development process is being administered, the reviewer is interested in three fundamental aspects of controls:

- Controls over the source or input data (correctness of data, proper transmittal, and validity tests)
- Controls over the processing of the data (tests for completeness of

[2] For a discussion of both types of audits, with emphasis placed on the developmental system audit, the reviewer is referred to *Audit and Control of Computerized Systems,* Management Advisory Publications, MAP-6. For guidelines on the audit of existing system applications, refer to *Computer Audit Guidelines,* published by the Canadian Institute of Chartered Accountants, Toronto, Canada. Both of these publications include procedural guidelines, and they also discuss system controls.

processing, error in handling audit trails, data security, and backup/recovery practices)

- Controls over the adequacy of programs and the integrity and accuracy of data files (program and file reviews and control procedures over program and file changes)

These subjects were essentially covered in the material on types of procedural controls, Chapter 18, although there the emphasis was on how the data center should handle these controls for effective and secure applications processing.

Smart organizations also adopt a structured methodology, based on risk analysis methods, for the planning and building of internal controls during the design phase.

Audit Tools and Techniques

The next topic to consider is the subject of tools available to assist the auditor in his review work during the development cycle. This whole area is in a stage of active evolution. Among others, the following are used:

1. Program code review
2. Transaction tagging and tracing
3. Test deck approaches
4. Integrated test facility
5. Parallel program simulation
6. Audit software packages
7. Test data generators
8. System simulation techniques (on-line systems)
9. Built-in audit and monitoring routines (dynamic auditing)
10. COMBI (COBOL missed branch indicator)
11. Structured walk-throughs
12. Controls documentation matrices
13. Prototyping
14. Generalized audit software packages
15. Transaction walk-through
16. Transaction conflict matrix

Many of these techniques of testing were discussed in Part I of this manual.

Project Management and Control and System Development Standards

As explained in Chapter 19, the unit of activity in most systems/programming activities is a project. Management and control of system development revolves around a project and the vehicle for its control is some form of project management and control procedure, in a similar fashion as organizations control construction projects. The other vehicle for control is the existence of a sound set of system development standards covering guidelines and procedures for system design and for controls building. Assuming that competent people are employed, the project management and control procedure and the system standards go a long way toward ensuring the quality and timeliness of a project and they promote adherence to sound practices and approved budgets by the project team. A review of the existence of and adherence to these project and technical standards is therefore very important.

A summary of system project control guidelines was given in Chapter 19, pages 312 to 313, and in the checklist for systems/programming activities on page 324.

Testing Procedures

Objectives

Another area of importance in system reviews is testing. The objectives of system/program testing are to minimize the possibility of (a) erroneous conditions, (b) omissions, and (c) unauthorized conditions being present in the finished system. The objective of the **review** of the system test stage, by a person other than the designer, is to ensure that an adequate system test program has been provided to accomplish the above. Another important mission of testing is to set the foundation for acceptance or rejection of the system. As explained in Part I, the same methodology discussed here for testing internal controls applies also to testing systems.

Types of Tests

There are a number of test situations encountered, such as testing:

- Small or extensive modifications to a single program
- Changes to chains of programs
- Additions to a train of programs
- A whole new system
- Whether a program meets system specifications

Concerning depth of testing one may consider testing:

a. A component or module of a program
b. A whole program, made of several modules
c. Program links or series (domino test) to ensure interfaces work (regression testing)
d. A full system, from raw input to output results

In connection with this, refer also to Chapter 2. There is also the need to test or verify the data and files and eventually "volume" test the programs and the system files at installation (cut over) time.

The tools for program test usually involve the use of test decks, program code review, parallel program simulation, and specially made or generalized audit programs. For certain systems and on-line systems the use of ITF, Integrated Test Facility, may be considered.[3] (See the material under "Audit Tools and Techniques" in this chapter; also see Chapters 6 and 8.)

Test Standards

The EDP department should have a set of standards for programs and system testing. These standards should, in turn, provide the basis for the development of ad-hoc test plans for each system, based on the system and programming specifications. The absence of test standards reveals a weakness in control. Failure to develop well-prepared test plans or a test program signifies an even worse weakness in control, which can lead to insufficiently tested systems with attendant consequences at a later stage.

The auditor/reviewer should evaluate the test standards, the test plans for each application, and the manner and thoroughness with which the tests are conducted. For further information on testing, the reviewer is referred to Part I of this manual. A systems test checklist is included at the end of this chapter. For a checklist of **test conditions** frequently encountered or considered in testing, see page 359.

System Documentation

Objectives and Scope

The objectives of documentation are manifold. Documentation:

- Improves internal control
- Ensures proper procedures are followed
- Preserves know-how and provides a means for communication (reduces **exposure** caused by turnover)
- Improves effectiveness (training, a basis for changes and maintenance, helps operations)
- Helps satisfy regulatory requirements and provides a basis for protection in case of litigation

---

[3] Refer also to W. E. Perry and J. F. Kuong, *Developing and Implementing an Integrated Test Facility to Test Computerized Systems* (Wellesley Hills, MA: Management Advisory Publications, 1979).

This chapter emphasizes systems documentation. Other forms of documentation are covered under the discussion of EDP standards and practices in Chapter 13.

Importance of Documentation

Documentation is essential to both EDP administration and to users and auditors outside of EDP. Good documentation enables the EDP manager to ensure that documentation standards are being followed and assists others in reviewing documentation and operating practices. For each system application, documentation provides a vital source of factual information necessary to be able to determine (a) what is encompassed in a given system application, (b) what is the flow of data through **manual** and **machine** operations, and (c) what controls were provided for in the system. Poor documentation is glaring evidence of weaknesses in internal control. Unfortunately, in the press of daily EDP activities, the reviewer will often find that documentation is often sacrificed by the EDP department. It is often (a) nonexistent, (b) inadequate, if available, or (c) outdated relative to the way actual operations are being run. Any of these conditions signifies exposure of the organization to potential loss of knowledge if employees leave or in case of disaster, mistakes for lack of standard instructional guidelines, and lack of uniformity in operations. Another benefit of documentation is that it can serve as an aid in planning and controlling the system development efforts. Another point worthy of mention is the fact that the auditor or reviewer will find, frequently, that the EDP documentation available is written strictly from an EDP technician's viewpoint. It is not oriented toward the user and certainly not adequate enough for review purposes. This makes documentation review quite laborious and awkward because it fails to consider the points of interface or review for the auditor or user. EDP documentation is usually machine and technically oriented whereas the user/reviewer's needs are problem-oriented. This, in turn, stems from lack of EDP standards that take into account the needs of users and auditors during the system development stage. As things stand today, system development practices and documentation will be inadequate from the auditor's viewpoint until EDP personnel and reviewers get together and define points of interface and areas of mutual understanding. Another serious and common deficiency is that internal controls documentation is unavailable. System documentation should have a separate section on the internal controls provided in the system.

Types of System Documentation

We will deal chiefly with **systems documentation.** Since documentation should be generated **during** the development cycle, it follows that system documentation should be available for each and every stage of the development cycle. In other words, it should follow the development cycle stages. At this point, we should distinguish between documentation for details of the whole development cycle and system application documentation for the operating **finished product.** Although in theory they could be the same, in practice there are likely to be differences between the "process" of documenting all the evolving working details throughout the development cycle by various individuals, and the self-contained summary documentation for the operational system itself. The first one should be more voluminous as it is a record of the development process itself.

This fine difference is important depending upon whether we are (a) evaluating **how** the EDP department goes about documenting and controlling the development process and their standards, or (b) auditing a specific system, about to become or already operational, for its contents, operability, and controls.

From a **developmental system review** viewpoint, documentation should follow the three main phases presented under "System Development Phases and Stages" earlier in this chapter. When reviewing how the systems/programming goes about developing and controlling development, one should seek evidence of documented facts as the system evolves, both chronologically and by development stage. A summary or checklist of system development documentation is presented in the checklist section as Figure 21-2.

System Application Documentation

When the reviewer inspects a system already operational, he or she is probably more concerned with the documentation as it applies to the working systems, after it has been designed and implemented, and less with the record and chronology of the system development phase. From an **individual system application** review point of view, we can distinguish the following major documentation components that should be present in ideal documentation.

1. System feasibility and requirements
2. System
3. Programming
4. Operations
5. User
6. Management summary
7. Controls

1. The **system feasibility and requirements** section amounts to essentially background information on project initiation, project purpose and scope, a brief description of the system it replaced and how this system fits in the scheme of other related systems, as well as the justification for the project.

2. **System documentation** comprises the following elements:
   a. Narrative of the system and its logic
   b. System flowcharts (data flow diagrams, if structured design methods are used)

c. Input and output streams and formats
d. File descriptions and design (data structures in data base systems)
e. Set of controls used
f. Quality control (accuracy) procedures
g. Timeliness requirements (data due-in and results due-out dates)
h. Backup and recovery procedures

3. **Programming documentation/specifications** consist of the following:
a. Structure of programs (program design; physical design, if structured programming is used)
b. Narrative of each program and logic
c. Program flowcharts/logic diagrams or decision tables
d. Input/output formats
e. File descriptions and accesses/data base structure, data base dictionary
f. Program sequence, for processing purposes
g. Program listings
h. Halts and special instructions

4. **Operations documentation** is prepared for the purposes of facilitating day-to-day operation of the system. It contains:
a. Data preparation instructions
b. Control section procedures/job control language
c. Library and file set-up instructions
d. Job assembly instructions and equipment configuration
e. Descriptions by specific job
f. Input and output with samples
g. Operator console keying instructions
h. "Halt" instructions, job aborting
i. Job balancing instructions
j. Report preparation and distribution
k. Due-in/due-out times
l. Error handling procedures, suspense files, and correction procedures

5. **User documentation** usually consists of a condensation of all the above but written in nontechnical terms and in narrative and schematic style. It emphasizes what the system can and cannot do and provides guidelines for system use. It contains:
a. System specifications
b. General flowcharts
c. Brief description of what each program does
d. Instructions for data input preparation
e. Balancing procedures
f. Handling of errors and reentry procedures
g. Due-in/due-out dates
h. System limitations do's and don'ts
i. Samples of reports

j. User responsibilities in the running of the system, including data element maintenance
k. How to use the system reports

6. **Management summary** is a special, small section intended for managerial personnel. It explains in a succinct, practical, and nontechnical manner the purpose of the system, the scope, and the benefits, as well as what the system helps accomplish as regards business functions. It is often desirable to indicate what previous systems or modus operandi the new system replaces. It is also possible to include an overall flowchart depicting the nature and scope of the system along with whatever narrative material that may be required.

7. The **controls section** is normally not encountered in a great majority of systems. Essentially, it consists of a condensation of all the "control" aspects of the system as regards information on control points, data processing and flow, operating procedures controls, recovery provisions, and security and privacy considerations. This section would be immensely useful to reviewers and to auditors in determining control weaknesses. The use of control matrices to summarize control provisions can also be very useful. At present auditors have to delve through the documentation maze to obtain controls information. The use of controls matrices stating control points, control objectives, and control solutions and techniques is highly recommended.[4]

System Development Checklist

System Development Standards

General

1. Is there a manual which governs the development of systems from conception to installation?
2. Does this manual include a procedure for project management and control? Are key review points and milestones identified and known by all?
3. Are responsibilities, including user involvement, clearly spelled out for the user and for the EDP project team?
4. Are there provisions for handling system changes in a controlled and secure manner?

---

[4] J. F. Kuong, *How To Design and Build EDP Internal Controls* (Wellesley Hills, MA: Management Advisory Publications, 1986).

Systems Controls (Refer to Chapters 16, 17, and 18.)

1. Do the programs standards specify procedures for:
   a. File label checking
   b. Master file sequence checking
   c. Record, character, and block counts
   d. Batch totals
   e. Update summaries
   f. Transaction summaries
   g. Transaction listing
   h. Exception reporting
2. Do system control standards specify guidelines for:
   a. Control over adequacy of input data
      –Input data correctness?
      –Data transmittal procedures and documents (including data communications and terminals)?
      –Tests of data input validity?
   b. Control over processing steps
      –Data completeness checks?
      –Programmed controls for data correctness?
      –Editing provisions and error rejection?
      –Handling of errors and rejects?
      –Audit trails?
      –Checkpoint and restart provisions?
   c. Controls over handling of programs and files (See Chapter 17.)
      –Program and file changes?
      –File retention schedules?
      –Backup and recovery? (See Chapter 16.)

Program Control Guidelines During Development

(These also apply to most operational programs.)

1. Operators should not know the contents of the development programs. They should not attempt to debug the system.
2. All test work should be done by operators under specific written instructions of the programming group.
3. Programs at the test stage should be kept **separate** from operational programs. Test-stage programs should not be catalogued in the library; if so, it should be done under specially authorized instructions.
4. Programmers should not catalog programs themselves. A formal procedure should be adhered to which routes cataloging requests through the control group after suitable signed approvals.
5. Testing should not be done with live data until the system is fully approved and documentation is completed and accepted.

6. New or updated programs should enter the program library through a librarian package for added control and done at the source language level.
7. There should be no **direct** patching of object decks under any circumstances. Changes to programs should be done at source language level with subsequent compilation of source language and controlled cataloging when the new program is accepted.
8. Once accepted by users and EDP operations the system ceases to be the responsibility of the systems/programming group. The latter should have no access to the operational system except through properly authorized procedures, such as when maintenance changes are duly authorized.

Testing Checklist

1. Are there standards for program and system testing which specify minimum test requirements and guidelines for testing, program modules, programs, program sequences, and integrated systems?
2. Are written test plans prepared for each important application for subsequent review with the user (whose involvement is needed) and the auditor? Where there is a system quality assurance group, this should also review the test plan.
3. Do test plans include test strategy, test data sources, specific "conditions" to be tested (both logic and possible error conditions), and test procedures?
4. Are test responsibilities spelled out for users and EDP?
5. Do test plans include individual program and module tests, program trains (domino test) to evaluate interfaces?
6. Is there a total system test from source documents to completed output?
7. Are appropriate methods used to validate test results, such as using precomputed results or parallel computations with a test program or audit software?
8. Are test results reviewed by someone **other** than the programmer? By the auditor?
9. Are programmers allowed to test their own programs in the computer? (Should be done by operators for duty separation reasons.)
10. Are tests allowed with "live" files? (Usually never, except under special and supervised conditions.)
11. Are tests normally made with specially prepared "test" files containing representative conditions rather than using "live" full volume files for economy in testing?

12. Are the results of tests and test data duly documented and kept up-to-date as well as beyond the reach of unauthorized people?
13. Are test results reviewed in detail with users and are users involved in the test phase?
14. Are file tests or validations performed on new files or on files subject to many changes between creation time and the time when they are declared operational? Is master file accuracy tested to ensure test results are not misleading?
15. Are corrections made by responsible parties (users/EDP)?
16. Are program deficiencies corrected and are there procedures to ensure these changes are made **before** acceptance?
17. Are sound provisions made to protect the privacy of files and avoid unauthorized access? (See Chapter 17 checklists.)
18. What test methods/techniques are used?
    a. Test decks (made up vs. live data)?
    b. Test data generators?
    c. Program simulation?
    d. Other?
19. Is a review made of system auditability provisions, preferably by the auditor?
20. Upon completion of the system test, are written guidelines for system test prepared for future use? Are these updated when system changes are made?
21. Are human engineering aspects of a system tested to ensure the system is workable on a routine basis for the man-machine operational system?
22. For the volume or full-scale test, are there system test acceptance criteria specified by which the user, management, EDP operations, and auditors can accept/certify the system?
23. Are there test sign-off or acceptance procedures spelled out as part of the standards?[5] Are these enforced?
24. Is a summary of test problems or unchanged conditions that were spotted during the test documented for future reference and/or improvements?
25. Are guidelines prepared on how to test and audit the system when it becomes operational?

[5] "EDP System Acceptance Testing—A Neglected Topic in the System Development Cycle and What You Can Do To Improve It," *COM-AND, Computer Audit News and Development,* December 1986, Management Advisory Publications.

Figure 21-2
System Development Documentation Guidelines[1]

PHASE 1. FEASIBILITY AND PROPOSAL

1. General
   - 1.1 Title and table of contents
   - 1.2 Important systems correspondence
   - 1.3 Project request/initiation/authorization form
   - 1.4 Statement of need and objectives and time goals
2. Feasibility Study
   - 2.1 Existing system description and review and flow charts
   - 2.2 Document and volume analysis, growth rates
   - 2.3 Alternative analysis
   - 2.4 Cost/benefit analysis
   - 2.5 Preliminary requirements for new system
   - 2.6 Recommendations
3. System Definition/Proposal
   - 3.1 Objectives and parameters of system
   - 3.2 Proposed system and functions to be affected
   - 3.3 Flow charts, costs/benefits in fine detail
   - 3.4 Project organization and responsibilities
   - 3.5 Time schedule/tasks
   - 3.6 User functional specifications outlining an understanding of what EDP is to do for the user
   - 3.7 Approval, signatures of sponsor or user

PHASE 2. IMPLEMENTATION, DESIGN AND ACCEPTANCE

4. Design Specifications
   - 4.1 Purpose and capabilities of the system
   - 4.2 Narrative description of the system and logic/Data flow diagrams in structured programming
   - 4.3 System flow charts
   - 4.4 Input/output formats
   - 4.5 File, codes, table descriptions
   - 4.6 Management report layouts
   - 4.7 System controls and audit trails
   - 4.8 Due-in/due-out times
   - 4.9 System test guidelines
   - 4.10 Calculations and decision rules, accuracy specifications
5. Program Specifications (before programming)
   - 5.1 Structure of programs in relation to system (physical design documentation)
   - 5.2 Description of each program, functions and logic
   - 5.3 Program flow charts/decision tables
   - 5.4 File layouts

[1] Applies to documentation produced during the development cycle. Chapters 15 to 21 apply to operational systems.

Documentation Standards Checklist

1. Is there a documentation standards manual which governs how documentation should be prepared and controlled for all system development stages and for every application? How good is it?
2. Are documentation standards being followed?
3. Do the system development standards specify that internal controls,

Figure 21-2
System Development Documentation Guidelines[1] (Continued)

- 5.5 Input/output formats
- 5.6 List of transactions
- 5.7 Interaction between related programs
- 5.8 Computations, rounding off provisions and accuracy specifications
- 5.9 Error handling, halts

6. Programs
   - 6.1 List of actual programs/correspondence
   - 6.2 Narratives and logic
   - 6.3 Flow charts/decision tables
   - 6.4 File formats, file sequencing
   - 6.5 Samples of input/output, printer layout
   - 6.6 Program listings (source level)
   - 6.7 Tables of elements used, cross references, etc.

7. System Test Plans
   - 7.1 Narrative of system/program test strategy/criteria and procedures
   - 7.2 Responsibility for tests of each system function
   - 7.3 Input/output, sample calculations
   - 7.4 Time tables
   - 7.5 Test records, acceptance tests

8. Conversion Plan
   - 8.1 Narrative of conversion plans, personnel training
   - 8.2 Conversion responsibilities
   - 8.3 Conversion record
   - 8.4 Acceptance record by operations, user, auditor

9. Operating Instructions
   Control Section and User
   - 9.1 I/O receipt and control
   - 9.2 Schedules (due-in/due-outs)
   - 9.3 Procedures for:
     - library and job assembly, job control cards
     - quality control, batch balancing, checklists
     - Distribution and security instructions (no. of copies, names, form no., frequency)
     - Error rejection handling and reentry
     - Procedures for reviewing output
     - Master file change procedures

   Data Preparation
   - 9.4 Data preparation at user end
   - 9.5 Data conversion instructions and controls
   - 9.6 Keying forms for source documents

   Computer Operations
   - 9.7 Operator run books
     - Configuration (cpu and peripherals)
     - Console keying/run sheets/job abort
     - Operational checks/halts, run-times
     - Sort parameters
     - Sequence of jobs
     - Error messages and disposition
     - Forms
     - Report samples
     - Console sheets samples
     - Sample input pictures
     - Program and file identification data

10. Internal Controls and Auditability Provisions
    - 10.1 Detailed specification of internal controls, control matrices and control flowcharts
    - 10.2 Audit trails and data retention cycles.

auditability, and audit trail provisions be documented for future reference?

4. Are system development documentation contents complete? A guideline for good system documentation which follows the development stages of Figure 21-1 is shown in Figure 21-2.
5. Is documentation reviewed periodically to ensure it is up-to-date?
6. Are there sound backup procedures for documentation in off-site locations?
7. Is there good control over access to system documentation?

System and Program Documentation Review Procedure

1. Take a sample of systems documentation manuals. Obtain some statistics. For example, "in eight out of ten systems sampled there was some form of documentation."
2. Request a set of documentation standards. If there are standards, evaluate how good they are and whether they are being observed. One way to do this is to compare what is available against a sound documentation checklist (Figure 21-2 can be of assistance.)
3. Prepare a checklist of documentation and prepare a documentation "assessment" matrix. This is made by listing the desirable documentation checkpoints or elements across the top and the list of systems vertically. Next put a check mark in the grid whenever the documentation element is present. On this basis, statistics can be taken again on, say, percentage of times that a desirable documentation element is present or not. Low percentages or nonexistence of a documentation element suggests either poor documentation standards or failure to follow the rules. Further inquiries can help determine whether the standards are incomplete or whether they are not being followed.
4. Another approach is to review a few system folders of frequently run systems and follow the questionnaire route.

DOCUMENTATION CHECKLIST

Programs

1. Is there a program file for each computer program containing the following information:
   a. Specific program name and number?
   b. The purpose of the program?
   c. Narrative description of program. What data is the user receiving?
   d. Systems flowchart showing portion of the system the program represents and equipment used?

e. Program flowchart, logic of program instructions?
f. Program listing (printout of the source deck)?
g. Reference lists:
   - A list itemizing all source documents and forms, and identifying the source of each
   - A list of all output reports, indicating the program which produces each
   - A list of all files, showing the programs in which each is used.
h. Each program should have a control sheet which contains:
   - Program identification number
   - Description of program function
   - Program language description
   - Date of testing and final approval
   - Program changes, dates, and approvals
i. Memory requirements
j. Where the program is normally run, which depends on the operating systems in use

2. Are procedures for users to specify changes in rate schedules available that do not require programmer help (handled as parameters)?
3. Test data
   a. Test data and results of tests should be evident.
   b. Approvals by user should be recorded.
   c. Before becoming operational, new systems should be approved by:
      - User departments
      - EDP manager
      - Senior executive
   d. The auditor only endorses the programs from a controls viewpoint.
4. All program changes and a record of all changes should be listed indicating change number, nature of change, by whom made, and by whom authorized.

Controls

1. A separate section describing all the pertinent controls contained in the systems should be included. Most EDP documentation does not present a section on controls. Controls are usually described in the bulk of the documentation for each program. Thus the reviewer or auditor has to extract or retrieve such information at great expenditure of effort. This section should spell out all types of controls (manual or EDP) from data source to receipt of reports by the user. A matrix of controls could also be included.
2. Operating instructions. There should be specifications and agreements as to:
   a. When source data is to be ready for processing

b. What output is required, format, etc.
c. When reports are due
d. How various transactions and exceptions are to be handled
e. What coding will be used.

(Written documents containing this information should be reviewed and should be signed by all department heads concerned. This assures that the problem has been thoroughly investigated and agreement has been reached before programming begins.)

3. Operator instructions. There should be complete operating directions. These instructions should be clear and simple.
   a. Is a run manual prepared for each computer run?
   b. Are operator instructions prepared for each run?
   c. Are operator instructions complete? They should be so complete that no oral instructions are required to operate the program. These instructions for each job should:
      –Identify all machine components in layout form
      –Identify all input/output forms
      –Explain the purpose of the run
      –Identify tape units on which various input and output files will be mounted
      –Describe any action required regarding external tape labels
      –Specify console switch settings
      –List all program halts with prescribed action for each
      –Describe restart procedures if other than standard
      –Describe any exception to other standard routines
      –Provide a description of all input data required
      –Provide a description of output data required: form numbers, approximate quantity, number of copies, etc.
      –Detail disposition of input material, defining exactly what is to be done with all input material; where to deliver; how long to retain
      –Detail record layouts (data included in tape and punched card fields)
      • Tape input records
      • Tape output records
      • Punched-card input and output format
      • Printed output including samples
      –Describe layout of storage locations and buffer areas, including:
      • Input, output, and work areas
      • Subroutines
      • Constants and variables
      –Describe and provide an example of any control card which may be necessary
      –Include a sample of printer carriage tapes, if any are used
      –Provide instructions for a dump of the program now in use
      –Switch settings

–Indicate programmed halts and ends-of-runs
–Provide job control cards (JCL)
–Specify end-of-reel and end-of-file procedures

Checklist of Test Conditions Commonly Used for Test Decks

1. Duplicate payments
2. Fictitious payee names (payroll, accounts payable)
3. Unreasonable payments
4. Can payees not on a master file be paid?
5. Can amounts be paid to the full limit of number of digits allowed? For example: For space reasons, you assign the following field: $XXXX.XX (good for $9999.99) but the maximum range of validity may be only $5000.00. Can $9999.99 be paid out without having specified the upper limit of the range?
6. Can obsolete payees be paid?
7. Can overtime be paid on exempt employees?
8. Can the same individual exist with two social security numbers or two payroll numbers?
9. Can customers exceeding credit limits be extended further credit and obtain goods?
10. Can new vendor name, code, and address be added to the vendor file without the specific administrative and edit controls built into the system?
11. Can shipments be authorized on insufficient, zero, or negative inventory? From reserved stock?
12. Can blank checks with proper amount but no payee name occur?
13. Can an employee who did not work be issued a check because of automated procedures?
14. Can processing of values or rates be processed beyond those in an authorized table (in the logic)?
    Example: Discount rates are limited to 10, 20, and 30% only. Can a 40% discount be granted?
15. Invalid fields and other common error conditions subject to testing are:
    –Incomplete record/data (missing account number)
    –Alpha instead of numeric or vice versa
    –Signed vs. unsigned
    –Out of sequence

–Invalid codes or dates (too long, too short, wrong structure, etc.)
–Missing input
–Duplicate record
–Same code or amount for different entity number
–Digit transposition
–Fields slide-over one or more columns into neighboring field
–Input file storage or output (printer) field too small to hold data (truncation errors)
–Data beyond normal range of validity
–Inconsistent data
–Input records out of sequence
–Transaction against nonexistent master file item (name, part number, item code, project, product category)
–Use of *missing* or *nonexistent* item in a reference table
–Erroneous batch or group total or record count. Example: Test for last transaction. It is often not processed
–Missing document number
–Reentering of previously processed data
–Duplication of a given item or transaction which can be processed by different segments of a program
–Zero division, due to either input error or as a product of a computational step
–Overflow quantities which either can be truncated on the file or are too large to print in the allowed printer space
–Missing codes that are unauthorized in the programs
–Edit routine conditions violation
–Wrong file (volume) loaded
–Out-of-sequence processing of data in a program chain (programs, job stream)
–Erroneous JCL for certain desired operations of the system

PART B: POSTINSTALLATION REVIEW

Objectives

The objectives of the "postimplementation" or "postinstallation" review are to :

a. Ascertain whether the newly developed system meets the original expectations as measured by goals and objectives specified at the outset
b. Determine deviations from intended goals, and the reasons
c. Identify areas and controls requiring improvement

d. Provide an "independent" aggregate assessment of the operability of the system
e. Evaluate the system team and user interface effectiveness and their performance
f. Improve future decisions

General Approach

This review is usually conducted a few months after the system was declared operational and was accepted by both users and EDP operations personnel. Since the system is already in operation, this is an **after-the-fact** review. At this stage it is highly unlikely that the organization would consider reverting to the previous situation. Thus the review is addressed to determining whether the system lived up to its expectations and whether it can be improved in important areas because of unforeseen problems or oversights during the development cycle.

Measures of Performance

In order to conduct the evaulation the reviewer should define a set of measures of effectiveness or performance. These could be the set of performance criteria established at the system feasibility/proposal phase adjusted perhaps for necessary changes in scope since the time the system design was frozen, and the set of criteria by which the system was accepted by the user.

As for data centers, the four basic measures of performance listed in Chapter 19, page 311 also apply to evaluating the system, with adequate subcategories for systems, for example:

1. QUALITY
   a. Were user requirements (functional specifications) met?
   b. Is the system accurate, reliable?
   c. Does it fit the operational boundaries?
   d. Is the system flexible, with capacity for growth?
   e. Were forecast savings or other benefits met?
   f. Is the system easy for both users and data center operations people to operate?
   g. Were human engineering aspects properly considered?
   h. Are there other intangible benefits or drawbacks?
2. TIMELINESS
   a. Was the system delivered on time?
   b. Is the on-line response time within the expected range?
   c. Are due-in and due-out dates being met?
3. COST/RESOURCE UTILIZATION
   a. Was the system developed within budget?

b. Was the amount of resources estimated for the project exceeded?
–Manpower for systems and programming?
–Equipment requirements/configuration (memory/peripherals)?
–Run time?

c. Does the system interfere with other data center operations or did it cause changes in priorities, schedules, resource use?

4. CONTROLS AND SECURITY
   a. Are system controls adequate and functioning well?
   b. Are data security/privacy provisions sound and workable?
   c. Are backup and recovery provisions sound?
   d. Was the system adequately tested?
   e. Is documentation complete and up-to-date?
   f. Are there any inherent remaining weaknesses?

Other factors that can be evaluated are organizational and administrative in nature. For example:

- Was the project organized and staffed properly with the right skills?
- Was the project leader effective?
- Did the user get involved and lived up to his responsibilities?
- Did the project team interface well with users and other groups?

An inventory of major problem areas encountered during development and how they were handled could also be drawn up and used as additional criteria of evaluation.

Reviewer Independence

In order to conduct an objective postinstallation review, the reviewer must be independent of the system team and, hopefully, not a previous part of it. The auditor will need to obtain the review facts from:

- Interviews of source data, user, and EDP operations departments
- Actual system data and reports and operating statistics available
- Cost and project accounting information

Review Depth and Procedures

Depending upon the scope of the audit, and who the reviewer is (internal or external to EDP), some independent verification steps or tests may be conducted, using special audit tools such as audit software packages and test decks or on-line terminals in on-line systems.

Concerning procedures for evaluation of the system itself, the guidelines and checklists presented throughout this manual would be applicable in most cases, particularly those in Chapter 16–"Backup and Recovery Program,"

Chapter 17–"Data and Program Protection," Chapter 18–"Procedural and System Controls," and Chapter 19–"EDP Administration and Control." Much of the material presented in Chapter 21, Part A, would also apply, except bear in mind that we are now dealing with an operational, as opposed to a developmental, system. (For example, the checklists for testing and documentation would also apply, to a large extent.)

Audit Results

The results of the audit should be summarized and reviewed with each affected party and plans for resolution made in areas where this is deemed necessary. The results and recommendations should next be presented to the appropriate level of management which is in a position to do something about the disposition of recommendations. Finally, the auditor should prepare an audit guidelines manual describing how the system should be reviewed in the future and the areas of weakness or remaining vulnerability for testing when the system is audited under whatever audit cycle or audit program has been devised for the system in question.

22

EDP Fraud Control

INTRODUCTION

The advent of EDP has not eliminated the possibilities of fraud. We could state simply that EDP has changed the nature of the possibilities. EDP fraud, for instance, may tend to be less frequent than minor miscellaneous types of conventional frauds. However, it tends also to be more massive and of a higher impact. This is because, in order to commit EDP fraud, the effort and the tools required to accomplish it tend to be more demanding and complex. In a few instances, the introduction of EDP has been credited with preventing, discovering, or thwarting fraud. For example, upon computerizing systems, previous fraudulent schemes have sometimes been discovered. In other cases, the fact that the records were computerized eliminated the possibility that conventional manual fraud schemes could be practiced.

One area of major danger in EDP fraud is that of program manipulation and alteration. It should be remembered that a program is nothing but a set of procedures incorporated into a processable package for the computer. If a programmer alters these procedures for personal advantage, which, technically, he can easily do, he could transfer monetary value from one account to another personal or fictitious account. He could also alter asset inventory value for whatever schemes he deems important to his goals.

EDP-RELATED FRAUD CASES

EDP Fraud Possibilities

The types and varieties of EDP-related fraud are many, and new schemes are being uncovered all the time. Future advanced developments in automation of business operations will no doubt bring their share of opportunities for fraud perpetration. Many are already concerned about the fraud possibilities of electronic funds transfer systems (EFTS) and of advanced multiaccess, on-line systems which have become increasingly popular, many of which are probably being rushed into operational status without adequate controls.

Figure 22-1
Types of EDP-Related Fraud

FRAUD BY MANIPULATION OF INPUT

- Increase in account through credit and charge of debit to another account where suspicion is not aroused (manipulation of account balances)
- Manipulation of "inactive" accounts (checking and savings accounts, stock ownership)
- Adding phantom vendor names or payroll accounts
- Changing rate tables through input parameters (prices, discounts, commissions, salary rates)
- Changing credit limits or limit tests
- Changing number of exceptions
- Changing the code structure
- Use of open-ended code of accounts (code 99)
- Adding fictitious data (accounts, policies, inventory items)

INPUT DATA AND CODES ARE STRONG CANDIDATES FOR FRAUD PERPETRATION

CONSOLE INTERVENTION

- Program patches from console
- Program override to reset computer
- Temporary program change (a fraudulent routine)
- Temporary master file change
- Fictional transaction or deletion of a legitimate one
- Operating system option manipulations

ILLEGALLY MODIFIED PROGRAM OR MASTER FILE

- Fraudulent subroutine inserted into the program:
  a. By the systems supervisor
  b. By anyone forging authorization
  c. By someone including it in the original program
- Schemes:
  a. Changing edit tests routines
  b. Violating reasonableness checks
  c. Violating inactive (dormant) accounts
  d. Rounding down fractions of pennies and accumulating such amounts in a fraudulent account
  e. Programming special conditions which are activated under special conditions or codes or by the programmer
  f. Programming certain bypasses in the normal or official logic
  g. Changing control total balancing
  h. Deleting items in exception reports
  i. Bypassing built-in audit routines
  j. Changing decision tables
  k. Altering item codes in relation to corresponding value or price for the item (refrigerator priced as a tie)
  l. Suppressing payee name on payable name but not payable amount (blank name check)
  m. Illicit use of programmed switches
  n. Planting "time bombs" to systematically destroy programs or files

The possibilities in this area are unlimited.

(Continued)

Figure 22-1
Types of EDP-Related Fraud (Continued)

PROGRAM THEFT

- Removing copies of programs without authorization
- Modifying proprietary programs for sale to external agencies (programmers, outside programming services personnel, vendor personnel)
- Stealing physical tape/disk volumes

Sometimes poor housekeeping practices may lead to inadvertent release of program or file listings by not destroying discarded printed listings.

COMPUTER TIME THEFT

- Unauthorized use of computer time
- Unauthorized use of time-sharing terminals
- Hacker penetrating a system to have free use of its capabilities

PRIVACY VIOLATIONS

- Breaking password codes in terminals
- Compromising authorization tables
- Altering private individual records (personnel, medical, legal data)

ESPIONAGE

- Stealing computerized confidential records (oil exploration, strategic plans, cost data)

LINE TAPPING

- Tapping telephone lines not protected by encryption methods

HACKING

- This type of computer abuse is most often associated with the penetration of mainframe computers via the use of micro- or personal computers by unauthorized persons, hobbyists, and other types of intruders. This is made possible by the easy availability of inexpensive personal computers and data communications devices which permit connecting PCs to target mainframes via modems and even software packages that enable the PC to behave as a terminal device using what is termed "terminal emulation" techniques. The outside intruders often manage to obtain passwords or access codes for the target mainframe from so-called "underground electronic bulletin boards" where intercepted, captured, or stolen passwords are posted. Under the hacking technique a number of possible illicit functions can be performed, such as browsing through files, downloading information from the main files to the attacking PC (files transfers), conceivably changing the information status on credit, or personal information, violation of privacy, and affecting the integrity of the information on the main target files.

Cases of Documented EDP Fraud

The number and variety of **documented EDP fraud and abuse** cases is in the hundreds already. However, these do not, of course, include those cases of which we are not even aware or that, if uncovered, organizations do not disclose for understandable public image reasons. The most complete investigation of EDP fraud and abuse cases has been conducted by Donn Parker at Stanford Research Institute. One of the first and most publicized cases of computer-aided fraud is the Equity Funding case which occurred in the early seventies. Since then the magnitude and variety of fraud schemes have been rather interesting. The advent of microcomputers has added new dimensions through so-called "hacking" to penetrate mainframe computers.[1]

TYPES OF EDP-RELATED FRAUD

It is beyond the scope of this manual to review all possibilities for EDP fraud. Further, many potential schemes are only now being discovered. Figure 22-1 summarizes some common possibilities.

FRAUD CONTROL

There is not a single guideline or measure effective enough to prevent all possibilities of fraud and EDP abuse. Perhaps another way to put it is to suggest

Figure 22-2
Factors Which Aid in Controlling Fraud

- Existence of sound EDP standards and administrative control procedures (Chapters 13, 18, 19)
- An effective personnel security program (Chapter 20)
- Balancing cash and accountable items frequently (Chapter 18)
- Use of input controls and validation methods enforced through the input control unit (Chapter 18)
- Establishing and enforcing strict program acceptance and change procedures (Chapters 18, 21)
- Establishing and enforcing strict file update procedures (Chapters 18, 21)
- Logging and monitoring computer operator activities (program overrides, file actions, reruns) (Chapters 18, 19)
- A strong physical security/access control program (Chapters 14, 17)
- Stressing separation of functions (Chapters 13, 18, 19, 20, 21)
- Spreading knowledge of critical systems to several individuals (keep instruction manuals away from unauthorized individuals) (Chapters 13, 18, 19, 20, 21)
- Safeguarding access to on-line systems via terminal controls. Using file scanning and balancing approaches off-line (Chapters 17, 23)
- Supporting an active internal audit program
- Practicing remote testing for programmers (Chapters 18, 19, 21)
- Controlling the system development cycle (Chapters 19, 21)

---

[1] J. F. Kuong, et al, *Microcomputer Security, Auditability and Control* (Wellesley Hills, MA: Management Advisory Publications, 1985) Chap. 10.

that all of the areas covered in this manual, and more, are necessary to reduce the incidence of fraud. Authorities seem to agree, however, that a sound and comprehensive network of internal (administrative, system, and procedural) controls goes a long way toward deterring fraud possibilities. The other important tool is an active and vigorous internal audit program with strong support from management and the board of directors. Finally, common sense administrative controls can be very effective relative to cost of implementation.

Figure 22-2, although not the ultimate in scope, gives a clue as to some of the basic types of controls that would be desirable to combat fraud. They can be useful mostly as an indication of whether some of thcsc fundamental protective measures are in existence. The notes in parentheses indicate those chapters of the manual where relevant information can be found for protection and control.

23

Advanced/On-Line and Data Communication Systems

OBJECTIVE

The objective of this chapter of the manual is to discuss key elements of advanced/on-line/data communication systems, to identify the most important audit and control implications, and to suggest the most significant points of review.

In the past decade the use of advanced/on-line and data base systems which rely heavily on data communications systems for the transfer of data from a whole variety of remote locations as near as one floor above the data center to data source and information-receiving units located all over the world, and even in outer space with the use of satellite communications, has become quite widespread and a common occurrence. In many cases these systems have replaced and vastly improved the capabilities of previous batch-oriented systems. In other cases, these advanced systems represent newly conceived approaches to performing altogether new functions for the purpose of improving business effectiveness, operations management and control, providing ongoing availability of information and of processing capabilities twenty-four-hours-a-day, seven-days-a-week, such as is the case with airline and hotel reservation systems, and other on-line monitoring systems.

The control dimensions of these new advanced systems are much greater than those of conventional batch and manual systems. The array of threats and exposures to organizations has also become much greater. This has given rise to the need to conceive new control postures, new control techniques, and new standards for managing and controlling this new technology. Accordingly, the review approaches and testing postures for auditing these systems are indeed considerably more complicated and continuously evolving. The technology and its potential applications are still in a state of flux as new possibilities for information transfer, processing, and storage become available all the time, such as:

- *Computer networks,* whereby several mainframe and small computers can be linked by means of data communication networks to share information and/or processing and potentially serve as backup capabilities for each other. These networks can be intradivision, intracompany, and intercompany in scope and can span the whole world for that matter.

- *Distributed data base systems,* whereby important corporate information can be made to reside in multiple and dispersed data bases or files so that there is not only distributed processing, but also, distributed information storage which can pave the way to multiple-site updating of data, which in turn, could lead to data dis-synchronization. This also means that data can be intercepted at many locations.
- *Linkage of microcomputers or personal computers (PCs) to company or outside mainframe computers* for various purposes ranging from access to mainframe processing power, to access to and downloading of important corporate data to the microcomputer systems. With the portability of these small systems, information from large mainframe data bases can indeed be made available to micros residing in homes, hotel rooms, and offices anywhere on the company premises.

Granting that these developments are exciting and virtually unlimited, the other side of the coin is the vast array of threats and of events that can compromise company assets, approved functions, and information integrity.

SCOPE

Considering the many possibilities and schemes for advanced systems, the scope of this chapter will be limited to highlighting some of the most common and important control and review aspects which apply to most of the advanced system situations. Highly specific situations must be dealt with on a case-by-case basis as many volumes of information would be needed to deal with every possible arrangement.[1]

The major areas requiring enhancement and change are those related to:

- Access security (an extension of considerations in Chapter 17)
- File (data base) integrity controls
- Provisions to maintain systems continuity through modified versions of backup and recovery (Chapter 16)
- Data communications security and reliability

This chapter of the manual will deal with most of these topics in an incremental fashion. That is to say, by adding information on these new systems over what has been covered in other sections of this manual which applies to all systems, but in particular to the more conventional batch systems.

---

[1] For a two-volume book containing a comprehensive list of internal controls for advanced/on-line/data base systems, see *Controls for Advanced/On-Line/Data Base Systems* (Wellesley Hills, MA: Management Advisory Publications, 1985) Vols. 1 and 2.

ENVIRONMENT AND KEY COMPONENTS OF ADVANCED ON-LINE SYSTEMS

Figure 23-1 shows the environment and key components of an advanced/on-line data communications system.

Checklist for Reviewing On-Line System Security and Data Integrity

The control and continuing review of access to on-line/data base systems is of vital importance to the security of such systems. This is due to the fact that in an on-line/multiuser environment the user is *remote* and *invisible* compared to the situation as it existed with batch or manual systems. This requires that there be controls for:

- Identification
- Authentication or positive identification
- Authorization (to delimit activities or functions)
- Concealment (encoding and encryption to protect message contents).

The checklist below will aid you in reviewing the level of control and security provided to meet the above control requirements.

Access and Authentication

1. Is there a roster of authorized personnel and is it kept up-to-date?
2. Are users assigned a unique identification code? (number, card, etc.)
3. Are passwords assigned to each authorized user? What type? (mnemonic, algorithmic, variable length)
4. How are passwords protected:
   a. Frequent change?
   b. Limit number of trials to three?
   c. Logging of illegal accesses or erroneous entries?
   d. Are password management procedures adhered to?
   e. Are passwords assigned to previous employees invalidated?
   f. Are passwords changed for employees transferred to other areas?
   g. Are passwords print-suppressed, scrambled, underprinted, etc.?
   h. Are passwords protected upon transmission, storage, and generation?
   i. When using algorithmic changes for previous passwords, are different algorithms used for different persons?
   j. Are time-delay techniques used when a person tries many passwords?

Figure 23-1
Main Components and the Environment in an On-Line/Data Base/Data Communications System

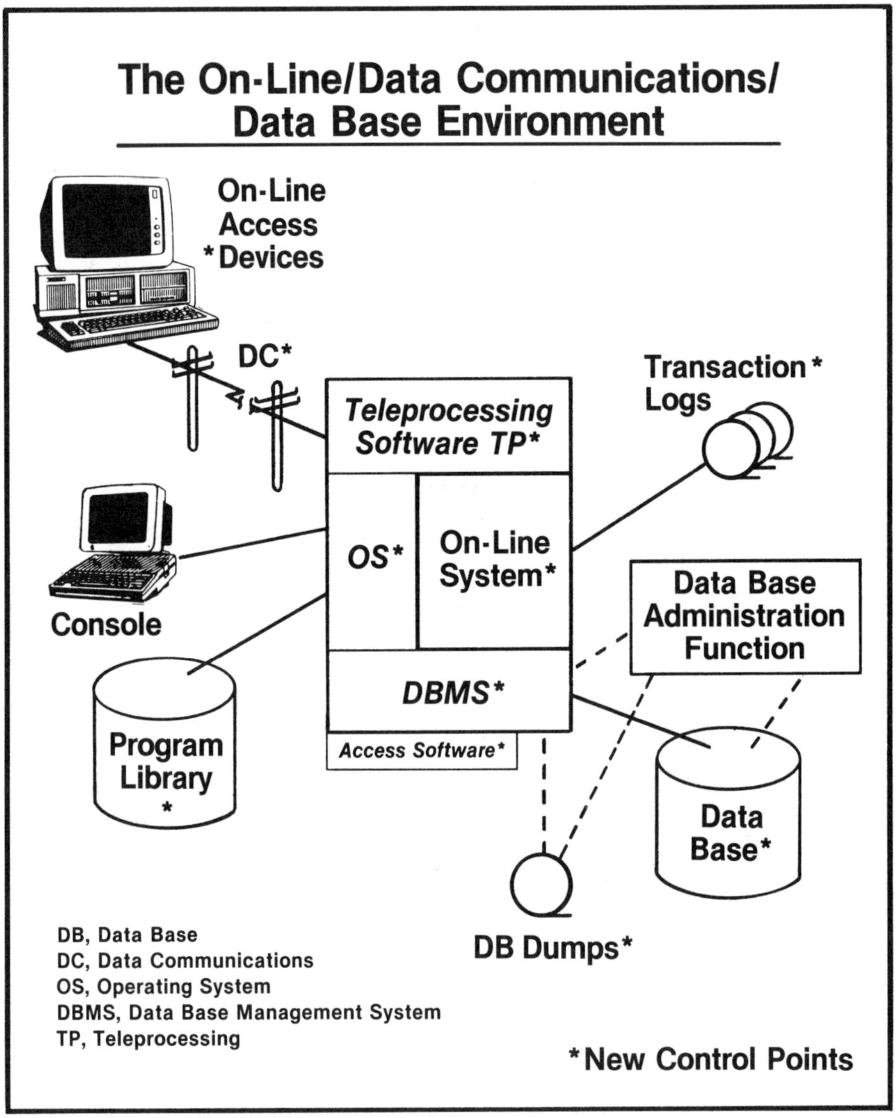

5. Are multilevel passwords used for sensitive operations?
6. Are passwords concealed on printing terminals or CRT's?
7. Do terminals log-off automatically after a period of no activity?
8. Are all illegal terminal operations reviewed, such as frequent illegal password trials, unsuccessful log-ons?
9. Is responsibility for password change and maintenance clear and enforced?
   a. Security officer?
   b. User?
   c. Mixed strategy user/security?
10. Are procedures for issuance and upkeep of passwords maintained?
11. Is the terminal area for sensitive terminals well-guarded and under containment control?
   a. Are only authorized people allowed?
   b. Are logs kept of user activity and entry?
   c. Are these terminals kept locked and under surveillance when not in use?
   d. Is after-hours use duly cleared?
12. Do remote terminals have lockable keyboards or physical locks on the terminal switches?
13. Are functional keys used for sensitive functions?
14. Are there physical access and fire protection provisions?
15. Are procedures for log-off and for leaving the terminal area clearly stated and enforced? (carbon removals, nonwriting of passwords, notification of area security personnel upon leaving terminal?)
16. Are the sensitive-use terminals restricted?
   a. Input or output only
   b. Sysgened for authorized receipt of sensitive data when not normally used for confidential purposes?
17. Are confidential terminal procedures kept in a secure area and marked confidential?

Authentication/Positive Identification

1. Are positive identification means used for confidential access to data? (palm identifier, voice, signature?)
2. Are automatic identifiers/authentication procedures in force for terminals? (e.g. Can the CPU interrogate the terminal for its hard-wired authenticator code to ensure the proper terminal is reached?)
3. Are reauthentication procedures used at sensitive data transmission time? (request hardwired authentication at random and frequently?)

4. Are handshaking passwords or algorithmic password methods used? (Handshaking means using a uniquely known feature, such as the user's hair shampoo. Algorithmic means the computer asks the user to give an answer to a given number using a formula known only to the user and to the computer. The answers must match for permission to access the system to be granted.)

Password Processing Control

1. Is a terminal used to load passwords into the password file? If so, is it locked when not in use?
2. Who has access to password files? Are these persons cleared?
3. Are password files locked after work hours, and is their use controlled during the day?
4. Are double passwords used to update or change passwords?
5. Are procedures available to ensure passwords are issued to legitimate users?
6. Are data security personnel properly cleared for the data center and restricted to prevent unauthorized use of privileges?
7. What personnel provides programming support to data security personnel? Are these people cleared and possible collusion monitored?
8. Are there adequate logs and audit trails of data security personnel activities? Are these reviewed by other than security personnel?
9. Are passwords periodically purged to ensure outdated passwords are deactivated? (previous employees, transferred employees?)
10. Are passwords used for sensitive functions/files encrypted in case of dumps from ABENDS to prevent scavenging and browsing?
11. Are the telephone numbers for sensitive terminals changed periodically?
12. Are terminals under repair monitored and disconnected from use and their later reinstatement duly certified?
13. Are the backup terminals for sensitive operations properly controlled? Are log-on procedures or sysgen procedures for alternate terminals properly followed?

Concealment (Encryption) Controls

1. Are encryption provisions used at the terminal area?
2. Are key management procedures closely adhered to?
3. Are terminals with encryption/decryption devices secured and watched?

4. Are neighboring areas inspected for possible:
    a. Tapping
    b. Impersonation
    c. Electromagnetic radiation
5. Is terminal area shielded if a candidate for emanation?
6. Are decrypted messages disposed of properly? No carbons produced? (to avoid scavenging?)
7. Are encryption security personnel properly cleared and identified?
8. Are encryption procedures safely locked and restricted in circulation?
9. Are encryption keys properly backed up and in safe storage?

File/Data Base Integrity

1. Is there a set of standards for data base design and documentation?
2. Is there a data cleaning program in place before data is loaded onto data bases to eliminate invalid, misspelled, erroneous, duplicate, and obsolete data?
3. Is the data base administrator responsible for developing and issuing standard practices for data base integrity, data element maintenance, and error correction, including training of all appropriate personnel?
4. Are there adequate controls to ensure that data entering the system from the remote terminals is correct, complete, and valid to avoid "data base corruption"?
5. Does the system make use of "conversational" or "dialogue" controls to check the accuracy and validity of data, such as, descriptive readback, algorithmic checks, checks against previous transaction, logical sequence checks, etc.?
6. Are the on-line data screens designed in a manner conducive to avoid data entry operator errors, confusion, and eye fatigue?
7. Are there stringent error checking and correction procedures to deal with rejected data?
8. Are there procedures to detect and report invalid data in the data base to prompt correction by the appropriate party?
9. Are there file balancing routines provided to ensure file integrity and to account for asset value or money?
10. Are there data item validation controls to ensure correctness of data input?
11. Are file "scanning" techniques used to locate and report erroneous or invalid data to reduce data base corruption?
12. Are there provisions to permit balancing of transactions sent to the data base by terminal or activity area (e.g., bank branch), using daily management reports?

13. When the data base is reorganized, are there control provisions to ensure data integrity is preserved via human and computerized procedures, such as by including item counts, file scanning procedures, file balancing procedures, control records, etc.?
14. Are there control measures to minimize the potential for "data base degradation"? (A condition that occurs when the rate of erroneous input data exceeds the rate at which the human system corrects rejected transactions, so that the data base status does not reflect the latest information that was sent to the system, as a result of rejected transactions remaining in suspense outside the system.)

Business Continuity

1. Is there a comprehensive contingency and recovery plan to minimize potential loss of the on-line system, contain damage, and permit recovery and restoration of the on-line system in case of a major disaster?
2. If applicable to the type of on-line system in question, are there provisions for alternate operation, such as a standby "hot-site" facility?
3. For interim system break-downs, are there provisions to recover the data base in case of destruction by: (a) disk crashes, (b) power failures, (c) major software errors?
4. Are there transaction logs to capture all the on-line real-time transactions to permit data base reconstruction to the point before the disruption occurred and to provide audit trail information? Are the transaction log tapes kept in safe storage?
5. Are file "dumps" of the data base taken periodically at predetermined frequencies and placed in safe storage?
6. Are there reconciliation procedures to ensure that data is not lost and to ensure that all transactions are accounted for from the time of the disruption to the time when recovery takes place?
7. Are retention cycles for data from the system clearly specified to take care of contractual, legal, regulatory, and auditing needs?
8. Are all the recovery procedures for the on-line system and its data base properly documented in the contingency plan and adequately backed up in an off-site storage facility?

Data Communications Security and Reliability

1. Are there adequate message accuracy and completeness controls to ensure message integrity? (parity bits, echo checks, message retransmission, beginning and end of message etc.)

2. Are there provisions to handle data transmission in case of equipment failures or disruptions? (backup modems, alternate lines, dial-up backup capabilities)
3. If the data is sensitive, are there provisions to encrypt data transmission sessions? If encryption is used, is there a sound "key" management and control program and is there a given individual charged with responsibility for encryption management?
4. If hacking and outside intruders are considered a threat, are there dial-back transmission port protection controls to ensure that only authorized individuals and not hackers enter the system?
5. If there is a communications control terminal, are there security provisions to limit access control to it?
6. Are there control provisions to ensure the security of communications software?
7. Is the telephone lines switch area properly protected against unauthorized access?
8. If access to the mainframe data base is permitted, are there adequate provisions to ensure that outside, would-be intruders do not penetrate the system via personal computers? (See question 4 on hacking above.)
9. If a front-end processor is used, are controls provided for this unit?

Bibliography

Part I

This section provides users of this manual with selected references for supplementary reading and for reference. The bibliographic material has been drawn mostly from the annotated bibliography and digest section of *COM-SAC, Computer Security, Auditing and Controls,* the semiannual journal on these subjects published by Management Advisory Publications. It is supplemented by other known sources of information gathered by the author over the years. Addresses for many of these publications and organizations are given in Figures 10-13 and 10-14 on pages 138 and 140 respectively.

As can be appreciated, the literature related to internal control is quite widespread and varied. The specific subject of internal control testing and integrity in EDP systems is dealt with in a number of publications in a rather scattered fashion and with varying levels of depth of coverage.

1. AICPA, *Audit Approaches for a Computerized Inventory System,* American Institute of Certified Public Accountants, New York, NY, 1980.
2. AICPA, *Audit Considerations in Electronic Fund Transfer Systems,* American Institute of Certified Public Accountants, New York, NY, 1979.
3. AICPA, *Guidelines to Assess Computerized General Ledger and Financial Reporting Systems for Use in CPA Firms,* American Institute of Certified Public Accountants, New York, NY, 1979.
4. AICPA, "Management, Control and Audit of Advanced EDP Systems," American Institute of Certified Public Accountants, New York, NY, 1977.
5. AICPA, *Statement on Auditing Standards No. 3, The Effects of EDP on the Auditor's Study and Evaluation of Internal Control,* American Institute of Certified Public Accountants, New York, NY, 1974.
6. AICPA, *The Auditor's Study and Evaluation of Internal Control in EDP Systems,* American Institute of Certified Public Accountants, New York, NY, 1977.
7. Andersen, Arthur, "A Guide for Studying and Evaluating Internal Accounting Controls," Arthur Andersen and Co., Chicago, IL, 1978. This publication deals with accounting controls evaluation using the transaction flow approach.
8. Cash, J. I., A. D. Bailey, and A. B. Whinston, "A Survey of Techniques for

Auditing EDP-Based Accounting Systems," *The Accounting Review,* October 1977, pp. 813–832. This is a fairly complete survey of audit techniques for EDP systems, commenting on their relative validity. It mentions a new approach being developed by the authors to evaluate the system of internal controls, called TICOM (The Internal Control Model) presently in its conceptual form.

9. Chapman, M., "Audit and Control in a Data Base/IMS Environment," *COM-SAC, Computer Security, Auditing and Controls,* Vol. 6, No. 2, July 1979, pp. A-9 to A-14.
10. CICA, *Computer Audit Guidelines,* Canadian Institute of Chartered Accountants, Toronto, Ontario, Canada, 1975.
11. CICA, *Computer Control Guidelines,* Canadian Institute of Chartered Accountants, Toronto, Ontario, Canada, 1971.
12. Clary, J. B., and R. A. Sacane, "Self-testing Computers," *IEEE Computer,* October 1979, pp. 45–59. This unique paper presents a summary of computer test approaches by built-in and external tests and by software and hardware means to build automatic test systems.
13. Connor, J. E., and B. H. De Vos, "Guide to Accounting Controls—Establishing, Evaluating and Monitoring Control Systems," *Warren, Gorham & Lamont, Inc.,* 210 South Street, Boston, MA 02111, 1980. Covers internal controls as mandated by the Foreign Corrupt Practices Act.
14. Davis, G., "Ensuring On-Line System Integrity Using Parallel Simulation on a Continuing Basis." *COM-SAC, Computer Security, Auditing and Controls,* Vol. 7, No. 2, July 1978, pp. A-9 to A-11. The use of parallel simulation on a separate computer using code prepared by a distinct group is described as applied to an on-line betting operation.
15. EDP Auditors Foundation, Control Objectives—1980, EDP Auditors Foundation, Streamwood, IL, 1980. A manual on control objectives for EDP.
16. Forsyth, A., "An Approach to Audit an On-Line System," *COM-SAC, Computer Security, Auditing and Controls,* Vol. 7, No. 1, January 1980, pp. A-1 to A-4. Describes methods used to audit an on-line betting operation, including the use of parallel simulation and the transaction logs for auditing.
17. General Accounting Office, "Improvements Needed in Managing Automated Decision-making by Computers Throughout the Federal Government," *The Comptroller General of the United States,* Report FGMSD-76-5, 1976.
18. Glass, R. L., "Real-Time; The 'Lost World' of Software Debugging and Testing," *Communications of ACM,* Vol. 23, No. 5, May 1980, pp. 264–271. This paper points out the limitations of present testing methods and exhorts all concerned to use more advanced techniques and approaches for testing advanced systems.
19. Grimes, J. and E. A. Gentile, "Maintaining Internal Integrity of On-Line Data Bases," *EDPACS Newsletter,* February 1977, pp. 1–14. This paper discusses the preparation of analytical audit programs to review the integrity of data bases on an after-the-fact basis. The audit programs are run against the massive data base to uncover errors and inconsistencies.
20. Hubbert, J., "Data Base Concepts," *The EDP Auditor,* Spring 1980. This paper introduces concepts of data base and suggests ways to audit data bases.

21. Hulme, K. and M. E. Aiken, "The Normative Approach to Internal Control Evaluation of On-Line/Real-Time Systems," *The Chartered Accountant in Australia,* July 1976, pp. 7–16. The case of a large-scale application of parallel simulation to test internal control is described for a savings bank application. The paper indicates that conventional test methods are not good enough for testing large on-line systems and that the simulation model is a better approach.

22. IIA, "How to Acquire and Use Generalized Audit Software," The Institute of Internal Auditors, Altamonte Springs, FL, 1979.

23. IIA, "Systems Auditability and Control—Audit Practices," The Institute of Internal Auditors, Altamonte Springs, FL, 1977.

24. IIA, "Systems Auditability and Control—Control Practices," The Institute of Internal Auditors, Altamonte Springs, FL, 1977.

25. IIA, "Systems Auditability and Control—Executive Report," The Institute of Internal Auditors, Altamonte Springs, FL, 1977.

26. Kuong, J. F., "Audit and Control of Computerized Systems" (MAP-6), Management Advisory Publications, P.O. Box 151, Wellesley Hills, MA 02181, 1977. This manual covers standards for auditing and controlling existing and development stage systems. Chapters 4 and 5 include material on system testing and acceptance.

27. Kuong, J. F., *Computer Auditing and Security Manual—Operations and System Audits* (MAP-5), Management Advisory Publications, 1976. A detailed manual on how to conduct an operational audit of a data center (including the EDP function) along with an introduction to system development and existing audits.

28. Kuong, J. F., *Checklists and Guidelines for Reviewing Computer Security and Installations* (MAP-4), Management Advisory Publications, 1976. A set of detailed guidelines and checklists for reviewing data centers, EDP, and application systems.

29. Kuong, J. F., *Audit and Control of Advanced/On-Line Systems* (MAP-7), Management Advisory Publications, 1980. A seminar manual on on-line system controls and testing, it covers approaches for the audit and control of advanced systems.

30. Kuong, J. F., "Approaches to Justifying EDP Controls and Auditability Provisions," *COM-SAC, Computer Security, Auditing and Controls,* Vol. 7, No. 2, July 1980, pp. A-1 to A-8. This paper presents the difficulties in justifying EDP controls and proposes approaches to risk analysis to aid in controls justification and assessment.

31. Kuong, J. F., "Advanced Tools and Techniques for System Auditing" (seminar notes course MC-8), Management Advisory Publications, 1978. Techniques for system auditing and for auditability building are discussed.

32. Kuong, J. F., "Computer Security, Auditing and Controls—Text and Readings," Management Advisory Publications, 1974. A text on the overall security and protection for EDP.

33. Kuong, J. F., *Controls for Advanced/On-line/Data-Base Systems* Vols. 1 and 2, 1985, Management Advisory Publications. A comprehensive compendium of

internal controls for advanced systems, including control objectives and specific control solutions.

34. Lainhart, J. W., and B. R. Snyder, "A Simultaneous-Parallel Approach to Testing Computerized Systems," *EDPACS Newsletter,* October 1977, pp. 7–12. This paper discusses the use of two programs, split and merge, and the use of extra tape drives to test computerized systems with live test data without incurring test data contamination.
35. Mair, W. C., K. Davis, and D. Wood, "Computer Control and Audit," The Institute of Internal Auditors, Altamonte Springs, FL, 1976. A text on the general aspects of EDP auditing and controls.
36. Martin, J., *Principles of Data Base Management,* Prentice-Hall, Inc., Englewood Cliffs, N.J., 1976.
37. Martin J., *Accuracy, Security and Privacy in Computer Systems,* Prentice-Hall, Inc., Englewood Cliffs, N.J., 1973. A text on controls for security and accuracy in computer systems. It includes control checklists.
38. National Bureau of Standards, "Guidelines for Automatic Data Processing Risk Analysis," U.S. Department of Commerce, FIPS Publication 65, August 1979.
39. Patrick R. L., "Performance Assurance and Data Integrity Practices," National Bureau of Standards, Washington, DC, 1978. This publication presents over sixty ideas on how to improve integrity in computer systems based on a survey.
40. Perry, W. E., "Auditing Computer Systems," FAIM Technical Products, Inc., Melville, N.Y., 1977.
41. Perry, W. E., "Internal Control," FAIM Technical Products, Inc., Melville, N.Y., 1980.
42. Perry, W. E., "Snapshot—A Technique for Tagging and Tracing Transactions," *EDPACS Newsletter,* March 1974, pp. 1–7. The technique of building snapshots to review internal control in systems is described at a good level of detail.
43. Perry, W. E., and J. F. Kuong, "Developing and Implementing an Integrated Test Facility for Testing Computerized Systems" (MAP-12), Management Advisory Publications, 1979. (Included as part of ECAP Manual, MAP-11.)
44. Perry, W. E., and J. F. Kuong, "Generalized Computer Audit Software—Selection and Application" (MAP-14), Management Advisory Publications, 1980. (Included as part of the ECAP Manual, MAP-11.)
45. Perry, W. E., and J. F. Kuong, "Effective Computer Audit Practices—ECAP Manual," Management Advisory Publications (MAP-11). This manual is available in installments and contains three main sections. Section 1 discusses EDP audit general practices. Section 2 presents key papers on applied EDP auditing written by practitioners. Section 3 consists of a series of in-depth monographs on EDP audit techniques.
46. Perry, W. E., and J. F. Kuong, *EDP Risk Analysis and Controls Justification,* Management Advisory Publications, 1981. A comprehensive methodology on how to conduct EDP risk analysis and controls justification.
47. Wess, B. P., and L. D. Hunt, "Virtual Transaction Testing (VTT)—An Auditing Technique for On-Line Data Bases and Computer Networks," *COM-SAC, Com-*

puter Security, Auditing and Controls,* Vol. 5, No. 2, July 1978, pp. A-3 to A-7. The authors describe the use of a twin data base and test programs for testing the internal control of on-line data base systems on an ongoing basis. The use of the twin data base avoids possible contamination of the main data base with test data.

48. Wilkins, B. J., *The Internal Auditor's Information Security Handbook,* Institute of Internal Auditors, Altamonte Springs, FL, 1979.

Part II

The literature references and bibliography that follow are intended to assist the interested reader in obtaining additional information on the subjects of organizing, developing, and training for EDP audit and control. Although this manual is self-contained and requires no additional references in order to practice the concepts and procedures provided, audit managers, EDP auditors, and control professionals will, nevertheless, benefit from reading some of the references furnished in their particular areas of interest.

The literature references were extracted from the nine published volumes of *COM-SAC, Computer Security, Auditing and Controls,* which surveys and digests all the literature on these subjects twice a year. Addresses for many of these publications and organizations are given in Figures 10-13 and 10-14 on pages 138 and 140 respectively.

1. Anderson, C. A., "Approach to Data Processing Auditing," *The Interpreter,* Insurance Accounting and Statistical Association, Mutual Plaza, Durham, NC 27701, April 1975, pp. 23–26.
2. Auerbach Staff, "What Every Auditor Should Know About DP," *Data Processing Management Service,* Auerbach Publishing Co., Portfolio 3-09-03, 1975, 14 pp. A review of auditor areas of involvement, plus the skills and training required.
3. Bar-Hava, N., "Training EDP Auditors," *Information and Management,* No. 4, 1981, pp. 39–42. Presents a good discussion of training of EDP auditors as experiment in a university in Israel.
4. Barrett, M. J., "Education for Internal Auditors," *EDP Auditor,* Spring 1981, pp. 11–20. A review of training in EDP auditing. Not very clear or explicit.
5. Canadian Institute of Chartered Accountants Committee, "Competence and Professional Development in EDP for the CA," *CA Magazine,* 250 Bloor St., Toronto, Canada, M4W 1G5, September 1974, pp. 26–70. Covers a proposal on training requirements in EDP for future chartered accountants in Canada.
6. Caputo, C. A., "Managing the EDP Audit Function," *COM-SAC, Computer Security, Auditing and Controls,* Vol. 8, No. 1, January 1981, pp. A-1 to A-8. Discusses the author's experience in managing EDP auditing in a large bank. Points out type of audits and the need to develop EDP auditors.

7. Cheney, P. H., "Educating the Computer Audit Specialist," *The EDP Auditor,* Fall 1980, pp. 9–15. Review of EDP auditor training needs.

8. Dorricott, K. O., "Organizing a Computer Audit Specialist," *CA Magazine,* May 1979, pp. 66–68. Discusses strategic decisions the audit firm must use in setting up an audit specialty. Tries to answer the what, who, where, how much, and do what questions that arise in EDP audit organization. Applies mostly to external auditing.

9. Emens, K. L., "A Survey of Internal EDP Audit Activity Among EDPAA Member Companies," *EDP Auditor,* Fall 1976, pp. 11–17. A survey of EDP Auditor Association members' activity in EDP audit.

10. Frank, E., "Integrating Reviews of EDP Systems with Regular Audit Project," *The EDP Auditor,* Summer 1974, pp. 10–11. Some limited suggestions on how to blend audit and system project reviews.

11. Horwitz, G., "Needed: A Computer Audit Philosophy," *Journal of Accountancy,* April 1976, pp. 69–72.

12. Hopper, E. L., "Staffing of EDP Auditors on the Internal Audit Staff," *The Interpreter* (address in item 1), August 1975, pp. 24–26. Staffing alternatives and training requirements.

13. IIA Staff, "Establishing the Internal Audit Function," Institute of Internal Auditors, Altamonte Springs, FL 32701, 1974.

14. IIA Staff, "Hatching the EDP Audit Function," Institute of Internal Auditors, Altamonte Springs, FL 32701, 1975. Organization, job descriptions, and types of audits.

15. Jancura, E. G., "Developing Concepts of Technical Proficiency in EDP Auditing," *The Ohio CPA,* Spring 1979. Comments on competency requirements of auditors to meet SAS 3 audit standards of the American Institute of Certified Public Accountants.

16. Kearns, J., "Are We Ready for Continuous Process Auditing," *CA Magazine,* September 1980, pp. 68–71. A good discussion of embedded auditability is given.

17. Kuong, J. F., "A Framework for EDP Auditing," *COM-SAC, Computer Security Auditing and Controls,* Vol. 3, No. 2, 1976, pp. A-1–A-8. Discusses directional priorities for EDP auditing.

18. Kuong, J. F., "Organizing, Managing and Controlling the EDP Auditing Function." Seminar Text, Management Advisory Publications, 1980.

19. Kuong, J. F., "Managing the EDP Audit Function." Paper presented at the First Regional EDP Auditors Conference, Tel-Aviv, Israel, May 29–June 3, 1982.

20. Kuong, J. F., "Audit and Control of Computerized Systems" (MAP-6), Management Advisory Publications, 1979. A manual on the subject which discusses training, organization, and skills for system development audits.

21. Kuong, J. F., "Computer Audit and Security Manual" (MAP-5), Management Advisory Publications. Chapters 4 and 5 cover organizing for EDP auditing.

22. Kuong, J. F., "Organizing and Staffing for EDP Auditing," *COM-SAC, Computer Security, Auditing and Controls,* Vol. 2, No. 1, 1975. Organization and staffing aspect of EDP auditing are covered.

23. Kuong, J. F., "Advanced Tools and Techniques for Systems Auditing" 1978, Management Advisory Publications. Covers advanced tools and techniques for auditing simple and advanced systems.

24. Kuong, J. F., "Audit and Control of Advanced/On-Line Systems," (MAP-7), Management Advisory Publications. A course manual on the subject and on advanced system audit approaches. 1980.

25. Kuong, J. F., "Auditor Involvement in System Development and the Need to Develop Effective, Efficient, Secure, Auditable and Controllable Systems." Keynote speech at the First Regional EDP Auditors Conference, Tel-Aviv, Israel, June 3, 1982.

26. Lagan, J. J., "The Development of an EDP Audit Function in a Complex Environment," Employment Research Management, 680, 1978.

27. Langmead, J. M., and R. V. Boos, "How Do You Train EDP Auditors?", Management Focus, September–October, 1978, pp. 6–11. In question-and-answer fashion, describes how internal audit could approach the training of EDP auditors.

28. Litecki, C. R., and J. E. McEnroe, "EDP Audit Job Definitions: How Does Your Staff Compare?" *The Internal Auditor,* April 1981, pp. 57–61. Based on results from survey questionnaires, tasks are given for EDP audit specialist and auditor with EDP audit responsibilities.

29. Macchiaverna, P. R., "Auditing Corporate Data Processing Activities," The Conference Board, Inc., 845 Third Avenue, New York, NY 10022, 1980. A monograph on the subject with a section on training of EDP auditors which is not very complete.

30. Marks, R. C., "Performance Appraisal of EDP Auditors." Speech given at the 11th Conference on Computer Auditing, Security and Control, ATC/IIA, New York, May 4–8, 1981.

31. McGuire, P. T., "EDP Auditing—Why? How? What?," *The Internal Auditor,* June 1977, pp. 28–34. The author summarizes his experiences in getting EDP auditing started in his company. Pointers on staffing and training are given.

32. Miller, T. L., "EDP—A Matter of Definition," *The Internal Auditor,* July–August 1975, pp. 31–38. A good discussion of types of EDP audits, objectives, time, and expertise required, payback and techniques used.

33. Morris, R., III, "The Internal Auditors and Data Processing," *The Internal Auditor,* August 1978.

34. Norris, P. N., "EDP Audit and Control—A Practitioner's Viewpoint," *The EDP Auditor,* Winter 1976, pp. 8–14. A good paper which covers nine types of audits and what they entail.

35. Pabst, C. A., "What's All the Fuss About EDP?" *California CPA Quarterly,* June 1975, pp. 10–16. Steps to develop EDP auditors as applied to the external auditor's profession.

36. Perry, W. E., "Trends in EDP Auditing," *EDPACS Newsletter,* December 1976, pp. 1–6. A survey of EDP audit practices among American Petroleum Institute (API) member companies.

37. Perry, W. E., "The Making of Computer Auditor," *The Internal Auditor,* November–December 1974, pp. 11–22.
38. Perry, W. E., "Adding a Computer Programmer to the Audit Staff," *The Internal Auditor,* July 1974, pp. 1–7.
39. Perry, W. E., "Career Advancement for the EDP Auditor," *EDPACS Newsletter,* February 1975, pp. 1–6.
40. Perry, W. E., and J. F. Kuong, "Effective Computer Audit Practices Manual (ECAP)," Management Advisory Publications, P.O. Box 151, Wellesley Hills, MA 02181. This is a most comprehensive manual with in-depth treatment of EDP audit techniques.
41. Polanis, M. F., "Choosing an EDP Auditor," *Bank Administration,* January 1973, pp. 52–53. Suggests using programmers to audit EDP as opposed to teaching EDP to auditors.
42. Reilly, R. F. and J. A. Lee, "Developing an EDP Audit Function: A Case Study," *EDPACS Newsletter,* May 1981, pp. 1–10. Offers one way to establish EDP auditing based on one company's experience.
43. Savich, R. S., "The Care and Feeding of an EDP Auditor," *EDP Auditor,* Summer 1974, pp. 12–13. The EDP auditor needs academic and practical education to be a professional.
44. Sulcas, P., "Planning Timing of Computer Auditing," *The South African Chartered Accountant,* July 1975, pp. 232. Suggestions are given for planning the timing of EDP audits with special regard to the external auditor vantage point. Some points apply to internal auditing as well.
45. Schneidman, A., "A Need for Auditors' Computer Education," *The CPA Journal,* New York, June 1979, pp. 29–35. Provides information on audit training requirements of auditors to meet SAS standards. Presents a list of training subjects which is not comprehensive.
46. Scoma, I., Jr., "The EDP Auditor," *Data Management,* May 1977, pp. 14–17. The roles of EDP auditing are discussed. Some suggestions on staffing and on the background of candidates for EDP auditing are presented. Paper does not cover the subject in depth.
47. Tussing, R. T. and G. L. Helms, "Training Computer Audit Specialists," *Journal of Accountancy,* July 1980, pp. 71–74. Outlines a program for training EDP auditors conducted on an experimental basis at Illinois State University.
48. Vasarhelyi, M. A., C. A. Pabst, and I. Daley, "Organizational and Career Aspects of the EDP Audit Function," *EDP Auditor,* 1980, pp. 35–43.

Index